AF765246

Financial Skills *for* Professionals

Financial Skills *for* Professionals

Vern Krishna, CM, QC, FRSC, FCPA
BCom (Manchester), MBA, LLB (Alberta),
DCL (Cambridge), LLM (Harvard)

Barrister at Law
Tax Chambers LLP (Toronto)
Professor of Law, University of Ottawa

UNIVERSITY OF TORONTO PRESS
Toronto Buffalo London

© Verkrish Investments Ltd. 2020
Irwin Law
An imprint of University of Toronto Press
Toronto Buffalo London
utorontopress.com
Printed and bound by CPI Group (UK) Ltd, Croydon, CR0 4YY

ISBN 978-1-5522-1559-3 (paper)   ISBN 978-1-5522-1560-9 (PDF)

All rights reserved. No part of this publication may be reproduced, stored in or introduced into a retrieval system, or transmitted in any form or by any means (electronic, mechanical, photocopying, recording, or otherwise) without the prior written permission of both the copyright owner and the above publisher of this book.

Cataloguing in Publication available from Library and Archives Canada

Title: Financial skills for professionals / Vern Krishna, CM, QC, FRSC, FCPA, BCom (Manchester), MBA, LLB (Alberta), DCL (Cambridge), LLM (Harvard), Barrister at LawTax Chambers LLP (Toronto), Professor of Law, University of Ottawa.
Other titles: Understanding financial statements
Names: Krishna, Vern, author.
Description: Previously published under title: Understanding financial statements. Toronto, ON : Irwin Law, 2013. | Includes bibliographical references and index.
Identifiers: Canadiana (print) 20200307940 | Canadiana (ebook) 20200307959 | ISBN 9781552215593 (softcover) | ISBN 9781552215609 (PDF)
Subjects: LCSH: Financial statements — Canada.
Classification: LCC HF5681.B2 K75 2020 | DDC 657/.30971—dc23

We wish to acknowledge the land on which the University of Toronto Press operates. This land is the traditional territory of the Wendat, the Anishnaabeg, the Haudenosaunee, the Métis, and the Mississaugas of the Credit First Nation.
University of Toronto Press acknowledges the financial support of the Government of Canada and the Ontario Arts Council, an agency of the Government of Ontario, for its publishing activities.

Canada Council for the Arts   Conseil des Arts du Canada

ONTARIO ARTS COUNCIL
CONSEIL DES ARTS DE L'ONTARIO
an Ontario government agency
un organisme du gouvernement de l'Ontario

Funded by the Government of Canada   Financé par le gouvernement du Canada   Canada

2 3 4 5 27 26 25 24

To Savitri, Linda, Nicola,
Sacha, Vivian, and Biggie

Summary Table of Contents

Detailed Table of Contents

Preface

Accounting is the forbidden fruit in the garden of business, which, if eaten without appreciation of its ingredients, can lead to unfortunate consequences for investors.

All commercial arrangements have financial implications. Professionals and businesspersons need to understand financial transactions. Lawyers draft contracts; managers and employees enter into compensation agreements; family lawyers negotiate matrimonial settlements. Civil litigation is essentially dispute resolution about monetary claims in which one party receives, and the other pays, compensation. Litigation lawyers carry the burden of persuasion to advise judges on the financial consequences of their legal positions.

Investors need to appreciate financial jargon that they are asked to sign off on by their investment advisors. For example, on 30 July 2020, Apple Inc announced a 4-for-1 stock split for its shares, which were trading at $400 per share. On 24 August, all investors who owned Apple's stock received three additional shares for each share held, which began trading on a split-adjusted basis on 31 August. The new price for holders would be around $100 on a split adjusted basis. This was Apple's fifth stock split since it went public. It also split on a 7-for-1 basis on 9 June 2014; a 2-for-1 basis on 21 June 2000; and on a 2-for-1 basis on 16 June 1987. In contrast, Warren Buffett's Berkshire Hathaway has never split the price of its A shares, which on the same day were trading at around $291,362. Why did Apple Inc split its stock and what would happen to call options on the stock after the split? (See Chapter 15 for stock splits and reverse splits.)

Even criminal lawyers dealing with tax fraud, money laundering, and securities crimes must understand the implications of the finance underlying alleged crimes. Hence, the inextricable link between law, finance, and accounting.

The purpose of this primer is to help professionals understand financial statements. To do so, users must understand the ingredients that go into their preparation and the unspoken assumptions and principles that determine their ultimate outcomes. This is not an accounting text. It is a primer on *understanding* financial statements and the basic principles of finance that explain accounting concepts.

Sutton's law, which medical students learn early in their careers, is that when diagnosing patients, one should first consider the obvious and most likely diagnosis. The law is named after the bank robber Willie Sutton, who reputedly replied to a reporter's inquiry as to why he robbed banks by saying "because that's where the money is." The same answer applies to securities fraud in the publicly listed markets. That is where really big money resides.

The events of the past two decades illustrate the lure of the forbidden fruit of accounting. Securities fraud is now the single most lucrative form of financial abuse of investors. The high profile reported corporate disputes and trials of the past two decades are merely the tip of the iceberg. Much remains hidden from view. *WorldCom* (2002), *Tyco* (2005), *Enron* (2006), *Livent* (2009), *Madoff* (2009), *Nortel* (2014), *Hollinger* (2015), and *Sino-Forest* (2018) are just a few examples. In each of the above cases, accountants, auditors, and management signed off on the veracity of their financial statements. However, it was the shareholders, investors, lawyers, and advisors who had to interpret the information and, ultimately, litigate for compensation.

In response to the financial scandals, the United States enacted *The Sarbanes-Oxley Act of 2002* (SOX). Section 302 of SOX requires senior corporate officers to personally certify in writing that the company's financial statements "comply with SEC disclosure requirements and fairly present in all material aspects the operations and financial condition of the issuer." Officers who sign off on financial statements that they know to be inaccurate are subject to criminal penalties, including prison terms. Canada abstained from enacting similar measures, leaving investors even more exposed to securities fraud.

As we go to press, the NASDAQ stock market has delisted Luckin Coffee Inc, an upstart rival to Starbucks in China, for allegedly reporting USD$300 million in fictitious sales to non–arm's length companies linked to its executives. In July 2020, Wirecard AG, the darling of Germany's fintech industry, valued on the German stock exchange at more than USD$14 billion, reported that $2 billion of its revenue, which it had told its auditors resided in a pair of Philippine banks, wasn't really there at all! The company filed for bankruptcy. The company's auditors, Ernst & Young GmbH, said "there are clear indications that this was an elaborate and sophisticated fraud involving multiple parties around the world in different institutions."[1] Criminal charges are pending. Investors will lose again.

Although there are many texts on accounting, there are no primers aimed specifically at professionals and non-technical users of financial information. This work is intended to fill that void. The primary objective is in understanding, rather than preparing, financial statements. However, just as a chef must understand the role that each ingredient contributes to a recipe, understanding finance requires an appreciation of its ingredients.

We cover the following dimensions in this primer:

- Fundamental concepts, accounting principles, and conventions underlying financial statements (chapters 1–4);
- The time value of money in financial decisions and retirement planning (chapters 5 and 18);
- Each of the financial statements: balance sheet, income statement, and statement of cash flows, together with the notes attached to them (chapters 6–13);

1 Patricia Kowsmann, Paul J Davies & Juliet Chung, "Wirecard Scandal Puts Spotlight on Auditor Ernst & Young" *Wall Street Journal* (27 June 2020), online: www.wsj.com/articles/wirecard-scandal-puts-spotlight-on-auditor-ernst-young-11593286933.

- The role of auditors and the scope of their reports to management and shareholders (Chapter 14);
- Interpretation of financial statements and their use in commercial decisions (Chapter 15);
- The intersection of law and accounting in business, and judicial limits on the liability of auditors to investors (chapters 16 & 17);
- Retirement and investment planning for individuals (Chapter 18); and
- A comprehensive glossary of accounting and finance terms, to allow readers to work through some of the jargon.

I am acutely aware that some people, particularly lawyers, suffer elevated blood pressure when they see numbers. I have deliberately used plain English to describe the meaning of technical terms in financial statements and include simple examples to illustrate the application of the principles and rules involved. I hope that these will lower the readings of "non-numerical" persons. Ultimately, this is a primer for students, professionals, and businesses.

I welcome constructive comments: vern.krishna@taxchambers.ca or at vkrishna@uottawa.ca

The text is current as of September 1, 2020.

Vern Krishna, CM, QC, FRSC, FCPA
www.vernkrishna.com

Chapter 1: Introduction

"*Without mathematics there is no art.*" — Luca Pacioli

We start with some preliminary questions.

- What is "accounting"?
- Who invented accounting and why?
- How does accounting relate to "finance"?
- Why do we need to have a basic understanding of accounting?

A. WHAT IS ACCOUNTING?

Accounting is the language of business. It involves orderly assimilation of numbers for the purposes of preparing financial statements and communicating with users of such statements. This involves measurement of historical financial information and its allocation to fiscal periods. Measurement requires a systematic process of recording financial transactions in quantitative and relevant format so that users can make decisions.

We refer to the initial mechanical process of recording financial transactions as "bookkeeping," so-called because the information was recorded in books of accounts. The information is summarized according to accounting rules and principles in financial statements, which managers, directors, trustees, and advisors use to discharge their fiduciary duties according to their legal mandates.

Businesses record transactions at each stage of their business cycle to determine the profitability of the enterprise, track cash flows, and determine what they own and owe. At the end of the enterprise's fiscal period, accounting statements will present a snapshot of the business's status and its profitability for the fiscal period.

The primary emphasis of financial statements is on information about past economic transactions and events that are financial in nature and can be expressed in financial terms. However, it is often necessary to estimate future transactions and events. Hence, in a nutshell, accounting is financial language and, as with all language, is governed by rules, conventions, and principles. The process has four distinct aspects:

- Identification,
- Measurement,
- Recording, and
- Communication.

Although all four of the above aspects are important in producing fair and reliable statements, it is the fourth element (communication) that is of greatest interest to end users of financial statements, such as business persons, investors, and professionals.

As with any language, accounting can be misunderstood. Hence, this text focuses on *understanding* financial statements and not as much on their preparation. However, to understand and interpret financial statements, users must have at least a modest understanding of the general concepts and principles that underlie their preparation. This is particularly important as accountants often use arcane terms and opaque language. They speak an obscure language that few of them will translate for the world at large. That should neither surprise nor disappoint. Every profession seeks to ring its territory with a wide moat. For example, it was not entirely accidental that lawyers in medieval England drafted pleadings in Latin and presented oral arguments in Norman French, which effectively prevented all but a few from understanding their "science."

Accounting is not a new discipline. The mathematics of modern accounting had their origins in Renaissance Italy, where the merchants of Venice, which at the time was the world's commercial centre, were trading all over the world, shipping goods out and bringing back treasures from the East. They needed a system of tracking their business transactions to account to their owners, investors, and bankers.

Modern-day accounting began in 1494. Fra Luca Bartolomeo de Pacioli (sometimes *Paccioli* or *Paciolo*) was an Italian mathematician, Franciscan friar, collaborator with Leonardo da Vinci, and early contributor to the field now known as accounting. He is referred to as "The Father of Accounting and Bookkeeping" in Europe. He was also called Luca di Borgo after his birthplace, Borgo Sansepolcro, Tuscany.

Pacioli's system of double-entry bookkeeping remains the foundation of sophisticated spread sheet architectures now used in computerized processes. Today, San Sepolcro is famous for at least three things: (1) tasty dried mushrooms; (2) the *Resurrection of Piero della Francesca*, one of the world's great paintings; and (3) the statue of Luca Pacioli.

Pacioli held the first chair in mathematics at Perugia University. His treatise, *Summa*, which he wrote at the height of the Italian Renaissance, was one of the first books published by Gutenberg Press. It contained only one chapter on double-entry bookkeeping in which he developed the fundamental accounting equation (A = L + E) that underpins all accounting to this day (more on the equation in Chapter 2).

But Pacioli was much more than a mathematician. He considered mathematics as the foundation of art. He is reputed to have said, "Without mathematics there is no art," and that:

> The Ancients, having taken into consideration the rigorous construction of the human body, elaborated all their works, as especially their holy temples, according to these proportions; for they found here the two principal figures without which no project is possible: the perfection of the circle, the principle of all regular bodies, and the equilateral square.[1]

---

1 Widely attributed to Luca Pacioli, *De divina proportione* (1509) [translator unknown].

In the course of his career, Pacioli taught Leonardo da Vinci of Florence and influenced the latter's work portrayed in "The Last Supper."[2]

See the video "Luca Pacioli: Father of Accounting" for more information (www.youtube.com/watch?v=OoTc3wLTqkk).

B. ACCOUNTING & FINANCE

Finance is the study of how to value businesses and raise and use capital for optimum returns. Hence, finance is a mode of analysis to value assets and businesses. Since all value depends upon time of payment or receipt of funds, the "time value of money" is the single most important concept in finance. We use the time value of money to value property, bonds, preferred shares, and common shares of a going concern business. However, finance requires reliable information from accountants on the profit, income, net income, earnings, and, most importantly, forecasted cash flows of the enterprise.

Financial analysts then determine the intrinsic value of a business or property. For this purpose, they use the most recent financial data to determine whether a business or publicly traded stock is fairly priced by taking the forecasted future cash flows of the enterprise and discounting them back to today's value. We refer to this as the Discounted Cash Flow (DCF) model, which is the most widely accepted method to calculate the fair value of a company and its stock price. It is based on the premise that the fair value of a company is the total value of its incoming cash flow minus its expenses, technically called Free Cash Flows (FCF), discounted to today's value.

Financial accounting provides the information that analysts need to use in business valuations. We see this regularly in announcements about the past financial performance of publicly listed securities and estimates about their future values. See, for example, Intel's (NYSE) announcement on 24 January 2020:

---

2 For more information, see Paul Jackson, David Tinius & William Weis, *Luca Pacioli: Unsung Hero of the Renaissance* (Cincinnati: South-Western Publishing Company, 1990), online: YouTube, posted by ACCT201bCSUF (4 March 2014) www.youtube.com/watch?v=OoTc3wLTqkk.

> For the fourth quarter [2019] Intel reported earnings, excluding certain items, of $1.52 per share, topping the $1.25 average estimate, according to analysts . . . Revenue of $20.21 billion beat the $19.23 billion average estimate. Intel is forecasting first-quarter earnings of $1.30 per share and revenue of $19 billion, beating Refinitiv survey estimates of $1.04 in earnings and $17.19 billion in revenue.[3]

On the same day, Intel stock closed at USD$68.47. This shows us Intel's financial accounting earnings for the last quarter of 2019 and the market's financial valuation of the stock as at the close of business on 24 January 2020.

C. BUSINESS CYCLES

Business cycles have various stages. The typical cycle of a manufacturing or production business generally comprises seven stages:

1) Injection of cash;
2) Purchase of raw materials for cash or credit;
3) Conversion of raw materials into work in progress (WIP);
4) Completion of finished goods or products for sale;
5) Sales for cash or on account;
6) Collection of accounts receivable from customers; and
7) Return of cash to the business and payment of accounts payable to creditors.

The length of each cycle depends upon the nature of the business. The cycle may be short, for example, a fast-food business catering to customers in a downtown business area, or long, for example, a company producing scotch whisky that matures for thirty years before it comes onto the market. Short or long, each business requires financial information as it proceeds.

3 Ari Levy, "Intel Stock Soars to Dot-com Era Levels Even as Warning Signs Flash for 2020 and Beyond" *CNBC (24 January 2020)*, online: www.cnbc.com/2020/01/24/intel-intc-stock-soars-to-dot-com-era-levels-after-q4-earnings.html.

D. USERS OF FINANCIAL STATEMENTS

The following chart lists some of the primary users of financial information and the uses to which they put that information:

Lawyers and professionals	Evaluate entity's resources and obligations; draft contracts and financial covenants such as legal clauses in buy-sell arrangements and estate planning. Criminal lawyers engaged in prosecuting or defending white-collar criminals must assess dense financial information to be presented to a judge or jury. (See below for types of lawyers and legal practices).
Bankers	Assess whether borrower has sufficient collateral as insurance for a potential loan. Determine whether borrower has sufficient future cash flows to service principal and interest.
Shareholders	Assess company's performance and future prospects to maintain, sell or buy stock.
Owners	Assess entity's performance for growth or shrinkage and identify strengths and weaknesses.
Managers and employees	Determine whether, and how much, of a bonus they should expect based on profits.
Suppliers and creditors	Assess whether the entity will be able to pay its outstanding debts.
Potential investors and advisors	Assess current conditions and predict future cash flows. Determine intrinsic value of a business and its rate of return and compare these to alternative investments in determining "income" and the value of assets.
Canada Revenue Agency (CRA)	Assess compliance with tax laws and payment of all proper taxes. Determine that entity used appropriate accounting and financial methodologies.
Regulators	Assess financials as part of rate-setting processes to determine appropriate rates of return.

E. LAWYERS

Amongst professional groups, lawyers use accounting information in a variety of legal practices. If accounting is the language of business, lawyers who deal with commercial issues should understand the rudimentary concepts of the discipline.

For example, Rule 3.1 of the Law Society of Ontario's Rules of Professional Conduct states:[4]

> "competent lawyer" means a lawyer who has and applies relevant knowledge, skills and attributes in a manner appropriate to each matter undertaken on behalf of a client including . . . (h) recognizing limitations in one's ability to handle a matter or some aspect of it, and taking steps accordingly to ensure the client is appropriately served.

There are similar rules in all other rules of provincial law societies.

The professional obligation to be "competent" requires commercial lawyers to have at least a modest understanding of the principles of accounting and finance so that they can recognize potential pitfalls for their clients. It is difficult to conceive of lawyers who act in business, commercial, family, or other financial transactions who do not get involved with numbers at one level or another. Lawyers deal with businesses, partners, shareholders, creditors, debtors, governments, tax authorities, and regulatory bodies.

Law students, lawyers, and judges tend to be apprehensive of financial statements. The mere mention of numbers elevates blood pressure and causes numbness in critical nerve centres. Brilliant legal minds suffer hyper-anxiety when presented with financial information that requires an understanding of basic math. The stress is entirely understandable. Law schools attract many students from diverse backgrounds, including the arts, humanities, social sciences, and philosophy, which, generally, are non-quantitative disciplines.

Hence, for many lawyers, the world of financial accounting is a mystery that is best left to accountants. The accounting profession welcomes the lawyer's aversion to numbers because it allows them to benefit from the mysterious "science" of numbers. So, what kinds of lawyers need to understand financial statements?

---

4 Law Society of Ontario, *Rules of Professional Conduct*, Adopted by Convocation on 22 June 2000, effective 1 November 2000 (as amended), online: https://lso.ca/about-lso/legislation-rules/rules-of-professional-conduct.

1. Business Lawyers

It is easy to build the case for the need for business lawyers to understand the language of accounting and finance. Corporate lawyers deal every day with corporations, banks, financial statements, shareholder rights, partnership agreements, insolvency and bankruptcy trustees, mergers, and acquisitions. Every one of these areas involves digesting financial information, sometimes fairly simple and other times, complex and sophisticated.

Commercial lawyers need to understand the handling of securitization and other financial transactions that rely on the value of assets and the impact of their transactions on client financial statements.

Lawyers encounter accounting issues and terminology in a variety of negotiated agreements. Even drafting a simple bonus contract that promises an executive a percentage of "net margin" or "net profit" involves subtle issues, many of which end up in litigation. Of course, lawyers performing due diligence must also be sensitive to the possibility that an enterprise has engaged in, or been a victim of, financial fraud or money laundering, which, almost inevitably, involves financial statements.

Hence, it is virtually impossible for business lawyers to avoid accounting concepts, such as "net income," "profit," "net book value," "adjusted net book value," and "net worth." They must also understand the scope and limitations of Generally Accepted Accounting Principles (GAAP) in drafting their contracts. For example, employment contracts, union contracts, lending agreements, buy-sell agreements all refer to material related to financial statements and concepts. Even a simple contract that provides a manager with a bonus equal to 10 percent of their division's "net income" for the year implicitly engages a financial accounting concept that someone must interpret.

We recognize that there are fundamental differences in the cultures of lawyers and accountants. Lawyers rely heavily upon the form of their transactions for legal effect. For example, a 999-year lease is just what it says, a "lease" without transfer of legal title. Accountants often rely on economic substance in characterizing transactions for financial statement purposes. In economic substance, a 999-year lease is the financial equivalent of an absolute transfer in fee simple title. Unfortunately, proving this proposition requires familiarity with finance, the time value of money, and net present value concepts.

The form versus substance approach is particularly relevant in timing recognition of revenue in financial statements. Transfers of property with side agreements can raise subtle issues as to whether or not there has been a "true sale" involving a transfer of the risks and rewards of ownership.

Enron for example, recognized revenues on its books after transferring certain assets to special purpose entities (SPEs). The various side agreements resulted in the company retaining all the risks of ownership after the transfers. For example, in one transaction Enron sold an interest in a Polish company to LJM2 for $30 million on 21 December 1999. Enron had intended to sell the interest to an unrelated party but could not find a buyer before the end of the year. Enron then recorded a gain of $16 million on the transaction, which it could not close with an arm's length third party. After the year end, Enron bought back LJM2's interest for $31.9 million after it failed to find an outside buyer. Enron used the related-party transactions with the special purpose entity (SPE) at the end of its fiscal period to manipulate its income and to meet earnings expectations to sustain its stock price.

In fact, Enron did not really "earn" the revenues that it reported on its financial statements, which ultimately led to its downfall. At Enron's peak, its shares were worth $90.75. When the firm declared bankruptcy on 2 December 2001, they were trading at $0.26. Investors, pension funds, and employees discovered this in the litigation that followed, but by then they were fighting over the company's carcass (See Chapter 16.B, "The Enron Debacle").

In addition, the Enron scandal led to the demise of its accounting firm (Arthur Andersen LLP) which oversaw Enron's accounts. As one of the five largest accounting firms in the United States at the time, Andersen had a reputation for high standards and quality risk management.

A lawyer's duty to their client includes the obligation to object when the client proposes or uses questionable accounting policies or practices. Clearly, the lawyer must first recognize that there is a problem.

Although solicitor-client privilege prevents the lawyer from disclosing client confidences, it does not prevent the lawyer from "going up the ladder" or, in an appropriate case, withdrawing from the file.

2. Civil Litigators

Civil litigation is essentially a fight over money. Whether in contract, tort, securities, insolvency, corporate, family law, or tax disputes, litigation inevitably draws upon accounting, finance, and tax law in calculating damages or remedies contingent upon financial performance.

Commercial litigators often retain forensic accounting experts to testify in fraud cases, and valuation experts to assess economic damages. They can be helpful in litigation. The key is to find one who can speak plain English to the lawyer, judge, and jury.

3. Family Lawyers

Family law inevitably requires lawyers to assess the valuation of family assets and the earning capacity of spouses in arriving at spousal and child support arrangements. Of course, family lawyers handling support agreements must understand not only the legal, but also the financial, character of "income" for family law and tax purposes. Many family law disputes involve evaluation of the net worth of private companies to determine settlements under family law and matrimonial agreements. They must also understand the nuances of the statements and the financial and tax implications of property and pension divisions.

4. Tax Lawyers

Tax law and accounting are inextricably linked to each other. It is impossible to escape financial concepts in tax law. At its most basic level, a business is taxable on its "profit" for the year.[5] The determination of profit is dictated by accounting and commercial principles, as modified by complex statutory provisions. A dispute with the Canada

---

5 *Income Tax Act*, RSC, 1985, c 1 (5th Supp), s 9.

Revenue Agency (CRA) on a tax assessment inevitably draws on the proper measurement of "taxable income," the value of assets, and the timing of income recognition. Similarly, buy-sell agreements in estate planning and deemed disposition provisions of the *Income Tax Act* rely upon the valuation of assets at particular points in time.

5. Investment Advisors

Investment advisors and trustees of estates need to evaluate the quality of investments under their supervision in making recommendations to investors and beneficiaries on their portfolios. Such advice is usually predicated on the evaluation of financial statements and public securities filings.

6. Estate Planners

Estate planners think about death. They take into account not only the net wealth of their clients' estate, but also the financial and tax impact of property distributions to beneficiaries, who may be individuals, foundations, corporations, or charities.

7. Criminal Lawyers

Even criminal lawyers must understand financial statements, particularly if they prosecute or defend white-collar crime. The Madoff Ponzi scheme, the largest in history, netted the mastermind (Bernie Madoff) nearly USD$50 billion. On 12 March 2009, Madoff pleaded guilty to eleven federal felonies and admitted to turning his wealth management business into a massive Ponzi scheme. As the scheme unravelled, it became clear that for twenty-five years he had sucked in some very sophisticated investors as enthusiastic disciples into his grand plan. He was ultimately sentenced to 150 years in prison.

Similarly, in 2012 the criminal trial of three Nortel senior executives focused almost exclusively on accounting entries and principles on using "reserves" to measure income in particular years, which had a substantial impact on bonus payments and stock prices.

Insider trading, stock market manipulation, stock option price fixing, and even old-fashioned looting of corporate assets all impact financial statements. Prosecuting and defence counsel in such cases must manoeuvre through dense financial data in long trials, assisted by the dense testimony of "forensic" accountants. In such cases, the fraudster does not use accounting for the purpose of communication. Quite the contrary, the fraudster (with the aid of their financial advisors) uses accounting to cloud the financial picture from regulators and investors in order to continue their wrongdoing.

8. The Regulators

Regulators are concerned with all sorts of businesses: for example, companies that sell securities (stocks, bonds, and derivatives), providers of utility and telecom services to the public, and government monopolies, such as liquor boards and hospitals. Labour unions are also interested in financial information, which they use in labour negotiations.

Poor accounting can violate the law and lead to criminal prosecution. See, for example, Canada's *Corruption of Foreign Public Officials Act*,[6] an anti-corruption law passed in 1999, ratifying the OECD *Convention on Combating Bribery of Foreign Public Officials in International Business Transactions*, and the SNC-Lavalin affair, alleging attempted political interference with the justice system by the Prime Minister of Canada, Justin Trudeau, and the Prime Minister's Office (PMO). The Parliament of Canada's Ethics Commissioner, Mario Dion, found that Trudeau improperly influenced then-Minister of Justice and Attorney General Jody Wilson-Raybould to intervene in an ongoing criminal case against Quebec-based construction company SNC-Lavalin. The Trudeau government maintained that there was no undue pressure or law broken, that offering SNC-Lavalin a deferred prosecution agreement (DPA) would save jobs, and that the controversy resulted from a misunderstanding.

---

6 SC 1998, c 34 (*CFPOA*).

See, for example, *R v Karigar*.[7] Karigar was convicted for his leading role in a conspiracy to bribe India's Minister of Civil Aviation and certain Air India officials to ensure that Cryptometrics Canada was successful in its bid for a contract from Air India for the supply of facial recognition software. First Canadian case to go to trial; three previous prosecutions resulted in guilty pleas.

See also the United States *Foreign Corrupt Practices Act* (*FCPA*), passed in 1977, which prohibits US firms and individuals from paying bribes to foreign officials in furtherance of a business deal. The *FCPA* places no minimum amount for a punishment of a bribery payment.

The primary focus of securities regulation is on stockholders. Canada has a plethora of securities regulators (thirteen in fact) one for each province and territory, that "regulate" securities law and prosecute offenders. The field of securities regulation is a patchwork of rules that reflect provincial political concerns.

9. Securities Regulation

Attempts to "unify" securities regulation in Canada have had limited success. In 2012, the Supreme Court of Canada turned back an attempt by the federal government to form a unified National Securities Regulator.[8] The Court held that the proposed Act was not valid under the general branch of the federal power to regulate trade and commerce. Instead, it focused on the day-to-day regulation of all aspects of contracts for securities within the provinces, including all aspects of public protection and professional competences. These matters were essentially provincial concerns falling within property and civil rights in the provinces and were not related to trade as a whole. Paragraph 122 states:

> Canada's problem is that the proposed Act reflects an attempt that goes well beyond these matters of undoubted national interest and concern and reaches down into the detailed regulation of all aspects

7 2013 ONSC 5199.

8 *Reference re Securities Act*, 2011 SCC 66, [2011] 3 SCR 837.

> of securities. In this respect, the proposed Act is unlike federal competition legislation, which has been held to fall under s. 91(2) of the *Constitution Act, 1867*. It would regulate *all* aspects of contracts for securities within the provinces, including *all* aspects of public protection and professional competence within the provinces. Competition law, by contrast, regulates *only* anti-competitive contracts and conduct—a particular aspect of economic activity that falls squarely within the federal domain. In short, the proposed federal Act overreaches the legislative interest of the federal government.

Here, the Court underestimated the increasing internationalization of capital markets and the risks inherent in fragmented securities regulation. Instead, it emphasized the constitutional division of powers between federal and provincial (territorial) governments rather than on the economic substance of the "trade and commerce" power.

Since then, the provinces have been "talking" but are unable to agree on a unified approach to securities legislation in Canada. The fragmentation of securities regulation results in a proliferation of administrative rules and dilution of expertise. It is extremely unlikely that all the provinces will ever agree to a uniform securities regime. Quebec will never come on board with a national regulator. Securities law in Canada remains fragmented and susceptible to fraud and abuse.

In the United States, the Securities and Exchange Commission (SEC), an independent agency created under the authority of the *Securities Acts* of 1933 and 1934, is a major player in the development of accounting principles for public companies. The role of the SEC is to ensure full and fair disclosure by corporations and issuers of securities to the public and monitor the integrity of public markets.

Accountants are also regulators concerned with the preparation of financial statements. The Chartered Professional Accountants (CPAs) of Canada has the responsibility for the development of accounting principles, which it publishes in its *Handbook* as Generally Accepted Accounting Principles (GAAP) and IFRS. Canadian corporate statutes recognize CPAs as the authoritative source of accounting principles for public and private corporations.

Canada has also adopted International Financial Reporting Standards (IFRS) issued by IASB and has converted its GAAP to harmonize with the European Union. The conversion became effective for Canadian public companies after 1 January 2011.

In the United States, the accounting profession created the Financial Accounting Standards Board (FASB) in 1973 as the independent, private-sector, not-for-profit organization that establishes financial accounting and reporting standards for public and private companies and not-for-profit organizations that follow Generally Accepted Accounting Principles (GAAP). The board issues Statements of Financial Accounting Standards (SFAS), which are the highest authority of the accounting profession on accounting principles.

The Securities and Exchange Commission (SEC) recognizes the FASB as the designated accounting standard setter for public companies. FASB standards are recognized as authoritative by many other organizations, including state Boards of Accountancy and the American Institute of CPAs (AICPA).

Equally significant, for American publicly traded companies, the *Sarbanes-Oxley Act* (SOX) of 2002, the most significant piece of accounting legislation since the enactment of the *Securities Act* in 1933, adds a new level of complexity, cost, and criminal sanctions for listed companies in the United States.

Lawyers must pay attention to domestic and international standards in drafting agreements. Although organizations such as the CPAs and FASB play an important role in the development of accounting standards and principles, there is also room for development of accounting by businesses. As businesses enter into new transactions, they must develop methods for recording the transactions on their books. Absent specific guidance from the regulatory and supervisory authorities, businesses must make their own decisions about the appropriate method for recording such transactions. The businesses' auditors must then determine whether the new reporting method is appropriate and one on which they can express a favourable opinion. As more businesses employ the same method of reporting similar transactions, the method used becomes generally accepted for future transactions.

At the same time, there is continuing division between accounting standards setting bodies. The International Accounting Standards Board (IASB) and the American Financial Accounting Standards Board (FASB) have not yet managed to agree on all accounting principles in financial reporting. Absent some consensus between standard-setting bodies, there will be reduced comparability between international financial statements.

F. EVOLUTION OF ACCOUNTING

Accounting has two distinct roles: reporting financial statements that focus on stewardship of corporate assets and providing financial information for decision making. Both roles, however, rely on historical data. The stewardship aspect of accounting in reporting to the owners of capital remains an important function in the development of the modern corporation and the raising of capital in the public markets. As public financial markets opened and expanded, however, investors and their advisors came to rely on financial information to evaluate public companies.

As ownership of capital separated from management of capital, the need for accounting to the owners of capital (the stewardship function) became more important. Public accountants—that is, accountants from outside the business—were needed to audit and certify financial statements and render an opinion on them. In England and Canada, such accountants are known as "licensed public accountants"; in the United States they are called "certified public accountants."

Traditionally, financial statements focused primarily on their stewardship function. Management is the steward of capital supplied by the owners (shareholders) and creditors who contribute or lend money to the business. The key aspect of stewardship reporting is on the measurement of historical "profits" or "net income."

In the past fifty years, however, the perspective of accounting has shifted from economic income measurement to an informational approach. The objective of the informational approach is to facilitate decision making by investors. Informational reporting also allows other users, such as creditors and contracting parties, to structure their contracts by reference to financial reporting data. For example, management bonuses and incentive contracts often rely upon the accounting entity's "net income" or the "profit" of a division of the entity. Similarly, holders of stock options in corporations are keenly interested in its "net income," which will drive the market price of the stock and, therefore, determine the value of their options. Thus, accounting has evolved from its initial role of stewardship reporting to providing information to existing and potential investors in the capital markets.

G. THE THREE Cs OF ACCOUNTING

Accounting concerns three *C*s:

- Characterization;
- Classification; and
- Communication.

Characterization is the proper identification of revenues and expenses and their relationship to financial reporting periods. Improper characterization can seriously distort financial results. For example, we must decide whether inflows should be considered revenues in the current fiscal period or deferred sales in a subsequent period. Similarly, we must characterize expenditures as being current costs or future costs. Current costs would be expenses relevant to the current financial reporting period; future costs would be capital costs relevant to future time periods. Ultimately, the income statement must match current revenues against current costs in order to determine net income in the current period.

Having characterized a transaction properly, the next step is to classify it into its appropriate category. For example, an expenditure on account of assets must be further classified based on whether the asset is current or long-term and, in the case of the latter, then into the particular type of long-term asset, such as tangible or intangible. Misclassifications can distort financial ratios, which may affect financial covenants in contracts.

Classification means pigeonholing the particular financial item into its appropriate slot. Thus, we must ask questions such as:

- Where does the item belong?
- In which entity do we put the item?
- In which division within the entity should we classify the item?
- In which department within the division should we classify the item?
- Where should we allocate overhead costs?

We characterize transactions according to their fundamental nature. For example, a business must characterize its expenditures as expenses relevant to the current financial year or as capital outlays that pertain to future financial periods. Characterization errors result in misleading financial statements. In 2002, for example, WorldCom Inc characterized USD$8 billion of its expenses as assets in order to inflate its income, resulting in a massive fraud and the largest bankruptcy protection in US history.

Finally, having characterized and classified accounting information into a manageable form, we must communicate the information to potential users. Effective communication requires full, fair, and clear disclosure of all relevant and material items for decision making. Thus, financial statements should use such form and terminology to ensure that significant information is readily understandable.

Investors, creditors, members, partners, government, and regulatory bodies all use various kinds of information to make their decisions, although each of these users has a different focus and requires varying degrees of detail. For example, a tax authority requires much more detailed information than that released in public filings. Information for tax purposes is strictly confidential whereas public filings are intended for a wide audience. Nevertheless, there is a substantial degree of commonality between user needs. The principal difference between users is the degree of detail in the financial statements.

As in all communication, language is susceptible to linguistic error. Thus, we should not blindly believe everything we read or hear in the media. Phrases in financial statements may have subtle undertones. For example, on 30 December 2002, Tyco International, a public company filed a report with the Securities & Exchange Commission in the United States in which it said it was reducing previously reported earnings. Its auditors, PricewaterhouseCoopers, approved the financial disclosures at Tyco, despite the company's use of "aggressive accounting that, even when not erroneous, was undertaken with the purpose and effect of increasing reported results above what they would have been if more conservative methods were used"![9] What was PWC telling its audience of readers?

Obfuscation is an art. Politicians, lobbyists, and communications consultants practise it routinely. But so too can business and accountants. For example, Research in Motion Ltd (RIM), a Canadian multinational company specialising in enterprise software and the Internet of things, suffered a disastrous year in 2011. The company introduced underwhelming products and had service disruptions and blackouts. The company's stock fell 78 percent and the shares closed at $13.97 on Friday, 16 December 2011, a level not seen since 2004. In the face of such performance, co-chairman Jim Balsillie issued the following statement in a conference call with investors:

> While we have remained solidly profitable and delivered significant unit volume during this transition, we recognize that our shareholders may feel that we have fallen short in terms of product execution, market share and financial performance.[10]

RIM closed at $7.59 on 23 October 2012, or a 46 percent drop. RIM changed its name to BlackBerry in 2013, which traded at USD$5.25 on 12 June 2020.

---

9 Tyco International Ltd report to the United States Securities and Exchange Commission, "Quarterly Report Pursuant to Section 13 or 15(d) of the Securities Exchange Act of 1934" commission file number 001-13836 (30 December 2002), online: www.sec.gov/Archives/edgar/data/833444/000095013002008787/d8k.htm.

10 Reported in Matt Hartley, "Key BlackBerry Phones Delayed" *Financial Post* (15 December 2011), online: https://financialpost.com/technology/rim-shares-slide-after-hours-on-weak-q4-outlook.

H. WHAT IS USEFUL INFORMATION?

We find useful information in a commercial context in several financial statements. Some examples:

Economic resources	What does a business own?	Balance Sheet: Assets [Chapter 7]
Obligations	What does a business owe?	Balance Sheet: Liabilities [Chapter 8]
Owners' investments	What is the owner's investment in the business?	Statement of Equity [Chapter 9]
Changes in the preceding fiscal period	How did the business perform?	Income Statement [Chapter 10]
Solvency	How much cash did the business generate?	Statement of Cash Flows [Chapter 12]
Economic performance	How do we measure performance?	Financial ratios [Chapter 15]

The answers to these questions must be understandable, relevant, reliable, comparable, and timely. Only then can they be useful. We examine each of these aspects of financial information and reporting in following chapters.

Chapter 2: Overview of Financial Statements

A. OVERVIEW

In this chapter, we introduce financial statements and their basic functions, which we will examine in greater detail in subsequent chapters. At this time, we first need to understand the language of accounting. Indeed, why is it even called "accounting"? Why does a businessperson or professional need to know anything about accounting and finance?

The four quantitative financials are:

1) The Balance Sheet;
2) The Income Statement;
3) The Statement of Retained Earnings;
4) The Statement of Cash Flows.

Each of these quantitative statements summarizes an entity's financial results, but from different perspectives. Although the information in the statements is interrelated, each statement provides a different picture of the entity's results, for different time frames.

The accompanying Notes to financial statements, which are an integral part of the financial statements, are qualitative and add explanatory information that explain principles and methods used in preparing the quantitative. The Notes are essential reading as that is often where management will bury its skeletons.

Unfortunately, we add to the novice's initial confusion by using various terminology to describe the same financial statements. For example, the following are some of the alternatives used to describe conventional financials:

- Balance Sheet:
  - » *Statement of Financial Position*
- Income Statement:
  - » *Statement of Profit and Loss*
- Statement of Retained Earnings:
  - » *Statement of Owner Equity*
  - » *Statement of Earned Surplus*
- Statement of Cash Flows:
  - » *Sources and Uses of Cash Statement*
  - » *Statement of Changes in Financial Position*

These are all essentially identical statements. In this text, we will use the main headings to describe the financials.

B. WHAT IS A BALANCE SHEET?

The balance sheet is a point in time picture of an entity's financial position. It is based on the fundamental accounting equation: Assets (A) = Liabilities (L) + Equity (E), where:

- Assets
  - » Assets are economic resources controlled by an entity as a result of past transactions or events and from which future economic benefits may be obtained.[1]
  - » Hence, assets are resources controlled by the entity that represent future benefits.

- Liabilities
  - » Liabilities are obligations of an entity arising from past transactions or events, the settlement of which may result

1 *CPA Canada Handbook – Accounting*, Chartered Professional Accountants of Canada (2018) [*Handbook*] at para 1000.24.

in the transfer or use of assets, provision of services, or other yielding of economic benefits in the future.[2]

- Equity
  - » Equity is the ownership interest in the assets of a profit-oriented enterprise after deducting its liabilities.
  - » Equity of a profit-oriented enterprise in total is a residual and includes specific categories of items (for example, types of share capital, contributed surplus, and retained earnings).[3]
  - » Equity is the net nominal amount (not necessarily in cash) available for distribution to the owners of the business.

The following is a simplified illustration of a balance sheet for the first fiscal period of a corporation:

XYZ Corporation Inc

Balance Sheet as at 31 December 20-1

Assets:	($)	($)
Cash		1,600
Accounts receivable		23,000
Inventory		35,000
Total assets:		**59,600**

Liabilities & Shareholders' Equity:		
Accounts payable		20,000
Stated capital, 1000 Class A shares	25,000	
Retained earnings	14,600	
Total shareholders' equity		39,600
Total liabilities & shareholders' equity		**59,600**

The first point to observe is that the balance sheet balances.

Assets (A) = Liabilities (L) + Equity (E)
$59,600 = $20,000 + $39,600

2 *Handbook* at para 1000.28.
3 *Handbook* at para 1000.31.

This is not due to any magical manipulation of the numbers. Instead, it is the inevitable result because it reflects all of the entity's resources (assets), which the company has financed from external sources (liabilities) and internal investments (equity).

Stated another way, an entity can only finance its resources (assets) from two sources, external and internal. We refer to the external sources as liabilities owed to third parties and internal sources as owner's equity. In the above example, XYZ Corporation Inc has financed its assets of $59,600 through debt of $20,000 (accounts payable to third parties), share capital of $25,000 that the owners provided, and $14,600 earnings retained as undistributed profits in the company.

We can restate the equation to emphasize other aspects of the enterprise. For example, we can restate the equation to emphasize its net worth:

Equity (E)	=	Assets (A)	–	Liabilities (L)
$39,600	=	$59,600	-	$20,000

Equity, which represents the interests of owners in the business, has two components:

Equity	=	Share capital	+	Retained earnings
$39,600	=	$25,000	+	$14,600

We will examine the legal and financial aspects of these components in subsequent chapters (see Chapter 9).

Observe also that we prepare the balance sheet as of a particular date, in this case, 31 December 20-1. Hence, it is "point in time" statement.

C. WHAT ARE ASSETS?

Assets have three essential characteristics:

1) They embody a future benefit that involves a capacity, singly or in combination with other resources to contribute directly or indirectly to future net cash flows;
2) The entity can control access to the future benefit; and

3) The transaction or event giving rise to the entity's right to, or control of, the benefit has already occurred.[4]

The balance sheet is essentially a summary position statement. As we will see later, the details of a balance sheet can be expanded to disclose more categories and classes of information. However, regardless of the number of categories, the fundamental equation, A = L + E, always prevails.

D. WHAT IS AN INCOME STATEMENT?

An income statement summarizes the enterprise's revenues and expenses during a fiscal period. As per the *Handbook*:

> Revenues are increases in economic resources, either by way of inflows of assets or reductions of liabilities, resulting from the ordinary activities of an entity, such as the sale of goods, the rendering of services, or the use by others of entity resources yielding rent, interest, royalties, or dividends.[5]
>
> Expenses are decreases in economic resources, either by way of outflows or reductions of assets or incurrences of liabilities, resulting from an entity's ordinary revenue generating or service delivery activities.[6]
>
> Gains are increases in equity, from peripheral or incidental transactions and events affecting the entity and from all other transactions, events, and circumstances affecting the entity *except* those that result from revenues or equity contributions.[7]
>
> Losses are decreases in equity from peripheral or incidental transactions and events affecting the entity and from all other transactions, events, and circumstances affecting the entity *except* those that result from expenses or distributions of equity.[8]

4 *Handbook* at para 1000.25.
5 *Handbook* at para 1000.32.
6 *Handbook* at para 1000.33.
7 *Handbook* at para 1000.34.
8 *Handbook* at para 1000.35.

The following is an example of an income statement:

XYZ Corporation Inc
Income Statement for the month ended 31 December 20-1

Sales revenues		$125,000
Subtract: Cost of sales		$75,000
Gross margin		$50,000
Subtract: Operating expenses		
Rent	$8,000	
Salaries	$15,000	
Other expenses	$11,600	
Total operating expenses		$34,600
Net income before taxes (NIBT)		**$15,400**
Earnings per share (EPS)		$15.40

The income statement is a "period" statement. In the above example, it covers the month from 1 to 3 December 20-1. During this time, sales of $125,000 increased assets (such as cash and receivables) and expenses of $109,600 reduced cash or, if unpaid, increased liabilities. Total revenues minus total expenses equals net income or loss during the period of time.

Hence, the balance sheet portrays the picture at a point in time and the income statement shows how the entity performed during a period of time. In effect, the income statement is the connecting link between successive balance sheets. In the above example, the income statement tells us that the company earned $125,000 from sales of products that cost $75,000, leaving a gross margin of $50,000. However, the company had various operating expenses, which totalled $34,600. This left net income before taxes of $15,400.

The above simplified example does not show the tax cost payable on the net earnings of $15,400. Taxes are a real and substantial cost of business, which would show on a more detailed and comprehensive income statement (more on taxes later).

Ultimately, net income increases owners' equity. A net loss would decrease owner's equity. In the above example, the income statement connects the balance sheets of XYZ Corporation Inc for the month of December 20-1 and shows positive net income before taxes of $15,400. Since the company had issued 1,000 shares (assumed), the business earned $15.40 per share for the owners. Basic earnings per share (EPS), or net income per common share, are earnings attributable to the residual owners of the enterprise, the common stockholders (see Chapter 15, Interpretation of Financial Statements and EPS).

E. WHAT ARE RETAINED EARNINGS?

The third financial statement is the statement of retained earnings, which explains the change in retained earnings balances between successive balance sheets:

XYZ Corporation Inc

Statement of Retained Earnings for the month ended 31 December 20-1

Retained earnings, 1 December 20-1		$0
Net income for the period	$15,400	
Subtract: dividends declared	$800	
Net increase in retained earnings		$14,600
Retained earnings, 31 December 20-1		$14,600

F. WHAT IS SHAREHOLDERS' EQUITY?

Shareholders' equity represents the residual interest of the shareholders after the enterprise pays off all of its debts. It comprises two components: retained earnings (RE) and share capital. Return on equity (ROE) measures the shareholder's investment in the corporation and tells us how well it is doing when compared to alternative investments.

XYZ Corporation Inc's opening balance of RE was $0 as at 1 December 20-1. The opening RE balance equals the closing RE balance of the immediately preceding fiscal period. In the next statement as at 1 January 20-2, the opening balance of retained earnings will be $14,600, the closing balance of the previous month.

The statement of retained earnings has important legal consequences. It is the *starting* point for determining how much an entity can legally distribute to its shareholders as dividends or in redeeming its shares. There are significant corporate and tax consequences, which we examine in Chapter 9. However, for present purposes, the important point is that retained earnings do not reflect market values and are not necessarily available in cash. They are simply a cumulative record of past earnings minus distributions. XYZ Corporation Inc, for example, has only $1,600 in cash at 31 December 20-1, whereas it has $14,600 in retained earnings. Cash and earnings are distinct concepts.

Where a corporation changes its stated capital between fiscal periods, such as by selling additional shares, the retained earnings statement will reflect the changes and be retitled as Statement of Shareholders' Equity.

Assume that on 1 January 20-2, XYZ Corporation Inc issues 500 additional Class A shares for $30 per share.

XYZ Corporation Inc

Statement of Shareholders' Equity as at 1 January 20-2

Stated capital 31 December 20-1	$25,000	
500 Class A shares issued 1 January 20-2	$15,000	
Stated capital, 1500 Class A shares		$40,000
Opening balance, retained earnings		$14,600
Net income for the period	$0	
Subtract: dividends declared	$0	
Closing balance, retained earnings		$14,600
Shareholders' Equity		**$54,600**

Summary

Balance Sheet	**Income Statement & Statement of Cash Flows**
Describes economic resources, obligations, and equity of an entity.	Describe changes in economic resources, obligations and equity of an entity.
At a point in time.	Over a period of time.

G. STATEMENT OF CASH FLOWS

The fourth major financial statement is the statement of cash flows, which provides details about the changes in the business's cash balances for the period covered by the income statement. The first point, which we shall repeatedly state in this text, is that net income according to accounting principles is not the same as cash (see Chapter 3). A successful business with a strong earnings history may, nevertheless, be short on cash. Conversely, a failing business with falling earnings may accumulate large amounts of cash on its downcycle.

The statement of cash flows provides supplementary information about the sources and uses of cash during a fiscal period, which coincides with the span of the income statement. The statement is divided into three main segments:

1) Cash flow from operating activities, such as primary business operations (revenues from sales and costs of running the business) and adjustments for changes in current assets and liabilities. This segment modifies income for changes in assets and liabilities that do not reflect cash changes and expenses that do not involve cash, such as, for example, depreciation.
2) Cash flow from investing activities, such as the purchase and sale of operating assets (buildings, investments etc.).
3) Cash flow from financing activities, including amounts received from issuing stock and debt.

The following is a simple statement of cash flows for XYZ Corporation Inc, which has been in business for only one month:

XYZ Corporation Inc

Statement of Cash Flows the month ended 31 December 20-1

Opening cash balance		$0
Net income before taxes	$15,400	
Subtract: net changes in current assets and liabilities from operations	−$38,000	
Cash from operations		−$22,600
Investing activities		$0
Financing activities: sale of Class A shares	$25,000	
Dividends paid	−$800	
Cash from financing activities		$24,200
Ending cash balance		**$1,600**

The statement reflects the increase in XYZ Corporation Inc's cash balance from zero on 1 December 20-1 to $1,600 by the end of the month. It shows a different picture than the net income from operations of $15,400, which was determined according to accounting principles.

H. CHARACTERIZATION OF TRANSACTIONS

We saw in Chapter 1 that financial statements involve:

- characterization;
- classification; and
- communication.

The proper categorization of items informs the reader as to the nature of the underlying transaction. For example, revenue (from ordinary business activities) and a gain (from an incidental or peripheral transaction) both increase equity. However, the categorization of a transaction under the appropriate heading provides relevant information about how equity may continue to grow in the future. Hence, we see financial analysts often report separately on net income from operations and extraordinary gains, which may not occur in the future.

A common issue in characterizing transactions is whether the transaction involves an expenditure on account of an asset or an expense. Mischaracterization can lead to disastrous financial results for investors. See, for example, WorldCom, which mischaracterized USD$8 billion of expenses as assets and increased its income. The company's apparent growth turned out to be largely illusory, facilitated by accounting trickery of reporting expenses as assets and, therefore, enlarging current profits, which propelled the company's stock price. At the 2005 trial, held in Manhattan, former employees testified that Ebbers (the CEO) had urged them to inflate WorldCom's financial results to make the company appear more profitable than it was.

WorldCom had USD$107 billion in assets when it applied for bankruptcy protection in July 2002—the largest bankruptcy filing in US corporate history at the time—and its rapid fall reverberated throughout the industry. As in all such debacles, thousands of employees lost their jobs, insurance, pensions, and retirement savings when the price of the company's stock plummeted. Ebbers's defence was that he relied on experts: "I'm not an engineer by training; I'm not an accountant by training," he said. "I'm the coach. I'm not the point guard who shoots the ball."[9] Despite his argument that he had been misled by subordinates and in the dark about any wrongdoing, the jury were not convinced and convicted him of securities fraud, conspiracy, and filing false reports.

The characterization of expenses and capital assets is also important for tax purposes. The *Income Tax Act*[10] permits the deduction of expenses in computing business income[11] but prohibits the deduction of capital expenditures.[12] This plays a key role in determining net income subject to tax in the year.

The ultimate irony of financial arrangements like this is that the company would pay higher taxes based on its fictitious profits than it would have if it had used proper accounting for net income. In the

9 Katharine Q Seelye & Daniel Victor, "Bernard J. Ebbers, WorldCom Chief Jailed in Fraud, Dies at 78" *The New York Times* (3 February 2020), online: www.nytimes.com/2020/02/03/business/bernard-ebbers-dead.html.

10 RSC, 1985, c 1 (5th Supp) [*ITA*].

11 *ITA*, s 9.

12 *ITA*, s 18(1)(b).

result, the tax authorities gained excessive tax revenues, management benefited from its inflated stock options, and the investors ultimately lost.

The WorldCom scandal was the largest accounting scandal in American history until Bernie Madoff's Ponzi scheme, involving billions of dollars and thousands of victims, was revealed in 2008.

I. ADDITIONAL INFORMATION

1. The Notes

In addition to the quantitative statements discussed above, there are additional qualitative principles specifically selected and applied to the financials. They are a form of financial "alerts" that may, for example, provide information on pending lawsuits, viability of pension and retirement plans, stock option dilutions, income tax assessments, and contingent liabilities. The Notes should be carefully reviewed as that is where management often discloses its skeletons.

2. Sample Extract of Notes from Royal Bank of Canada (2019)

The following is Note 2 of the Royal Bank of Canada's Annual Report for the year ended 31 October 2019:

> The significant accounting policies used in the preparation of these Consolidated Financial Statements, including the accounting requirements prescribed by OSFI, are summarized below. These accounting policies conform, in all material respects, to IFRS. Except where otherwise noted, the same accounting policies have been applied to all periods presented.
>
> In preparing our Consolidated Financial Statements, management is required to make subjective estimates and assumptions that affect the reported amount of assets, liabilities, net income and related disclosures. Estimates made by management are based on historical experience and other assumptions that are believed to be reasonable. Key sources of estimation uncertainty include:

determination of fair value of financial instruments, the allowance for credit losses, insurance claims and policy benefit liabilities, pensions and other post-employment benefits, income taxes, carrying value of goodwill and other intangible assets, litigation provisions, and deferred revenue under the credit card customer loyalty reward program. Accordingly, actual results may differ from these and other estimates thereby impacting our future Consolidated Financial Statements. Refer to the relevant accounting policies in this Note for details on our use of estimates and assumptions.

3. Management's Discussion & Analysis (MDAs)

Public companies that report under securities laws to regulatory bodies, such as the Ontario Securities Commission or the Securities & Exchange Commission (US), will also include management's explanation of operating and financial matters as well as detail on some financial figures. These disclosures assist in understanding the financial statements and making forecasts.

SEDAR is the name of the official website that provides access to most public securities documents and information filed by issuers with the thirteen provincial and territorial securities regulatory authorities (Canadian Securities Administrators or CSA) in its filing system. The statutory objective of making this information public is to enhance investor awareness of the business and affairs of issuers and to promote confidence in the transparent operation of capital markets in Canada. Achieving this objective relies heavily on the provision of accurate information on market participants.

The following is a sample extract from MD&A of Royal Bank of Canada in its third quarter 2019 Report filed with SEDAR:

Overview

Our focus is to maximize total shareholder returns (TSR) through the achievement of top half performance compared to our global peer group over the medium-term (3–5 years), which we believe reflects a longer-term view of strong and consistent financial performance.

Maximizing TSR is aligned with our three strategic goals discussed earlier and we believe represents the most appropriate measure of shareholder value creation.

TSR is a concept used to compare the performance of our common shares over a period of time, reflecting share price appreciation and dividends paid to common shareholders. The absolute size of TSR will vary depending on market conditions, and the bank's relative position reflects the market's perception over a period of time of our overall performance relative to our peers.

Financial performance objectives are used to measure our performance against our medium-term TSR objectives and are used as goals as we execute against our strategic priorities.

We review and revise these financial performance objectives as economic, market and regulatory environments change. By focusing on our medium-term objectives in our decision-making, we believe we will be well-positioned to provide sustainable earnings growth and solid returns to our common shareholders. . . .

2019 vs. 2018

Net income of $12,871 million increased $440 million or 4% from a year ago. Diluted EPS of $8.75 was up $0.39 or 5% and ROE of 16.8% was down 80 bps. Our Common Equity Tier 1 (CET1) ratio was 12.1%, up 60 bps from a year ago.

Our results reflected strong earnings in Personal & Commercial Banking and Wealth Management, and solid results in Insurance, partially offset by lower results in Investor & Treasury Services and Capital Markets. Our results also reflected the impact in the prior year of the U.S Tax Reform which resulted in the write-down of net deferred tax assets, as well as an increase due to the impact of foreign exchange translation.

Personal & Commercial Banking earnings increased mainly due to average volume growth of 7% and higher spreads. These factors were partially offset by higher PCL and an increase in staff-related costs as well as technology and related costs.

Wealth Management results increased mainly due to higher average fee-based client assets, an increase in net interest income and a gain on the sale of the private debt business of BlueBay of $134 million (after-tax). These factors were partially offset by increased costs in support of business growth, higher variable compensation commensurate with revenue growth and higher PCL.

Insurance earnings were up mainly due to the impact of new longevity reinsurance contracts, partially offset by higher claims costs.

Investor & Treasury Services results decreased primarily due to lower funding and liquidity revenue, severance and related costs associated with repositioning of the business, as well as lower revenue from our asset services business.

Capital Markets results were down driven by lower revenue in Corporate and Investment Banking, higher PCL and higher technology and related costs. These factors were partially offset by a lower effective tax rate largely reflecting changes in earnings mix, higher revenue in Global Markets and the impact of foreign exchange translation.

Corporate Support net loss was $28 million, largely due to the impact of an unfavourable accounting adjustment, residual unallocated costs and unfavourable tax impacts, partially offset by asset/liability management activities. Net loss was $155 million in the prior year, largely due to the impact of the U.S. Tax Reform of $178 million as noted above, partially offset by asset/liability management activities.

J. THE AUDIT REPORT

The audit report is a key element of financial statements. Unlike the other financial statements for which management is responsible, the audit report belongs to the auditor, who should be independent of the company on which it reports. This independence is the basis on which investors and users rely to make their decisions. As Chairman, Arthur Levitt of the Securities & Exchange Commission (US) said in a speech to New York University Center for Law and Business (10 May 2000):[13]

---

13 Arthur Levitt, "Speech by SEC Chairman: Renewing the Covenant With Investors," presented at the US Securities & Exchange Commission (New York University:

> The accounting profession must be like Caesar's wife. To be suspected is almost as bad as to be convicted. There has always been this higher standard for the auditor. It is not enough that the accountant on an engagement act independently. For investors to have confidence in the quality of the audit, the public must *perceive* the accountant as independent.

The report contains the auditor's opinion on the financials and notes any deficiencies if the financials do not comply with accounting and disclosure principles. The report typically follows a standard format, which will set out the scope of the audit work performed, adherence to generally accepted accounting principles, fair presentation of the information in the financials, and any material deficiencies noted.

1. Sample Audit Opinions

1) "In our opinion, the accompanying financial statements present *fairly*, in all *material* respects, the financial position of . . . as at December 31, 20-1 and the results of its operations and its cash flows for the year then ended in accordance with *Canadian accounting standards* . . ."
2) "In our opinion, the financial statements referred to previously present *fairly*, in all *material* respects, the financial position of XYZ Company as of December 31, 20-2, 20-1 and 20-0, and the results of its operations and its cash flows for the years then ended in conformity with *accounting principles generally accepted* in the United States of America."

Despite minor variations, we note the similarity between Canadian and US audit opinions. Both emphasize "fairness" (not absolute accuracy), "materiality" (not absolute accuracy), and compliance with "accounting standards and principles," which may differ between the two countries.

Center for Law and Business (10 May 2000), online: www.sec.gov/news/speech/spch370.htm.

K. DOUBLE-ENTRY BOOKKEEPING

The mere mention of "double-entry bookkeeping" strikes terror in the hearts of most people. The whole idea of "debits and credits" is a chilling experience, even for grown adults who can be reduced to tears after a five-minute discourse on the subject.

We saw above the fundamental accounting equation: Assets (A) = Liabilities (L) + Equity (E), where:

> Assets are economic resources controlled by an entity as a result of past transactions or events and from which future economic benefits may be obtained;
>
> Liabilities are obligations of an entity arising from past transactions or events, the settlement of which may result in the transfer or use of assets, provision of services, or other yielding of economic benefits in the future; and

Equity is the ownership interest in the assets of a profit-oriented enterprise after deducting its liabilities.

Practically speaking, double-entry bookkeeping simply means that every transaction has two entries for accounting purposes: (1) the use of funds, and (2) the source of financing (What got? How got?). Thus, by definition, since every transaction is recorded from the same two perspectives, the result must be that the sum of all uses of funds will exactly equal the sum of all sources of financing. This is a metaphysical truth.

The only point that we should note at this time is that even balanced books can be completely wrong. Balancing is simply a mathematical by-product of the double entry system. Wrong and fraudulent books will still balance. Indeed, it would be a foolish corporate fraudster who would not first balance the books. A balance sheet out of balance is a red flag. But a balanced balance sheet should not be a sedative.

Financial statements provide information about an economic entity's financial performance, economic resources and legal obligations to investors, creditors, management, tax authorities, and other regulators. Thus, we use financial statements to assess management's performance, predict the entity's ability to generate future cash flows to meet obligations, assess the return to shareholders, and measure tax liabilities.

The Balance Sheet and the Income Statement are closely interrelated and must be read together in order to present a complete and meaningful picture of the profitability and solvency of a business.

1. Bookkeeping Examples

The following transactions illustrate the operation of the fundamental Balance Sheet accounting equation A = L + E.

Assume that A and B open a retail business on 1 January, Year 1 with each contributing $2,500, and take out a bank loan of $10,000. The opening balance sheet *as at* 1 January Year 1, would appear as follows:

Balance Sheet as at 1 January Year 1 ($)			
Assets:		Liabilities & Equity:	
Cash	15,000	Bank loan	10,000
		Owners' equity:	
		Capital A	2,500
		Capital B	2,500
Total	**15,000**		**15,000**

We see that the Balance Sheet balances: the left side of the statement, which lists all the property that the business owns, is *exactly equal* to the right side of the statement, which lists its sources of financing. In other words, the statement informs the reader as to *what* the business owns (assets) and discloses *how* it financed the assets (liabilities and equity). Hence, the Balance Sheet informs any reader without further explanation that the business entity (the retail business) owned $15,000 of property (assets) as at 1 January Year 1, and that it held it in the form of cash. Further, it informs the reader that two individuals and an outsider financed the firm from two sources—one external (bank loan of $10,000) and the other internal (owners' equity of $5,000).

On 2 January Year 1, the business leases office space at an annual rent of $6,000 and pays two months' rent on that date.

Balance Sheet as at 2 January Year 1 ($)			
Assets:		**Liabilities & Equity:**	
Cash	14,000	Bank loan	10,000
Prepaid rent (two months)	1,000	Owners' equity:	
		Capital A	2,500
		Capital B	2,500
Total	**15,000**		**15,000**

Here, the business exchanged one type of asset, cash, for another asset, prepaid rent. The prepaid rent is an asset because it is an *unexpired* cost as at 2 January that will benefit future operations. It will become an expense as time passes.

On 4 January Year 1, the business acquired office furniture at a cost of $3,000, paying $1,500 in cash with a promise to pay the balance in ninety days.

Balance Sheet as at 4 January Year 1 ($)			
Assets:		**Liabilities & Equity:**	
Cash	12,500	Accounts payable	1,500
Prepaid rent (two months)	1,000	Bank loan	10,000
Office furniture	3,000	Owners' equity:	
		Capital A	2,500
		Capital B	2,500
Total	**16,500**	**Total**	**16,500**

Here, the business acquires an asset, furniture, and finances it by paying with another asset (cash) and by credit (accounts payable). The accounting equation continues and the balance sheet balances.

On 15 January Year 1, the business hired two employees at a monthly salary of $1,000 each and paid their salaries on 31 January Year 1.

Balance Sheet as at 31 January Year 1 ($)			
Assets:		**Liabilities & Equity:**	
Cash	11,500	Accounts payable	1,500
Prepaid rent (two months)	500	Bank loan	10,000
Office furniture	3,000	Owners' equity:	
		Capital A	1,750
		Capital B	1,750
Total	**15,000**	**Total**	**15,000**

The points to note in the 31 January Balance Sheet are: First, the prepaid rent is now only $500 because one month has passed and the rent for January is now an expired cost or an expense. Second, cash is $1,000 lower than before because the business paid $500 to each of two employees for half a month's salary. Third, retained earnings has dropped by $1,500 because the business has incurred $1,500 in expenses (salary $1,000 and rent $500) but without any corresponding sales income.

Rent	$500
Salaries	$1,000
Total	**$1,500**

During the month of February Year 1, the business sold merchandise and collected $6,000 cash, again paying its staff $2,000 in salary.

Balance Sheet as at 28 February Year 1 ($)			
Assets:		**Liabilities & Equity:**	
Cash	15,500	Accounts payable	1,500
Prepaid rent (two months)	0	Bank loan	10,000
Office furniture	3,000	Owners' equity:	
		Capital A	3,500
		Capital B	3,500
Total	**18,500**	**Total**	**18,500**

Cash has gone up by $4,000 because the business had cash sales of $6,000 and salary expense of $2,000. Note that by the end of February, all of the prepaid rent has now expired and become an expense.

Each of the transactions described used the fundamental equation: A = L + E. We see that the business owns property (assets) that cost $18,500, now held in two forms, cash and office furniture, and that the firm is financed, at 28 February Year 1, by outsiders to the extent of $11,500, with insiders (owner's equity) providing the balance of $7,000.

The balance sheet does not, however, disclose any information as to *how* and *why* the owners' interest in the business increased from $5,000 (2 January) to $7,000 (28 February) during the two months of operations. The balance sheet tells only half of the story. Based on the balance sheet alone it would be difficult, if not impossible, for any user to assess the profitability of the business. Should the owners, A and B, for example, be required to pay income tax on the increase in their equity of $2,000, or on some other amount? We look to the income statement to find the answer.

The purpose of the income statement is to disclose *how* a business has performed between two successive points in time. In this sense, it is a connecting link between successive balance sheets. Whereas a balance sheet informs a reader *where* a business stands as at a given time, an income statement reveals *how* the business moved from its opening position to the closing balance sheet.

Continuing with the previous illustration, the income statement reveals the following information:

Income Statement for the two months ended 28 February Year 1 ($)		
Sales revenue		6,000
Expenses:		
Wages	3,000	
Rent	1,000	
		4,000
Net income		**2,000**
Allocation of net income to A	1,000	
Allocation of net income to B	1,000	

This statement now informs the reader *how* the owner's equity increased by $2,000 from 2 January to 28 February. Specifically, the business generated revenues of $6,000 and incurred expenses of $4,000 in the process of generating those revenues, leaving an excess of revenues over expenses (net income) of $2,000. The purpose of the income statement is to match revenues earned with expenses incurred to generate the revenue. The statement usually explains the change in the owners' equity between successive points in time.

L. ACCOUNTING METHODS

Accounting principles and conventions deal with the methodology behind the task of matching revenues and expenses. To this point, we have used the term "income" to denote the excess of revenues earned over expenses incurred to generate those revenues. Hence, in one sense income is an increase in net wealth; conversely, a loss is a decrease in net wealth. This definition is terse and obvious but mathematically demonstrable. The essence of the concept is thereby reduced to "gain during an interval of time." "Gain" is the *sine qua non* of income. While this definition satisfies the purpose of conceptual explanation, it is necessary to adapt it to use it in the preparation of financial statements.

1. Time Intervals

As a preliminary matter, it is essential to select the appropriate "interval of time" between successive financial statements. For no other reason than that of administrative convenience, we conventionally prepare financial statements at least annually. Thus, annual financial statements for external reporting and tax purposes are now, with limited exceptions, the general rule. It is the statutory requirement of annual reporting that gives rise to several income measurement problems.

2. Cash vs Accrual Accounting

The first of the measurement problems is to determine whether we should prepare financial statements on a "cash basis" or on an "accrual basis." The principal distinction between the two methods of accounting arises in connection with the treatment of accounts receivable and payable.

Accounts receivable from customers and employers are not included in income under the cash method until the entity actually receives the cash. In contrast, under the accrual method, we must report income when the entity completes its services and bills for them, regardless of when the customer actually pays the account. Thus, the distinction between the two is one of timing.

In cash basis accounting, we record business transactions at the time, and in the accounting period, when the business receives the cash or disburses the amount.

Example

Assume an accounting period of 1 January to 31 December and the sale of merchandise on 15 December Year 1 for $3,000 with payment received on 15 January, Year 2. A cash basis business would record and report the $3,000 revenue in Year 2. Further assume that the cost of the merchandise that the business sold was $1,000, which it paid in cash at time of purchase on 1 December Year 1. A cash basis business would record and report the cost of merchandise sold in Year 1. The effect of the purchase and sale of merchandise would be reflected in the income statements of the business as follows:

Cash Basis	**Year 1** ($)	**Year 2** ($)	**Combined** ($)
Sales revenue	0	3,000	3,000
Cost of goods sold	−1,000	0	−1,000
Net income (loss)	−1,000	3,000	2,000

Regardless of the accounting method, the *combined* net income of the business in the forgoing circumstances would always amount to $2,000. However, there is a difference in timing net income.

The disadvantage of the cash basis method lies in the mismatching in a particular accounting (fiscal) period of revenues earned and expenses incurred to earn those revenues. Thus, Year 1 shows a net loss of $1,000 due to the combined effect of early expense recognition and delayed revenue recognition. A year later, the statement shows net income of $3,000 by ignoring the earlier expense write-off. Each of Years 1 and 2 viewed in isolation presents a distorted result of the underlying business transaction: namely, an economic increase of $2,000 in net wealth.

We can only determine net income with absolute accuracy when the reporting period for financial statements covers the entire life of a business. The selection of a time period shorter than the life of the business changes the task from income determination to allocation and estimation of net income. We justify the sacrifice in mathematical accuracy, however, by the regulatory and business convenience that results from timely financial statements.

In most situations, cash basis accounting distorts the financial statements of an entity and conceals the true impact of business transactions. A notable exception is in the reporting of employment income for tax purposes. Individuals must report employment income on a cash basis. This requirement results from a balancing of the enhanced administrative convenience to the employee, the employer, and the Canada Revenue Agency, and the minimal distortion that occurs in measuring employment income on a cash basis.

In contrast with the cash basis of accounting, accrual accounting recognizes revenue when an entity realizes and reports expenses in the same time period as the revenues for which they were incurred. The accrual basis is premised on the rationale that reporting revenues earned and expenses incurred in the same accounting period provides a better "matching," and that such matching more accurately depicts the underlying business transaction. Using the same figures as in the previous example, an income statement prepared on an accrual basis would disclose the following:

Accrual Basis	Year 1 ($)	Year 2 ($)	Combined ($)
Sales revenue	3,000	0	3,000
Cost of goods sold	–1,000	0	–1,000
Net income (loss)	2,000	0	2,000

Although the combined net incomes of the two years is the same in both the cash basis and accrual basis methods of reporting, the latter method more accurately reflects the increase in net wealth in each period. (The outstanding accounts receivable of $3,000 as at 31 December Year 1 represents debt that increases net wealth.)

Regardless of when the accounting entity actually receives cash, accrual accounting requires the reporting of revenue in the fiscal period in which the entity realizes it. The rationale that debt represents an increase in wealth is one that is particularly appropriate to any modern economy. At the same time, the accrual method requires that an entity should match expenses with corresponding revenues earned in the same fiscal period.

The accrual method also generally prevents tax deferral. For example, if a person pays five years' worth of lease payments in advance, the lump sum is capitalized and written off over a five-year period. Similarly, the lessor will treat the prepaid rents as an asset and recognize only one-fifth of the lump sum in each of the five succeeding years.

Unfortunately, tax and commercial accounting do not always arrive at the same solution. Tax accounting puts the lessor on the cash method and compels them to recognize the full five-year lump-sum payment as income in the year that they receive it.[14] The lessee, however, is not entitled to deduct the lump sum in the year that they pay it but must spread it out over five years. Not surprisingly, this asymmetric policy works to the advantage of the government and against the taxpayer.

M. DISCLOSURE OF FINANCIAL INFORMATION

Berkshire Hathaway Inc's letter to its shareholders is the model for comprehensive disclosure of management's analysis in plain language. A portion of Warren Buffett's (Chairman) annual letter to shareholders of Berkshire Hathaway is reproduced below for illustrative and educational purposes. Buffett is often referred to as the "Oracle of Omaha."

---

14 *ITA* §12(1)(a).

Excerpt from Warren Buffett's (Chairman) 2018 annual letter to shareholders of Berkshire Hathaway[15]

Berkshire earned $4.0 billion in 2018 utilizing generally accepted accounting principles (commonly called "GAAP"). The components of that figure are $24.8 billion in operating earnings, a $3.0 billion non-cash loss from an impairment of intangible assets (arising almost entirely from our equity interest in Kraft Heinz), $2.8 billion in realized capital gains from the sale of investment securities and a $20.6 billion loss from a reduction in the amount of unrealized capital gains that existed in our investment holdings.

A new GAAP rule requires us to include that last item in earnings. As I emphasized in the 2017 annual report, neither Berkshire's Vice Chairman, Charlie Munger, nor I believe that rule to be sensible. Rather, both of us have consistently thought that at Berkshire this mark-to-market change would produce what I described as "wild and capricious swings in our bottom line."

The accuracy of that prediction can be suggested by our quarterly results during 2018. In the first and fourth quarters, we reported GAAP *losses* of $1.1 billion and $25.4 billion respectively. In the second and third quarters, we reported *profits* of $12 billion and $18.5 billion. In complete contrast to these gyrations, the many businesses that Berkshire owns delivered consistent and satisfactory operating earnings in *all* quarters. For the year, those earnings exceeded their 2016 high of $17.6 billion by 41%.

Wide swings in our quarterly GAAP earnings will inevitably continue. That's because our huge equity portfolio—valued at nearly $173 billion at the end of 2018—will often experience one-day price fluctuations of $2 billion or more, all of which the new

---

15 Warren E Buffett, *To the Shareholders of Berkshire Hathaway Inc* (23 February 2019), online: Berkshire Hathaway Inc www.berkshirehathaway.com/letters/2018ltr.pdf.

rule says must be dropped immediately to our bottom line. Indeed, in the fourth quarter, a period of high volatility in stock prices, we experienced several days with a "profit" or "loss" of more than $4 billion.

Our advice? Focus on operating earnings, paying little attention to gains or losses of any variety. My saying that in no way diminishes the importance of our investments to Berkshire. Over time, Charlie and I expect them to deliver substantial gains, albeit with highly irregular timing.

* * * * * * *

Long-time readers of our annual reports will have spotted the different way in which I opened this letter. For nearly three decades, the initial paragraph featured the percentage change in Berkshire's per-share book value. It's now time to abandon that practice.

The fact is that the annual change in Berkshire's book value—which makes its farewell appearance on page 2—is a metric that has lost the relevance it once had. Three circumstances have made that so. First, Berkshire has gradually morphed from a company whose assets are concentrated in marketable stocks into one whose major value resides in operating businesses. Charlie and I expect that reshaping to continue in an irregular manner. Second, while our *equity holdings* are valued at market prices, accounting rules require our collection of *operating companies* to be included in book value at an amount far below their current value, a mis-mark that has grown in recent years. Third, it is likely that—over time—Berkshire will be a significant repurchaser of its shares, transactions that will take place at prices above book value but below our estimate of intrinsic value. The math of such purchases is simple: Each transaction makes per-share intrinsic value go up, while per-share book value goes down. That combination causes the book-value scorecard to become increasingly out of touch with economic reality.

In future tabulations of our financial results, we expect to focus on Berkshire's market price. Markets can be extremely capricious: Just look at the 54-year history laid out on page 2. Over time, however, Berkshire's stock price will provide the best measure of business performance.

* * * * * * *

Before moving on, I want to give you some good news—really good news—that is not reflected in our financial statements. It concerns the management changes we made in early 2018, when Ajit Jain was put in charge of all insurance activities and Greg Abel was given authority over all other operations. These moves were overdue. Berkshire is now far better managed than when I alone was supervising operations. Ajit and Greg have rare talents, and Berkshire blood flows through their veins.

Now let's take a look at what you own.

Focus on the Forest—Forget the Trees

Investors who evaluate Berkshire sometimes obsess on the details of our many and diverse businesses—our economic "trees," so to speak. Analysis of that type can be mind-numbing, given that we own a vast array of specimens, ranging from twigs to redwoods. A few of our trees are diseased and unlikely to be around a decade from now. Many others, though, are destined to grow in size and beauty.

Fortunately, it's not necessary to evaluate each tree individually to make a rough estimate of Berkshire's intrinsic business value. That's because our forest contains five "groves" of major importance, each of which can be appraised, with reasonable accuracy, in its entirety. Four of those groves are differentiated clusters of businesses and financial assets that are easy to understand. The fifth—our huge and diverse insurance operation—delivers great value to Berkshire in a less obvious manner, one I will explain later in this letter.

Before we look more closely at the first four groves, let me remind you of our prime goal in the deployment of your capital: to buy ably-managed businesses, *in whole or part*, that possess favorable and durable economic characteristics. We also need to make these purchases at sensible prices.

Sometimes we can buy control of companies that meet our tests. Far more often, we find the attributes we seek in publicly-traded businesses, in which we normally acquire a 5% to 10% interest. Our two-pronged approach to huge-scale capital allocation is rare in corporate America and, at times, gives us an important advantage.

In recent years, the sensible course for us to follow has been clear: Many stocks have offered far more for our money than we could obtain by purchasing businesses in their entirety. That disparity led us to buy about $43 billion of marketable equities last year, while selling only $19 billion. Charlie and I believe the companies in which we invested offered excellent value, far exceeding that available in takeover transactions.

Despite our recent additions to marketable equities, the most valuable grove in Berkshire's forest remains the many dozens of non-insurance businesses that Berkshire controls (usually with 100% ownership and never with less than 80%). Those subsidiaries earned $16.8 billion last year. When we say "earned," moreover, we are describing what remains after *all* income taxes, interest payments, managerial compensation (whether cash or stock-based), restructuring expenses, depreciation, amortization and home-office overhead.

That brand of earnings is a far cry from that frequently touted by Wall Street bankers and corporate CEOs. Too often, their presentations feature "adjusted EBITDA," a measure that redefines "earnings" to exclude a variety of all-too-real costs.

For example, managements sometimes assert that their company's stock-based compensation shouldn't be counted as an expense. (What else could it be—a *gift* from shareholders?) And restructuring expenses? Well, maybe last year's exact rearrangement won't recur. But restructurings of one sort or another are common in business—Berkshire has gone down that road dozens of times, and our shareholders have always borne the costs of doing so.

Abraham Lincoln once posed the question: "If you call a dog's tail a leg, how many legs does it have?" and then answered his own query: "Four, because calling a tail a leg doesn't make it one." Abe would have felt lonely on Wall Street.

Charlie and I do contend that our acquisition-related amortization expenses of $1.4 billion (detailed on page K-84) are not a true economic cost. We add back such amortization "costs" to GAAP earnings when we are evaluating both private businesses and marketable stocks.

In contrast, Berkshire's $8.4 billion depreciation charge understates our true economic cost. In fact, we need to spend *more* than this sum annually to simply remain competitive in our many operations.Beyond those "maintenance" capital expenditures, we spend large sums in pursuit of growth. Overall, Berkshire invested a record $14.5 billion last year in plant, equipment and other fixed assets, with 89% of that spent in America.

Berkshire's runner-up grove by value is its collection of equities, typically involving a 5% to 10% ownership position in a very large company. As noted earlier, our equity investments were worth nearly $173 billion at year end, an amount far above their cost. If the portfolio had been sold at its yearend valuation, federal income tax of about $14.7 billion would have been payable on the gain. In all likelihood, we will hold most of these stocks for a long time. Eventually, however, gains generate taxes at whatever rate prevails at the time of sale.

Our investees paid us dividends of $3.8 billion last year, a sum that will increase in 2019. Far more important than the dividends, though, are the huge earnings that are annually retained by these companies. Consider, as an indicator, these figures that cover only our five largest holdings:

	Year-end	Berkshire's Share in $ millions of	
Company	**Ownership**	**Dividends**[1]	**Retained Earnings**[2]
American Express	17.9%	237	997
Apple	5.4%	745	2,502
Bank of America	9.5%	551	2,096
Coca-Cola	9.4%	624	(24)
Wells Fargo	9.8%	809	1,263
Total		**2,966**	**6,837**

(1) Based on current annual rate.
(2) Based on 2018 earnings minus common and preferred dividends paid.

GAAP—which dictates the earnings we report—does not allow us to include the retained earnings of investees in our financial accounts. But those earnings are of enormous value to us: Over the years, earnings retained by our investees (viewed as a group) have eventually delivered capital gains to Berkshire that totaled more than one dollar for each dollar these companies reinvested for us.

All of our major holdings enjoy excellent economics, and most use a portion of their retained earnings to repurchase their shares. We very much like that: If Charlie and I think an investee's stock is underpriced, we rejoice when management employs some of its earnings to increase Berkshire's ownership percentage.

Here's one example drawn from the table above: Berkshire's holdings of American Express have remained unchanged over the past eight years. Meanwhile, our ownership increased from 12.6% to 17.9% because of repurchases made by the company. Last year, Berkshire's portion of the $6.9 billion earned by American Express was $1.2 billion, about 96% of the $1.3 billion we paid for our stake in the company. When earnings increase and shares outstanding decrease, owners—over time—usually do well.

A third category of Berkshire's business ownership is a quartet of companies in which we share control with other parties. Our portion of the after-tax operating earnings of these businesses—26.7% of Kraft Heinz, 50% of Berkadia and Electric Transmission Texas, and 38.6% of Pilot Flying J—totaled about $1.3 billion in 2018.

In our fourth grove, Berkshire held $112 billion at year end in U.S. Treasury bills and other cash equivalents, and another $20 billion in miscellaneous fixed-income instruments. We consider a portion of that stash to be untouchable, having pledged to always hold at least $20 billion in cash equivalents to guard against external calamities. We have also promised to avoid *any* activities that could threaten our maintaining that buffer.

Berkshire will forever remain a financial fortress. In managing, I will make expensive mistakes of commission and will also miss many opportunities, some of which should have been obvious to me. At times, our stock will tumble as investors flee from equities. But I will never risk getting caught short of cash.

In the years ahead, we hope to move much of our excess liquidity into businesses that Berkshire will permanently own. The immediate prospects for that, however, are not good: Prices are sky-high for businesses possessing decent long-term prospects.

That disappointing reality means that 2019 will likely see us again expanding our holdings of marketable equities. We continue, nevertheless, to hope for an elephant-sized acquisition. Even at our ages of 88 and 95—*I'm the young one*—that prospect is what causes my heart and Charlie's to beat faster. (Just writing about the possibility of a huge purchase has caused my pulse rate to soar.)

My expectation of more stock purchases is *not* a market call. Charlie and I have no idea as to how stocks will behave next week or next year. Predictions of that sort have *never* been a part of our activities. Our thinking, rather, is focused on calculating whether a portion of an attractive business is worth more than its market price.

* * * * * * *

I believe Berkshire's intrinsic value can be *approximated* by summing the values of our four asset-laden groves and then subtracting an appropriate amount for taxes eventually payable on the sale of marketable securities.

You may ask whether an allowance should not also be made for the major tax costs Berkshire would incur if we were to sell certain of our wholly-owned businesses. Forget that thought: It would be foolish for us to sell any of our wonderful companies even if *no* tax would be payable on its sale. Truly good businesses are exceptionally hard to find. Selling any you are lucky enough to own makes no sense at all.

The interest cost on *all* of our debt has been deducted as an expense in calculating the earnings at Berkshire's non-insurance businesses. Beyond that, much of our ownership of the first four groves is financed by funds generated from Berkshire's fifth grove—a collection of exceptional insurance companies. We call those funds "float," a source of financing that we expect to be cost-free—or maybe even better than that—over time. We will explain the characteristics of float later in this letter.

Finally, a point of key and lasting importance: Berkshire's value is maximized by our having assembled the five groves into a single entity. This arrangement allows us to seamlessly and objectively allocate major amounts of capital, eliminate enterprise risk, avoid insularity, fund assets at exceptionally low cost, occasionally take advantage of tax efficiencies, and minimize overhead.

At Berkshire, the whole is greater—considerably greater—than the sum of the parts.

Repurchases and Reporting

Earlier I mentioned that Berkshire will from time to time be repurchasing its own stock. Assuming that we buy at a discount to Berkshire's intrinsic value—which certainly will be our intention—repurchases will benefit both those shareholders leaving the company and those who stay.

True, the upside from repurchases is very slight for those who are leaving. That's because careful buying by us will minimize any impact on Berkshire's stock price. Nevertheless, there is *some* benefit to sellers in having an extra buyer in the market.

For continuing shareholders, the advantage is obvious: If the market prices a departing partner's interest at, say, 90¢ on the dollar, continuing shareholders reap an increase in per-share intrinsic value with every repurchase by the company. Obviously, repurchases should be price-sensitive: Blindly buying an overpriced stock is value destructive, a fact lost on many promotional or ever-optimistic CEOs.

When a company says that it contemplates repurchases, it's vital that all shareholder-partners be given the information they need to make an intelligent estimate of value. Providing that information is what Charlie and I try to do in this report. We do not want a partner to sell shares back to the company because he or she has been misled or inadequately informed.

Some sellers, however, may disagree with our calculation of value and others may have found investments that they consider more attractive than Berkshire shares. Some of that second group will be right: There are unquestionably many stocks that will deliver far greater gains than ours.

In addition, certain shareholders will simply decide it's time for them or their families to become net consumers rather than continuing to build capital. Charlie and I have no current interest in joining that group. Perhaps we will become big spenders in our old age.

* * * * * * *

For 54 years our managerial decisions at Berkshire have been made from the viewpoint of the shareholders who are staying, not those who are leaving. Consequently, Charlie and I have *never* focused on current-quarter results.

Berkshire, in fact, may be the only company in the Fortune 500 that does not prepare monthly earnings reports or balance sheets. I, of course, regularly view the monthly financial reports of most subsidiaries. But Charlie and I learn of Berkshire's overall earnings and financial position only on a quarterly basis.

Furthermore, Berkshire has no company-wide budget (though many of our subsidiaries find one useful). Our lack of such an instrument means that the parent company has *never* had a quarterly "number" to hit. Shunning the use of this bogey sends an important message to our many managers, reinforcing the culture we prize.

Over the years, Charlie and I have seen all sorts of bad corporate behavior, both accounting and operational, induced by the desire of management to meet Wall Street expectations. What starts as an "innocent" fudge in order to not disappoint "the Street"—say, trade-loading at quarter-end, turning a blind eye to rising insurance losses, or drawing down a "cookie-jar" reserve—can become the first step toward full-fledged fraud. Playing with the numbers "just this once" may well be the CEO's intent; it's seldom the end result. And if it's okay for the boss to cheat a little, it's easy for subordinates to rationalize similar behavior.

At Berkshire, our audience is neither analysts nor commentators: Charlie and I are working for our shareholder-partners. The numbers that flow up to us will be the ones we send on to you.

Non-Insurance Operations — From Lollipops to Locomotives

Let's now look further at Berkshire's most valuable grove — our collection of non-insurance businesses — keeping in mind that we do not wish to unnecessarily hand our competitors information that might be useful to them. Additional details about individual operations can be found on pages K-5–K-22 and pages K-40–K-51.

Viewed as a group, these businesses earned pre-tax income in 2018 of $20.8 billion, a 24% increase over 2017. Acquisitions we made in 2018 delivered only a trivial amount of that gain.

I will stick with pre-tax figures in this discussion. But our after-tax gain in 2018 from these businesses was *far* greater — 47% — thanks in large part to the cut in the corporate tax rate that became effective at the beginning of that year. Let's look at why the impact was so dramatic.

Begin with an economic reality: Like it or not, the U.S. Government "owns" an interest in Berkshire's earnings of a size determined by Congress. In effect, our country's Treasury Department holds a special class of our stock — call this holding the AA shares — that receives large "dividends" (that is, tax payments) from Berkshire. In 2017, as in many years before, the corporate tax rate was 35%, which meant that the Treasury was doing very well with its AA shares. Indeed, the Treasury's "stock," which was paying nothing when we took over in 1965, had evolved into a holding that delivered billions of dollars annually to the federal government.

Last year, however, 40% of the government's "ownership" (14/35ths) was returned to Berkshire — free of charge — when the corporate tax rate was reduced to 21%. Consequently, our "A" and "B" shareholders received a major boost in the earnings attributable to *their* shares.

This happening materially increased the intrinsic value of the Berkshire shares you and I own. The same dynamic, moreover, enhanced the intrinsic value of almost all of the stocks Berkshire holds.

Those are the headlines. But there are other factors to consider that tempered our gain. For example, the tax benefits garnered by our large utility operation get passed along to its customers. Meanwhile, the tax rate applicable to the substantial dividends we receive from domestic corporations is little changed at about 13%. (This lower rate has long been logical because our investees have already paid tax on the earnings that they pay to us.) Overall, however, the new law made our businesses and the stocks we own *considerably* more valuable.

Which suggests that we return to the performance of our non-insurance businesses. Our two towering redwoods in this grove are BNSF and Berkshire Hathaway Energy (90.9% owned). Combined, they earned $9.3 billion before tax last year, up 6% from 2017. You can read more about these businesses on pages K-5–K-10 and pages K-40–K-45.

Our next five non-insurance subsidiaries, as ranked by earnings (but presented here alphabetically), Clayton Homes, International Metalworking, Lubrizol, Marmon and Precision Castparts, had aggregate pre-tax income in 2018 of $6.4 billion, up from the $5.5 billion these companies earned in 2017.

The next five, similarly ranked and listed (Forest River, Johns Manville, MiTek, Shaw and TTI) earned $2.4 billion pre-tax last year, up from $2.1 billion in 2017.

The remaining non-insurance businesses that Berkshire owns—and there are many—had pre-tax income of $3.6 billion in 2018 vs. $3.3 billion in 2017.

Insurance, "Float," and the Funding of Berkshire

Our property/casualty ("P/C") insurance business—our fifth grove—has been the engine propelling Berkshire's growth since 1967, the year we acquired National Indemnity and its sister company, National Fire & Marine, for $8.6 million. Today, National Indemnity is the largest property/casualty company in the world as measured by net worth.

One reason we were attracted to the P/C business was the industry's business model: P/C insurers receive premiums upfront and pay claims later. In extreme cases, such as claims arising from exposure to asbestos, or severe workplace accidents, payments can stretch over many decades.

This collect-now, pay-later model leaves P/C companies holding large sums—money we call "float"—that will eventually go to others. Meanwhile, insurers get to invest this float for their own benefit. Though individual policies and claims come and go, the amount of float an insurer holds usually remains fairly stable in relation to premium volume. Consequently, as our business grows, so does our float. And how it has grown, as the following table shows:

Year	Float (in millions)*
1970	$39
1980	$237
1990	$1,632
2000	$27,871
2010	$65,832
2018	$122,732

* *Includes float arising from life, annuity and health insurance businesses.*

We may in time experience a decline in float. If so, the decline will be very gradual—at the outside no more than 3% in any year. The nature of our insurance contracts is such that we can *never* be subject to immediate or near-term demands for sums that are of significance to our cash resources. That structure is by design and is a key component in the unequaled financial strength of our insurance companies. That strength will *never* be compromised.

If our premiums exceed the total of our expenses and eventual losses, our insurance operation registers an underwriting profit that adds to the investment income the float produces. When such a profit is earned, we enjoy the use of free money—and, better yet, get paid for holding it.

Unfortunately, the wish of all insurers to achieve this happy result creates intense competition, so vigorous indeed that it sometimes causes the P/C industry as a whole to operate at a significant underwriting *loss*. That loss, in effect, is what the industry pays to hold its float. Competitive dynamics almost guarantee that the insurance industry, despite the float income all its companies enjoy, will continue its dismal record of earning subnormal returns on tangible net worth as compared to other American businesses.

Nevertheless, I like our own prospects. Berkshire's unrivaled financial strength allows us far more flexibility in investing our float than that generally available to P/C companies. The many alternatives available to us are always an advantage and occasionally offer major opportunities. When other insurers are constrained, our choices expand.

Moreover, our P/C companies have an excellent underwriting record. Berkshire has now operated at an underwriting profit for 15 of the past 16 years, the exception being 2017, when our pre-tax loss was $3.2 billion. For the entire 16-year span, our pre-tax gain totaled $27 billion, of which $2 billion was recorded in 2018.

That record is no accident: Disciplined risk evaluation is the daily focus of our insurance managers, who know that the benefits of float can be drowned by poor underwriting results. All insurers give that message lip service. At Berkshire it is a religion, Old Testament style.

* * * * * * *

In most cases, the funding of a business comes from two sources—debt and equity. At Berkshire, we have two additional arrows in the quiver to talk about, but let's first address the conventional components.

We use debt sparingly. Many managers, it should be noted, will disagree with this policy, arguing that significant debt juices the returns for equity owners. And these more venturesome CEOs will be right *most* of the time.

At rare and unpredictable intervals, however, credit vanishes and debt becomes financially fatal. A "Russian Roulette" equation—usually win, occasionally die—may make financial sense for someone who gets a piece of a company's upside but does not share in its downside. But that strategy would be madness for Berkshire.

Rational people don't risk what they have and need for what they don't have and don't need.

Most of the debt you see on our consolidated balance sheet—see page K-65—resides at our railroad and energy subsidiaries, both of them asset-heavy companies. During recessions, the cash generation of these businesses remains bountiful. The debt they use is both appropriate for their operations and *not* guaranteed by Berkshire.

Our level of equity capital is a different story: Berkshire's $349 billion is unmatched in corporate America. By retaining all earnings for a very long time, and allowing compound interest to work its magic, we have amassed funds that have enabled us to purchase and develop the valuable groves earlier described. Had we instead followed a 100% payout policy, we would still be working with the $22 *million* with which we began fiscal 1965.

Beyond using debt and equity, Berkshire has benefitted in a major way from two less-common sources of corporate funding. The larger is the float I have described. So far, those funds, though they are recorded as a huge net *liability* on our balance sheet, have been of more utility to us than an equivalent amount of equity. That's because they have usually been accompanied by underwriting earnings. In effect, we have been *paid* in most years for holding and using other people's money.

As I have often done before, I will emphasize that this happy outcome is far from a sure thing: Mistakes in assessing insurance risks can be huge and can take many years to surface. (Think asbestos.) A major catastrophe that will dwarf hurricanes Katrina and Michael *will* occur—perhaps tomorrow, perhaps many decades from now. "The Big One" may come from a traditional source, such as a hurricane or earthquake, or it may be a total surprise involving, say, a cyber attack having disastrous consequences beyond anything insurers now contemplate. When such a mega-catastrophe strikes, we will get our share of the losses and they will be big—*very* big. Unlike many other insurers, however, we will be looking to add business the next day.

The final funding source—which again, Berkshire possesses to an unusual degree—is deferred income taxes. These are liabilities that we will eventually pay, but that are meanwhile interest-free.

As I indicated earlier, about $14.7 billion of our $50.5 billion of deferred taxes arises from the unrealized gains in our equity holdings. These liabilities are accrued in our financial statements at the current 21% corporate tax rate, but will be paid at the rates prevailing when our investments are sold. Between now and then, we in effect have an interest-free "loan" that allows us to have more money working for us in equities than would otherwise be the case.

A further $28.3 billion of deferred tax results from our being able to accelerate the depreciation of assets such as plant and equipment in calculating the tax we must currently pay. The front-ended savings in taxes that we record gradually reverse in future years. We regularly purchase additional assets, however. As long as the present tax law prevails, this source of funding should trend upward.

Over time, Berkshire's funding base—that's the right-hand side of our balance sheet—should grow, primarily through the earnings we retain. Our job is to put the money retained to good use on the left-hand side, by adding attractive assets.

GEICO and Tony Nicely

That title says it all: The company and the man are inseparable.

Tony joined GEICO in 1961 at the age of 18; I met him in the mid-1970s. At that time, GEICO, after a four decade record of both rapid growth and outstanding underwriting results, suddenly found itself near bankruptcy. A recently installed management had grossly underestimated GEICO's loss costs and consequently underpriced its product. It would take many months until those loss-generating policies on GEICO's books—there were no less than 2.3 million of them—would expire and could then be repriced. The company's net worth in the meantime was rapidly approaching zero.

In 1976, Jack Byrne was brought in as CEO to rescue GEICO. Soon after his arrival, I met him, concluded that he was the perfect man for the job and began to aggressively buy GEICO shares. Within a few months, Berkshire bought about ⅓ of the company, a portion that later grew to roughly ½ without our spending a dime. That stunning accretion occurred because GEICO, after recovering its health, consistently repurchased its shares. All told, this half-interest in GEICO cost Berkshire $47 million, about what you might pay today for a trophy apartment in New York.

Let's now fast-forward 17 years to 1993, when Tony Nicely was promoted to CEO. At that point, GEICO's reputation and profitability had been restored—but not its growth. Indeed, at year-end 1992, the company had only 1.9 million auto policies on its books, far less than its pre-crisis high. In sales volume among U.S. auto insurers, GEICO then ranked an undistinguished seventh.

Late in 1995, after Tony had re-energized GEICO, Berkshire made an offer to buy the remaining 50% of the company for $2.3 billion, about 50 times what we had paid for the first half (and people say I never pay up!). Our offer was successful and brought Berkshire a wonderful, but underdeveloped, company and an equally wonderful CEO who would move GEICO forward beyond my dreams.

GEICO is now America's No. 2 auto insurer, with sales 1,200% greater than it recorded in 1995. Underwriting profits have totaled $15.5 billion (pre-tax) since our purchase, and float available for investment has grown from $2.5 billion to $22.1 billion.

By my estimate, Tony's management of GEICO has increased Berkshire's intrinsic value by more than $50 billion. On top of that, he is a model for everything a manager should be, helping his 40,000 associates to identify and polish abilities they didn't realize they possessed.

Last year, Tony decided to retire as CEO, and on June 30, he turned that position over to Bill Roberts, his long-time partner. I've known and watched Bill operate for several decades, and once again Tony made the right move. Tony remains chairman and will be helpful to GEICO for the rest of his life. He's incapable of doing less.

All Berkshire shareholders owe Tony their thanks. *I* head the list.

Investments

Below we list our 15 common-stock investments that at year end had the largest market value. We exclude our Kraft Heinz holding—325,442,152 shares—because Berkshire is part of a control group and therefore must account for this investment on the "equity" method. On its balance sheet, Berkshire carries its Kraft Heinz holding at a GAAP figure of $13.8 billion, an amount reduced by our share of the large write-off of intangible assets taken by Kraft Heinz in 2018. At year end, our Kraft Heinz holding had a market value of $14 billion and a cost basis of $9.8 billion.

				12/31/18
Shares*	Company	Percentage of Company Owned	Cost**	Market
			(in millions)	
151,610,700	American Express	17.9%	$1,287	$14,452
255,300,329	Apple	5.4%	$36,044	$40,271
918,919,000	Bank of America	9.5%	$11,650	$22,642
84,488,751	The Bank of New York Mellon	8.8%	$3,860	$3,977
6,789,054	Charter Communications	3%	$1,210	$1,935
400,000,000	Coca-Cola Co.	9.4%	$1,299	$18,940
65,535,000	Delta Air Lines	9.6%	$2,860	$3,270
18,784,698	Goldman Sachs	4.9%	$2,380	$3,138
50,661,394	JPMorgan Chase	1.5%	$5,605	$4,946
24,669,778	Moody's	12.9%	$248	$3,455
47,890,899	Southwest Airlines	8.7%	$2,005	$2,226
21,938,642	United Continental Holdings	8.1%	$1,195	$1,837
146,346,999	U.S. Bancorp	9.1%	$5,548	$6,688
43,387,980	USG Corp.	31%	$836	$1,851
449,349,102	Wells Fargo	9.8%	$10,639	$20,706
	Others		$16,201	$22,423
	Total Common Stocks Carried at Market		**$102,867**	**$172,757**

* Excludes shares held by pension funds of Berkshire subsidiaries.

** This is our actual purchase price and also our tax basis.

Charlie and I do *not* view the $172.8 billion detailed above as a collection of ticker symbols—a financial dalliance to be terminated because of downgrades by "the Street," expected Federal Reserve actions, possible political developments, forecasts by economists or whatever else might be the subject *du jour*.

What we see in our holdings, rather, is an assembly of companies that we partly own and that, on a weighted basis, are earning about *20%* on the net tangible equity capital required to run their businesses. These companies, also, earn their profits without employing excessive levels of debt.

Returns of that order by large, established and understandable businesses are remarkable under any circumstances. They are truly mind-blowing when compared against the return that many investors have accepted on bonds over the last decade—3% or less on 30-year U.S. Treasury bonds, for example.

On occasion, a ridiculously high purchase price for a given stock will cause a splendid business to become a poor investment—if not permanently, at least for a painfully long period. Over time, however, investment performance converges with business performance. And, as I will next spell out, the record of American business has been extraordinary.

The American Tailwind

On March 11th, it will be 77 years since I first invested in an American business. The year was 1942, I was 11, and I went all in, investing $114.75 I had begun accumulating at age six. What I bought was three shares of Cities Service preferred stock. I had become a capitalist, and it felt good.

Let's now travel back through the two 77-year periods that preceded my purchase. That leaves us starting in 1788, a year prior to George Washington's installation as our first president. Could anyone then have imagined what their new country would accomplish in only three 77-year lifetimes?

During the two 77-year periods prior to 1942, the United States had grown from four million people—about [0.5%] of the world's population—into the most powerful country on earth. In that spring of 1942, though, it faced a crisis: The United States and its allies were suffering heavy losses in a war that we had entered only three months earlier. Bad news arrived daily.

Despite the alarming headlines, almost all Americans believed on that March 11th that the war would be won. Nor was their optimism limited to that victory. Leaving aside congenital pessimists, Americans believed that their children and generations beyond would live far better lives than they themselves had led.

The nation's citizens understood, of course, that the road ahead would not be a smooth ride. It never had been. Early in its history our country was tested by a Civil War that killed 4% of all American males and led President Lincoln to openly ponder whether "a nation so conceived and so dedicated could long endure." In the 1930s, America suffered through the Great Depression, a punishing period of massive unemployment.

Nevertheless, in 1942, when I made my purchase, the nation expected post-war growth, a belief that proved to be well-founded. In fact, the nation's achievements can best be described as breathtaking.

Let's put numbers to that claim: If my $114.75 had been invested in a no-fee S&P 500 index fund, and all dividends had been reinvested, my stake would have grown to be worth (pre-taxes) $606,811 on Jan. 31, 2019 (the latest data available before the printing of this letter). That is a gain of *5,288 for 1.* Meanwhile, a $1 million investment by a tax-free institution of that time—say, a pension fund or college endowment—would have grown to about $5.3 *billion.*

Let me add one additional calculation that I believe will shock you: If that hypothetical institution had paid only *1%* of assets annually to various "helpers," such as investment managers and consultants, its gain would have been *cut in half,* to $2.65 billion. That's what happens over 77 years when the 11.8% annual return actually achieved by the S&P 500 is recalculated at a 10.8% rate.

Those who regularly preach doom because of government budget deficits (as I regularly did myself for many years) might note that our country's national debt has increased roughly 400-fold during the last of my 77-year periods. That's 40,000%! Suppose you had foreseen this increase and panicked at the prospect of runaway deficits and a worthless currency. To "protect" yourself, you might have eschewed stocks and opted instead to buy [a few ounces of] gold with your $114.75.

And what would that supposed protection have delivered? You would now have an asset worth about $4,200, *less than 1% of what* would have been realized from a simple unmanaged investment in American business. The magical metal was no match for the American mettle.

Our country's almost unbelievable prosperity has been gained in a bipartisan manner. Since 1942, we have had seven Republican presidents and seven Democrats. In the years they served, the country contended at various times with a long period of viral inflation, a 21% prime rate, several controversial and costly wars, the resignation of a president, a pervasive collapse in home values, a paralyzing financial panic and a host of other problems. All engendered scary headlines; all are now history.

Christopher Wren, architect of St. Paul's Cathedral, lies buried within that London church. Near his tomb are posted these words of description (translated from Latin): "If you would seek my monument, look around you." Those skeptical of America's economic playbook should heed his message.

In 1788—to go back to our starting point—there really wasn't much here except for a small band of ambitious people and an embryonic governing framework aimed at turning their dreams into reality. Today, the Federal Reserve estimates our household wealth at $108 trillion, an amount almost impossible to comprehend.

Remember, earlier in this letter, how I described retained earnings as having been the key to Berkshire's prosperity? So it has been with America. In the nation's accounting, the comparable item is labeled "savings." And save we have. If our forefathers had instead consumed all they produced, there would have been no investment, no productivity gains and no leap in living standards.

* * * * * * *

Charlie and I happily acknowledge that much of Berkshire's success has simply been a product of what I think should be called *The American Tailwind.* It is beyond arrogance for American businesses or individuals to boast that they have "done it alone." The tidy rows of simple white crosses at Normandy should shame those who make such claims.

There are also many other countries around the world that have bright futures. About that, we should rejoice: Americans will be both more prosperous and safer if *all* nations thrive. At Berkshire, we hope to invest significant sums across borders.

Over the next 77 years, however, the major source of our gains will almost certainly be provided by The American Tailwind. We are lucky—gloriously lucky—to have that force at our back.

The Annual Meeting

Berkshire's 2019 annual meeting will take place on Saturday, May 4th. If you are thinking about attending—and Charlie and I hope you come—check out the details on pages A-2–A-3. They describe the same schedule we've followed for some years.

If you can't join us in Omaha, attend via Yahoo's webcast. Andy Serwer and his Yahoo associates do an outstanding job, both in covering the entire meeting and interviewing many Berkshire managers, celebrities, financial experts and shareholders from the United Stateds and abroad. The world's knowledge of what goes on in Omaha the first Saturday of every May has grown dramatically since Yahoo came on board. Its coverage begins at 8:45 a.m. CDT and provides Mandarin translation.

* * * * * * *

For 54 years, Charlie and I have loved our jobs. Daily, we do what we find interesting, working with people we like and trust. And now our new management structure has made our lives even more enjoyable.

With the whole ensemble—that is, with Ajit and Greg running operations, a great collection of businesses, a Niagara of cash-generation, a cadre of talented managers and a rock-solid culture—your company is in good shape for whatever the future brings.

February 23, 2019

Warren E. Buffett
Chairman of the Board

Chapter 3: Fundamental Accounting Concepts

References

See generally: *CPA Canada Handbook—Accounting*, Chartered Professional Accountants of Canada (2018) [*Handbook*] at Chapter 2, Part II, Section 1000, Financial Statement Concepts.

A. OVERVIEW

The objective of financial statements is to communicate accounting information that is useful to investors, creditors, and other users in allocating resources and/or assessing management stewardship.[1] Accounting comprises a spectrum of financial concepts, conventions, postulates, and axioms that, collectively, provide the reference points that accounting bodies, regulatory agencies, and auditors use to formulate their decisions and opinions. Hence, we need to understand these fundamental concepts, their limitations, and their parameters.

We saw in Chapter 2 that the auditor's opinion on the financials will comment on the audit work performed, adherence to generally accepted accounting principles, and fair presentation of the information. We examine these concepts in this chapter as a stepping stone to discussing the financial statements in greater detail in following chapters.

1 *Handbook* at para 1000.12.

B. BASIC CONCEPTS

The basic concepts are "silent" in that they are not formally stated as part of the financial statements but underlie all financials and are an integral part of them.

1. Judgments and Estimates

First and foremost, all financials involve judgments, estimates, and selection between equally acceptable alternatives. An audit report does not guarantee the accuracy of financial statements. Even an "unqualified" or "clean" opinion provides only "reasonable assurance" that the financials "present fairly" the entity's position and results of operations. This means that financial results should not be interpreted as "absolutes." The final numbers can vary depending upon choices between alternatives, which may be equally acceptable in appropriate circumstances. This is usually stated in the formal auditor's opinion as follows: "As part of an audit in accordance with Canadian generally accepted auditing standards we exercise professional judgment and maintain professional skepticism throughout the audit" (see, for example, Chapter 14, Reports on Financial Statements).

2. Notes

Second, and less well known, is that the accompanying Notes are an integral part of the financial statements. This is often misunderstood because the Notes use qualitative terms that expand on some of the choices and consequences embedded in the quantitative segments of the financials. Unfortunately, readers often overlook the Notes as they are long, boring, and often drafted to obfuscate sensitive issues. Hence, they warrant close scrutiny.

C. BUSINESS ASSUMPTIONS

1. Going Concern

A cardinal concept of financial statements is that, unless otherwise expressly stipulated, they are prepared on the assumption that the enterprise will continue operations in the future as a viable "going concern." This concept of continuity of operations, and its implied presumption of business stability, determines the selection of alternative methods in allocating costs between fiscal periods, such as depreciation.

A corollary of this concept is that in the event that it does not apply, for example, in a situation of anticipated liquidation, that fact will be specifically disclosed. Where a business is to be liquidated, we value its assets according to their liquidation values, which, in turn, will depend upon whether the liquidation is voluntary and orderly or involuntary and compelled. For example, a "fire sale" liquidation usually produces lower values than an ordinary liquidation.

Similarly, we value inventory at the lower of cost or market value. If the entity is a going concern into the indefinite future, it matters little in the measurement of net income in a year. The market value of the inventory will show up in the selling price that the company charges for its products.

The valuation of "purchased goodwill" also depends on the going concern assumption. Goodwill is the premium that a purchaser pays for a business over and above the monetary fair market value of the assets or shares purchased. Purchased goodwill is the difference between the fair market value of shares purchased and the price that the purchaser pays for them. In 2011, for example, Interbrand estimated Coca-Cola's brand value at approximately $72 billion, which will contribute to its goodwill if the company is sold.

2. Separate Entity

Financial statements are prepared on the basis of business entities rather than legal entities. Hence, we separate businesses from their owners. For example, if Jane owns a laundry business and a pizza business, the financials for each business would be separate even though Jane owns both businesses.

3. Monetary Measurements

Financial statements record only facts expressed in monetary terms. They do not record other information that may be highly relevant in determining the viability or success of an enterprise. For example, a law firm's balance sheet will show only how much property the firm owns as assets: cash, receivables, work-in-process, investments, computers, furniture, art, land, and buildings. The firm's balance sheet will not disclose anything about its "real," and most valuable, resource: the talent pool of its lawyers who are the core of the business and generate its revenues. Hence, in evaluating and valuing a business we should be mindful that some of its most valuable resources, such as management, are not quantified in the financials.

4. Objectivity

Accounting statements should reflect objective and verifiable data. Generally, arm's length market prices are objective. *Verifiable* means supported by evidence. Estimates should be based on rational considerations and realistic expectations.

5. Constant Dollars

Another aspect of money measurement is that conventional financial statements assume that all dollars are equal and have constant values. For example, if a business bought ten acres of land in downtown Toronto in 1950 for $1 million and purchased one acre of adjacent land in 2019 for $1 million, the eleven acres of land will show on the books at a cost of $2 million. For accounting purposes, we assume that the 1950s dollar is the same as the 2019 dollar. This is clearly unrealistic.

We know that $1 in 1950 was worth $10.57 in 2019, a percentage change of 957 percent.[2]

Hence, the second purchase of land would be worth $10,570,000 in 1950 dollars. Recent developments in International Financial Reporting Standards (IFRS) require disclosure of market values, but only for certain assets.

We know from empirical evidence that the assumption of constant dollars is not realistic. Nevertheless, we rely on the concept of constant dollars. Hence, for the purposes of valuations, we must be sensitive to the nature of assets shown and the mixing of dollars. It does not matter much if we mix dollar values of certain assets, such as receivables, because of their short life. A March account receivable mixed with a July accounts receivable does not significantly distort the financial statements because the change in value, assuming normal inflation, is slight. The issue is important, however, when we mix capital assets (such as land) that are on the books for many years, sometimes decades or even centuries.

6. Historical Costs

Subject to certain IFRS requirements, the convention is that financial statements are based primarily on the historical cost of assets at the time that the business acquires them. Thereafter, the asset may appreciate or depreciate in value. With certain exceptions for diminution in value of property, plant and equipment, for example, subsequent changes do not usually show up in the balance sheet. Financial statements do not generally reflect the market value of a business or its assets.

The traditional argument in favour of historical cost accounting is that costs are objectively determinable based upon consummated transactions and actual values at the time that the entity purchased the asset. To be sure, historical cost statements are objective and more readily verifiable. Thus, they serve a useful purpose for fiduciary reporting duties by custodians of assets. Historical cost statements,

---

2 Statistics Canada, *Consumer Price Indexed for Canada*, online: www.statcan.gc.ca/eng/subjects-start/prices_and_price_indexes/consumer_price_indexes.

however, are largely irrelevant in the context of fixed asset valuations for other purposes, such as financing, securitization, and purchase and sale of businesses.

Example

If a company acquires a building for $10 million, the asset is on the balance sheet at that cost. The company will depreciate the building over its useful life by allocating the cost of the asset to several accounting periods. For example, if the building has an estimated useful life (with zero residual value) of fifty years, it may allocate $200,000 per year for depreciation. If the building appreciates in value to $80 million in thirty years, the balance sheet will still reflect its original cost minus accumulated depreciation. Unless revalued, the potential gain of $70 million will not show on a conventional balance sheet prepared on the basis of historical costs.

The historical cost model can produce hysterical results. For example, the Disney company carries all the land on its books at their 1930s costs. This information may be objectively verified, but is of limited use to a reader of the company's current financial statements. Similarly, Disney has no cost on its books for all of its "classic" animated features released over the past sixty years. The costs related to these classics have all been written off. Hence, the company clearly has valuable "hidden assets."

Asset values on a balance sheet become increasingly dated the further one moves out in time. A balance sheet prepared according to conventional historical accounting principles for fiduciary reporting to shareholders does not help us in valuing the business for the purposes of obtaining loan financing or in issuing its securities in a public offering.

There are some exceptions to the use of historical cost depending upon the type of asset and the type of business. For example, accounting principles requires that inventory should be valued at the lower of cost or market value. This rule imposes on the historical cost principle to reflect another fundamental assumption of accounting, namely conservatism. Hence, a company may use replacement cost to measure "market value." Similarly, a company may use the discounted present value of future expected cash flows to measure pension liabilities.

Although there is a trend, particularly by the International Accounting Standards Board (IASB), which developed IFRS, towards fair value or current value accounting in an effort to provide more relevant information, the prevalent norm remains historical cost valuation.

D. TIMING ASSUMPTIONS

1. Annual Reporting

We produce financial reports on a regular basis for various reasons, such as statutory requirements under the *Income Tax Act*, *Canada Business Corporations Act*, and various securities statutes. For external reporting purposes, public companies will produce annual audited financial statements for shareholders and reporting to regulatory bodies. Companies may, however, also have to file interim financials (unaudited) with regulators, such as securities commissions.

The thorniest problems in the annual reporting requirement concern the allocation of revenues and costs to appropriate time periods. Current costs are allocated to the income statement and deducted as expenses from revenues earned in computing net income. Costs that will benefit future operations are allocated to the balance sheet, where they will appear as assets to be assigned to future time periods.

We could dispense with allocation problems, if we measured the income of an entity only over its entire life. If the only reporting was at the beginning and at the end of the life of the business, the process is quite simple. To measure the income of the business over its entire life, we would look at the initial investment of cash into the business (stage 1 of the business cycle) and compare it to the ultimate distribution of cash to the owners (stage 7 of the business cycle) when it is liquidated. The excess amount, with appropriate adjustments for interim distributions or additional contributions of cash, would be the income of the business. However, the information would not be particularly relevant and useful to users of the statements.

However, we produce financial statements annually. The shorter the financial reporting period, the more difficult it is to make accurate allocations. In an annual financial report covering the calendar year, it does not matter very much whether we allocate expenses to October, November, or December of the year. In each case, the expenses will be in the appropriate calendar year. However, in preparing annual financials, costs that cross the fiscal year must be allocated to separate reporting periods. A misallocation of expenses, for example, from December to January of the following year will distort financial results.

2. Basis of Reporting

Financial statements have meaning in the context of time. There are three concepts of timing in accounting:

- Cash basis;
- Accrual basis; and
- Time value.

(a) Cash Basis

In the cash basis we record transactions when the enterprise receives or disburses cash. There is no need to match revenues and expenses and the process of income measurement under this method is quite straightforward. It is easy to identify cash receipts and disbursements with certainty. As we shall see, we use this concept in the cash flow statement (see Chapter 12).

(b) Accrual Basis

The accrual concept requires a matching of revenue and expenses according to when the business *earns* its revenues and *incurs* expenses to earn the revenues, regardless of when it actually collects or dispenses cash. The accrual concept requires judgmental decisions and estimates as to when the business should recognize its revenues and identify the appropriate expenses to match with those revenues. Misallocating revenues and expenses will distort annual financial results.

For example, a company that earns revenue of $30 million in Year 1 but assigns expenses of $20 million that it incurs to earn the revenue to Year 2, will overstate income by $10 million in the first year and understate it in the following year. The balance sheet will overstate assets by an equal amount. Although the amounts will balance out over two years, the results will be distorted for each year.

That is what happened to WorldCom.[3] The company's CFO, Scott Sullivan, fraudulently took billions of dollars in operating expenses and spread them out across so-called capital property accounts. This allowed WorldCom to spread the expenses in smaller amounts over a span of years, instead of reporting them immediately. As a result, in 2001, the company reported USD$1.4 billion as profits. Had the operating costs been correctly reported, WorldCom would have lost money for fiscal 2001 as well as in the first quarter of 2002. It was as simple as that: timing manipulation of expenses between time periods that deferred current expenses to the future and increased current profits.

WorldCom's CEO, Bernard Ebbers, was sentenced to twenty-five years in jail for his role in the fraud. Sullivan was sentenced to five years for his cooperation with prosecutors. The company went bankrupt, recording the largest bankruptcy in American history until the financial crisis of 2008. Thousands of people lost their jobs. WorldCom emerged from bankruptcy and re-emerged as MCI, now a subsidiary of Verizon (VZ/NYSE).

Notwithstanding the allocation difficulties that annual reporting creates, it is the most defensible system of financial reporting. Financial reports must be timely in order to be relevant for decision makers. All of the problems of allocations in annual reporting are the price that we pay for making information relevant for users.

---

3 See, generally, Joshua Kennon, "The Worldcom Scandal Explained: How One of the World's Largest Companies Made $3.8 Billion Disappear" *The Balance* (28 May 2020), online: www.thebalance.com/worldcom-s-magic-trick-356121; "WorldCom Ex-CFO Surrenders: Scott Sullivan and Ex-Controller Turn Themselves in to Feds; Ashcroft Hints More Charges May Follow" *CNN Money* (2 August 2002), online: money.cnn.com/2002/08/01/news/worldcom; and "Sullivan Gets Five Years for WorldCom Fraud: Fifth WorldCom executive sentenced to prison in $11 billion scandal" *Associated Press* (11 August 2005), online: NBC News www.nbcnews.com/id/8907976/ns/business-corporate_scandals/t/sullivan-gets-five-years-worldcom-fraud/#.Xv3rVpNKgdk.

(c) Time Value

Money has no monetary value except in the context of time. A dollar today is worth more than a dollar tomorrow. Time value underlies the discipline of finance and is relevant in determining the value of assets, shares, bonds, and long-term liabilities, such as future pension benefits for retirees. Hence, the principle is at the heart of investment, retirement, and tax planning.

The time value concept discounts future earnings and expenses to their present value based on the timing of the estimated receipts and the relevant discount factor, which is linked to interest rates. However, we use time value of money only in limited circumstances in conventional accounting statements. Nevertheless, it is fundamental in the valuation of businesses (see Chapter 5, Time Value of Money and Chapter 18, Retirement Planning).

E. MATCHING PRINCIPLE

The matching principle requires matching of revenues against the costs that the business incurs to earn the revenues. Thus, timing revenue recognition and the matching principle are the heart of proper income measurement. This raises two related issues:

- Timing of revenues; and
- The realization principle.

As a general rule, we recognize revenues only when the business exchange process is substantially complete, and the amount realized and collectability of the consideration is reasonably certain. This usually occurs at point of sale.

An important correlative aspect of revenue recognition is that we should recognize expenses and match them with the revenues for which the business incurred them. Hence, revenues and expenses arising from the same event or transactions should be recorded in the same fiscal period.

Thus, the matching principle allows management and accountants considerable latitude in exercising their judgment on timing of revenue recognition and appropriate matching. The following illustrates the latitude that accountants have in applying the matching principle.

Example

A company buys a business and its intangible assets for $10,000,000. Assume that management determines that the company will benefit from the intangibles for, alternatively, ten years or five years. Using equal write-offs, the annual amortization will be as follows:

Cost of intangibles	$10,000,000
Ten-year amortization	$1,000,000
Five-year amortization	$2,000,000

The point to observe here is that the term of the write-off is largely management's decision, and it can manage to adjust net income by deciding to lengthen or shorten the amortization period.

The mathematics simply adjust to management's estimate of the useful life of the intangibles. If management chooses a ten-year life, its annual expenses will be reduced by $1,000,000 per year, which will boost net income in each year. This flexibility in estimating the life of the asset sometimes leads to "earnings management" of the financial statements.

Summary

- Recognize revenue according to revenue principle;
- Then match expenses in the same period;
- If revenue is deferred, defer expenses;
- Deferred costs will be applied against future revenues.

F. CONSISTENCY

Consistency requires one to prepare financial statements using the same method of accounting between different time periods, unless there is a sound reason for change. The concept of consistency in financial statements is important if we use them to compare numbers over time.

Consistency facilitates comparability. We want to compare apples with apples. Where there is a change in the method applied in valuing assets or determining income between two time periods, the effect of the change should be fully explained in the Notes to the financial statements (see Chapter 15, Interpretation of Financial Statements).

G. MODIFYING PRINCIPLES

1. Conservatism

It is not entirely coincidental that accountants have a reputation for being conservative. Conservatism is in fact one of the basic concepts underlying financial statements, a core accounting value and a fundamental principle of income measurement.

Simply stated, conservatism means that where there is uncertainty about recording a transaction or the value that one should attach to an asset, we should resolve the uncertainty with a "bias" in favour of understating income or assets. Stated another way, one should not anticipate gains, but one may anticipate losses.

Hence, where there is uncertainty, estimates of a conservative nature attempt to ensure that assets, revenues, and gains are not overstated and, conversely, that liabilities, expenses, and losses are not understated. However, conservatism does *not* mean deliberate understatement of assets, revenues, and gains or the deliberate overstatement of liabilities, expenses, and losses.[4]

See, for example, the expert's opinion in the *Nortel* trial:

> Frequently assets and liabilities are measured in the context of significant uncertainties; historically; managers, investors, and accountants have generally preferred that possible errors in measurement be in the direction of understatement rather than overstatement of net income and net assets. This has led to the convention of Conservatism.[5]

---

4 See *Handbook* at paras 2–27.

5 *R v Dunn*, 2013 ONSC 137 at 210, citing Accounting Principles Board Statement No 4, "Reporting Gains and Losses from Extinguishment of Debt: An Amendment of APB Opinion No 30" *Financial Accounting Standards Board* (March 1975), online: www.fasb.org/pdf/fas4.pdf at para 17.

Similarly, in paragraph 35 of Accounting Principles Board Statement No 4:

> The uncertainties that surround the preparation of financial statements are reflected in a general tendency toward early recognition of unfavorable events and minimization of the amount of net assets and net income.

And in Financial Accounting Standards Board:[6]

> [W]here there is a range of accrued liabilities and no estimate within the range is better than any other, the lowest estimate in the range must be used . . . [paragraph 8 of the FAS 5] is not inconsistent with the accounting concept of Conservatism.

To summarize: where there are acceptable alternatives for accounting treatment, choose the one that:

- has the least favourable impact on owners' equity;
- reflects lower asset values;
- reflects higher liability values;
- avoids favorable exaggeration.

Example

Assume that a business purchased products at a cost of $10 per unit. The business has 10,000 units on hand at the end of the year. Due to market conditions, the unit cost of the product has fallen to $7 per unit as at the year-end.

Cost per unit of product	$10
Units on hand end of the fiscal period	$10,000
Face value of ending inventory	$100,000
Market value per unit of product	$7
Inventory write-down to market value	$30,000
Ending inventory at lower of cost or market	$70,000

6 "Accounting for Contingencies" *Financial Accounting Standards Board* (March 1975), online: www.fasb.org/pdf/fas5.pdf

In these circumstances, it is appropriate for the business to write-down its ending inventory to $70,000 on the balance sheet by charging $30,000 to the income statement as an expense. The replacement value of the inventory is less than its historical cost. Thus, by being conservative, we reduce net income by $30,000 and the inventory on the balance sheet by an equivalent amount.

Note, however, that over-conservatism can also be misleading. In the above example, it would be improper and misleading to use $5 per unit based entirely on pessimistic speculation that the future value of the inventory may fall even further.

Besides which, conservatism in asset valuation *costs* investors who hold shares in publicly listed companies. Conservative valuation leads to lower net income, which, in turn, leads to lower earnings-per-share (EPS), a key figure that financial analysts use in valuing the market price of shares. Excessive conservatism means that a person selling their shares in the market may not get their "real" value because management has depressed the earnings numbers through pessimistic valuations.

Excessive conservatism also creates "hidden reserves." As noted earlier, the Disney company, for example, carries its "classic" animated features at zero on its balance sheet. If assets are undervalued because of conservative estimates, the real value of the business is actually higher than its stated value. Thus, the real value of the assets is hidden because they are understated. That is why on the sale of a business, the vendor will insist upon the full value of the business and will not be satisfied with accepting an amount based solely on book values. Thus, business valuators use principles of finance to value assets and businesses based on future cash flows rather than accounting statements.

Conservatism also affects the income statement and net income. The general tenet of conservatism is to recognize revenues only when the business is reasonably certain that it has earned them and has realized the revenue. Hence the maxim is: Do not anticipate revenue recognition until there is substantial certainty; recognize expenses as soon as reasonably possible.

2. Materiality

The concept of materiality is simple. Financial statements should disclose all significant information and disregard insignificant events or amounts. However, we need to balance cost of theoretical purity with the utility of the information for decision makers.

The concept of materiality overrides all technical rules and principles of accounting. Materiality is one of those concepts that is difficult to define with precision. Materiality reflects pragmatic adaptation of theory. Thus, management, the accountant, and the auditor must determine whether an item is material or not in each case where the issue arises.

An item is material if it would have a significant effect upon an important judgment based on the statement. There is, however, no bright line test of "materiality." Materiality is a matter of professional judgment in the particular circumstances.

Paragraph 2-20 of the *Handbook* comments as follows:

> In preparing financial statements, the importance of information to the users of financial statements must be considered. The financial statement information presented or disclosed should be material to the users of the financial statements.

The key is whether the measurement, disclosure, or omission influence or change a user's decision-making process. If an item would influence or change the decisions of users, it is material.

The determination of whether information is material requires professional judgment and is not simply a quantitative measurement. For example, the loss of a distribution right or even a key employee who is critical to future operations could change a creditor's risk assessment and should be disclosed. The judgment is qualitative rather than quantitative.

Materiality is not a fine line where one dollar less is not material or one dollar more is material. It represents a gray area between what is very likely not material and what is very unlikely material. As the *Handbook* states:

> Quantitative guidelines for materiality do exist but are a matter of judgment. For example, CAS 320, *Materiality in Planning and*

> *Performing an Audit*, paragraph A7, states that auditors may consider 5% of profit before tax from continuing operations appropriate for a manufacturing entity. However, preparers of financial statements should use caution when using guidelines developed for auditors since the auditors are providing an opinion on financial statements prepared by others. Preparers of financial statements should attempt to be more accurate and not tolerate misstatements or omissions.[7]

There are two aspects to materiality: subjective and objective. The subjective aspect is that an item should be considered to be material if knowledge of the item would affect a user's decision. This is a difficult test to apply because one can never be certain of the audience of potential users of financial statements. At best, one might say that an item is material if a reasonable person's decision might be affected by knowledge of the particular item.

Given the difficulty of applying the subjective test, many accountants tend towards a mathematical solution, where one measures the particular item being considered for materiality against a base figure or reference number. For example, an item may be considered material if it is more than 1 percent of net income or 5 percent of assets.

Relying on such mathematical relationships gives the accountant a sense of greater certainty, but the method has traps. Even if a particular item is below the mathematical threshold (say 1 percent of net income), it is important to determine the cumulative effect of all other immaterial items to see if their total exceeds the threshold. For example, if there are ten items that are being considered for materiality and each of them represents 0.8 percent of net income, the cumulative effect of all ten (assuming they all pull in the same direction) might be 8 percent of net income.

In practice, there is a trade-off between qualitative characteristics, particularly between relevance and reliability. For example, there is often a trade-off between the timeliness of producing financial statements and the reliability of the information reported in the statements. Generally, the aim is to balance the characteristics in order to meet

7 *Handbook* at para 2-20.

the objective of financial statements. The relative importance of the characteristics in different cases is a matter of professional judgment.[8]

Hence, regardless whether the accountant uses a subjective or objective method of resolving materiality, they must exercise judgment. We can see how it is quite easy for various accountants reviewing the same information to arrive at different conclusions on the financial statements.

However, some items are always material, regardless of the amount and its relationship to net income or net assets. For example, transactions between related parties must be disclosed, regardless of the amounts involved. Bribes that contravene the *Corruption of Foreign Public Officials Act* must be disclosed regardless of the amount paid.

Similarly, uncertainties that relate to events or conditions that cast doubt upon the ability of an enterprise to continue as a going concern are always material.

3. Full Disclosure Principle

Financial statements should disclose all significant information in a complete and understandable form. They should ensure "fair" presentation so that a reasonably prudent investor would not be misled.

It is generally assumed that users of financial statements have a reasonable understanding of accounting and can exercise reasonable diligence in studying the information. However, there are aspects of financial statements that are inherently complex. For example, the statement of cash flows is not simple in the best of circumstances. Nevertheless, it is an important financial statement that should be included as part of fair disclosure. Its complexity does not make it acceptable to exclude such a statement and care should be taken to make it as understandable as possible.

Finally, the Notes to financial statements should disclose and not obfuscate or hide significant information.

---

8 *Handbook* at para 1000.21.

H. FAIR VALUE ACCOUNTING

We saw above that, as a general rule, traditional financial statements are prepared based on historical costs. Hence, for example, if a company invests $10 million on a new factory, the standard accounting practice is to initially record that factory at $10 million and depreciate it on that cost over time.

We justify the historical cost principle on the basis that it provides objective, measurable evidence. This is useful if the sole purpose of financial statements is on stewardship accounting for fiduciary obligations. But how useful is the principle if one of the objectives of financial reporting is also to provide the relevant information to providers of capital to make decisions?

There are a few exceptions to this generally accepted principle, such as, for example, in the case of marketable securities that are marked to market. We use fair value accounting mainly for easily marketable financial instruments, such as stocks or bonds. The idea is that it's more accurate to value those securities at the current market prices by "marking to market."

Fair value accounting would consider an asset's current value based on the price it would sell for in a notional orderly market transaction at that moment. However, that does not mean that there necessarily is an actual market or a buyer for the particular asset. Instead, we would need to calculate the value based upon valuation yardsticks, such as the income and cash flows that it will generate.

A major objection to fair value accounting is that it would be based on estimates, rather than "hard facts," and that those estimates could be erroneous or intentionally manipulated (known as "earnings management").

However, most of accounting requires judgments and relies on estimates from management. For example, we estimate the useful life of property, plant, and equipment and its ultimate salvage value to allocate its cost through depreciation. We estimate the collectability of accounts receivable and provide for bad debts. Banks estimate impairments to their loan portfolios, and insurance companies estimate loss reserves.

However, pending the wholesale reform of the current accounting model, which is highly unlikely, the only important point to remember is the basis and assumptions upon which the current model operates.

I. MISCONCEPTIONS ABOUT ACCOUNTING

To this point we have examined the underlying fundamental concepts and principles of accounting and financial statements. Now, it is useful to summarize a few misconceptions. Some examples:

1) All dollars are equal
   No, costs are historical costs and co-mingled over time.

2) Accounting reflects values
   Not usually. Historical cost accounting measures the flow of costs, which may differ from market and fair values.

3) Balance Sheet assets represent market values
   No, with some exceptions, assets generally reflect only unallocated historical costs.

4) "Net Worth" really means net worth
   No, it is merely a residual figure, the difference between assets and liabilities, generally measured on historical costs rather than market or fair values.

5) Incurring an expense is the same as paying for the expense
   No, there can be timing differences between incurring an expense and paying for it.

6) Earning revenues is the same as getting paid
   No, earning and collection of revenues are different. There can be timing differences.

7) Depreciation, depletion, and amortization are cash expenses
   No, they are allocations of the historical costs of fixed assets, natural resources, and intangible assets.

Chapter 4: Accounting Principles

A. OVERVIEW

Accounting is the language of the world of commerce, law, finance, and taxation. As with all languages, there are certain rules and conventions that we follow to make the language universally understandable and acceptable. We refer to these rules as concepts and principles, which also provide the foundation for calculations of taxable income under the *Income Tax Act*. In this chapter we commence with general principles. In subsequent chapters, we will examine specific tax rules of accounting (see Chapter 17, Law and Accounting).

When accounting rules are generally accepted by business and the appropriate authorities, we refer to them as "generally accepted accounting principles" (GAAP), which are essentially the "rules" within which accountants are supposed to operate. GAAP comprise assumptions, principles, standards, rules and conventions for preparing and presenting financial statements. However, GAAP is not rigid and allows choices between permissible alternatives, which can produce varied results. As with all languages, there can be misinterpretations and distortions, whether accidental or deliberate. Hence, there is no shortage of accounting scandals in the world of business and securities markets (see Chapter 16, Accounting and the Law).

Professionals rely upon accountants to explain the technical details of particular principles. For example, in a lawsuit involving the accounting treatment of inventory valuation, lawyers can rely on professional opinions on the appropriate principles to apply. However, GAAP is not a set of "black and white" rules that always produce a single "bottom line" number. Management can use GAAP to "manage earnings." Although lawyers may not have detailed technical expertise in GAAP, they should be sufficiently familiar with them in drafting legal agreements and in financial or tax litigation.

B. SOURCES OF GAAP?

The Chartered Professional Accountants of Canada (CPA Canada), which publishes the *CPA Handbook* on accounting and auditing, is the leading source of Canadian GAAP. The *Canada Business Corporations Act* and regulatory statutes recognize the *Handbook* as the benchmark of accounting principles for financial reporting.

Section 1100 of the *Handbook* describes what constitutes GAAP:

> Generally accepted accounting principles (GAAP) encompass broad principles and conventions of general application as well as rules and procedures that determine accepted accounting practices at a particular time.[1]

The International Accounting Standards Board (IASB) has other GAAP. Canada has adopted international GAAP, known as IFRS, as formulated by the IASB.

Part I of the *Handbook* contains IFRS for "public enterprises," which are entities, other than not-for-profit organizations, that have issued, or are in the process of issuing, debt or equity instruments that are, or will be, outstanding and traded in a public market. Public enterprises must use IFRS in their reports.

Part II of the *Handbook* addresses accounting standards for private enterprises (ASPE). Private enterprises have a choice between applying ASPE in Part II or IFRS in Part I.

---

1 At para 1100.02(b)

Both GAAP and IFRS are broad principles and conventions that apply generally in accounting. They also refer to specific rules to determine accounting practices at particular times. However, all GAAP are not identical. Hence, for example, the United States has its own set of GAAP.

When the *Handbook* does not cover a particular matter, accountants refer to other sources of information, such as, for example, International Accounting Standards, Financial Accounting Standards Board (FASB) pronouncements in the United States, or academic accounting literature. Unfortunately, these sources do not always agree on what constitutes GAAP. The *Handbook* addresses potential differences by saying, "the relative importance of these various sources is a matter of professional judgment in the circumstances."

Accounting bodies develop GAAP by exercising professional judgment and analyzing the advantages and disadvantages of alternative methods of accounting and reporting. Since accounting cannot produce precise answers to every question, GAAP provide rules and guidelines that are generally acceptable. Hence, GAAP may offer choices between allowable alternatives or may be entirely silent on the particular point. However, the basic standard of ASPE is mandatory:

> An entity *shall* apply every primary source of GAAP that deals with the accounting and reporting in financial statements of transactions or events encountered by the entity.[2]

Lawyers often refer to GAAP in legal contracts. For example, contracts that contain negative covenants relating to financial status or ratios, such as working capital or debt/equity ratios, frequently state that the relevant financial statements must be prepared in accordance with GAAP. In these circumstances, it is best to specify which GAAP (Canadian, American, or International) should apply to the particular contract.

---

2 *Handbook* at para 1100.03.

C. THE AUDIT OPINION

The auditor's report will refer specifically in its audit opinion to GAAP. See, for example, the auditor's report for the hypothetical company Duggan Inc:[3]

> In our opinion, the financial statements present fairly, in all material respects, the financial position of Duggan Inc. as at September 30, 20-2 and 20-1, and its financial performance and its cash flows for the years ended September 20-2 and 20-1 in accordance with Canadian generally accepted accounting principles and International Financial Reporting Standards.

D. HIERARCHY OF GAAP SOURCES

There are various sources for GAAP. The official statements from organizations that the accounting profession designates as the official body to determine appropriate accounting treatment for financial transactions are the primary official source of GAAP in Canada. These are discussed in the CPA's *Handbook*.

1. Regulatory Agencies

Regulatory bodies can also stipulate GAAP or other principles for their specific purposes.

(a) Canada

Securities Commissions may require public companies to file financial statements in compliance with GAAP. See, for example, section 78(1) of the *Ontario Securities Act*:[4]

> Every reporting issuer that is not a mutual fund and every mutual fund in Ontario shall file annually within 140 days from the end of its last financial year comparative financial statements relating separately to,

3 See Chapter 14, Reports on Financial Statements.

4 RSO 1990, c S.5, s 78 (1)

(a) the period that commenced on the date of incorporation or organization and ended as of the close of the first financial year or, if the reporting issuer or mutual fund has completed a financial year, the last financial year, as the case may be; and
(b) the period covered by the financial year next preceding the last financial year, if any, made up and certified as required by the regulations and in accordance with *generally accepted accounting principles.*

(b) United States

The official body for determining the appropriate accounting treatment of transactions in the United States is the Financial Accounting Standards Board (FASB), an independent body created to establish and improve standards for financial accounting and reporting. FASB includes a cross-section of accountants, academics, and users of financial statements. In order to enhance the independence of the board, the seven members of FASB cannot hold private employment during their tenure of service on the board.

The Securities and Exchange Commission (SEC) regulates the sale of securities and securities markets in the United States. Therefore, publicly listed companies must file regular financial statements according to specified criteria with the SEC.

The SEC does not routinely develop accounting principles and generally leaves the development of such principles to the independent accounting bodies, such as FASB. Nevertheless, the SEC will, on some occasions, promulgate accounting principles if it is of the opinion that the accounting bodies are not acting fast enough on their own.

E. ROLE OF MANAGEMENT IN SELECTING GAAP

Management has a key role in determining the nature, format, and underlying principles of its financial statements. Indeed, the General Representation Letter (see Chapter 14) that corporate management submits to its auditors usually states in the first paragraph, generally:

> We are responsible for the fair presentation in the financial statements of financial position, results of operations and changes in financial position in conformity with generally accepted accounting principles.

To discharge its responsibility, management must select accounting principles, determine asset life, and decide reporting policies.

Interaction between management and the corporation's auditors is delicate and, sometimes, can be tense. Accounting firms are first and foremost businesses that value client retention. They realize, however, that corporations can "opinion shop" if the audit firm is being difficult in respect of particular items on the financial statements. Hence, corporations can pressure auditors to their point of view. In 2000, for example, Enron paid Arthur Andersen $52 million, $25 million for auditing services and $27 million for non-auditing services, and ranked as Andersen's second-largest client.

Thus, at the very least, a lawyer who uses financial statements should have a general understanding of GAAP and IFRS that the audit opinion addresses. The Notes to the financial statements will set out the corporation's selection of GAAP and IFRS and their impact on the financial statements.

F. ARE GAAP GOOD FOR YOU?

GAAP and IFRS are rules of content that deal with compiling and disclosing information in the financial statements. The first item in the Notes to the financial statements will usually describe the principles that the particular enterprise applies in the preparation of its financial statements.

GAAP and IFRS provide considered and properly researched principles that accountants can adhere to and readers can use with reasonable confidence in understanding financial statements. They also make financial statements more comparable if the underlying GAAP are the same for all statements. There are, however, some limiting aspects of GAAP. We saw in Chapter 3, for example, that conservatism is one of the basic underlying concepts of accounting, which generally tends to understate income and assets. Although this may be a desirable aspect for stewardship and fiduciary accounting, conservatism can lead to lowered valuations, which can mislead investors.

Given the variety of GAAP that one may apply to measure or report upon the same situation, we can have many net income figures, each of which is equally valid according to GAAP. This is an important consideration in drafting legal agreements. In a sense, consistent application is just as important as the particular GAAP that one applies in a contract. Thus, in many situations, cash flow is a much more reliable figure because it eliminates the need to select between alternative accounting principles. Ultimately, cash is king and difficult to manipulate.

G. ACCOUNTING STANDARDS

The two key accounting standard–setting bodies in the world are the International Accounting Standards Board (IASB) and the Financial Accounting Standards Board (FASB) of the United States. The two bodies do not have identical standards. Indeed, they differ quite significantly in some areas such as "fair value" accounting.

Broadly speaking, fair value accounting standards value a firm's assets and liabilities based upon market value rather than historical cost. The difference is particularly important in the valuation of financial instruments, property, plant, and equipment on the balance sheet.

Canada adopted International Financial Reporting Standards (IFRS) for public companies in 2011 even though our economy is more closely linked to the United States, which primarily uses FASB pronouncements.

1. Framework of IFRS

IFRS refers to the body of authoritative literature of the International Accounting Standards Board (IASB) designed principally for use by profit-oriented entities. The IFRS Foundation oversees the IASB. The IASB developed a *Conceptual Framework* for the development of IFRS and for guidance to accountants in preparing public enterprise financial statements.

The objective of the IASB is to narrow the differences among accounting standards, procedures, and regulations that apply in the preparation of financial statements in different countries. Harmonization facilitates economic decision making and international comparisons of companies. Reporting entities must comply with all of the standards and interpretations (including disclosure requirements) and make a positive statement of explicit and unreserved compliance in the audit opinion.

The framework recognizes that the overall objective of general-purpose financial reporting is to provide financial information about the reporting entity that is useful to existing and potential investors, lenders, and other creditors in making decisions about providing resources to the entity. According to IASB, general purpose financial reports are not designed to show the value of a reporting entity. However, they provide useful information to help existing and potential investors, lenders, financial analysts, and other creditors to estimate the value of the reporting entity.

Financial statements prepared according to IFRS will involve:

- Accounting policy choices;
- Professional judgment in making estimates;
- Fair value measures in the financial statements; and
- Disclosures in the Notes.

The overall objective of IFRS is fair presentation in the financial statements. In this aspect, there is no underlying difference in principle between IFRS and Canadian GAAP. However, absent specific prohibition, IFRS admits deviation and provides for a "true and fair" override if complying with IFRS would produce misleading information. In contrast, there is no such concept of a true and fair view override in Canadian GAAP.

Financial reports are based on estimates, judgments, and models rather than exact depictions. The Conceptual Framework of IFRS establishes the concepts that underline those estimates, judgments, and models. The fundamental qualitative characteristics of useful financial information are relevance and faithful representation.

Financial statements, *per se*, are not predictions or forecasts. However, relevant and faithful representation of material financial information is the foundation used by investors, management, and financial analysts to make predictions and forecasts. Thus, accounting is a stepping stone to financial valuation.

Faithful representation does not imply perfect accuracy in all respects, but the information should be relevant and faithfully represented. Financial information in reports should be material. Materiality means that omission or misstatement of the information could influence decisions that users make based on the information about a specific reporting entity.

Materiality is an entity-specific aspect of relevance based on the nature or magnitude, or both, of the items to which the information relates in the context of its financial report. The IASB does not specify a uniform quantitative threshold for materiality. Whether an item is material or not is a matter of professional judgment in the circumstances of the entity's financial information.

Both IFRS and Canadian GAAP rely on a conceptual framework of accounting standards, which preparers of financial statements can refer to in the absence of specific guidance. IFRS states that it does not apply to items that are "immaterial." Although Canadian GAAP does not contain a similar explicit statement, that, in practice, is how accountants apply GAAP.

2. Who Is Affected by IFRS?

The underlining objective of the IFRS is to produce global accounting standards that are transparent and provide comparable information on financial statements. By having a single set of global standards, public corporations can eliminate multiple GAAP reconciliations between countries.

Both IFRS and Canadian GAAPs are comprehensive sets of principles-based standards that have a similar form and structure and share similar basic concepts of income recognition and measurement principles. However, IFRS requires more professional judgment and a greater volume of disclosures.

Canadian GAAPs are simpler to apply and, therefore, less costly. They also have fewer disclosure requirements than IFRS. However, Canada adopted IFRS for "publicly accountable enterprises" (PAE), which include "profit-oriented" enterprises with publicly issued securities and enterprises that hold assets in a fiduciary capacity for a broad group of outsiders. PAE also includes government business enterprises, such as the Ontario Securities Commission.

Not-for-profits are not required to adopt IFRS.

IFRS and Canadian GAAP require that management account for financial transactions based upon their substance, rather than their legal form. Thus, accountants should recognize transactions with shareholders in their capacity as shareholders directly in the equity portion of the financial statements rather than through the income statement.

However, there are differences between IFRS and Canadian GAAP. Generally, there are fewer bright lines and rules in IFRS. Hence, there are more accounting policy choices and fewer interpretative matters. In particular, there are substantial differences in valuation and disclosure of impaired assets and securitizations.

3. IFRS and US GAAP

In Canada, IFRS affects large multinational public companies and small private corporations differently. The big four Canadian accounting firms and their multinational corporate clients like IFRS because it simplifies transnational accounting and makes it easier for them to raise corporate capital in international markets. On the other hand, IFRS is more complex and expensive to administer and, therefore, not particularly attractive to smaller companies that operate only in Canada.

The SEC continues to study the implications for US companies. It appears, however, that the United States will not adopt a full-blown changeover to IFRS because of the cost and burden of any such change. Instead, the United States may, like Canada, adopt a compromised "endorsement" model that would gradually incorporate IFRS into the US system of rules, while maintaining authority to modify or reject any international rules if it saw fit.

H. FAIR VALUE MEASUREMENT

Most items are disclosed in the financial statements based on their historical costs. In some circumstances, such as inventories, an enterprise may reduce historical cost to reflect a loss if fair market value is less than cost. In other cases, such as property, plant, and equipment, an entity may reduce or increase amounts to reflect their fair value.

IFRS 13 defines fair value and has a framework for measuring and disclosing it in the financials.

Fair value is the price that an entity would receive if it sold an asset or paid to transfer a liability in an orderly transaction between market participants as at the measurement date. Thus, fair value is a market-based measurement, not an entity-specific measurement. When measuring fair value, an entity uses the assumptions that market participants would use to price the asset or liability under current market conditions. As such, the entity's intention to hold the asset is not relevant when measuring fair value. The measure is what the buyer will pay for the benefit that it expects to generate from the use (or sale) of the assets, regardless of the entity's actual intentions.

I. GAAP AND TAX LAW

The key to an efficient tax system is the accurate measurement of the taxable base on which taxes are payable. For example, sales taxes must identify taxable sales of goods and services. Usage taxes, such as highway tolls, must identify the consumer's use of the particular facility. Gasoline taxes are based on the quantity of gas pumped into the automobile.

The general measure of the taxable base in commerce is the profit that the business earns. Hence, we start with basic commercial principles as understood by Venetians and first articulated by Fra Luca Bartolomeo de Pacioli, a fifteen century Italian mathematician, Franciscan friar, collaborator with Leonardo da Vinci, and early contributor to the field now known as accounting. He is considered "The Father of Accounting and Bookkeeping."

Section 9 of the *Income Tax Act* also starts with the premise of measuring "profit" for a business—that is, how much "better off" in economic terms a taxpayer has become during the fiscal period. By "better off" we mean the excess of the taxpayer's revenues over expenses, as adjusted for consumption. The objective of the process is to produce "an accurate picture" of the taxpayer's *profit* for a taxation year.[5]

Since the Act does not define the term "profit," we determine the profit of a business by applying ordinary commercial principles. With rare exceptions, the Act does not refer specifically to accounting principles but only to books of account and records. For example, section 230(1) simply states:

> Every person carrying on business and every person who is required, by or pursuant to this Act, to pay or collect taxes or other amounts shall keep records and books of account (including an annual inventory kept in prescribed manner) at the person's place of business or residence in Canada or at such other place as may be designated by the Minister, in such form and containing such information as will enable the taxes payable under this Act or the taxes or other amounts that should have been deducted, withheld or collected to be determined.

The initial objective of tax accounting is to obtain a "fair," "true," and "accurate picture" of a taxpayer's profit for a taxation year.

"Income" and "profit" are measures of net economic gain. Hence, we must identify the amount of the gain, relate it to the appropriate time period, and recognize the gain for tax purposes according to specific tax rules. We measure, recognize and time income by applying accounting and legal principles to economic transactions.

The important point to note, however, is that determining business income for the purposes of income tax is ultimately a question of law.[6]

See Chapter 17, Law and Accounting.

---

5 See *Canderel v Canada*, [1998] 1 SCR 147.

6 *Ibid*.

1. Overview of Tax Structure

The following is an overview of the structure for measuring income for tax purposes. It highlights the interaction between commercial principles, such as GAAP, and statutory rules.

Overview

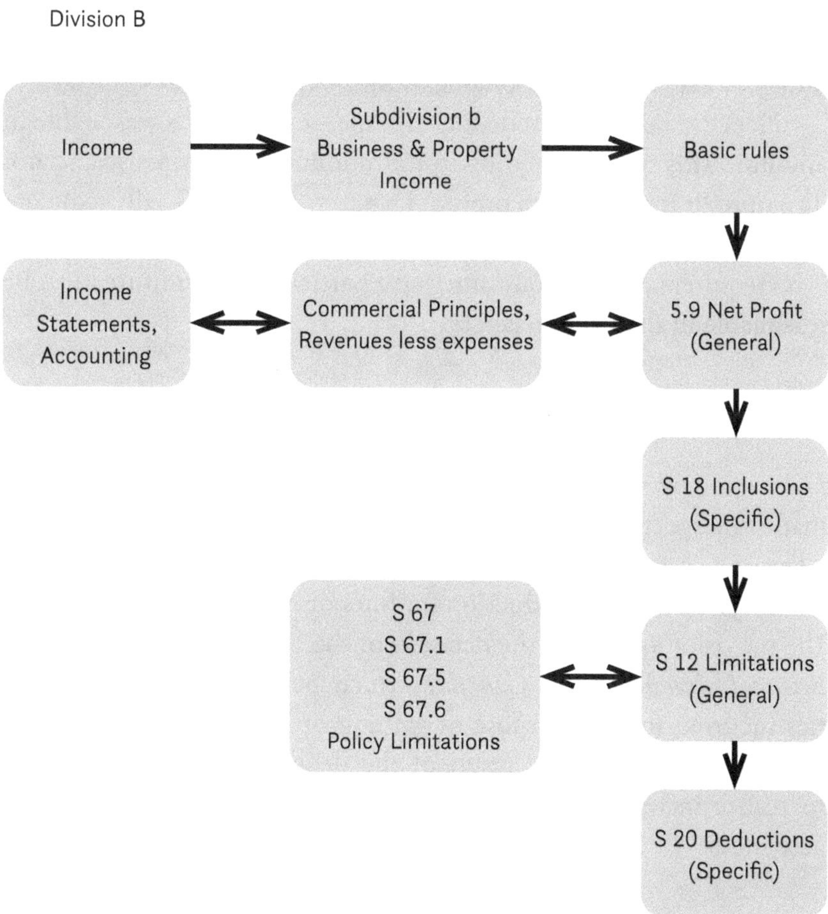

We see the central role of commercial principles in determining business profit under section 9 of the Act. However, the Act is more than the embodiment of GAAP and commercial practices. It contains a vast body of "policy limitations" and "incentive provisions"

to promote other socio-economic, cultural, and political objectives, which have nothing to do with the "fair" or "accurate" measure of net gains or profit. The following are some examples.

2. Unreasonable Expenses

Section 67: "In computing income, no deduction shall be made in respect of an outlay or expense in respect of which any amount is otherwise deductible under this Act, except to the extent that the outlay or expense was reasonable in the circumstances."

Hence, a taxpayer can deduct an expense only if it is reasonable in amount. This rule relates only to the amount of the expense and not its nature. It is intended to prevent taxpayers from artificially reducing their income for tax purposes through unreasonable expenses. There is no requirement in accounting that a particular expenditure must be reasonable in the circumstances.

3. Fines and Penalties

ITA section 67.6 states: "In computing income, no deduction shall be made in respect of any amount that is a fine or penalty imposed under a law of a country or of a political subdivision of a country."

This rule denies a deduction for fines or penalties imposed by law. The provision overturns the decision of the Supreme Court in *65302 British Columbia Ltd v Canada*,[7] which held that fines and penalties incurred for the purpose of gaining or producing income were deductible expenses as a result of the deliberate business decisions to realize income, regardless that they were incurred on improper activities.

7 [1999] 3 SCR 804, [2000] 1 CTC 57, 99 DTC 5799 (SCC): an over-quota levy imposed on an egg-producing poultry farm by the BC Egg Marketing Board on an allowable deduction pursuant to section 9(1) and paragraph 18(1)(a) of the *ITA*. The levy was incurred as part of the taxpayer's day-to-day operations. Since the fine was imposed to remove the profit of over-quota production, it was allowable as a deductible current expense.

4. Bribes and Illegal Payments

ITA section 67.5 (1) states: "In computing income, no deduction shall be made in respect of an outlay made or expense incurred for the purpose of doing anything that is an offence under section 3 of the *Corruption of Foreign Public Officials Act* or under any of sections 119 to 121, 123 to 125, 393 and 426 of the Criminal Code, or an offence under section 465 of the Criminal Code as it relates to an offence described in any of those sections."

ITA section 67.5(1) prohibits the deduction of bribes paid to foreign public officials. The provision is based exclusively on grounds of public policy and morality and has nothing to do with the earning of net gains.

Chapter 5: Time Value of Money

"Time is money."

A. OVERVIEW

Money has no monetary value except when it is put in the context of time. Stated alternatively: A dollar today is worth more than a dollar tomorrow. The value of money depends upon the effect of time on interest on investments. This basic principle of finance is the key to investment, retirement, and tax planning.

Interest is the rental cost of borrowing money. For the borrower, interest is the rent that they pay for borrowing money. For the lender, interest is the income earned from lending money. They are just different sides of the same coin. Hence, the time value of money pervades finance, accounting, law, and taxation.

B. IMPLICATIONS

There are two dimensions of value: future and present. Given a sum of money, we can determine its value at some future date if we know the interest rate at which we can invest the money. Conversely, if we know that we are to receive a sum of money in the future, we can determine its value today if we know the rate at which it is, or can be, invested. Thus, all money has "time value."

There are three factors to consider in determining the present or future value of a sum of money: (1) the prevailing interest rate; (2) time; and (3) the net tax effect of earning or paying interest. In lawsuits, it is counsel's responsibility to raise time value issues to determine the discounted value of judgments looking to lost profits or anticipated future earnings. Judges do not make such calculations on their own initiative. Counsel must educate them.[1]

C. UNDERLYING FACTORS

The value of money depends upon three factors:

1. Principal amount (P);
2. Interest rate (r); and
3. Time (n).

"Principal" is the amount of money originally borrowed or loaned. "Interest" is compensation for use of money (similar to rent). Time refers to the period of borrowing, lending, or investing.

All assets, tangible and intangible, can be expressed in terms of their future or present value if we can determine the rate at which the principal amount of the asset is invested or discounted over a period of time.

The appropriate rate is usually the market-determined interest or investment rate. In economic terms, "interest" is the rental cost of borrowing money. As with all rentals, the cost of renting money may be fixed in advance, determinable at a future time, or variable according to specified conditions. Thus, interest and time are inextricably related. An interest rate is relevant if, and only if, it is related to time.

Although most of us learned about simple and compound interest in school, we are less intuitive about the concept of the discounted value of future sums of money. This is because we are taught to think intuitively of investing for the future, but not of the present value of sums of money to be received in the future. Yet, mathematically

1 *Lehrman v Gulf Oil Corp*, 500 F.2d 659, 672 (5th Cir 1974, *cert denied*, 420 US 929 (1975)).

speaking, future and present values are mirror images of each other looked at from the opposite ends of a telescope. The primary purpose of determining future and present values is to measure money in comparable terms across time by translating future dollars into economically equivalent current dollars, and vice versa.

D. IMPLICATIONS FOR LAWYERS

Lawyers deal with assets that have "time value" in virtually all aspects of practice, including their billable hours. The following are some common areas of law practices involving time value issues:

- Matrimonial settlements;
- Damages in litigation;
- Value of charitable donations;
- Value of life and remainder interests of trusts;
- Truth in lending laws [interest on credit cards];
- Usury laws under the *Criminal Code*;
- Funding for children's education;
- Annuities in life insurance products;
- Retirement planning and tax shelters;
- Compound interest on outstanding tax assessments;
- Tax deferral; and
- Estate planning.

Although the context may vary, the underlying principle is invariable: Time is money.

E. FINANCIAL IMPLICATIONS

There are two underlying aspects of the time value of money: simple interest and compound interest.

1. Simple Interest

We start with the concept of interest and simple arithmetic. We refer to interest paid only on the amount originally invested, but not on any interest that accrues subsequently, as simple interest. Simple interest is a function of the principal sum (*P*) multiplied by rate (*r*) multiplied by time (*n*):

$$\text{Interest} = P \times r \times n$$

Example 1

Suppose that Sonny has $1,000, which he can invest at 10 percent simple interest per year. If he invests the $1,000 for one year, he will earn $100 at the end of the year. If he invests for the second year, his interest will be determined on the *original* principal amount ($1,000) but without any added interest. He will continue to earn the same amount of interest ($100) each year according to the formula:

$$\text{Interest} = P \times r \times n$$

Where:

P = the principal amount invested;
r = the rate of interest for the time period; and
n = the time period.

The "*n*" in the formula is always equal to 1. At the end of four years, he will have earned $400, which equals 40 percent on his original principal of $1,000.

Year (n)	Principal (P)	Interest rate (r)	Interest earned
1	$1,000	10%	$100
2	$1,000	10%	$100
3	$1,000	10%	$100
4	$1,000	10%	$100

2. Compound Interest

When we compound interest, the interest earned each year is calculated on the principal amount (*P*) *and* the interest earned in the preceding year.

The formula to determine future compound values is:

$$FV = P(1+r)^n$$

Where:

FV = future value
P = the principal amount invested;
r = the rate of interest for the time period; and
n = the time period.

However, the formula in compounding is exponential in that the variable (n) is now the power, rather than the base.

Example 2

Suppose that India invests $1,000 for four years compounded at 10 percent per year. Then, at the end of year 1, she will earn $100 (same as simple interest), which is then added to the principal amount at the beginning of year 2. Hence, *P* in year 2 now equals $1,100. Then she earns 10 percent on the enhanced principal of $1,100 and will receive $110 at the end of year 2, and so on. At the end of four years, she will have earned $464, which is 46 percent on her original investment of $1,000.

Year (n)	Principal (P)	Interest rate (r)	Interest earned per year
1	$1,000	10%	$100
2	$1,100	10%	$110
3	$1,210	10%	$121
4	$1,331	10%	$133

The compounding effect increases her rate of return by 6 percent over four years.

Example 3

Suppose that Milo invests $10,000 for four years compounded at 10 percent per year. Then, at the end of year 1, he will earn $1000 (same as simple interest), which is then added to the principal amount at the beginning of year 2. Then he earns 10 percent on the enhanced principal of $11,000 and will receive $1100 in year 2, and so on. At the end of four years, Milo would have earned $4,640 (rounded), which is 46 percent on his original investment of $10,000.

We see the impact of exponential growth in the graphic below.

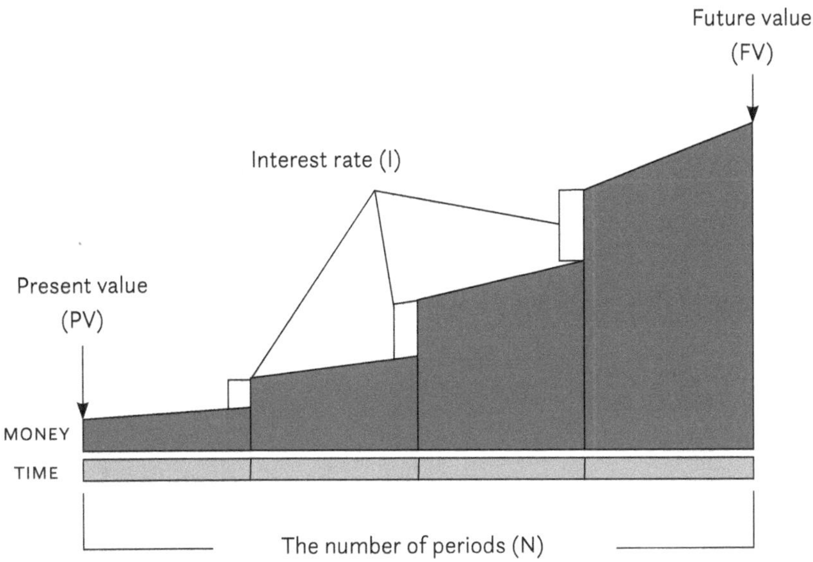

Note, despite their different absolute earnings, the ratio of India's and Milo's earnings remains the same at 1.46. In other words, regardless of the principal amount, the ratio for 10 percent for 4 years remains the same.

Fortunately for the less mathematically inclined, someone pre-calculated the numbers in the body of Future Value Tables for different Rates (*r*) and Times (*n*), so that each ratio represents the shortcut for a specified combination of Rate and Time (see Table 5.1).

3. The Rule of 72

The Rule of 72 allows us to calculate the approximate length of time or interest rate that it will take to double an investment using compound interest. For example, assuming a compound interest rate of 8 percent, it will take approximately nine years (72/8) to double an investment (see Table 5.1). We can estimate the rate of interest required to double money in a specified number of years. For example, if we want to double our money in twelve years (72/6), we need to earn 6 percent annually (see Table 5.1).

F. RETIREMENT PLANNING

How much money will an individual require on retirement? Assume that Sasha invests $30,000 at 8 percent (average long-term rate of return on equities) in a tax-free account when she is 25 years old.

Age (years)	Investment @ 8 percent ($)
25	30,000
34	60,000
43	120,000
52	240,000
61	480,000
70	960,000

Without ever investing another dollar, Sasha will accumulate $960,000 by the time she is seventy.

Berkshire Hathaway Inc's performance illustrates the power of compounding. For the period of 1965–2019, Berkshire's compounded annual gain equalled 20.3 percent compared to the S&P 500 (dividends included) gain of 10.0 percent. The overall gain for the company was 2,744,062 percent (see Berkshire's *2018 Report to Shareholders* in Chapter 2).

We explore retirement planning further in Chapter 18.

G. COMPOUNDING LONG-TERM DEBT

We see the dramatic impact of compounding in a reported incident in the sleepy hamlet of Mittenwalde in Eastern Germany. According to Reuters, the town historian (Vera Schmidt) uncovered a centuries-old debt slip dating back to 1562 in the archives where it had been filed. Mittenwalde apparently lent Berlin 400 Guilders on 28 May 1562 which was to be repaid with 6 percent interest per year. According to Radio Berlin Brandenburg, adjusting the debt for compound interest and inflation, the total debt now lies in the trillions. Apparently, the Mayor of Mittenwalde and his predecessors have asked Berlin for the return of their money and have made such a request every fifty-five years since 1820, but always to no avail. Mittenwalde, which had a population in 2012 of 8,800 people, would benefit enormously from repayment. Berlin, however, is not playing along. Why?

H. FUTURE VALUE

Future value is the sum to which an amount, or a series of periodic equal amounts, will grow at the end of a period of time, invested at a particular *compound* interest rate. The future value of a principal sum of money depends upon the rate of interest, the mode of calculation of the interest, and the duration of investment.

Hence, *future value (FV)* is the amount to which a current Principal (*P*) will grow at the end of a period of time (*n*) invested at a compounded rate (*r*) of interest. The formula is:

$$FV = P(1+r)^n$$

The longer the time horizon for investment and the more frequent the compounding intervals, the greater the future value of a present sum of money.

Example 4

Suppose that Nicola deposits $10,000 in a guaranteed investment certificate (GIC) for a period of one year at 6 percent, the GIC will be worth $10,600 at the end of the year. The interest earned is $600, or 6 percent of the principal amount for one year. If she invested at 6 percent simple interest for four years, the total sum of interest will be $2,400, and the GIC will be worth $12,400 in four years.

In contrast, compound interest refers to the process whereby interest is earned not only on the amount originally invested but also on subsequently accrued interest. Compound interest starts out with exactly the same formula as simple interest but extends it to account for the reinvested interest. Thus, the interest on the second and subsequent time periods is calculated exponentially on the initial principal amount *and* any interest accumulated in preceding time periods.

Example 5

Suppose India invests $10,000 in a GIC at 8 percent compounded annually for two years, the GIC is worth $11,664 at the end of the second year. At the end of the first year the principal and the interest are $10,800 (the same as with simple interest). But the interest for the second year is calculated as 8 percent of $10,800, which is $864.

Future Value Tables specify the value of $1 (*P*) at various interest rates (*r*) over various periods of time (*n*). The tables are a simple way of applying the formula. Alternatively, one can use a financial calculator.

Example 6

Jasmine invests $5,000 in a TFSA, which will earn 8 percent net interest compounded for twenty years. The future value of $1 at 8 percent for 20 years is a factor of **4.66**. Hence, $1 will grow to $4.66 in twenty years. Therefore $5,000 will grow to $23,300 in that time.

Future value tables typically relate interest rates (*r*) and time (*n*) on an annual basis. Where the compounding is more frequent, we must adjust the *r* and *n* factors to accommodate for more frequent compounding effects (see Table 5.1).

Example 7

Suppose that in example 6, Jasmine's investment at the net 8 percent annual rate is compounded semi-annually instead of annually. Then we adjust *r* to 4 percent ($^8/_2$) and *n* to 40 (20×2) semi-annual periods to accommodate semi-annual compounding. Now the appropriate future value factor of $1 is **4.80**. Hence, $1 will grow to $4.80 and $5,000 will grow to $24,000. The semi-annual compounding yields $700 simply by compounding more frequently.

The more frequent the compounding, the higher the cost of borrowing or the rate of return. We can generalize the future value factor when a contract requires interest compounding more than once a year and still use the tables. When interest is compounded *c* times a year, multiply the number of years that (*P*) will be invested by *c*, and divide the interest rate (*r*) by *c* and then see where the two lines intersect on Table 5.1.

Example 8

Suppose that Ravi deposits $2,000 in a tax-free account that pays 6 percent per year, compounded semi-annually, for five years. The bank will pay 3 percent every six months (6% /2) over 10 time periods (5 × 2). A future value table tells us that 3% intersects with 10 time periods for a factor of **1.34**. Hence, the $2,000 will grow to $2,680 in five years.

The message is simple: a lender will benefit from compounding interest as frequently as possible and the borrower will pay more for frequent compounding. Thus, in an open and competitive market, the borrower and the lender should negotiate *both* the interest *rate* and the frequency of compounding intervals. When you see banks advertising different rates of return on the same invested amount, check the frequency of compounding and the advertised rate of interest.

I. ANNUITIES

An *annuity* refers to a series of periodic and equal amounts pursuant to a contractual arrangement. For example, a retiree can purchase an annuity contract from a life insurance company to provide a stream of annual income in retirement. In the simplest case, the buyer of a single-premium life annuity pays a lump sum upfront in return for an annual stream of payments that will last for the buyer's entire life. Thus, an annuity is essentially a form of risk transfer from the annuitant to the issuing life insurance company. The value of the annuity depends upon the amount invested, prevailing interest rates, and investment returns.

1. Forms of Annuities

There are many forms of annuities. For example:

- *Single life annuity*: provides guaranteed income for a lifetime of one individual, regardless of market conditions or interest rate fluctuations.

- *Joint Life Annuity* (Last Survivor Annuity): provides guaranteed income for the lives of two people regardless of market conditions or interest rate fluctuations. When the first person dies the income is paid to the surviving individual.
- *Annuity Certain*: provides guaranteed income for a predetermined period of time or until a certain age.

Annuities may be indexed to inflation and may either be immediate or deferred. Each variation affects the cost and payout ratios.

Example 9 (Single Life Annuity)
Seventy-year old Linda buys an annuity from Life Insurance Company for $1 million today in return for an annual payment of $100,000 for as long as she lives. The annuity is an actuarial bet on how long she will live and the investment return that the Life Insurance Company will earn on the $1 million. If Linda lives to age 90, the insurance company loses the bet because she will collect $2,000,000. If she dies at age 75, the insurance company wins because it pays out only $500,000. Sophisticated actuaries calculate the odds for insurance companies, which seldom lose their overall bets, in much the same way that casinos in Las Vegas never lose in the long run.

Investors also use annuities in planning for retirement. In an annuity investment, the investor deposits a series of payments into a savings vehicle (tax-sheltered or otherwise) on an annual basis. In an *ordinary annuity* (*annuity in arrears*), the investor makes their payments at the end of the first period. In contrast, under an *annuity due* (*annuity in advance*), the investor makes the payments at the beginning of the period. The future value of both annuities is calculated using the principles of determining future values (see also Chapter 18 on tax sheltered Retirement Planning).

2. Ordinary Annuity

The future value of an *ordinary annuity* represents the sum accumulated at the *end* of the last payment.

Example 10

Suppose that Jennifer contributes $1,000 at the *end* of each year for a period of four years, which accumulates at 5 percent each year. Then, using Table 5.1:

First payment, will compound for three years (4-1)	1.16
Second payment, will compound for two years (4-2)	1.10
Third payment, will compound for one year (4-3)	1.05
Final payment, no interest	1.00
Total annuity factor	**4.31**

Hence, Jennifer's annual contribution of $1,000 would accumulate to $4,310 at the end of four years. Alternatively, we obtain the same result in Table 5.4 where 5% and four years intersect to provide a factor of 4.31. Table 5.4 uses the future value factors from Table 5.1 to provide a quick answer.

3. Annuity Due

With an *annuity due* the investor makes payments at the beginning of the period. The future value of an annuity due represents the sum accumulated one period *after* the last payment. Since the last payment is invested for one extra year, the accumulated amount will be greater than that of an equivalent ordinary annuity.

Example 11

Suppose from the previous example that Jennifer contributes $1,000 at the *beginning* of each year for a period of four years, which accumulates at 5 percent each year. Then, using Table 5.1:

First payment, will compound for four years	1.21
Second payment, will compound for three years	1.16
Third payment, will compound for two years	1.10
Final payment, will compound for one year	1.05
Total	**4.52**

Jennifer's annuity payment of $1,000 for four years will accumulate to $4,520, which is $210 more than the equivalent ordinary annuity. The reason for the increase is that her last payment of $1,000 has one extra year to earn interest.

Hence, there is a significant difference in making payments at the beginning of each period (annuity due) rather than waiting to make annual payments at the end of each period (ordinary annuity).

J. PLANNING FOR COLLEGE

We can also use annuities for planning other purposes that will require the use of accumulated capital funds, such as, for example, education.

Example 12

Frankie's grandparents plan to invest $2,000 at the *beginning* of each year for the next fifteen years in his college fund. Assuming the fund earns 6 percent annual compound interest, how much will the fund have in fifteen years?

Using Table 5.4, because Frankie's grandparents are making fifteen payments to an annuity due, we find that the future value factor for *sixteen* payments is 25.67 for an ordinary annuity due, minus 1 equals 24.67. Hence, the $2,000 annuity will grow to $49,340 in fifteen years.

K. PRESENT VALUE

We can evaluate the time value of money in two ways: the future value of a present sum of money or the present value of a future sum. Although this may seem obtuse, both values are in fact merely different ways of looking at the same thing. The future value is the sum to which an amount, or a series of periodic and equal amounts, will grow at the end of a certain amount of time if compounded at a particular interest rate. The present value is the discounted value at a particular rate of interest of a sum of money to be received in the future. Both forms of analysis flow from the fundamental principle that a dollar today is worth more than a dollar tomorrow because one can invest the money today and earn interest on it. In other words: Time is money. If $1,000 compounded at 10 percent will equal $1,331 in four years, then $1,331 due in four years must be equal to $1,000 today.

The present value formula simply restates the future value formula to solve for *PV*.

$$PV = FV / (1+r)^n$$

Where:

- *PV* is present value
- *FV* is future value
- *r* is the interest rate (as a decimal)
- *n* is the number of years

Example 14

Year (n)	Principal (P)	Interest rate (r)	Interest earned per year
1	$1,000	10%	$100
2	$1,100	10%	$110
3	$1,210	10%	$121
4	$1,331	10%	$133

Table 5.2 shows pre-calculated amounts of the present value of $1 at specified rates of interest (*r*) at the end of specified future years (*n*). Present value calculations are always done on the basis of cash flows and not on accrual accounting profits.

L. LEGAL SETTLEMENTS

Lawyers need to determine the time value of money in a variety of circumstances, most notably in litigation, where the issues have to be presented clearly and simply to judges *before* they arrive at their judgments.

Example 15

Suppose that a plaintiff's lawyer is offered a choice between taking an immediate cash settlement of $500,000 or six successive annual payments of $100,000, payable at the end of each year, for a total of $600,000. Should she accept the lump-sum settlement or the extended payment plan? Ignoring questions of risk, insolvency, and income tax considerations, the financial answer depends upon the prevailing interest rate associated with the two alternatives. At an interest rate of 10 percent, the factor for six annual payments is 4.35 (Table 5.3). The six annual payments of $100,000 have a present value of only $435,000. Hence, the plaintiff would be better off with the immediate lump-sum settlement. However, if, instead, the interest (discount) rate is 4 percent, the factor for the six payments is 5.24 (Table 5.3). Hence, the $100,000 annual payments have a net present value of $524,000.

We can arrive at the above answers in two ways. We can add the present values of each of the payments for six years at 10 percent (Table 5.2).

Years (n)	Rate (r) @ 10%
1	.909
2	.826
3	.751
4	.683
5	.620
6	.564
Total (rounded)	4.350

Hence, the present value of $100,000 payable in six installments is $435,300.

Alternatively, we arrive at the same answer by looking at Table 5.3. Reading down the 10 percent column and across the six-year row, we see that the present value of an annuity of $1 payable at the end of each year is $4.35. Hence, the present value of a $100,000 annuity is $435,000 (rounded). At 4 percent it would be $524,000.

Similarly, the defendant in a lawsuit involving future lost profits of a business enterprise may ask the court to reduce the size of any lump-sum award to the plaintiff to consider the accelerated value of receiving the money today, rather than over an extended period in the future.

Example 16

Suppose that one can establish that the defendant's actions will cause the plaintiff a loss of $100,000 of business profits annually for a period of five years? Should the defendant be required to pay the nominal amount of the damages ($500,000) up front, or some lesser discounted amount because of the time value of money? At an interest rate of 12 percent, the annual loss of $100,000 spread over five years is worth only $360,000 today if the payments are receivable at the end of each year (see Table 5.2).

Years (*n*)	Rate (*r*) @ 12%
1	.893
2	.797
3	.711
4	.636
5	.567
Total (rounded)	3.600

Alternatively, Table 5.3 provides a factor of 3.60 as the present value of an annuity. Ignoring the time value of money would penalize the defendant and provide the plaintiff with a windfall gain.

M. TAX CONSIDERATIONS

Time value considerations also raise income tax considerations, depending on the characterization of the terms of settlement or judgment. Where the lump-sum amount is a substitution of a taxable stream of earnings, the discounted value would be on similar account. Where the amount is on account of a non-taxable capital settlement, the lump sum would not normally be taxable if we followed the substitution theory. There can, however, be other considerations if the amount that would otherwise be taxable is paid as lump sum upon death. Thus, time value considerations should be considered in structuring damage settlements to account for the net present value of money *and* the related tax costs and savings.

The more distant the time when an amount has to be paid on account of taxes, the lower its present value. Hence, a fundamental principle of tax planning is to legally delay or defer the payment of taxes as long as possible so as to minimize the net present value of the obligation today. This basic principle of finance is at the root of legitimate tax shelter schemes. Unfortunately, the principle is also used to promote dubious tax shelter arrangements, such as leveraged charitable donation schemes, with unfortunate consequences for investors.

Example 17

For example, the present value of $1 invested at 8 percent at the end of years 1 through 5 is as follows:

Years (*n*)	Rate (*r*) @ 8%
1	.93
2	.86
3	.79
4	.74
5	.68

Hence, when we say that the interest rate is 8 percent per year, we mean that we should be able to exchange 93 cents today in return for $1 a year from now, and 86 cents in return for $1 two years from now, and so on. If we can defer $1,000 in taxes today for five years, the present value of the tax liability to pay is only $680. Although the face amount of the legal obligation to pay remains the same, $1,000 in five years, its economic value varies depending upon when it will be paid. Stated another way, if we invested $680 in a deposit that compounded tax free at a rate of 8 percent, we would accumulate $1,000 at the end of five years with which to pay the tax liability. By deferring the tax payable for five years we reduce the economic value of the tax liability by $320.

Example 18

To continue with the same example above, assume that we can defer tax payable for a period of fifty years. The present value of $1,000 payable in fifty years at a discount rate of 8 percent is $21. In other words, if we invest $21 today and compound it for fifty years at *net* 8 percent annually, we will have $1,000 at the end of the investment period.

The discounted amount shrinks as a function of two factors: time (*n*) and the discount rate (*r*). The longer the period of deferral and the higher the interest rate, the lower the discounted present value. For example, $1,000 payable in fifty years and discounted at 20 percent has a present value today of (effectively) zero.

N. UNDERLYING ASSUMPTIONS

In determining present and future values, we must be clear about the assumptions of the mathematical calculations. Since time value calculations require an interest rate, an error in estimating the rate can significantly distort results. There is no easy way to minimize this risk other than to rely upon responsible predictions.

Example 19

For example, if one earns 10 percent (instead of 12 percent) over ten years, $10,000 invested in an RRSP would grow to $25,900 instead of $31,100 (rounded). The 2 percent difference in interest rates reduces the investment return by $5,200, a reduction of 16.5 percent over ten years. The longer the investment horizon, the greater the risk that inaccurate assumptions will creep into the reinvestment formula. Hence, long-term retirement plans should be based on conservative estimates of future reinvestment rates.

It is also important in time value calculations to consider the income tax effect of payments. As noted above, reinvestment rates can vary substantially depending upon whether the funds are invested in a tax shelter or in a currently taxable investment. With some marginal tax rates above 53 percent, ignoring taxes can be even more significant than the miscalculation of anticipated inflation.

Example 20

Under a proposed settlement agreement, a plaintiff is offered three options:

1. An immediate cash settlement of $200,000;
2. A deferred cash payment of $400,000 at end of ten years; or

3. A five-year annuity of $50,000 beginning one year after the plaintiff signs the settlement agreement.

Ignoring income tax considerations and assuming an interest rate of 7 percent compounded annually, the best option for the plaintiff at the present time would be option 3.

	Time	Total Cash Paid	Present Value
Option 1	$200,000 payable *immediately*	$200,000	$200,000
Option 2	$400,000 payable in *10 years*	$400,000	$203,200
Option 3	$50,000 payable at end of each year for *5 years*	$250,000	**$205,000**

Option 1: *PV* of $200,000 payable immediately equals $200,000.
Option 2: *PV* of $400,000 payable at end of ten years equals 0.508.
Option 3: *PV* of annuity at 7 percent for five years equals 4.10.

O. CONTINGENCY FEES

A lawyer acting on a contingency fee arrangement should clearly specify the mode of calculation of the fee payable upon success, preferably in her engagement letter. For example, assuming a contingency fee of 30 percent in *Example 20*, should the lawyer get 30 percent of $205,000 immediately ($61,500) or 30 percent of each annual payment of $50,000 as received, which would be $15,000 annually for a total of $75,000 over five years? The present value of the deferred payments in option 3 is $61,500. Where the settlement is discounted to its present value, it would be "reasonable" to discount the contingency fee according to the same timeline. However, in such circumstances, it is best to state the terms precisely in the engagement letter and not rely on determining what is "reasonable" in subsequent fee litigation.

P. BUSINESS VALUATION

1. Return on Invested Capital (ROIC)

A business is the sum of the values of all of its *net* assets, which can be more or less than the values shown on its balance sheet. We value businesses as a whole, generally by valuing the stock of the enterprise. We value businesses by analyzing them to perpetuity. This theoretical analogy is useful if the business will create a fairly constant and indefinite level of cash flows. However, in any other case, the analogy becomes troublesome.

In the abstract, one might suggest that the total value of a company's stock should be equal to the value of the company's total *net* assets. A share of stock should be equal to its proportionate share of the total stock value. In fact, there are many reasons why this is not so.

First, there may be hidden and undisclosed assets on the balance sheet, such as goodwill and reputation associated with the company's corporate brand. Think of Coca Cola, Amazon, or Apple Inc. Second, it is usually the case that a large block of stock is worth more proportionately than the sum of the values of the individual shares because of the premium attributable to control of the corporation. Third, there may be significant income tax considerations embedded in the asset values on the balance sheet that may not be readily apparent. For example, there may be significant deferred income taxes because of past tax write-offs of tangible and intangible assets or current taxes on unrealized gains.

Companies with a long-term strategic horizon create more value. Hence, we restate the principle of creating value as maximizing value for *current and future* shareholders. Shareholder value is the difference between cash inflows and the cost of invested capital, adjusted for the time value of money and the riskiness of future cash flows. As noted above, tomorrow's cash flows are worth less than today's. The ultimate value of a company is its ROIC, revenue growth, and its ability to sustain both over time.

2. Capitalized Values

We refer to the discounted present value of a stream of future payments as the "capitalized" value. The interest rate (r) used in capitalizing the payments is the "capitalization rate" or "Cap Rate." For example, the perpetuity valuation model is:

Value = PMP/r
Cap Rate (r) = PMP/Value.

In the simplest case, a share that provides the shareholder with $1 per year in year-end dividends forever (and no other return) resembles a perpetuity. Assuming a 10 percent annual yield, the share is worth $10, which is PMP/*r*.

3. The Multiplier

We refer to the ratio of the capitalized value to annual future payments as the "multiplier," that is, the amount one multiplies the future payments by in order to determine the capitalized value. Hence, the multiplier is equal to 1/Cap Rate. For example, with a 10 percent annual yield the multiplier is 10; with a 5 percent annual yield the multiplier is 20. Stated another way, with a 10 percent yield, it would take ten years to recover one's investment; with a 5 percent yield, it would take twenty years to recover the investment.

The simple perpetuity valuation method requires only two numbers: The Cap Rate and the Expected Payment. The Cap Rate is a function of risk. The Expected Payment schedule is where finance and accounting intersect because both types of business valuations use "profit," "income," or "earnings" to measure expected cash flows. Hence, the relationship between accounting and finance. Finance needs information to value businesses. Accounting provides the information. Thus, finance is an important consumer of accounting information.

There is, however, tension between finance and accounting principles. Finance looks to the future and focuses on valuations based on prospective cash flows. The past is irrelevant except to the extent that it provides information about the future. In contrast, accounting looks exclusively to the past in measuring the performance of the enterprise on an accrual basis. This explains why stocks can go up even when profits go down and go down even when profits go up. Stock prices are a function of future earnings. Accounting profits reflect past performance.

An enterprise may report lower earnings and see its stock go up because finance values future earnings and stock values depend upon expectations about the future. When expectations disappoint, stock values can go down even when reported profits go up. Conversely, when a company exceeds expectations, stocks can go up even if reported profits have fallen.

TIME VALUE TABLES

Table 5.1

Compound Amount of $1: Amount to Which $1 Now Will Grow by End of Specified Year at Compounded Interest

Year	3%	4%	5%	6%	7%	8%	10%	12%	15%	20%
1	1.03	1.04	1.05	1.06	1.07	1.08	1.10	1.12	1.15	1.20
2	1.06	1.08	1.10	1.12	1.14	1.17	1.21	1.25	1.32	1.44
3	1.09	1.12	1.16	1.19	1.23	1.26	1.33	1.40	1.52	1.73
4	1.13	1.17	1.22	1.26	1.31	1.36	1.46	1.57	1.74	2.07
5	1.16	1.22	1.28	1.34	1.40	1.47	1.61	1.76	2.01	2.49
6	1.19	1.27	1.34	1.41	1.50	1.59	1.77	1.97	2.31	2.99
7	1.23	1.32	1.41	1.50	1.61	1.71	1.94	2.21	2.66	3.58
8	1.27	1.37	1.48	1.59	1.72	1.85	2.14	2.48	3.05	4.30
9	1.30	1.42	1.55	1.68	1.84	2.00	2.35	2.77	3.52	5.16
10	1.34	1.48	1.63	1.79	1.97	2.16	2.59	3.11	4.05	6.19
11	1.38	1.54	1.71	1.89	2.10	2.33	2.85	3.48	4.66	7.43
12	1.43	1.60	1.80	2.01	2.25	2.52	3.13	3.90	5.30	8.92
13	1.47	1.67	1.89	2.13	2.41	2.72	3.45	4.36	6.10	10.7
14	1.51	1.73	1.98	2.26	2.58	2.94	3.79	4.89	7.00	12.8
15	1.56	1.80	2.08	2.39	2.76	3.17	4.17	5.47	8.13	15.4
16	1.60	1.87	2.18	2.54	2.95	3.43	4.59	6.13	9.40	18.5
17	1.65	1.95	2.29	2.69	3.16	3.70	5.05	6.87	10.6	22.2
18	1.70	2.03	2.41	2.85	3.38	4.00	5.55	7.70	12.5	26.6
19	1.75	2.11	2.53	3.02	3.62	4.32	6.11	8.61	14.0	31.9
20	1.81	2.19	2.65	3.20	3.87	4.66	6.72	9.65	16.1	38.3
25	2.09	2.67	3.39	4.29	5.43	6.85	10.8	17.0	32.9	95.4
30	2.43	3.24	4.32	5.74	7.61	10.0	17.4	30.0	66.2	237
40	3.26	4.80	7.04	10.3	15.0	21.7	45.3	93.1	267.0	1470
50	4.38	7.11	11.5	18.4	29.5	46.9	117	289	1080	9100

Table 5.2

Present Value of $1: What a Dollar at End of Specified Future Year Is Worth Today

Year	3%	4%	5%	6%	7%	8%	10%	12%	15%	20%
1	.971	.962	.952	.943	.935	.926	.909	.893	.870	.833
2	.943	.925	.907	.890	.873	.857	.826	.797	.756	.694
3	.915	.890	.864	.839	.816	.794	.751	.711	.658	.578
4	.889	.855	.823	.792	.763	.735	.683	.636	.572	.482
5	.863	.823	.784	.747	.713	.681	.620	.567	.497	.402
6	.838	.790	.746	.705	.666	.630	.564	.507	.432	.335
7	.813	.760	.711	.665	.623	.583	.513	.452	.376	.279
8	.789	.731	.677	.627	.582	.540	.466	.404	.326	.233
9	.766	.703	.645	.591	.544	.500	.424	.360	.284	.194
10	.744	.676	.614	.558	.508	.463	.385	.322	.247	.162
11	.722	.650	.585	.526	.475	.429	.350	.287	.215	.134
12	.701	.625	.557	.497	.444	.397	.318	.257	.187	.112
13	.681	.601	.530	.468	.415	.368	.289	.229	.162	.0935
14	.661	.577	.505	.442	.388	.340	.263	.204	.141	.0779
15	.642	.555	.481	.417	.362	.315	.239	.183	.122	.0649
16	.623	.534	.458	.393	.339	.292	.217	.163	.107	.0541
17	.605	.513	.436	.371	.317	.270	.197	.146	.093	.0451
18	.587	.494	.416	.350	.296	.250	.179	.130	.0808	.0376
19	.570	.475	.396	.330	.277	.232	.163	.116	.0703	.0313
20	.554	.456	.377	.311	.258	.215	.148	.104	.0611	.0261
25	.478	.375	.295	.232	.184	.146	.0923	.0588	.0304	.0105
30	.412	.308	.231	.174	.131	.0994	.0573	.0334	.0151	.00421
40	.307	.208	.142	.0972	.067	.0460	.0221	.0107	.00373	.000680
50	.228	.141	.087	.0543	.034	.0213	.00852	.00346	.000922	.000109

Table 5.3

Present Value of Annuity of $1, Received at End of Each Year

Year	3%	4%	5%	6%	7%	8%	10%	12%	15%	20%
1	0.971	0.960	0.952	0.943	0.935	0.926	0.909	0.890	0.870	0.833
2	1.91	1.89	1.86	1.83	1.81	1.78	1.73	1.69	1.63	1.53
3	2.53	2.78	2.72	2.67	2.62	2.58	2.45	2.40	2.28	2.11
4	3.72	3.63	3.55	3.46	3.39	3.31	3.16	3.04	2.86	2.59
5	4.58	4.45	4.33	4.21	4.10	3.99	3.79	3.60	3.35	2.99
6	5.42	5.24	5.08	4.91	4.77	4.62	4.35	4.11	3.78	3.33
7	6.23	6.00	5.79	5.58	5.39	5.21	4.89	4.56	4.16	3.60
8	7.02	6.73	6.46	6.20	5.97	5.75	5.33	4.97	4.49	3.84
9	7.79	7.44	7.11	6.80	6.52	6.25	5.75	5.33	4.78	4.03
10	8.53	8.11	7.72	7.36	7.02	6.71	6.14	5.65	5.02	4.19
11	9.25	8.76	8.31	7.88	7.50	7.14	6.49	5.94	5.23	4.33
12	9.95	9.39	8.86	8.38	7.94	7.54	6.81	6.19	5.41	4.44
13	10.6	9.99	9.39	8.85	8.36	7.90	7.10	6.42	5.65	4.53
14	11.3	10.6	9.90	9.29	8.75	8.24	7.36	6.63	5.76	4.61
15	11.9	11.1	10.4	9.71	9.11	8.56	7.60	6.81	5.87	4.68
16	12.6	11.6	10.8	10.1	9.45	8.85	7.82	6.97	5.96	4.73
17	13.2	12.2	11.3	10.4	9.76	9.12	8.02	7.12	6.03	4.77
18	13.8	12.7	11.7	10.8	10.1	9.37	8.20	7.25	6.10	4.81
19	14.3	13.1	12.1	11.1	10.3	9.60	8.36	7.37	6.17	4.84
20	14.9	13.6	12.5	11.4	10.6	9.82	8.51	7.47	6.23	4.87
25	17.4	15.6	14.1	12.8	11.7	10.7	9.08	7.84	6.46	4.95
30	19.6	17.3	15.4	13.5	12.4	11.3	9.43	8.06	6.57	4.98
40	23.1	19.8	17.2	15.0	13.3	11.9	9.78	8.24	6.64	5.00
50	25.7	21.5	18.3	15.8	13.8	12.2	9.91	8.30	6.66	5.00

Table 5.4 Future Value of an Annuity

n/i	1%	2%	3%	4%	5%	6%	7%
1	1.0000	1.0000	1.0000	1.0000	1.0000	1.0000	1.0000
2	2.0100	2.0200	2.0300	2.0400	2.0500	2.0600	2.0700
3	3.0301	3.0604	3.0909	3.1216	3.1525	3.1836	3.2149
4	4.0604	4.1216	4.1836	4.2465	4.3101	4.3746	4.4399
5	5.1010	5.2040	5.3091	5.4163	5.5256	5.6371	5.7507
6	6.1520	6.3081	6.4684	6.6330	6.8019	6.9753	7.1533
7	7.2135	7.4343	7.6625	7.8983	8.1420	8.3938	8.6540
8	8.2857	8.5830	8.8923	9.2142	9.5491	9.8975	10.2598
9	9.3685	9.7546	10.1591	10.5828	11.0266	11.4913	11.9780
10	10.4622	10.9497	11.4639	12.0061	12.5779	13.1808	13.8164
11	11.5668	12.1687	12.8078	13.4864	14.2068	14.9716	15.7836
12	12.6825	13.4121	14.1920	15.0258	15.9171	16.8699	17.8885
13	13.8093	14.6803	15.6178	16.6268	17.7130	18.8821	20.1406
14	14.9474	15.9739	17.0863	18.2919	19.5986	21.0151	22.5505
15	16.0969	17.2934	18.5989	20.0236	21.5786	23.2760	25.1290
16	17.2579	18.6393	20.1569	21.8245	23.6575	25.6725	27.8881
17	18.4304	20.0121	21.7616	23.6975	25.8404	28.2129	30.8402
18	19.6147	21.4123	23.4144	25.6454	28.1324	30.9057	33.9990
19	20.8109	22.8406	25.1169	27.6712	30.5390	33.7600	37.3790
20	22.0190	24.2974	26.8704	29.7781	33.0660	36.7856	40.9955
21	23.2392	25.7833	28.6765	31.9692	35.7193	39.9927	44.8652
22	24.4716	27.2990	30.5368	34.2480	38.5052	43.3923	49.0057
23	25.7163	28.8450	32.4529	36.6179	41.4305	46.9958	53.4361
24	26.9735	30.4219	34.4265	39.0826	44.5020	50.8156	58.1767
25	28.2432	32.0303	36.4593	41.6459	47.7271	54.8645	63.2490
26	29.5256	33.6709	38.5530	44.3117	51.1135	59.1564	68.6765
27	30.8209	35.3443	40.7096	47.0842	54.6691	63.7058	74.4838
28	32.1291	37.0512	42.9309	49.9676	58.4026	68.5281	80.6977
29	33.4504	38.7922	45.2189	52.9663	62.3227	73.6398	87.3465
30	34.7849	40.5681	47.5754	56.0849	66.4388	79.0582	94.4608

8%	9%	10%	11%	12%	13%	14%	15%
1.0000	1.0000	1.0000	1.0000	1.0000	1.0000	1.0000	1.0000
2.0800	2.0900	2.1000	2.1100	2.1200	2.1300	2.1400	2.1500
3.2464	3.2781	3.3100	3.3421	3.3744	3.4069	3.4396	3.4725
4.5061	4.5731	4.6410	4.7097	4.7793	4.8498	4.9211	4.9934
5.8666	5.9847	6.1051	6.2278	6.3528	6.4803	6.6101	6.7424
7.3359	7.5233	7.7156	7.9129	8.1152	8.3227	8.5355	8.7537
8.9228	9.2004	9.4872	9.7833	10.0890	10.4047	10.7305	11.0668
10.6366	11.0285	11.4359	11.8594	12.2997	12.7573	13.2328	13.7268
12.4876	13.0210	13.5795	14.1640	14.7757	15.4157	16.0853	16.7858
14.4866	15.1929	15.9374	16.7220	17.5487	18.4197	19.3373	20.3037
16.6455	17.5603	18.5312	19.5614	20.6546	21.8143	23.0445	24.3493
18.9771	20.1407	21.3843	22.7132	24.1331	25.6502	27.2707	29.0017
21.4953	22.9534	24.5227	26.2116	28.0291	29.9847	32.0887	34.3519
24.2149	26.0192	27.9750	30.0949	32.3926	34.8827	37.5811	40.5047
27.1521	29.3609	31.7725	34.4054	37.2797	40.4175	43.8424	47.5804
30.3243	33.0034	35.9497	39.1899	42.7533	46.6717	50.9804	55.7175
33.7502	36.9737	40.5447	44.5008	48.8837	53.7391	59.1176	65.0751
37.4502	41.3013	45.5992	50.3959	55.7497	61.7251	68.3941	75.8364
41.4463	46.0185	51.1591	56.9395	63.4397	70.7494	78.9692	88.2118
45.7620	51.1601	57.2750	64.2028	72.0524	80.9468	91.0249	102.4436
50.4229	56.7645	64.0025	72.2651	81.6987	92.4699	104.7684	118.8101
55.4568	62.8733	71.4027	81.2143	92.5026	105.4910	120.4360	137.6316
60.8933	69.5319	79.5430	91.1479	104.6029	120.2048	138.2970	159.2764
66.7648	76.7898	88.4973	102.1742	118.1552	136.8315	158.6586	184.1678
73.1059	84.7009	98.3471	114.4133	133.3339	155.6196	181.8708	212.7930
79.9544	93.3240	109.1818	127.9988	150.3339	176.8501	208.3327	245.7120
87.3508	102.7231	121.0999	143.0786	169.3740	200.8406	238.4993	283.5688
95.3388	112.9682	134.2099	159.8173	190.6989	227.9499	272.8892	327.1041
103.9659	124.1354	148.6309	178.3972	214.5828	258.5834	312.0937	377.1697
113.2832	136.3075	164.4940	199.0209	241.3327	293.1992	356.7868	434.7451

Chapter 6: The Balance Sheet — General

A. OVERVIEW

Accounting is concerned with assimilating and disseminating financial information for various purposes and users. The "financial statements" assemble data derived from accounting records, which summarize an entity's economic resources and sources of financing at a point in time and its operations for a period of time. The overarching objective of statement preparation is to provide full and fair disclosure of relevant and material information of the enterprise's financial position and activities.

There are five components to a set of financial statements:

1) The Balance Sheet (also known as a Statement of Financial Position);
2) The Income Statement;
3) The Statement of Cash Flows;
4) The Statement of Shareholders' Equity; and
5) Notes to the Statements.

Each of these components discloses aspects of financial information about an entity, but from different perspectives.

The fundamental principles underlying these statements are reasonably uniform between entities and industries. Thus, when reduced to a common size, they facilitate interpretation and analysis, regardless of the size of the entity, the nature of its business, or its location.

The six principal components of the financial statements are:

1) Assets;
2) Liabilities;
3) Owners' equity;
4) Revenues;
5) Expenses; and
6) Cash flows.

The first three segments (Assets, Liabilities, and Owner's equity) appear on the Balance Sheet, which is a point in time statement, that is, a snapshot of an enterprise as at one moment. In this chapter, we start with an overview of the balance sheet, which we explore in greater detail in chapters 7, 8, and 9.

B. THE BALANCE SHEET EQUATION

The fundamental premise of the balance sheet is that at any point in time an entity's "resources" (R) must equal its "sources" of financing (S). Thus, R always equals S. This is an immutable law. All resources, which we call "assets," are financed either by creditors, which we describe as "liabilities," or the owners of the business, which we call "equity." Thus, we can think of the balance sheet as a list of what the business owns, and what it owes (crudely, a "what got," "how got" statement).

As its name implies, a balance sheet "balances." Thus, the fundamental balance sheet equation is:

$$A = L + E$$

Where:

A = Assets
L = Liabilities
E = Equity

The equation describes the financial position of an enterprise at a point in time.

There is really no mystery about why a balance sheet balances. After all, a balance sheet tells us what assets the entity owns and how it financed the assets. Since we finance everything that we own, either with debt (liabilities) or our own money (owners' equity), the relationship must always be in balance. It is metaphysically impossible for a properly prepared balance sheet not to balance.

1. Assets

"Assets" are resources that represent future benefits from past transactions and that are under the control of the accounting entity. The entity may be an individual, partnership, corporation, trust, or charitable organization. The three essential requirements are:

1) The entity controls the resources,
2) The entity expects that the resources will provide future benefits, and
3) The resources can be measured in monetary terms.

Example

Sandra Loeb, a recently qualified lawyer, sets up her practice as *Loeb Law* as a sole proprietor on January 1. She invests $1,000 in the business and obtains a bank loan, guaranteed by her mother, of $20,000. She purchases furniture and fixtures for $2,000 and a computer for $1,200.

Balance Sheet of Loeb Law as at January 1

Assets (A)	**$**
Cash	17,800
Computer	1,200
Furniture and fixtures	2,000
Total Assets	21,000

Liabilities (L)	
Bank loan	20,000
Equity (E)	1,000
Liabilities and Equity	21,000

The balance sheet for Loeb Law as a sole proprietorship accounting entity is distinct and separate from Sandra Loeb, the owner of the business. Loeb Law's assets all represent resources that it will use in its business in the future. The cost of each of the assets is objectively determinable from market transactions.

2. Liabilities

Liabilities are legal obligations to other entities that result from past transactions and that the entity has no discretion to avoid. They may arise from borrowings, purchases on credit, breaches of contract, or torts. Liabilities have three characteristics:

1) A present duty or legal responsibility;
2) The entity is obliged to discharge the obligation in the future; and
3) The legal obligation arises from an event or transaction that can reasonably be measured.

Loeb Law is financed from two sources: (1) a legal obligation payable to the bank ($20,000) and (2) Sandra's own investment of $1,000.

3. Equity

Equity represents the owner's investment in the entity, that is the amount by which its assets exceed its liabilities. A deficit would represent the excess of liabilities over assets. Thus, we can restate the basic balance sheet equation to determine equity as follows:

$$E = A - L$$

In law, the claims of the entity's creditors (liabilities) rank ahead of any "inside" claims by its owners. Hence, "equity" is essentially the residual ownership interest, which is the arithmetical amount that remains after the entity subtracts its liabilities ($20,000) from its assets ($21,000). Equity increases when the owner of the business invests in its assets. For example, Loeb Law's cash assets increased by $1,000 when Sandra invested that amount in her business. Equity decreases when the owner withdraws assets from the business.

The residual ownership interest goes by different names depending on the legal character of the entity. Loeb Law is a sole proprietorship that Sandra Loeb owns exclusively. Hence, we refer to the sole owner's interest as *proprietorship*.

A partnership arises when two or more persons engage in a business for profit.[1] The law relating to partnerships is governed by statute and the common law. A partnership does not have legal existence separate from its partners. However, for accounting purposes, the partnership is an entity and its residual ownership is known as *partners' equity*.

There are also hybrid variations of partnerships, such as *limited partnerships* and *limited liability partnerships*, which are governed by provincial laws. Residual ownership interests in these accounting entities are also known as *partners' equity*. Limited partnerships keep separate equity accounts for each partner.

A business can also be set up as a corporation by complying with the appropriate federal or provincial corporate statute, such as the *Canada Business Corporations Act*[2] or its provincial equivalent, the *Ontario Business Corporations Act*. All of the provinces have similar, but not identical, statutes.

The unique feature of a corporation is that it is a distinct legal entity separate from its owners, who are its shareholders.[3] For most purposes, with limited exceptions, the liability of shareholders is limited to their share contributions and that is the most that they can lose of their investment.[4] We measure the residual ownership interest

1 See, for example, *Ontario Partnership Act*, RSO 1990, c P5, s 2: "Partnership is the relation that subsists between persons carrying on a business in common with a view to profit, but the relation between the members of a company or association that is incorporated by or under the authority of any special or general Act in force in Ontario or elsewhere, or registered as a corporation under any such Act, is not a partnership within the meaning of this Act."

2 RSC, 1985, c C-44 [*CBCA*].

3 See *Salomon v Salomon & Company*, [1897] AC 22 (HL).

4 *CBCA* at s 45(1).

of shareholders by their "shares" in the corporation. Generally, shareholders share proportionally in the corporation's earnings through dividends. They also share proportionally in residual corporate assets upon liquidation. We refer to their residual ownership interest as *shareholders' equity*.

C. CLASSIFIED BALANCE SHEET

Balance sheets are broadly classified into categories of assets, liabilities and equity in accordance with the basic equation of A = L+E. For analytical purposes, we also classify the balance sheet into subcomponents that are useful in financial statement analysis and management decisions.

By classifying assets and liabilities into categories, we can analyze financial statements in a more meaningful way than if we simply had one aggregate figure for all assets and liabilities. The extent of detail, which should be meaningful and appropriate for the circumstances, depends upon the purpose for which the reader will use the financial statements.

Financial statements for public dissemination are relatively sparse and show only a few categories. They must balance the need for public disclosure against the protection of confidential information. Too much detail would disclose the company's proprietary information to competitors. Financial statements prepared for management, however, are more detailed because management uses the information to make its operational and financing decisions.

The following is an illustrative (and simplified) comparative Balance Sheet of a company, Duggan Inc, as at 30 September, divided into various segments.

Balance Sheet as at 30 September	**20-2**	**20-1**
(thousands of dollars)	$	$
Assets		
Current Assets:		
Cash	268	561
Cash equivalents	713	702
Marketable securities	1,100	1,000
Accounts receivable	5,835	5,621
Allowance for doubtful accounts	−467	−430
Inventories	4,031	4,164
Deferred tax assets	755	662
Prepaid expenses	216	86
Total current assets	**12,451**	**12,366**
Fixed Assets:		
Land	406	405
Buildings	10,657	10,212
Machinery & equipment	28,576	26,294
Leasehold improvements	3,086	3,026
Accumulated depreciation	−15,041	−13,310
Capital assets (net)	27,684	26,627
Intangible Assets:	1,287	533
Other Assets:		
Accrued benefits	949	624
Total Assets	**42,371**	**40,150**

Liabilities (thousands of dollars)	20-2 $	20-1 $
Current Liabilities:		
Current portion of long-term debt	210	157
Notes payable	3,672	1,962
Accounts payable	3,088	3,138
Accrued Liabilities:		
Income taxes	659	1,041
Salaries & wages	765	780
Advertising & promotion	2,338	2,280
Deferred revenue	1,414	1,352
Total current liabilities	**12,146**	**10,710**
Long-term Liabilities:		
Long-term debt	5,216	3,149
Non-pension post-retirement benefits	4,509	4,076
Deferred income taxes	1,889	1,846
Capital leases	1,477	917
Total long-term liabilities	**13,091**	**9,988**
Total Liabilities	**25,237**	**20,698**

Shareholders' Equity (thousands of dollars)	20-2 $	20-1 $
Class A shares:		
Authorized - unlimited		
Issued and outstanding	1,496	1,467
Retained earnings	34,094	30,339
Treasury shares, at cost	–18,456	–12,354
Total shareholders' equity	**17,134**	**19,452**
Total Liabilities & Shareholders' Equity	**42,371**	**40,150**

1. Asset Classification

Accountants typically classify assets into three broad categories: *current assets*, *fixed assets*, and *intangible assets*. The assets appear on the balance sheet in the order shown. (Accountants may segregate *long-term investments* as a separate category.)

For example, as at 30 September 20-2, Duggan Inc's total assets of $42,371,000 are subdivided into current assets of $12,451,000; capital assets of $27,684,000; intangible assets of $1,287,000; and other assets of $949,000.

The *current assets* are divided into seven sub-categories:

- Cash;
- Cash equivalents;
- Marketable securities;
- Accounts receivable;
- Inventories;
- Deferred tax assets; and
- Prepaid expenses.

The assets are listed in order of liquidity, with cash being the most liquid of all assets provided that it is not restricted.

Current assets are a useful measure of an entity's short-term ability to pay its debts as they come due. For example, loan contracts often stipulate that the entity must maintain a certain minimum ratio of current assets to its short-term debt payment schedule.

In contrast, we classify resources that the accounting entity would not normally expect to convert into cash or use within one year as *long-term investments*. These would include stocks and bonds of other entities, long-term notes receivable, and prepaid expenses, such as insurance premiums paid in advance if they apply for several years.

Fixed Assets are tangible assets that the entity acquires to use in its business over an extended period. Duggan Inc has four sub-categories of such assets:

- Land;
- Buildings;
- Machinery & equipment; and
- Leasehold improvements.

The fixed assets, which total $27,684,000 in 20-2, are intended for use in the business rather than resale.

2. Liability Classification

Similarly, liabilities are subdivided into categories: current liabilities, long-term liabilities, and other liabilities. As at 30 September 20-2, Duggan Inc has current liabilities of $12,146,000 and long-term obligations of $13,091,000. The total is $25,237,000.

3. Equity Classification

Equity represents the residual claim that the owners of a company have against its assets after it satisfies all of its obligations to creditors. Shareholders' equity has two principal components: contributed capital and retained earnings. Contributed capital is the investment that shareholders have in the stock of the company. Retained earnings, as its name implies, are earnings or profits that the company retains in the corporate entity and does not distribute to its shareholders. The equity account also reflects transactions with shareholders, such as dividend payments and stock buybacks. Together, the contributed capital and retained earnings segments represent the owners' collective economic interest in the enterprise.

It is important to understand what equity is not. It is *not* a measure of:

- The market value of the entity;
- What the owners will receive if the entity is liquidated; or
- Future dividends.

The term "net worth," often used to describe owners' equity, is an unfortunate choice because it conveys the impression that it represents the "value" or "worth" of the company. In fact, net worth is nothing more than assets minus liabilities (NW = A – L). It is best to avoid the term in legal contracts. The term "net assets," that is, assets minus liabilities, is a more accurate description.

D. LIMITATIONS

1. Point in Time Statement

Since the balance sheet is a point in time statement, its utility diminishes as time passes and the information in it becomes stale. Thus, the balance sheet of an enterprise that is older than four to six months is of limited value for making operational decisions. Management would not use such stale-dated financial statements for its decisions.

Nevertheless, the statement is valuable for the purposes of historical reporting and stewardship accounting. For example, public companies are required to distribute their financial statements to shareholders annually and file the statements with regulatory agencies. The purpose of annual financial statements is to report on management's *past* stewardship of the company.

2. Only Monetary Values

An essential feature of the balance sheet is that it shows only assets that can be measured objectively in monetary terms. The balance sheet provides a lot of historical information about monetary assets and liabilities, costs, investments, obligations, and owners' equity (both initial and retained). However, it has limitations. For example, a law firm's balance sheet will show its assets (cash, receivables, work in progress, computer hardware, furniture, and equipment, etc.) but will not show its principal and most valued resources, its reputation for service, the ability and integrity of its lawyers, and its "brand." Thus, a balance sheet does not reflect an entity's "value" for sale purposes. A high rating in a legal directory such as Martindale Hubbell is a valuable "asset" in a business sense to the lawyer and their firm. For accounting purposes, however, we do not show the rating as an asset because we cannot accurately measure its monetary value.

Similarly, a balance sheet does *not* disclose the value of:

- Advantageous long-term contracts;
- Intrinsic goodwill; or
- Brand loyalty.

E. SUMMARY OF BALANCE SHEET

- Snapshot as a point in time;
- Balance sheet lists economic resources (Assets), sources of financing from creditors (Liabilities), and owners (Equity);
- Balance sheet equation is: A = L + E;
- E = A – L;
- Assets and liabilities generally carried at historical cost;
- Historical cost may differ from market value;
- *Current assets* are cash or assets that will be converted into cash or be used within the business in the next year or fiscal period;
- *Fixed Assets* are tangible assets that the entity acquires to use in its business over an extended period, generally over one year;
- *Liabilities* are legal obligations that result from past transactions that the entity has no discretion to avoid and can be measured;
- *Equity* is the net residual claim of the owners of the entity against its assets after it satisfies all of its liabilities;
- The balance sheet shows only assets, liabilities, and equity that have a measurable monetary value.

Chapter 7: The Balance Sheet — Assets

A. OVERVIEW

In Chapter 6, we introduced the balance sheet equation and its components: assets, liabilities, and equity and their respective roles in summarizing financial information. In this chapter we will look at the components in greater detail to examine their underlying accounting principles. Although balance sheets vary between industries, they share common characteristics and accounting principles, which we examine here.

Traditional financial statements use the historical cost model in recording assets and liabilities. Hence, they present a retrospective picture of an entity's financial condition and are useful for fiduciary and regulatory accounting purposes but have limited value for investment purposes. Accountants also use different accounting rules for different purposes. For example, an entity may use one set of rules for financial reporting purposes, another for regulatory purposes, and still another for tax purposes. Hence, there is nothing offensive about keeping different "books" for different purposes. The important point is that the reader should first understand the purpose for which the accountant prepared the statements.

There is a trend towards a "mixed-attribute model," which reports certain assets and liabilities, such as financial instruments, at fair value or current market value, which, although difficult to measure, are more relevant. The fair value of a financial instrument is the price that the enterprise would receive to sell an asset or pay to transfer a liability in an orderly transaction between market participants as at the measurement date. Accountants determine fair value by incorporating various factors that market participants would consider in setting a price, including commonly accepted valuation approaches.

B. HYPOTHETICAL BALANCE SHEET

The following is a partial (asset portion) of the Balance Sheet of Duggan Inc

Balance Sheet as at 30 September	**20-2**	**20-1**
(thousands of dollars)	$	$
Assets		
Current Assets:		
Cash	268	561
Cash equivalents	713	702
Marketable securities	1,100	1,000
Accounts receivable	5,835	5,621
Allowance for doubtful accounts	−467	−430
Inventories	4,031	4,164
Deferred tax assets	755	662
Prepaid expenses	216	86
Total current assets	**12,451**	**12,366**
Fixed Assets:		
Land	406	405
Buildings	10,657	10,212
Machinery & equipment	28,576	26,294
Leasehold improvements	3,086	3,026
Accumulated depreciation	−15,041	−13,310
Capital assets (net)	27,684	26,627
Intangible Assets:	1,287	533
Other Assets:		
Accrued benefits	949	624
Total Assets	**42,371**	**40,150**

C. CURRENT ASSETS

Assets are resources that a business uses in its operations to earn income. Current assets are a subset of assets that the business expects to use or consume within the next year or within the operating cycle of the business if the cycle is longer than one year. The operating cycle is the length of time that a business needs to acquire raw materials or other inputs, produce or sell its goods or services, and collect the cash generated from its revenue producing activities. The cycle can be short—for example, with a restaurant—or very long—for example, with a winery. Current assets typically include cash, marketable securities, accounts receivable, inventories, and prepaid expenses. These are listed on the balance sheet in order of their liquidity or how soon they can be converted into cash or utilized in the business.

1. Cash

Cash, the most liquid of all assets, includes all currency and bank accounts that an entity can withdraw at any time without restrictions. Cash also includes "cash equivalents," such as short-term, liquid instruments, money market funds, and commercial paper that is readily convertible into cash. Duggan Inc has a cash balance of $268,000 at the end of 20-2.

2. Cash Equivalents

Cash equivalents are short term, highly liquid money market instruments with a maturity of three months or less, such as commercial paper, treasury bills, and money market funds. Duggan Inc reported cash equivalents of $713,000 in 20-2.

3. Restricted Cash

Restricted funds are not included in cash. Restricted funds are amounts that an entity must set aside for specific purposes. For example, a bank may loan money to a business, but require that it maintain a minimum cash balance. In effect, the minimum compensating balance increases the effective rate of interest that the bank charges on its loan. Assume, for example, that a bank loans a business $1 million at 5 percent, but requires the business to maintain a minimum of $100,000 in its account. Then, ignoring time value of money considerations, the effective rate of interest on the loan is $50,000/$900,000 or 5.56 percent. Restricted funds are reported as "Other Assets."

Because cash is highly liquid, it can "disappear" easily. Hence, it is usual to have strict internal control and audit procedures to ensure that it is not used for unauthorized purposes. For example, auditors will usually confirm the amounts shown as cash balances with the bank and check for unrecorded loans, which may be used to conceal a cash shortage.

4. Marketable Securities

Marketable securities are liquid financial instruments, such as bonds and shares, that the business holds as temporary investments for excess cash. Marketable securities usually generate a higher rate of return than cash sitting in a savings account. The securities should be available for sale at any time in order to meet cash requirements for the business. Marketable securities held as "trading securities" are classified as current assets.

In a departure from historical cost accounting, an entity will report its marketable or "trading securities" on the balance sheet at market values. Duggan Inc's marketable securities as at September 30, 20-2 were $1,100,000, up by $100,000 from the previous year.

A business also may hold marketable securities that it does not intend to sell in the short term, or that it is restricted from selling by virtue of contractual obligations with financial institutions. Such instruments are classified in the non-current portion of the balance sheet.

5. Accounts Receivable

Accounts receivable, also called "trade receivables," arise from sales on credit in the normal course of business and are legal rights to receive cash in the future. For example, assume that a business sells $150,000 of merchandise on terms of 1/10, net 30. This means that the business has extended credit and will give a discount of 1 percent if the customer pays $148,500 within ten days; otherwise the full amount is due in thirty days.

A business will record its receivables initially at their face value at the time that it sells the goods or services. Under accrual accounting principles, the business should recognize the revenue from the sale ($150,000) and the resulting accounts receivable as an asset. If the purchaser does not take the discount of $1,500, the business should record that as "cash discounts not taken," which is a form of interest revenue.

(a) Reporting Receivables

Most businesses know that they will not collect all of their receivables. At year-end, following the principle of conservatism, a business will estimate the uncollectable portion of its accounts receivable and set-up an "allowance for doubtful accounts" to recognize their potential collectability. Thus, a business should report its accounts receivable at their "net realizable value" on the balance sheet date. Any estimated uncollectable receivables should be recognized as potential "bad debts" and charged to the income statement as an expense and set up as an allowance for doubtful accounts on the balance sheet.

In Duggan Inc, for example, we see an accounts receivable balance as at 30 September 20-2 of $5,835,000, against which the company has an allowance for doubtful accounts of $467,000. The charge for the increase in doubtful accounts is taken as an expense in the year in which potential collectability of the receivables is recognized. Duggan Inc increased its doubtful accounts from 20-1 by $37,000, which would have been charged as an expense to the 20-2 income statement and reduced profits by that amount.

The "allowance for doubtful accounts" is a "contra account" and is deducted from the accounts receivable balance on the balance sheet in the current assets section. This has the effect of showing the accounts receivable at their net realizable value. In Duggan Inc, for example, the net realizable value of the trade receivables is $5,368,000 as at September 30, 20-2.

(b) Bad Debts

An account receivable that goes from being "doubtful" to "bad" is written off and the accounts receivable balance and the allowance for doubtful accounts are both reduced by the amount. There is no expense charge to the income statement when the business writes off the account because, under accrual accounting principles, it provided for the charge when it estimated the allowance for doubtful accounts.

Example

Assume that X Ltd has sales revenues of $1 million in 20-0 and accounts receivable of $190,000 at its year end. The company estimates that it will not collect 5 percent of its accounts receivable. Then:

Income statement (partial) for year ended 20-0:	($)
Sales revenue	1,000,000
Bad debt expense	9,500
Effect on net income	990,500
Balance sheet (partial) as at year ended 31 December 20-0:	
Accounts receivable	190,000
Allowance for doubtful accounts	9,500
Net accounts receivable	180,500

(c) Estimating Bad Debts

There are various methods for estimating the amount of accounts receivable that the business will not collect. The method and amount will depend upon the particular industry and the state of the economy at the particular time. For example, based upon its past experience, a business may estimate a percentage of its total sales or loans receivable as uncollectable accounts (*percentage of sales method*).

Alternatively, it may "age" its accounts receivable, that is, categorize them by the number of days outstanding and then estimate the uncollectable portion (*aged receivable analysis*). The theory of "ageing" accounts receivable is that the older the account, the greater the risk of it becoming uncollectable.

Regardless of the method, a business should carefully review its estimate of uncollectable receivables from time to time to see that it is an appropriate amount. An underestimation of bad debts overstate income. An overestimate of bad debt reserves creates a "hidden reserve" and misleads investors. The number is one to watch carefully as it can affect executive compensation, management bonuses, and stock options.

(d) Assignment of Receivables

Where a business assigns or pledges its accounts receivable as collateral for a loan, the amount assigned should be shown separately from the unassigned accounts receivable. The assigned receivables remain as current assets but are segregated and shown as "Assigned Accounts Receivable."

Example

Assume that a business with $1 million accounts receivable borrows $500,000 from a bank and assigns a similar amount to the bank as security for the loan. The business estimates that it will not collect 5 percent of its total receivables.

Balance sheet (partial) as at year ended 31 December 20-0:	**($)**
Accounts receivable	500,000
Allowance for doubtful accounts	50,000
Net accounts receivable	450,000
Assigned accounts receivable (Note)	500,000
Total accounts receivable	950,000

(e) Tax Issues

The objective of accounting is to present fair disclosure of an entity's results in the financial statements. Hence, following the principle of conservatism, accountants anticipate certain events by setting up a reserve in determining the entity's "profit" for the year. The reserve reduces net income and receivables in the current fiscal period. The allowance for doubtful accounts is, in effect, a reserve against the uncollectable portion of the accounts receivable.

Accountants adjust the amount of the reserve each year by adding to, or subtracting from, the previous year's ending balance to bring it into line with current expectations. We saw above that Duggan

Inc increased its doubtful accounts from 20-1 by $37,000, which it would charge as an expense to the 20-2 income statement and reduce its profits by that amount.

However, the tax rules are different from accounting. The *Income Tax Act*[1] prohibits the deduction of *all* reserves *unless* they are specifically authorized. This is an outright prohibition against the deduction of accounting reserves. The tax authorities are concerned that taxpayers, and their accountants, may adopt an unduly pessimistic view of their accounts receivable collections in order to reduce income and, therefore, taxes payable in the current period.

In lieu of the accounting reserve, the Act has its own scheme. A taxpayer may deduct a "reasonable" amount as a reserve for doubtful debts that have been included in the taxpayer's income for the preceding year.[2] However, the entire reserve deducted at the end of one year must be included in computing the taxpayer's income in the next year.[3] In Duggan Inc's case, the entire reserve of $430,000 from 20-1 would be added back.

At the end of the next year, the whole procedure begins again, and the taxpayer may once more deduct the whole of a reasonable reserve ($467,000) in respect of trade debts regarded as of doubtful at that time. This structure is contrary to customary accounting practice in which only the increase (or decrease) in the reserve is reflected as a charge (or credit) to the profit and loss account. Thus, there can be a difference between accounting reserves for financial statement purposes and reserves for tax purposes.

(f) Notes Receivable

Notes receivable are more formal accounts receivable where the customer signs a note showing the amount of the receivable and any terms and conditions of the note. A note receivable may charge interest, which the business will recognize as interest revenue. Where a business is doubtful about collecting the full value of its notes, it should provide for a reserve.

1 *Income Tax Act*, RSC, 1985, c 1 (5th Supp) [*ITA*] at para 18(1)(e).
2 *ITA* at para 20(1)(l).
3 *ITA* at para 12(1)(d)

6. Inventories

Manufacturers, wholesalers, and retailers of goods almost always have unsold products on hand at the end of their fiscal year. In a service firm, such as a law or accounting practice, unbilled services at end of the year are work in progress (WIP) inventory. These unsold products and services are "inventory," which are "current assets" that will be converted into sales within the next fiscal year or operating cycle. The proper identification and valuation of inventory is critical as inventory is susceptible to accounting manipulations, which will affect both balance sheet values and net income (see Chapter 16, Accounting and Law).

(a) What is Inventory?

Inventories are assets:[4]

(i) held for sale in the ordinary course of business;
(ii) in the process of production for such sale; or
(iii) in the form of materials or supplies to be consumed in the production process or in the rendering of services.

A particular asset can be classified as inventory by one company and as a different type of asset such as plant or equipment by another company. A drill press, for example, would be a component of the plant, property, and equipment of most businesses. However, if a company is in the business of selling drill presses, it would be classified as inventory. Land, a building, or equipment purchased with no clear intentions for its use could be considered as inventory or property, plant, and equipment, and be reclassified when the business determines its purpose.

Manufacturing companies have several categories of inventory depending on where the product is in the manufacturing cycle. In a typical manufacturing operation, the enterprise purchases raw materials, which it uses to produce finished products that it will sell to its

4 *CPA Canada Handbook — Accounting*, Chartered Professional Accountants of Canada (2018) [*Handbook*] at para 3031.07(a).

customers. At the end of any fiscal period, the business will typically have on hand raw materials, work-in-progress, and finished goods inventory (see stages 2, 3, and 4 of the Business Cycle). Duggan Inc reported inventories of $4,031,000 for 20-2.

Accounting for inventories is critical in the preparation of financial statements as they affect both the balance sheet and the income statement. When inventories are sold, their cost is recorded as costs of goods sold and charged against the revenue from sales in the income statement. Hence, accrual accounting requires sales and the cost of goods sold to be properly matched in the same period.

Inventory accounting involves allocating costs over fiscal periods. We must allocate the total cost of purchases between current and future accounting periods. We express the relationship in an equation as follows:

Total cost of inventory = Current costs + Deferred costs

Where:

Current costs = cost of goods sold;
Deferred costs = ending inventory.

Alternatively, we can restate the equation as follows:

Total cost of inventory − Deferred costs = Current costs

By taking a physical count of inventory at the end of the accounting period, we can deduce the cost of goods applicable to the current period. This is essentially the equation that most businesses use when they employ the *periodic inventory method.* Hence, an accurate physical count is essential to proper accounting.

Current costs are the cost of goods sold in the period and appear on the income statement in determining net income. Deferred costs are ending inventory and appear on the balance sheet as current assets. Because of the inter-relationship between the balance sheet and income statement, distortion of either the cost of goods sold or ending inventory will affect both financial statements.

For example, premature recognition of sales revenue overstates current income and cost of goods sold and undervalues inventories on the balance sheet. The overstatement of income boosts the enterprise's "profit" for the year and, ultimately, its "retained earnings" on the balance sheet. Publicly traded corporations may overstate their earnings in this manner.

Similarly, understatement of cost of goods sold in the income statement will overstate inventory on the balance sheet, which will qualify management for larger bonuses or stock options based on net income.

Example

	Correct Ending Inventory	Overstate Ending Inventory	Understate Ending Inventory
Sales revenues	$300,000	$300,000	$300,000
Cost of goods sold:			
Opening inventory	$40,000	$40,000	$40,000
Add: Goods purchased	$210,000	$210,000	$210,000
Goods available for sale	$250,000	$250,000	$250,000
Subtract: Ending inventory	$50,000	$60,000	$40,000
Cost of goods sold (COGS)	$200,000	$190,000	$210,000
Gross margin	$100,000	$110,000	$90,000
Gross margin % of sales	33.3%	36.7%	30.0%

As we overstate ending inventory, we decrease the COGS and correspondingly overstate gross margin. Conversely, when we understate ending inventory, the COGS increase and we understate the gross margin. The errors will carry over to the next accounting period and distort results again. This is an important issue for anyone whose compensation is tied to the gross margin or net income.

(b) Cost of Goods Sold

As its name implies, "Cost of Goods Sold" in the income statement is the cost of the merchandise that the enterprise sells during the fiscal period. A proper matching of sales revenue and cost of goods sold is essential in calculating gross margin and net income in the particular accounting period. This raises two issues: (1) What costs to include in inventory? and (2) What value to assign to ending inventory?

We begin with the relationship between inventory on the balance sheet and cost of goods sold on the income statement.

Example

Opening inventory (asset)	$1,000
Add: purchases in the year	$700
Inventory available for sale	$1,700
Subtract: Ending inventory (asset)	$800
Cost of goods sold (expense)	$900

A misstatement of ending inventories will affect both the asset on the balance sheet and expenses on the income statement. For example, if we overstate ending inventory by $400, cost of goods sold falls by an equal amount and net income increases by $400.

Example

In January, Chubb T-Shirts Inc sells $20,000 of merchandise inventory, which it purchased for $4000 in the same month.

Sales revenue	$20,000
Subtract: Cost of goods sold	–$4,000
Gross margin	$16,000

This is a simple example because it assumes that Chubb T-Shirts Inc sold exactly the number of T-shirts that it purchased in January. A more likely scenario will be that Chubb will have some unsold T-shirts at the end of January, which it hopes it will sell in the following months.

Example

Now assume that Chubb T-Shirts Inc purchased 4,000 T-shirts for $4,000 and sold 2,500 at $8 each in January.

Sales revenue (January)	$20,000
Subtract: Cost of goods sold	–$2,500
Gross margin	$17,500

The remaining $1,500 invested in the T-shirts would show on the balance sheet as inventory as at January 31.

Example

In February, Chubb sells the remaining T-shirts at $6 each and earns sales revenue of $9,000. The Income Statement would show:

Sales revenue (February)	$9,000
Subtract: Cost of goods sold	–$1,500
Gross margin	$7,500

We see that the total cost of $4,000 of the T-shirts is charged as an expense over two months. However, each month shows a separate gross margin. Accurately determining ending inventory is a key element in calculating gross margin, net profit, taxes payable, and asset values.

Each of these examples raises the question: What costs to include in inventory? The cost of inventory includes not only the direct product costs, but also all other expenditures that the enterprise incurs in bringing the inventory to its existing condition and location. For example, if an enterprise purchases merchandise for $50,000 and pays $3,000 to ship it to its factory and $2,000 for customs brokerage fees and delivery, its landed inventory cost is $55,000, the total product cost of bringing the inventory to the enterprise's place of business from which it will use or sell the product to earn revenues.

In a manufacturing business, product costs include direct or prime costs, such as raw materials and labour. Product costs also include factory overheads or indirect expenses, such as heat, light, depreciation, and property taxes.

Improper valuation of inventory has serious consequences. In *Berkowitz v Baron*,[5] for example, an action for securities fraud under section 10(b) of the United States *Securities Exchange Act (1934)*, the vendor of a business included its shipping costs as a component of manufacturing overhead instead of operating expenses. If the costs

5 428 F Supp 1190 (1977) US District Court, Southern District of New York [*Berkowitz*].

were an operating expense, the deduction would have been against gross profit and reduced net income. However, by including the costs in inventory, the effect was to increase net profit. Hence, instead of showing a net income of $19,603 (as reported), the company would have had a loss of $24,960. The court found the financial statements to be "materially misleading" and, therefore, in violation of Rule 10(b-5) of the *Securities Act*.

> The most troublesome aspect of the financial statement is the treatment accorded certain items recorded therein. One such item is shipping cost and expenses totaling $145,281.76 [and which include shipping salaries, the costs of supplies, and charges incurred for express and parcel post]. This sum was included as a component of manufacturing overhead. Expert testimony established that this method of presentation was not in accord with generally accepted accounting principles of the time. The appropriate procedure would have been to treat such shipping costs as an operating expense, as was done in the 1969 financial statement, and take it as a deduction against gross profit, instead of including it in the cost of goods sold, above the gross profit line.
>
> The effect of this treatment was to cast a false picture of the companies' net income and inventory value. Because manufacturing overhead is a component of cost of goods sold, which in turn is one element of inventory value, improper incorporation of shipping costs and expenses in manufacturing overhead resulted in an overstatement of inventory computed to be approximately $44,560 by plaintiffs' expert witness. The enlarged inventory entry had the direct effect on the net loss/net income figure reported in the financial statement. Had the shipping costs and expenses been treated according to generally accepted accounting principles, the companies would have shown a net loss of approximately $24,960 (less the tax effect) for the fiscal year ending April 30, 1970, instead of a net income of $19,603 as was reported....
>
> [A] finding that the financial statement is "materially misleading" is fully supported.... [T]he net income/net loss and inventory value entries on a corporate financial statement are of material

importance to parties interested in purchasing all of the outstanding shares of the company.

There was no issue in *Berkowitz* as to the amount of the shipping costs. The only issue was where they appeared in the financial statements. The proper course was to deduct them as operating expenses. Instead, the companies deferred the costs to ending inventory, which had the effect of overstating both inventory and current profits. Inflated inventories increase the apparent worth of a business, which raises legal problems in purchase and sale agreements.

(c) Ending Inventory

The purpose of inventory accounting is to allocate costs between the portion that the enterprise will utilize in a future fiscal year (assets) and the portion that it incurs in the current fiscal year (expenses). There are two considerations that determine the value of inventory: 1) the cost of the inventory; and 2) the assumed flow of costs from time of purchase to recognition as a cost of goods sold.

There are two methods for determining the cost of ending inventory and the cost of goods sold: the perpetual inventory system and the periodic inventory method.

i. Perpetual Inventory Method

Under the perpetual inventory system, the enterprise keeps track of each item of merchandise that it purchases and sells. There are many sophisticated computer tracking programs that businesses use to keep count of their sales and inventories. If each product has a bar code, for example, the salesclerk will scan the code at point of sale. The computer will automatically log the transaction as a sale at the price that the sales clerk enters into the machine. At the same time, it will extract the cost of the product from inventory and enter it into a cost of goods sold account. Hence, the term "perpetual" to describe the system, which keeps a running balance of all transactions identified by their code numbers.

The perpetual system is useful for high value and unique products, each of which can be specifically identified and entered in the system.

However, a perpetual system is expensive to maintain and not appropriate for businesses that sell large amounts of similar or identical products, which they acquire at different prices during the year.

ii. Physical Count Method

An alternative method of determining inventory and the cost of goods is to physically count or "take inventory" of what is on hand at the end of the enterprise's fiscal period. The business can then determine the amount of cost of goods sold from the physical count. As a general rule, the count extends to all products to which the entity has title to the goods. This is an important issue if goods "belonging" to the company are in someone else's possession for storage.

Example

Assume that Chubb T-Shirts Inc started its fiscal year with an inventory of 1,500 T-shirts valued at their cost (at the end of the prior year) of $1,500. During the current fiscal month, Chubb acquires 4,000 additional T-shirts at a cost of $1 each. Hence, its total cost of goods of the 1,500 units available for sale is $5,500. If Chubb sells 4,800 of the T-shirts at $10 each, it would have sales revenue of $48,000 and 700 units of unsold T-shirts on hand. It would offset $4,800 as cost of goods sold against its revenues.

The income statement (partial) would appear as follows:

Opening inventory	$1,500
Add: purchases	$4,000
Units available for sale	$5,500
Physical count of units on hand (ending inventory)	-$700
Units sold during month	$4,800
Sales revenue	$48,000
Cost of Goods Sold (4,800 x $1)	$4,800
Gross Margin	$43,200

Since Chubb took a physical count and determined it had 700 T-shirts on hand at the end of the fiscal period, it concludes that it sold (assuming no "shrinkage") 4,800 units during the fiscal period.

Since all of the T-shirts cost $1 per unit, the cost of goods sold is $4,800 and the cost of the ending inventory on the balance sheet is $700. In fact, Chubb might have lost some inventory during the course of the fiscal period due to theft, obsolescence, and deterioration. We recognize these in cost of goods sold because inventory "shrinkage" is an intrinsic cost of business.

(d) Valuation

The above examples are simple because Chubb acquired all of its T-shirts at a cost of $1 each. Hence, there is no issue concerning the value of ending inventory, which is simply the number of units on hand (700) multiplied by their cost ($1).

However, valuation of inventory is more complicated if, as is likely, businesses buy identical products at different prices during the course of the fiscal year. The cost at which an enterprise values its ending inventory can be significant and has been the subject of many lawsuits and accounting frauds. Apart from blatant frauds, the issue often comes down to what should be included in the cost of inventory and which costs should be considered operating expenses. Overstated ending inventory may affect decisions on insurance claims and management of bonuses based on net profits. By including unrelated costs in inventory, an enterprise overstates its net income and asset values on the balance sheet.[6]

i. Flow of Costs

In theory, one might suggest that the most accurate method of identifying the cost of goods sold and ending inventory would be to specifically identify each unit of material or product as it physically flowed through the business. In fact, specifically identifying each item of inventory through a production process is difficult, expensive, and, in many cases, impossible. Specific identification of products would also permit cherry-picking items for cost manipulation. For example, one could pick low-cost items to increase profits or high-cost items to lower income.

---

6 See *ibid*.

To avoid income manipulation, accountants make assumptions about cost flows and then apply the assumptions consistently. Generally accepted accounting principles allow several different assumptions for valuing the flow of costs in order to determine cost of goods sold and ending inventory. Each assumption has its advantages and disadvantages. The important aspect is to understand the consequences of each method of valuation, apply the method consistently, and clearly disclose any changes in method (and financial consequences of the change) in the notes to the financial statements.

Example

In the first year of its operations, Young Stores Limited (Young), a retail store, orders 8,000 shirts for resale. The accounting records show the following:

Date 20-0	No of Units	Unit Price ($)	Total Price ($)
January 1	2,000	20	40,000
March 1	3,000	22	66,000
June 1	2,000	23	46,000
December 1	1,000	21	21,000
Total	8,000		173,000

At the end of its first accounting year (31 December), Young takes inventory and counts 3,000 shirts in its warehouse and on its shelves in its store. Thus, Young must determine the cost of the 5,000 shirts that it sold (or lost through "shrinkage") during the year and value its ending inventory, which will also determine its cost of the merchandise that it sold during the year.

To determine the value of its ending inventory, Young must make assumptions about its flow of costs. For example, Young can assume that the cost of the shirts flowed through on a first-in, first-out (FIFO) basis. Alternatively, it may assume that the costs flowed through on a last-in, first-out (LIFO) basis. Alternatively, it may assume that the flow of costs should be their weighted average during the year. Each assumption has consequences for the financial statements.

ii. FIFO

Under FIFO, the 5,000 units sold have a cost of $106,000—that is, the January and March costs, which were first in and assumed to be first out from the business. If we assume a selling price of $40 per unit, the gross margin is $94,000, or 47 percent of sales.[7]

FIFO presents a fair valuation on the balance sheet because the ending inventory (last-in, still-here) is priced at the most recent costs. The 3,000 units of ending inventory have a cost of $67,000. Thus, the balance sheet reflects the company's most current values. During periods of high inflation, however, FIFO distorts net income by putting through the earliest (and cheapest) product costs as cost of goods sold. Thus, in inflationary periods, FIFO boosts profits by understating the cost of goods sold. Nevertheless, in many businesses, goods do actually flow on a first-in, first-out basis to prevent inventory spoilage and obsolescence. Hence, the cost flow assumption often matches the actual physical flow of goods.

The increase in net income, however, is artificial because it does not properly reflect the operating results of the business and includes an element of "inventory profit" unrelated to its operating efficiency. Thus, even an inefficient business can show an increase in profits simply by virtue of the impact of inflation on its inventory.

In contrast to the circumstances in *Berkowitz*, where the transaction involved the sale of a business, the incentive for tax purposes is to understate ending inventory and overstate cost of goods sold so as to minimize current net income and, therefore, lower tax liabilities. Such understatements of inventories can prejudice employees who are compensated through profit sharing agreements. For example, a company may charge all of its "freight in" as a current expense instead of allocating the costs to inventories.[8]

---

7 ($94,000/200,000) × 100 = 47 percent.

8 See, for example, *D Loveman & Son Exp Corp v Comm'r*, 34 TC 776 (1960) affd 296 F 2d 732 (6th Cir 1961); the taxpayer could not deduct "freight in" as current expense and was required to treat costs as part of acquiring merchandise.

iii. LIFO

The LIFO method of inventory valuation emphasizes the impact of the most recent costs on the income statement. In times of rising prices (inflation), LIFO produces a lower net-income figure because the latest (most expensive) purchases go into determining the cost of goods sold during the year. Stated another way, LIFO means first-in, still-here. The earliest, and cheapest, inventory purchases show up on the balance sheet. Thus, LIFO can depress current net income and also understate the value of inventory on the balance sheet.

There are sound theoretical reasons for using LIFO in inflationary periods. When costs are rising, LIFO produces a conservative net income figure by showing the full impact of inflation on profits.

IFRS does not permit the use of LIFO for financial reporting, which is different from US generally accepted accounting principles (GAAP). Some US companies would pay higher income taxes if the United States adopted IFRS, which explains some of their resistance against IFRS.

Example

Using the same data for Young Stores Limited (above), ending inventory using LIFO would be determined as follows:

2,000 units @ $20 each	$40,000
1,000 units @ $22 each	$22,000
Ending inventory	$62,000
Cost of goods sold:	
Opening inventory	$0
Purchases during the year	$173,000
Goods available for sale	$173,000
Ending inventory (LIFO)	$62,000
Cost of goods sold in the year	$111,000

At a selling price of $40 per unit, the gross margin is $89,000, or 45 percent of sales, which is lower than under FIFO.

There are some disadvantages of LIFO. The inventory on the balance sheet is "understated" in that it reflects low prices that do not prevail in the market (first in, still here). The lower net income reported under LIFO can distort certain ratios, particularly ratios that use current assets, total assets, or equity. For example, the lower balance sheet value of inventory under LIFO will affect the working capital ratio, which can be important in loan agreements (see Chapter 15, Interpretation of Financial Statements).

LIFO also allows management to manipulate reported profits. Each addition to the inventory balance under LIFO is a "layer." Thus, the oldest layer may be the initial inventory balance from years past. Where a company increases the number of units in its inventory, each addition adds an additional layer. With the passage of time, the value of LIFO inventory on the balance sheet becomes dated. Thus, a business can significantly improve its net income by depleting its inventory and digging into its earlier lower costs as reflected in the inventory balance.

For example, a business that wanted to increase its net profits for a period might simply deplete its inventory, thereby releasing "inventory profits" resulting from lower inventory costs into the cost of goods sold. In effect, previously unrealized gains and losses from inventory appreciation would suddenly appear in the accounting year in which management depletes its inventory. A company that never depleted its inventory entirely would continue to show its earliest inventory costs on the balance sheet. Some of those inventory costs (first-in, still-here) would comprise costs from many years earlier.

iv. Weighted Average Cost

The weighted average cost method is simply a compromise between FIFO and LIFO. Under this method, a business determines the weighted average cost of all of its inventory available for sale in the fiscal period and uses that cost in determining its ending inventory and costs of goods sold. In the previous example, the weighted average cost of ending inventory is:

$$[\$173{,}000/8{,}000] \times 3{,}000 = \$64{,}875.$$

v. Lower of Cost and Net Realizable Value

GAAP usually requires inventory to be valued at its historical cost, be it FIFO, LIFO, or weighted average. However, the principle of conservatism requires that inventory values on the balance sheet be the lower of cost or market value. Thus, where market values fall below the costs of inventory, the business must write down its ending inventory and take the charge into its cost of goods sold. Following the principle of conservatism, increases in the value of inventory are not reflected on the balance sheet.

"Market value" can have several different meanings and the notes to the financial statement should disclose which meaning management uses in the particular circumstances. Market value can mean replacement value, that is, the costs at which the business can replace its inventory. For example, where a business acquired 1,000 units of inventory at $10 per unit, the total cost of inventory available for sale would be $10,000. If the ending inventory of 300 units can now be replaced at $8 per unit, the inventory has a replacement value that is $2 less than its original cost. Thus the business should write down its ending inventory by $600 to reflect the reduction in value of its ending inventory.

Market value can also mean "net realizable value," that is, anticipated selling price minus costs of disposal. When net realizable value falls below replacement costs, the lower number should be used for purposes of the inventory write-down. In the above example, if the units can only be sold at $7 per unit less $1 in disposal costs, the net realizable value is $6 per unit. In these circumstances, the 300 units of ending inventory should be written down by $4 per unit, for a total write-down of $1,200.

Example

Canadian Computer Inc (CCI) purchased 1,000 laptops in September 20-0 at $200 each. CCI sells most of these laptops at an average price of $500 each. At 1 December 20-0, the sales price of the laptops still on hand is reduced to $300 each. At 31 December 20-0, fifteen laptops are still unsold. At 31 December 20-1, five laptops remain unsold. CCI could liquidate these laptops for a net amount of $100 each. Selling costs are insignificant as CCI pays no commissions.

At 31 December 20-0, the inventory is valued at its cost of $3,000 ($200 × 15 laptops), since the cost is lower than the net realizable value. At 31 December 20-1, the five remaining laptops are valued at a net realizable value of $500 ($100 × 5 laptops), since the net realizable value is lower than the cost.[9]

vi. Risks of Misstatement

There is a risk, particularly with publicly traded companies, that management may inflate ending inventory in order to boost net income and therefore share prices and stock option values. An outside reader of the financial statements will not be able to detect such overstatements and must trust the company's management and auditors that the statements are fairly presented according to IFRS and GAAP.

For tax purposes, the behavioural incentive is exactly the opposite. Management is tempted to understate inventory, because understated inventory decreases net income and, therefore, current taxes payable. Similarly, for the purposes of profit-sharing arrangements with employees, management may shortchange employees by understating ending inventory to reduce profit-sharing payouts based upon net income.

The most common method of understating inventory is by charging as current expenses amounts that should otherwise properly be included in the cost of inventory. In this manner, expenses are increased, ending inventory is understated, and net income is reduced. For example, in *Loveman & Son Export Corp v Commissioner*, the taxpayer deducted "freight-in" on purchase as current expenses when the charges should have been included in the cost of its inventory. The taxpayer was not allowed to deduct the freight charges as a current expense.

Lawyers should be careful in drafting warranties and covenants. For example, in *Berkowitz*, the vendor warranted that the financial statement for the year ending 30 April 1970 fully and accurately presented companies' financial condition in assets and liabilities and the results of the companies' operations for the period indicated.

9 *Handbook* at para 3031.10.

When it comes to litigation, words such as "fully and accurately" are dangerous. GAAP permits alternative treatment for many items that are all acceptable under accounting principles. In such circumstances, it is advisable for representations and warranties to track the language of the audit opinion. For example, the warranty might state:

> The financial statements present fairly, in all material respects, the financial position of the Companies as of [date] and the results of operations for the year ended [date] in conformity with generally accepted accounting principles (or alternatively, in accordance with IFRS).

vii. Financial Statement Disclosure

GAAP requires that the breakdown of inventory by category (finished goods, work-in-progress, and raw materials) and their valuation method should be disclosed in the financial statements. An entity may disclose this information in the body of the balance sheet or, more usually, in the Notes to the statements.

For example, a Note on inventories may state:

> Inventories are stated at the lower of FIFO cost or market. The Company records inventory reserves for obsolete and slow-moving items and for estimated shrinkage between physical inventory counts.

GAAP generally prevents an entity from changing from one accounting principle to another unless the new principle is "preferable" to the old principle. Accounting principles include the methods applied to them. Changes in the method of inventory valuation and the effect of the changes on net income should be disclosed in the Notes to the financial statements.

viii. Tax Issues

Section 10 of the *Income Tax Act* states the general rule that inventory must be valued at whichever is the lower between cost or its fair market value. However, section 10(6) provides an exception for artists who may elect to value their inventory at nil. This allows artists to write off their costs immediately rather than waiting for sale of their artworks, which means that they are effectively taxed on a cash basis of accounting.[10] The provision was enacted after artist Toni Onley threatened to burn his works to reduce his inventory and tax bill! Who says that you cannot fight City Hall?

The work in process (WIP) of a professional person is inventory.[11] WIP includes the cost of employees but not fixed or indirect overheads and does not include the professional's own time. The FMV of contingency fees is nil until the amount is known.

The Act does not define either "cost" or "fair market value." Regulation 1801 permits a business (other than breeding and raising of animals) to value all of its inventory at fair market value. The taxpayer may thus value their inventory at cost, market, or perhaps a combination of the two. The CRA recognizes only the average cost and FIFO methods of determining the cost of inventories for income tax purposes. It does not recognize LIFO.

LIFO became popular in the United States because, since 1939, American businesses can use LIFO for tax purposes under certain conditions. Since, in inflationary periods, LIFO produces a lower net-income figure than FIFO, it is entirely understandable that corporations may opt for LIFO to reduce their income taxes.

ix. Anaconda American Brass Ltd v MNR

Since the decision of the Privy Council in *Anaconda American Brass Ltd v MNR*,[12] the CRA does not accept LIFO as a proper method for valuing inventory for tax purposes. The Exchequer Court, the Supreme Court of Canada, and the Privy Council all agreed that the LIFO method is, in certain conditions, a proper and generally accepted method of accounting. However, the Minister of National Revenue contended that no matter how appropriate the LIFO method might be for corporate purposes, it did not truly reflect profit for income

10 *Tramble*, [2001] 4 CTC 2160 (TCC); *Faber*, 2008 TCC 403. See section 10(6) of the *Income Tax Act* for the meaning of "artistic endeavour," which excludes the business of reproducing works of art.

11 *ITA*, s 10(5).

12 52 DTC 1111 at para 1126 [*Anaconda Brass*].

tax purposes because it did not reflect the physical flow of goods and, accordingly, assessed the company on the FIFO method.

Unfortunately, the Privy Council, which was the supreme judicial council in the era of the Empire, reversed the Supreme Court of Canada.[13] Although their Lordships accepted LIFO as a proper accounting method and appropriate in the case, they contended that the real issue was whether LIFO was permissible for *income tax purposes* or whether the method most correctly reflected income within the structure of Canadian income tax law. The Privy Council accepted that LIFO is based upon an accounting assumption of flow of costs, but not necessarily the actual flow of goods. They considered LIFO to be a "novel, and even revolutionary proposal."[14] Hence, in their view, it did not truly reflect the company's profit for income tax purposes.

The Privy Council relied upon Lord Loreburn's judgment in *Sun Insurance Office v Clark*[15] that determining the cost of goods by the first-in first-out method of inventory valuation disclosed the only true profit for income tax purposes:

> For many years before and ever since . . . *Whimster & Co.* v. *C.T.R.* 12 T.C. 813, what is to be valued at the beginning and end of the accounting period has for tax purposes to be taken to be the actual stock so far as it can be ascertained. It is in fact so far as tax law is concerned a novel, and even revolutionary proposal, that the physical facts should even, where they can wholly or partly be ascertained, be disregarded for the purpose of the opening and closing inventory and a theoretical assumption made which is based upon a supposed "flow of cost" and "unabsorbed residue of cost."[16]

Following *Anaconda Brass*, for pragmatic reasons, LIFO is not a popular method of inventory accounting in Canada for financial statements because it would involve two sets of records and affect published

---

13 *MNR v Anaconda American Brass Ltd*, [1956] 2 AC 85.

14 *The Minister of National Revenue (Appeal No 6 of 1955) v Anaconda American Brass Limited (Canada)*, [1955] UKPC 36 (13 December 1955) per Viscount Simonds at 5.

15 [1912] AC 443 at para 450.

16 *MNR v Anaconda American Brass Ltd*, above note 13 at para 101.

net income figures. Hence, despite any theoretical arguments in its favour, Canadian businesses shy away from LIFO for financial statement purposes. This saves them from having to show two different net-income figures, one for financial statement purposes and the other for tax purposes.

7. Prepaid Expenses

Short-term prepaid expenses are amounts that the business has paid for goods or services in advance of their delivery or service. Prepaid expenses, also known as deferred charges, are not generally convertible into cash but are consumed over time. For example, a business with a calendar year-end may buy an insurance policy on 1 July and pay $20,000 premium for one year's coverage. At 31 December, the business would have used only six months of coverage and would recognize $10,000 on its balance sheet. Typical expenses include prepaid rent, prepaid insurance, prepaid subscription services, prepaid taxes, and prepaid interest. Duggan Inc's prepaid expenses were $216,000 for 20-2.

8. Property, Plant, and Equipment

A fundamental principle underlying the measurement of income in accrual accounting is the matching of revenues with expenses during a fiscal period. The matching process requires a review of acquisition costs of long-term assets and their allocation between current expenses and deferred expenses. Long-term assets may be tangible or intangible.

Tangible fixed assets have physical substance, are acquired for their productive capabilities rather than resale, and benefit more than one accounting period. The critical question is: has the entity incurred an expenditure that will benefit future accounting periods? If so, then it has acquired an asset. If not, then the expenditure is an expense in the current period.

Where an enterprise purchases (or constructs) tangible fixed assets with a finite life, it must allocate their cost over their useful life in order to match the current portion of the cost as expenses against current revenues. Land does not have a finite life and its cost is not allocated.

Hence, the starting point is to determine whether the expenditure is on account of long-lived fixed or capital assets or current expenses. If the former, the enterprise must estimate the useful or productive life of the capital asset and its residual value (if any) at the end of its useful life, and decide on the manner in which it will allocate the cost over useful life. Management makes these decisions.

In the historical cost model, fixed asset acquisitions are recorded at cost on the balance sheet. Hence, for example, where a business acquires (or constructs) a building for $60 million, it will record the asset at that cost.

The next question is: how long will the building last and what will be its residual (salvage) value at the end of its expected useful life? Let us assume that professional experts estimate the building's useful life to be fifty years and estimate a $10 million salvage value.

Then, the next decision is the manner in which to allocate the net $50 million over the fifty years in each accounting period. We refer to the allocations of cost of long-lived tangible assets as "depreciation."

(a) Depreciation

There are four principal factors to consider in determining the amount of depreciation that an enterprise should record as a charge against revenues in a fiscal period:

1) Cost of the fixed (capital) asset;
2) Salvage value;
3) Useful life; and
4) Mode of calculation.

Observe that the calculation for depreciation involves two estimates, salvage value, and useful life. It also requires a judgment call by management on the method of allocating the net cost over useful life. Thus, although the final depreciation number in the financial statements appears numerically precise, it is only as good as the estimates and judgment that management makes in respect of useful life, salvage value, and mode of cost allocation.

The annual depreciation charge does not involve any cash charge or transfer on the books of the enterprise. The cash cost of acquisition or construction occurs when the enterprise pays out cash to acquire the asset. Depreciation is simply an allocation of the net cost of capital assets over their useful life and does not involve any cash accumulation by the enterprise. We see this in the statement of cash flows, where the annual depreciation charge is added back to operating income for the purposes of determining cash in-flows and out-flows (see Chapter 12, Statement of Cash Flows).

i. Cost of Fixed Assets

Fixed or capital assets are recorded initially at cost, which is the cash, or cash equivalent, price to bring the asset to its intended location and ready for use. Costs to set up the asset for its intended use are also included in the initial capital cost of the asset. Hence, for example, the recorded cost will include the asset's purchase price, taxes, freight, installation, and set-up charges. In the case of buildings, we segregate the cost of the land from the cost of the building because land is not a depreciable asset.

ii. Salvage Value

The salvage value of a tangible asset is the amount that one expects it will realize when the business ultimately disposes of it at the end of its useful life. The best that management can do is to estimate salvage value based upon its past experience with such assets, current market conditions, and professional opinions. The longer the expected life of the asset, the greater the difficulty in estimating its salvage value.

iii. Useful Life

Management must also estimate useful life at the time that the enterprise acquires the capital asset based upon its experience and evolving technology. Useful life can be the actual physical life of the asset or its utility based upon technological developments and considerations of efficiency. Thus, useful life of an asset can be shorter than its physical life.

Example

On 1 January, a business acquires a machine for $72,000. The machine can last for ten years, but management estimates that it will have a useful productive life of only four years at the end of which the business will sell it for $12,000. Hence, the *net* amount to be depreciated over the four years is $60,000. The annual depreciation charge over the four years will depend upon the method of depreciation that management selects (see below).

(b) Depreciation Methods

The method of depreciation that a business selects will affect the annual expense charge to the income statement. There are various methods for allocating depreciation, but they all have the same objective: allocate the *net* cost of the asset (initial cost minus salvage value) over its useful productive life to match revenues and expenses. Since fixed assets are not acquired for resale, depreciation does not reflect any diminution in the market value of the asset, other than in the estimate of its salvage value. Similarly, the net book value of the asset on the balance sheet does not necessarily reflect the market value of the asset, unless management opts to disclose the asset at its fair value.

There are various methods of calculating depreciation. Here we review three of the most common methods:

- Straight line;
- Declining balance; and
- Units of production.

i. Straight Line

Straight line is the simplest of all the methods and results in the business charging an equal amount of depreciation expense to the income statement over the useful life of the asset. The formula for this method is as follows:

$$\text{Depreciation expense} = \frac{[\text{Original Cost} - \text{Salvage value}]}{\text{Useful life in years}}$$

Example

Assuming the same facts for the machine as in the preceding example, the annual depreciation charge for each of the four years of useful life would be $15,000 per year calculated as follows:

Year	Beginning Book Value	Depreciation @ 25%	Ending Book Value
1	$72,000	$15,000	$57,000
2	$57,000	$15,000	$42,000
3	$42,000	$15,000	$27,000
4	$27,000	$15,000	$12,000 Salvage value

The straight-line method derives its name from the shape of the flat line on a graph when one plots the annual depreciation charge on the vertical axis and the number of years on the horizontal axis. The only adjustment that needs to be made to the straight-line computation is if the asset is purchased and placed in use partway through the first year. In such a case the annual depreciation charge is proportionately allocated for the number of months in the year that it is actually in use.

ii. Declining Balance Method

The declining balance method applies a fixed percentage to the initial cost of the asset in the first year, and subsequently the same percentage to the remaining book value of the asset at the beginning of each year. The book value of the asset in the beginning of each year is the original cost of the asset minus the accumulated amount of depreciation charged in prior years.

The most common percentage used in the declining balance method is double the percentage that one would use under the straight-line method. There is no immediate adjustment made for the salvage value under this method. In the preceding example, the annual straight-line percentage is equal to 25 percent (that is, 1 divided by the useful life of four years). Using the declining balance method, we would charge 50 percent of the cost of the asset in the first year. Thus, the charge in the first year would be $36,000. In each of the following years the 50 percent would apply only to the remaining book value of the asset, as in the example below.

Example

Year	Beginning Book Value	Depreciation @ 50%	Ending Book Value
1	$72,000	$36,000	$36,000
2	$36,000	$18,000	$18,000
3	$18,000	$6,000	$12,000
			Salvage value

There is no additional depreciation after Year 3 as asset has reached its salvage value of $12,000.

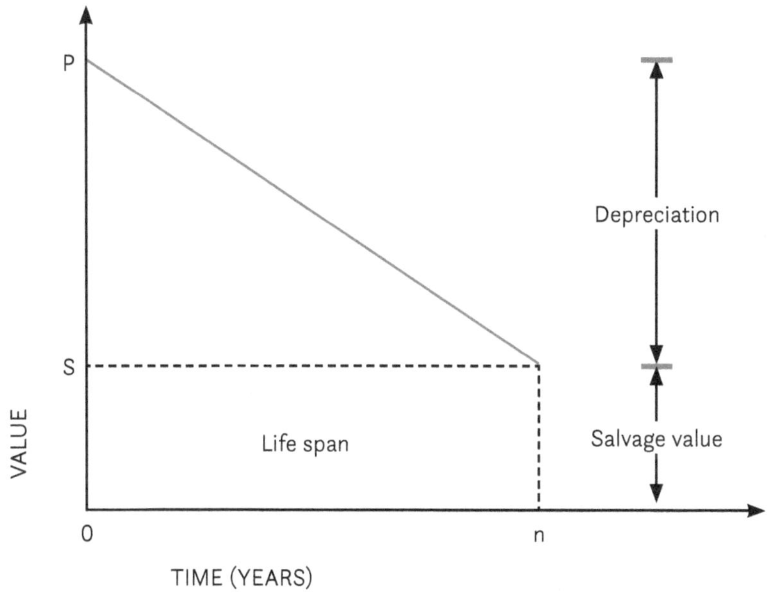

As with the straight-line method, the declining balance method derives its name from the shape of the graph when one plots the annual depreciation charge on the vertical axis and the number of years on the horizontal axis.

Now we see the difference in the amount of depreciation expense between the straight-line method and the declining balance method. Under the straight-line method, the annual charge was $15,000 per year, whereas under the declining balance method, the charge is $36,000 in the first year. Thus, the declining balance method produces a higher write-off rate in the early years of an asset's useful life. In later years, however (for example, Year 3), the annual depreciation charge ($15,000) under the straight-line method exceeds the amount charged ($6,000) under the declining balance method.

iii. Tax Issues

For tax purposes, a taxpayer is not allowed to deduct expenditures on account of capital outlays, depreciation, obsolescence, or depletion.[17] On preliminary examination, this prohibition against the deduction of depreciation (and similar expenses) flies in the face of accrual accounting principles in the computation of net income. The *Income Tax Act* does, however, allow for a compensatory deduction. In computing income from a business or property, a taxpayer may deduct[18] a portion of the capital cost of property as is allowed by the Regulations. In tax law, we refer to this deduction as capital cost allowance (CCA).

The basic concept underlying the capital cost allowance system is that it is a deduction from income, which approximately allocates the cost of capital assets over their useful lives. Thus, in a sense, the CCA system is nothing more than statutory depreciation but at pre-determined fixed rates.

CCA rates are generally set to reflect, as closely as possible, the useful life of assets and, in this sense, to accurately measure net income. However, because the rates are the same for all taxpayers, CCA does not offer the same flexibility and accuracy as accounting depreciation. The government also uses the CCA rates to implement other socio-economic and political policies and to remain competitive with the United States.

The CCA rates, which are the same for all taxpayers with similar assets performing similar activities, generally allow generous write-offs. The deduction for tax purposes in the early years of an asset's life usually exceeds the comparable depreciation for accounting and financial statement purposes. Thus, in part at least, the capital cost allowance system

17 *ITA* at para 18(1)(b).

18 *ITA* at para 20(1)(a), Regulations Pt XI (Regs 1100–1107). The phrase "capital cost allowance" refers to an allowance in respect of the capital cost of depreciable property.

compensates taxpayers for the effects of inflation on asset replacement costs. The system also permits taxpayers to defer taxes because of the difference between tax and accounting depreciation.

The difference between the two methods is important in considering the amount of income taxes payable during the life of the asset. The higher write-off under the declining balance method reduces net income and, therefore, income taxes payable in the early years. However, the higher write-off also creates a potential deferred income tax liability in the future when the write-off rate under the declining balance method drops below the amount charged under the straight-line method. Duggan Inc, for example, has deferred income taxes of $1,889,000, part of which may pertain to the difference between its CCA and book depreciation.

iv. Units of Production Method

The units of production method is conceptually similar to the straight-line method except that it is calculated on expected units of production from the asset, rather than on its years of service. Thus, the first step is to determine the rate of depreciation per unit as follows:

Depreciation per unit = [Original cost - Estimated salvage value]/ Expected total units of production

Example

Assuming the same data as given in the first example above, the original cost of the asset is $72,000 with a salvage value of $12,000. It is estimated that the asset will produce 200,000 units during its useful life. Thus, the depreciation per unit (net of salvage value) will be $0.30 per unit.

Year	Beginning Book Value	Units	Depreciation @ 0.30 cents per unit
1	$72,000	40,000	$12,000
2	$60,000	50,000	$15,000
3	$45,000	30,000	$9,000
4	$36,000	60,000	$18,000
5	$18,000	20,000	$6,000
Total	$12,000 Salvage value	200,000	$60,000

(c) Repairs and Improvements

Repairs and improvements to fixed assets pose a special problem in accounting. One must first determine whether an expenditure on account of repairs is a current expense or a capital expenditure. If it is a current expense, the cost goes to the income statement. If it is a capital expenditure, the cost is added to the capital asset and depreciated over time. The practical difficulty is in drawing the line between expenses and capital expenditures.

Repairs are generally costs that maintain an asset's operating efficiency and expected useful life. Repairs, which are usually small in amount and tend to recur, are considered current expenses because they tend to benefit only the current accounting period.

Capital expenditures generally increase the operational efficiency and productive capacity and extend the useful life of the asset. Hence, they also benefit future accounting periods.

The distinction between routine repairs and capital improvements can be highly subjective and have a material effect on net income. For example, assume that a business spends $20,000 to repair a machine that has an estimated useful life of five years prior to the repairs. However, the repairs to the machine extend its life by another year. Should the $20,000 be charged as an expense in the current year or capitalized into the cost of the machinery? If it is expensed in the current year, net income will fall by $20,000. This may, for example, affect a production manager's bonus payment based upon net income. What if the repairs extend useful life by four years? Here, the rationale for capitalizing the cost is more convincing and will not affect the manager's bonus. Management must make the decision.

i. Misstatements and Fraud

Repairs versus capitalization issues are judgmental issues, but they can also lead to deliberate misstatements and mislead investors and potential buyers of the business.

In *re Valley Systems, Inc*,[19] for example, Valley, a publicly traded corporation on the NASDAQ, provided industrial cleaning services

19 Securities & Exchange Commission, 1995, Fed Sec L Rep (CCH) at ¶ 74,222 (14 September 1995).

to companies engaged in heavy industry. As of 30 June 1992, *Valley* reported consolidated assets of $29.5 million, shareholders' equity of $10.7 million, consolidated revenues of $24.5 million, and a net loss of $2 million.

For the first three quarters of fiscal 1992, Valley's CFO arbitrarily capitalized current period expenses on the purported ground that they were incurred in the construction of capital equipment. There was no supporting documentation or analysis to justify the amounts capitalized. The amount of the excess capitalization and, consequently, the overstatement of pre-tax income was as follows:

Quarter	Improper Capitalization ($)
Q1	1,100,000
Q2	970,000
Q3	179,000

At the end of the first quarter, the CFO directed that $1.5 million of the previously capitalized expenses be reclassified from the Construction in Progress account to an Equipment account. The fixed assets were described as seventeen waterblasters and three ultra-high pressure (UHP) units, practically none of which existed. After receiving queries from Valley's auditors concerning the equipment entry, the CFO directed that Valley's records be altered to conceal the fact that the equipment did not exist. He directed his subordinates to "bury" or "spread" the costs of the seventeen waterblasters and three UHP units by allocating the costs to various other pieces of equipment. Valley then altered its books and records so that they did not show the existence of the waterblasters and UHP units. The SEC found that *Valley* violated section 10(b) of the *Exchange Act* and Rule 10b-5 thereunder.

ii. IFRS Disclosure

IFRS allows an entity to record property, plant, and equipment at its fair value less any subsequent accumulated depreciation and accumulated impairment. However, where an entity chooses to show its property, plant, and equipment at fair value, it must do so for all assets within the same class. Further, the entity must revalue the assets regularly to ensure that they are shown at current fair value.

(d) Depletion

Depletion refers to the consumption of natural resources and is similar in concept to the depreciation of tangible assets. Depletion allocates the costs to acquire natural resources to the accounting periods in which the enterprise consumes its wasting assets. The costs are charged as expenses as the natural resources are mined, extracted, or otherwise consumed.

The depletion rate is calculated in the same way as the units of production method for depreciation. The total cost of the natural resource is determined from the purchase documents. The salvage value (if any) is estimated. Finally, the total amount of the natural resource available is estimated. From these three figures we can determine the depletion rate per unit of the natural resource extracted.

Example

Assume that a company purchases a mine for $500 million and expects to extract 400,000 ounces of ore from the mine. Then each ounce of ore extracted will deplete the mine by $1,250. If the company extracts 60,000 ounces in the first year, the depletion expense will be $75 million, which will reduce the net book value of the mine to $425 million.

Depletion expenses reduce income and an equivalent amount of accumulated depletion shows on the balance sheet at the end of each year.

9. Intangible Assets

Intangible assets are assets (other than financial assets) that lack physical substance. Goodwill is typically excluded, unless it is purchased goodwill. Intangible assets typically include intellectual property and legal rights, such as patents, trademarks, certain computer software development costs, broadcast licences, and franchises.

The accounting for intangible assets depends on the manner in which the business acquires or develops them. Because intangibles lack physical substance, they raise difficult questions concerning their useful lives and estimates of their value. Intangibles are generally measured initially at cost and charged as expenses if the expenditure will produce future economic benefits. The cost of the asset may be amortized over its useful life.

If the fair value of the intangible can be measured by reference to an active market, the entity may revalue it at its fair value and show net of accumulated amortization and any impairment. Revaluation increases are recorded in the statement of comprehensive income and show on the balance sheet in the equity section as "Revaluation Surplus."

10. Goodwill

Goodwill refers to the excess cost that a purchaser pays for an entity over the net amount of its assets and any liabilities that it assumes. Goodwill is attributable to many amorphous factors that contribute to the competitive advantage of a business, but which cannot be separated from the business as a whole. It is the most intangible of intangibles. Lord Eldon described goodwill as "the probability that the old customers will resort to the old place."[20]

In effect, goodwill translates into the expectation of superior prospective earnings. Goodwill includes, for example, strong brand acceptance (e.g. Apple Inc's products, Coca Cola's brand loyalty, etc.), effective management, loyal employees, secure supply chains, or good labour relations. Following the principle of objective measurement of assets, accountants do not recognize internally generated goodwill as an intangible asset because it cannot be measured reliably.

For example, when *Amazon Inc* bought *Whole Foods Market Inc* for $13.7 billion in 2017, the e-commerce giant paid $9 billion more than the value of the supermarket's stores and other net assets. That amount was added to Amazon's books as goodwill. As things stand now, Amazon is supposed to evaluate that $9 billion every year to see if its value still holds. If not, they have to write down a portion of it, a move that would cut into its profit.

---

20 *Cruttwell v Lye*, 17 Ves 335, 346, 34 Eng Rep 129, 134 (Ch 1810).

Goodwill is the product of deals, but there's a debate about how to properly account for it. The current annual review process is time consuming and expensive. However, the old approach, which allowed amortization of goodwill year by year, allowed companies to mask problems and cost investors valuable information.

The Financial Accounting Standards Board (FASB), the accounting-rules maker in the US, is weighing whether to continue to assess goodwill by annual tests—or return to a similar approach of the old guidelines, when companies wrote down a set portion of goodwill each year for up to forty years.

11. Patents

A patent is a monopoly that the Government of Canada (and other governments in other countries) grants to inventors for a period of time for the exclusive right to make, sell, import, use, or otherwise commercially exploit a new invention. In most cases, the legal life of a patent is twenty years from the date of filing, during which period the patentholder enjoys exclusive rights for the use of the invention.

In the simplest case, as an asset, the cost of the patent may be written off or amortized over its protected life. The concept of amortization is similar to that of depreciation in that both involve an allocation of cost of the asset over its life. However, because of technological developments, the useful life of a patent can be less than its legal life.

12. Copyright

Copyright refers to the legally protected right to publish, sell, or perform from books, music, films, and recordings. The general duration of copyright protection in Canada is life-plus-fifty, or the end of the calendar year fifty years after the year in which the author died. Copyrights are amortized over their useful life.

13. Trademarks

A trademark is a mark that distinguishes goods or services in the marketplace, such as distinctive names, symbols, or designs that identify a particular product or service

A trademark may be a "wordmark" composed of a word or words, or a "design mark" that is composed of a design, with or without words. A trademark may be a name, logo, slogan, or design.

(a) Amortization

The cost of acquiring identifiable intangible assets should be capitalized. Cost includes the purchase price of the property and all legal expenses incurred to perfect title to the property. The legal cost to defend intellectual property rights should also be capitalized.

An intangible asset with a finite life (for example, a patent) should be amortized over its *useful* life. The useful life of an intangible asset does not necessarily coincide with the period during which it is legally protected. For example, although a patent may have a legally protected life of twenty years, the business may not enjoy its monopolistic protection of the patent for all those years because of changing technologies and competing products coming on the market. Thus, management must annually estimate the remaining useful life of the property and make the appropriate expense charge.

Amortization of intangibles is generally based on a straight-line on the full cost of the intangible. Unlike the charge for depreciation, which is accumulated in an account and shown as a deduction from capital assets on the balance sheet, amortization charges are usually written off directly against the cost of the intangible, with only the *net* remaining intangible cost showing on the balance sheet.

Example

Assume that a business purchases a patent for $1 million and that the patent has a remaining life of fifteen years. In the first year, the amortization charge would be $66,667 and the patent would show on the balance sheet as an intangible asset with a net capital cost of $933,333.

Chapter 8: Liabilities

A. OVERVIEW

Liabilities are the legal obligations of a business to persons other than the owners of the business. However, the owners of a business can also be its creditors where, for example, they lend it money.

Liabilities may be actual cash obligations payable sometime in the future, such as for example, accounts payable, notes payable, bonds, and mortgages. Such liabilities are usually settled in cash.

Liabilities may also arise in other ways. For example, prepaid revenues (also known as "deferred income" or "deferred revenues") are liabilities, which an entity usually discharges through the delivery of goods or services for which the business received the prepayment. In a legal practice, for example, client retainers are the classic form of deferred revenues. Until the lawyer renders the service for which they receive payment in advance, the funds remain in the trust account and belong to the client. The lawyer must "earn" the income before they can recognize it as revenue.

Liabilities may be due on different dates, accrue interest at various rates, and be secured by different means. We classify liabilities on the balance sheet according to their duration and timing for payment.

The following is the Liabilities section of the Balance Sheet of the hypothetical company, Duggan Inc.

Partial Balance Sheet for Duggan Inc as at September 30

Liabilities (thousands of dollars)	20-2 $	20-1 $
Current Liabilities:		
Current portion of long-term debt	210	157
Notes payable	3,672	1,962
Accounts payable	3,088	3,138
Accrued Liabilities:		
Income taxes	659	1,041
Salaries & wages	765	780
Advertising & promotion	2,338	2,280
Deferred revenue	1,414	1,352
Total current liabilities	12,146	10,710
Long-term Liabilities:		
Long-term debt	5,216	3,149
Non-pension post-retirement benefits	4,509	4,076
Deferred income taxes	1,889	1,846
Capital leases	1,477	917
Total long-term liabilities	13,091	9,988
Total Liabilities	**25,237**	**20,698**

B. CURRENT LIABILITIES

Current liabilities are known obligations (such as accounts payable and notes payable) or estimated amounts (such as product warranties), which the enterprise will satisfy in the near future, usually within one year. Current liabilities are a source of funding at no cost to the borrower. For example, where a business buys merchandise on credit and is required to pay within thirty days, it is, in effect, getting a thirty-day interest-free loan. Similarly, unearned subscription revenue prepaid to a publisher is, in effect, an interest-free loan from the subscribers to the publisher. Duggan Inc has total current liabilities of $12,146,000 at year end in 20-2.

1. Accounts Payable

Accounts payable are debts that an enterprise incurs when it purchases goods or services on terms that do not call for immediate payment. Most accounts payable (such as credit card purchases) are due and payable within a short time, generally 15–30 days, without interest charges. As such, they are a form of interest-free loan from the creditor.

Accounts payable are recorded at their face value and appear in the current liability section of the balance sheet. There is no imputed interest on the payable where the debt arises in the normal course of business and is due within one year of its creation. Duggan Inc has accounts payable of $3,088,000 at its 20-2 year end.

2. Notes Payable

Notes payable are a more formal type of accounts payable that are recorded in a note that usually provides for interest and stipulates a due date. Most notes payable arise from cash loans to the business, such as bank loans and commercial paper. The entity records the note at its face value and shows in the current liability section of the balance sheet. Any interest payable on the note is charged as interest expense. Duggan Inc has notes payable of $3,672,000 at year end 20-2.

3. Accrued Liabilities

Accrued liabilities arise when a business incurs an expense even though there is no immediate legal obligation to pay. Classic accrued liabilities are salaries and wages earned but not payable until a later payroll date. The expense is recognized in the income statement and the accrued liability shows on the balance sheet.

Accrued liabilities typically accumulate over time. For example, assume that a note payable of $100,000 has interest payable of 0.5 percent per month payable on the fifteenth day of each month. If the company's year-end is 31 December, there will be $250 accrued at that date for one-half month's interest, which the business will recognize as interest expense in the income statement for the year and show as an accrued liability on the balance sheet.

4. Deferred Revenues

The fundamental principle of revenue recognition is that a business should recognize revenue only when it *realizes* its revenue. This occurs when it has a *bona fide* exchange transaction and the earnings process from the exchange has been substantially completed.[1] Until such time, any amounts received in advance are considered deferred revenues, which appear as a liability on the balance sheet.

Example

Assume that a business rents out a portion of its premises for $30,000, payable in semi-annual installments of $15,000 on 1 October and 31 March. If the business has a calendar year-end, it will have deferred (unearned) revenues of $7,500 for the period of 1 January to 31 March. Hence, it would recognize the portion that it earns from 1 October to 31 December as revenues and defer recognizing the remaining $7,500 until the subsequent calendar year.

5. Estimated Liabilities

Estimated liabilities (or, as International Accounting Standards 37[2] calls them, "provisions") arise when a business knows that it will incur expenses in respect of its current sales but cannot absolutely determine the exact amount of the expenditure that will arise in the future.

For example, a car manufacturer may sell an automobile with a four-year warranty. The manufacturer knows that it will incur warranty expenses in the next four years but cannot be certain as to the exact amount of warranty work on each car sold. Hence, it will estimate its future warranty work as a reserve and recognize the

---

1 See Chapter 10, Income Statement.

2 International Accounting Standards 37, *Provisions, Contingent Liabilities and Contingent Assets* (September 1998), as amended, online: www.iasplus.com/en/standards/ias/ias37.

expenditure as a current expense to match against the revenue from the sale of the car. The estimate should be the amount required to settle the liability.

The use of estimates is part of the accounting process. The provision should be discounted to its present value using the appropriate pre-tax discount rate.

6. Contingent Liabilities

Accrual accounting requires the recognition of expenses and losses in the appropriate accounting period to match against revenues. This means that we should match a potential loss or expense in the current period against the revenues that the expense generates. However, there may be potential expenses and losses that may never occur. We refer to these as "contingencies."

Not everything about a business's financial results during a particular period of time is certain. There are many uncertainties about the future that may affect financial statements and where the business must estimate future losses.

The simplest example is accounts receivable. A company sells goods and services on credit, which create accounts receivable that will be payable in the future. Some of the accounts may never be collected. The company may not be certain which of its accounts it will not be able to collect, but past experience teaches it that it will not have a 100 percent collection record on its credit sales. Hence, the company will provide an "Allowance for Doubtful Accounts" and subtract the amount from its accounts receivable balance on the balance sheet. In 20-2, for example, Duggan Inc's balance sheet shows that the company provided $467,000 as an allowance of doubtful accounts, which reduced its accounts receivable from $5,835,000 to $5,368,000. In effect, the company provided for future default by taking a write-down of its receivables in the present.

Contingencies are another form of uncertainty, but which involve two uncertainties: (1) will the loss or liability arise at all? and (2) if it does, in what amount? The contingency depends upon events that have not been completed, but which create the distinct possibility that some amount may be created in the future if the event occurs. The *CPA Canada Handbook—Accounting*[3] defines a contingency as: "an existing condition or situation involving uncertainty as to possible gain or loss to an enterprise that will ultimately be resolved when one or more future events occur or fail to occur."[4]

Examples of Contingencies

- Obligations related to product warranties;
- Threat of expropriation of assets;
- Pending or threatened litigation;
- Actual or possible claims and assessments;
- Guarantees of indebtedness of others.

Example

A manufacturer provides a warranty in 20-4 that its product will function at a certain level of efficiency for at least five years until 20-9 and that, if it does not, it will refund 15 percent of the original purchase price to be applied against a replacement of the product. The potential unknown future liability of 15 percent should be matched against the revenues generated in 20-4. If it is not matched, net income for the year will be overstated and net income for later years will be understated.

The accounting and disclosure of future uncertain events depends upon the nature and degree of their uncertainty. Under GAAP, the critical distinctions depend upon whether the event is probable, reasonably probable, or remote.

A company should accrue its contingent losses from events by charging them against current income if:

- The event is probable and likely to occur; and
- The company can reasonably estimate the amount of the loss.

The accrual will reduce net income in the current period.

---

3 *CPA Canada Handbook—Accounting*, Chartered Professional Accountants of Canada (2018) [*Handbook*].

4 *Handbook* at para 3290.05.

If, however, the occurrence of the future event is not determinable but is reasonably possible, the company should disclose the contingency in the Notes to the financial statements and estimate the loss or range of losses that might occur. The company should use notes disclosure if:

- The future event is likely to occur;
- It cannot reasonably estimate the amount of the loss; or
- It is exposed to losses in excess of amounts already accrued in the income statement.

The company should not disclose or accrue any amount if the future event is remote.

Non-disclosure of contingencies can have significant legal consequences. In *Endo v Albertine*,[5] for example, the company was liable for damages because it failed to disclose contingent tax deficiencies and environmental liabilities in its financial statements.

(a) Handbook

The treatment of contingent losses depends upon the likelihood or probability of the event occurring. Paragraphs 3290.18 and .19 of the *Handbook* provide as follows:

Paragraph 3290.18:

> The existence of a contingent loss at the date of the financial statements shall be disclosed in notes to the financial statements when:
> (a) the occurrence of the confirming future event is *likely*, but the amount of the loss cannot be reasonably estimated;
> (b) the occurrence of the confirming future event is *likely*, and an accrual has been made but there exists an exposure to loss in excess of the amount accrued; or
> (c) the occurrence of the confirming future event is *not determinable*.

Paragraph 3290.19:

> *At a minimum*, the note disclosure shall include:
> (a) the nature of the contingency;

5 863 F Supp 708 (ND Ill 1994).

(b) an estimate of the amount of the contingent loss or a statement that such an estimate cannot be made; and
(c) any exposure to loss in excess of the amount accrued;
(d) Pending Litigation.

Litigation and tax audits are prone to difficult contingencies. As at the year-end, the business cannot be certain as to how litigation in which it is involved will eventually resolve and, in the case of an adverse judgment, in what amount. Based on the principle of conservatism, the business may provide an amount based upon the probability of future liability in the litigation and, to the best of its ability (based upon counsel's advice), estimate the potential damages and costs payable.

There are two possibilities. If it is likely and probable that the business will incur a liability in the future and it is possible to reasonably estimate its amount, the contingent liability is accrued as an expense in the income statement and shows as a liability on the balance sheet. For example, assume that a company is involved in a lawsuit in which the damages claimed are $5 million. Counsel advises that there is a likelihood that the company will be liable but, if it is, the damages will likely be no more than $500,000. The company would set up the $500,000 as a general liability expense and recognize $500,000 expense on the income statement. The contingent liability of $500,000 appears on the balance sheet. However, disclosure of the contingent liability creates potential problems for legal counsel defending the action.

If the likelihood of liability from the lawsuit is probable, but the amount cannot be reasonably estimated, the information about the contingent liability should be disclosed in the Notes to the financial statements, but without recognizing any current expense in the income statement.

Finally, where the likelihood of loss from the contingency is remote, no entry is required in the financial statements and there is no disclosure of the contingency in the Notes to the financial statement.

As the above criteria show, management has considerable discretion to determine whether a potential loss is or is not a contingent liability that warrants disclosure in the financial statements. However, where the financial statements do not follow GAAP (however vague the standard), the enterprise faces the risk of being sued for financial statement fraud or securities violations.

(b) Audit Inquiry Letters

Businesses that require audited financial statements usually receive a "management letter" from their auditors to disclose any asserted and unasserted claims against the business. In addition, the auditor will ask the lawyer for the business through an "audit inquiry letter" to respond to the auditor regarding asserted claims and their possible outcome in monetary terms.

There are problems with audit inquiry letters as auditors and lawyers have different objectives and professional standards within the legal system. Auditors are concerned with disclosure of information for the protection of the investing public. Full disclosure protects the auditor from legal liability if the client encounters financial difficulties and investors lose money.

Lawyers are concerned with solicitor-client privilege within the legal system, which the Supreme Court has characterized as a near constitutional right. Disclosure of information to third parties can destroy the privilege. The public interest is protected by maintaining the confidentiality of lawyer-client communications in giving legal advice. Disclosure of the client's legal position can damage its case and be used by the opposing party as an admission of potential liability. At the very least, any disclosure of the potential amount of damages ultimately anticipated will be highly prejudicial to the client's strategic legal position.

The traditional approach was covered by a joint policy statement of the Canadian Bar Association and the Canadian Institute of Chartered Accountants (CBA/CICA) (1978). Clients were asked to evaluate whether potential losses from claims or possible claims were "likely, unlikely, or not determinable." Clients were to report contingent liabilities that included claims that would not materialize until the occurrence of some future event beyond their control, unless there was only a remote possibility that there would be an outflow of resources.

Under new IFRS rules for public companies, disclosure requirements have been expanded to require reporting of existing claims where it is "more likely than not" that resolution will require some outflow of resources. It is not at all clear how the new IFRS standard varies from the previous "likely" standard based upon an evaluation of probabilities.

Further, whereas the 1978 (CBA/CICA) standard only required clients to report the ultimate amount of losses from any claims or possible claims "if reasonably estimable," the new rules require clients to provide the "best estimate" of what they would "rationally pay" to settle a claim or transfer to a third party. Schedules C and E of the 2016 JPS sets out sample letters that law firms can use in response to the auditor's request for information.

Finally, IFRS has a stricter threshold for non-disclosure of claims. Under the 1978 standard, entities could omit reportable information from their financial statements where disclosure would have a "significant adverse effect" on their businesses. Under IFRS, non-disclosure is restricted to extremely rare cases in which reporting the information could prejudice seriously the position of the client in a dispute with other parties on the subject matter of the claim.

Lawyers should be extremely cautious about the scope of disclosure to parties who are not able to claim legal privilege. Generally, potential or contingent claims that are not identified in the audit inquiry letter should be raised directly with the client and not routed to the client's auditors.

C. LONG-TERM LIABILITIES

Long-term liabilities refer to debts with a maturity date that exceeds one year from the date of the balance sheet. Any portion of the debt that is payable in less than a year from the balance-sheet date is classified as a current liability. At the end of its fiscal period, Duggan Inc has long-term debt of $5,216,000 and, in addition, $210,000 payable within the coming year.

There are many forms of long-term liabilities, but they have certain common characteristics. First, and foremost, they usually have a maturity date and stipulate an interest rate. The obligations go by various names, depending upon their features. They may be in the form of a note payable, a bond, or mortgage. Obligations that are unsecured by assets of the corporation are called "debentures." In contrast, bonds that are secured against the corporation's real property are referred to as "mortgage bonds."

1. Bonds

A bond is a formal loan evidenced by a certificate that promises to pay the bondholder a specified sum of money at a stated time (maturity date) and that pays interest at a specified rate (coupon rate). Bonds usually have a par value of $1,000. However, they may be issued at a discount or premium because of changes in interest rates. The annual interest rate on a bond is fixed once the coupon rate is set. Thus, interest payable = par value × coupon rate.

A mortgage is a bond secured by the borrower's pledged assets, usually land, buildings, or equipment, or some combination thereof.

Where the debt is issued to multiple lenders, the terms and conditions of the loan are usually incorporated in a formal document, such as a bond indenture. The indenture contains the essential terms pertaining to the debt, such as maturity date, interest rate, dates for payment of interest, security (if any), designated trustee, and terms and conditions on default.

(a) Issuance at Par

Where a corporation issues a bond at a rate of interest that is equal to the current market rate, it is said to be issued at par. For example, a corporation may issue $5 million of ten-year bonds at 6 percent when the market rate of interest is 6 percent. In these circumstances, the corporation will receive $5 million and will record the bonds on its books at their face value. If the bonds pay interest on 1 October and 31 March, bondholders will be entitled to 3 percent interest as of each pay date. If the corporation has a 31 December year-end, it will record 1.5 percent interest as an accrued liability for interest that will become payable for October, November, and December.

(b) Issuance at Other than Par

A corporation may issue a bond at a rate of interest that is either below or above the prevailing rate of interest in the market. The purpose of bond discounts and premiums is to increase or decrease the *effective* rate of interest from the nominal rate.

Where the bond is issued at less than the prevailing market rate, its face value will be discounted to account for the higher market rate. For example, a bond with a nominal interest rate that is less than the market rate must be discounted from its par (face) value so that the lender is compensated for the yield difference.

Where a corporation issues a bond at a rate of interest that is above the prevailing market rate, the issue price of the bond will command a premium over its face value to compensate for the differential in interest rates. For example, a corporation that issues a bond with a face value of $1,000 at a rate of 8 percent when the market rate is 6 percent will price the bond at a premium so as to lower the effective rate of interest payable to market rates.

Example

Selma Corporation Inc issues twenty-year bonds at 10 percent when the prevailing market rate is 8 percent. The market price of the bond will be $1,197 to reflect the current yield of 8 percent for any person who purchases the bond.

Present Value Factors	Amount ($)
PV of annual interest stream of $100×9.82 (Table 5.3)	982
PV of redemption proceeds on maturity, $1,000×0.215 (Table 5.2)	215
Market price of bond to yield 12%	1,197

Bond prices move inversely to interest rates. The inverse relationship is more pronounced the longer the remaining life of the bond. Hence, for example, the value of a thirty-year Treasury Bill will fluctuate more than the value of a ten-year bill in response to movements in market rates of interest. Similarly, a ten-year bond will be more volatile in response to changes in the market rate of interest than a two-year bond of equivalent risk.

(c) Bond Valuation

Bonds give their owner two distinct rights: (1) the right to periodic interest payments (an annuity) and (2) the right to repayment of the principal at the bond's maturity (single future amount). The market price of the bond is equal to the sum of (1) and (2).

There are four variables:

1) The principal amount (face value) of the bond;
2) The coupon (interest) rate;
3) Maturity date (periods until maturity);
4) Yield to maturity (market interest rate required on the bond).

We can value a bond using present value principles if we have the above information.[6]

Example

Assume that Alpha Limited borrows $10,000 on a bond that will pay the going market rate of interest of 10 percent at the end of each of five years, and then repay the principal amount at the end of the fifth year. Thus, the bond comprises five annual payments of $1,000 at the end of each of the years and $10,000 principal amount at the end of the fifth year. Using Table 5.2, we calculate the present value of each of these payments as follows:

Years	Amount Paid ($)	Present Value @ 10%	PV of Amount Paid ($)
1	1,000	.909	909
2	1,000	.826	826
3	1,000	.751	751
4	1,000	.683	683
5	11,000	.620	6,820
Total	15,000		10,000 (rounded)

As one might expect, the bond is worth its face amount of $10,000 because it yields 10 percent, which is equal to the market rate.

6 See Chapter 5, Time Value of Money.

We arrive at the same result if we multiply the annuity payments of $1,000 for five years by 3.79 (Table 5.3) and $10,000 by the present value factor of .620 (Table 5.2). Then:

Years	Amount Paid ($)	Annuity @ 10%	Present Value @ 10%	PV of Amount Paid ($)
1–5	1,000 per year	3.79		3,790
5	10,000		.620	6,200
Total	15,000			10,000 (rounded)

Bond values and interest rates are inversely related. When rates rise, bond values fall. When rates fall, bond values rise.

Example

If the market rate of interest rises to 12 percent after Alpha issues its bond, the value of the bond will be discounted to $9,274. We can check this by using Table 5.2 as follows:

Years	Amount Paid ($)	Present Value @ 12%	PV of Amount Paid ($)
1	1,000	.893	893
2	1,000	.797	797
3	1,000	.711	711
4	1,000	.636	636
5	11,000	.567	6,237
Total	15,000		9,274 (rounded)

We get the same result if we multiply the annuity payments of $1,000 for five years by 3.60 (Table 5.3) and $10,000 by the present value factor of .567 (Table 5.2). Then:

Years	Amount Paid ($)	Annuity @ 12%	Present Value @ 12%	PV of Amount Paid ($)
1–5	1,000 per year	3.60		3,600
5	10,000		.567	5,670
Total	15,000			9,270 (rounded)

The bond will be discounted because the current market rate of interest (12%) for equivalent quality bonds exceeds Alpha's coupon rate of 10 percent.

The annual effective yield of 12 percent is made up of two components: the annual coupon interest rate of 10 percent plus the gain upon maturity when the bond is redeemed for $10,000. This is an example of economic substance over legal form. Stated another way, why would anyone pay $10,000 for a bond yielding 10 percent when the market is paying 12 percent on comparable bonds?

Example

Conversely, if the market rate of interest falls to 6 percent, the value of the bond will rise to $11,681. The premium compensates for the reduction of the interest rate on comparable bonds.

Years	Amount Paid ($)	Present Value @ 6%	PV of Amount Paid ($)
1	1,000	.943	943
2	1,000	.890	890
3	1,000	.839	839
4	1,000	.792	792
5	11,000	.747	8,217
Total	15,000		11,681 (rounded)

Once again, we get the same result if we multiply the annuity payments of $1,000 for five years by 4.21 (Table 5.3) and $10,000 by the present value factor of .747 (Table 5.2). Then:

Years	Amount Paid ($)	Annuity @ 6%	Present Value @ 6%	PV of Amount Paid ($)
1–5	1,000 per year	4.21		4,210
5	10,000		.747	7,470
Total	15,000			11,680 (rounded)

The bond now sells at a premium because interest rates on comparable bonds have fallen to 6 percent.

(d) Amortization of Discounts and Premiums

Bonds issued at a discount or premium show on the balance sheet at their face value less or plus the discount or premium shown separately. There are two basic methods for calculating the amortization of bond discounts and premiums: the effective interest method and the straight-line method.

The effective interest method results in the same effective yield reported on the bonds for each interest payment period. The amount amortized in each period is calculated by multiplying the carrying value of the bonds, that is, their face value, minus any discount or plus any premium, at the beginning of the period by the effective interest rate or yield to maturity implied by the initial purchase price of the bonds to determine the interest expense to be reported for the period.

Bond discount and premiums may also be amortized using the straight-line method. Under this method, the bond discount or premium is amortized in equal amounts over the term of the bonds. The straight-line method is only used where the difference between the results that it yields is not substantially different from the effective interest rate method and is not material.

(e) Bond Yields

The yield on a bond is the rate of return that the bondholder earns from the bond. The return is made up of two parts: (1) the interest payments on the bond and (2) any difference that the investor pays for the bond and the proceeds that they receive when they sell the bond. This difference is the capital gain or loss on the bond. However, we must adjust both the interest payments and the future sale proceeds to their present values to be comparable with the current market price.

i. Current Yield

The current yield on a bond is the annual interest payment by the current price.

Example

Prescott Inc's 10 percent bonds are selling in the bond market at a price of 94—that is, $940. Then, the annual interest payment is $100, and the current yield is $100 / 940 or 10.6 percent.

ii. Yield to Maturity

The yield to maturity or the effective interest rate of a bond is the discount rate that makes the sum of (1) the present value of the series of future interest payments plus (2) the present value of the redemption proceeds equal to the current market price of the bond.

Example

Exactly ten years before their redemption, Starbuck's 10 percent bonds have a market price of $887. Starbuck's makes its $100 at year-end. The yield to maturity is the discount rate that will make the present value of the ten-year series of future $100 annual interest payments plus the present value of the $1,000 redemption proceeds equal to the bond's current market price of $887. The rate is 12 percent.

Present Value Factors	Amount ($)
PV of annual interest stream of $100×5.65 (Table 5.3)	565
PV of redemption proceeds on maturity, $1,000×0.322 (Table 5.2)	322
Market price of bond	887

We can obtain the yield to maturity through trial-and-error use of present value tables, which is a cumbersome process. Alternatively, we can use a business calculator or computer program, which is much easier.

(f) Tax Issues

Corporations generally issue bonds redeemable at par (face) values of $1,000. However, where interest rates change from the planning for issuance, corporations have to issue the bonds at a discount in order to increase their effective yield to maturity.

Example

Assume, for example, that a corporation issues a ten-year $1,000 bond with a coupon rate of 6 percent for $970. The investor will receive $600 in interest per year for ten years plus $30 upon its redemption, for a total of $630. The yield on the bond for each of the ten years is 6.49 percent, that is, 630 / 970 × 10. In economic substance, the entire $630 is on account of interest, as adjusted for market rates.

However, in tax law, the legal form would characterize $600 as interest and the $30 as a capital gain. The capital gain would effectively be taxable at 50 percent of the rate applicable to interest income. In tax law, "a buck is not a buck." Each source of income is subject to different rules and effective tax rates. This would encourage corporations to issue bonds at a discount so that the bondholders would benefit from lower effective tax rates.

The *Income Tax Act*[7] has a complex regime to discourage corporations from issuing bonds at a substantial discount to convert what would otherwise be taxable as interest into capital gains. Paragraph 20(1)(f) regulates the deductibility of bond discounts. In general terms, the issuer of the bond may deduct the full amount of the discount as interest expense if it issues the bond at a "shallow discount." A shallow discount is one where the taxpayer issues the bond for an amount that is *not less* than 97 percent of the face value thereof *and* the annual yield does not *exceed* ¾ of the bond's coupon rate of interest. Hence, there are two variables.

Example

In the above example, (1) at an issue price of $970, the discount on the bond is *not less* than 97 percent; and (2) the annual yield of 6.49 percent on the bond issued at $970 is *less* than 4⁄3 of the nominal rate of 6 percent, which would be 8 percent. Hence, the discount is considered a "shallow discount" and the issuer may deduct the entire amount of the interest expense of $60 per year plus the $30 discount as interest expense.

If, on the other hand, the corporation issued the $1,000 bond at $970 for only one year at 6 percent, the *annual* yield would be 9.28 percent (($60 + $30) / 970). Since the annual yield exceeds ¾ of 6 percent, or 8 percent, the discount would be a "deep discount." Then, only one half of the discount would be deductible as interest expense. In effect, the deep discount is treated as the equivalent of a capital gain and not as interest. In this case, we ignore the economic

7 RSC, 1985, c 1 (5th Supp) [*ITA*].

substance of the transaction and allow its form to prevail because of the different tax rules that apply to income and capital gains.

2. Leases

A lease is a contract whereby one of the parties (the lessor) grants to another party (the lessee) the use, possession, and enjoyment of an asset for a period of time in consideration of rental payments. The payment is the rental cost for the use of property.

A lease is a form of financing, the terms and conditions of which can be tailored to meet the financial needs of the lessor and the lessee. Almost any asset that can be purchased can also be leased. The most common forms of leases in business are for automobiles, furniture, equipment, and real property.

Long-term leases can be "operating" leases or "capital leases." Depending upon their terms, leases may be considered pure rental arrangements, or they may appear on the balance sheet as purchases and liabilities. The distinction between the two types depends upon the economic substance of the lease arrangement, which affects their financial reporting.

(a) Operating Leases

A "true" or "operating" lease is a rental agreement in which the lessor conveys to the lessee the right to use the property for a stated period in return for consideration in the form of rent. Such an arrangement does not require any immediate entry in the financial statements. The monthly rental costs will be treated as expenses and appear on the income statement. There is no corresponding entry on the balance sheet.

Example

Xavier agrees to lease a small office for fifty-five years. In exchange for the long lease, the landlord gives Xavier a fixed rental price of $10,000 per year. The agreement is a rental for the *use* of the office for fifty-five years. This is a "true lease" or an "operating lease."

Operating leases can be a form of "off-balance sheet" financing in certain circumstances. The popularity of leasing, as opposed to purchasing, assets is attributable to the financial advantage of keeping debt off the balance sheet, which may allow the lessee to maintain more favourable debt-to-equity ratios or avoid violating financial covenants.[8] Also, leasing does not drain the cash flow of an enterprise in the same way a purchase of assets does.

Advantages:

- Since leasing is an "off-balance sheet" form of financing, it does not affect debt/equity ratios, which are often covenants in debt instruments.
- Since leases are not reported as liabilities on the balance sheet, they do not reflect adversely on the enterprise's access to the credit markets.
- Small businesses do not usually have easy access to the capital markets in order to purchase substantial amounts of tangible assets. A lease is an alternative to long-term financing to purchasing equipment.
- Leasing terms and conditions can be flexible and, therefore, more easily adapted to the particular needs of the business.
- Lease payments can be linked to the enterprise's profits.

Disadvantages:

- Since the leased asset belongs to the lessor, any appreciation in the value of the asset belongs to the lessor, not to the lessee. This is a significant financial consideration in leases involving real property.
- Leases are fixed term contracts (albeit often with options to renew) and commit the lessee to the contract. It is not usually easy to exit from the contract without paying a penalty or premium. Thus, unlike the owner of an asset who may be able to dispose of it if circumstances change, a lessee is contractually locked in even when economic circumstances change or become unattractive.

---

8 Stephen B Cohen, "Even Before Enron" (2002) 5:4 *Green Bag* 387 at 389.

(b) Capital Leases

Where the "lease" transfers substantially all of the risks and benefits that accompany *ownership* of a property, the agreement is tantamount to the purchase of an asset and it, and the related liability, should appear on the balance sheet. Such a lease is in substance a "capital" lease and the lessee should treat the property acquired as an asset.

Example

Yasmine buys an office for $123,860 (the present value of $10,000 annually over fifty-five years at 8 percent) and finances the purchase through a 10-year mortgage at 8 per cent. The agreement is a *purchase* of real property. In substance, this is an installment purchase plan and is a "capital lease."

(c) Walks like a Duck, Quacks like a Duck

A "hybrid lease" is one that looks like a lease in form but has all the economic attributes of a purchase of property.

Example

Zoe leases an office for $10,000 per year, but also negotiates an option to purchase the property at the end of 55 years for $1. Until that time, the landlord retains full legal title to the property, but Zoe pays all of the maintenance, taxes, and utilities for the office. Zoe does not have title to the property but has all the costs of ownership. The agreement "looks like a lease and walks like a lease" but, in economic substance, it resembles an outright purchase.

Example

Assume the following balance sheet for a business:

Assets	$300,000
Liabilities	$150,000
Equity	$150,000
Total Liabilities and Equity	$300,000
Debt/Equity Ratio ($150/$150)	1:1

If the business enters into an "operating lease" for equipment of $100,000, there is no effect on the balance sheet.

However, if the business effectively "purchases" the equipment through a "capital lease," the balance sheet will appear as follows:

Assets	$400,000
Liabilities	$250,000
Equity	$150,000
Total Liabilities and Equity	$400,000
Debt/Equity Ratio ($250/$150)	1.67:1

The debt/equity ratio has increased because of the mode of reporting the lease.

(d) Accounting for Leases

For accounting purposes, from the perspective of the lessee, a lease transaction is characterized as a capital lease if it meets *any* of the four following tests:

1. Under the terms of the lease, the title to the property passes to the lessee by the end of the lease term.
2. The lease contains a "bargain purchase option" under which the lessee has the right to acquire the leased property for an amount expected to be substantially less than the fair market value of the property at the time of exercise of the option.
3. The present value of the minimum rent payments under the lease is 90 percent or more of the fair market value of the leased property.
4. The non-cancellable term of the lease is 75 percent or more of the expected useful life of the leased property at the inception of the lease.[9]

Accounting follows an "all or nothing approach" to lease reporting. If the transaction does not satisfy any of the four conditions above, the

9 "Accounting for Leases," Accounting Principles Board Statement No 4, *Financial Accounting Standards Board*, (November 1976) (as updated 1 October 1998), online: www.fasb.org/pdf/fas4.pdf at para 7.

lease is an "operating lease" and will not appear on the balance sheet. GAAP does not require the lessee to record the asset because the lessee does not "own" the underlying asset. This encourages lessees to negotiate their leases to bring them on side with the operating lease rules.

3. Tax Aspects

(a) The Cost of Borrowing

Debt is often the primary source of capitalization of a small business corporation in the early stages of its life. There are advantages to using debt capital to capitalize a small business corporation. If one structures the loan properly, interest on the debt is deductible for tax purposes. The owner of the business can also secure the debt and rank ahead of other creditors to the extent of the security.[10]

Thus, an individual can start an enterprise with a small amount of share capital and contribute the balance of the capital by way of a secured shareholder loan. External lenders (for example, banks) will, however, usually require the owner/shareholder to provide a personal and spousal guarantee for borrowed funds.

i. Meaning of Debt

The *Income Tax Act* does not define "debt" and we derive its meaning from the common law. Indebtedness requires an intention to create the debt, accompanied by an enforceable, provable, and unconditional obligation to legally repay it.

The following are some of the features to look at in determining the existence of debt:

1) the intent of the parties;
2) the existence of a written document or other evidence of the indebtedness;
3) the presence or absence of a fixed maturity date;
4) the presence or absence of a stated interest rate;
5) the right to enforce payment of principal and interest; and

10 Except against banks and lending institutions.

6) the expected ability of the borrower to satisfy the loan in accordance with terms at the inception of the loan.

No single factor is conclusive, and it is necessary to look at all the features to determine the character of the instrument under review. It is important, however, to retain the appropriate evidence for use at a later date in case of a challenge by the CRA.

ii. Interest Expenses

"Interest" is the return, or consideration for, the use or retention by one person of a sum of money belonging to or owed to another.[11] In effect, interest is a form of rental payment for the use of another person's money.

iii. Source of Income

Interest is deductible only if it relates to a source of income that exists.[12] For example, a taxpayer who finances the purchase of investment securities may claim any directly related interest expense as a deduction. The deduction is available so long as the taxpayer continues to hold the original investment or substituted securities. This is so even if the security declines in value or becomes worthless. However, in certain circumstances, a taxpayer may claim the deduction if they sell the investment and then use the funds for another eligible purpose.

Interest on money used to acquire income-earning property may be deductible even if one disposes of the property. However, there are two conditions for continued deductibility:[13]

- The borrowed money must have been used for the purpose of earning income from capital property (other than real or immovable property or depreciable property); and

---

11 *Ref re s 6 of Farm Security Act, 1944 of Sask*, [1947] SCR 394 at 411 (SCC); affd [1949] AC 110, (sub nom *AG Sask v AG Can*) (PC); *Riches v Westminster Bank Ltd*, [1947] AC 390 (UKHL).

12 *Emerson v The Queen*, [1986] 1 CTC 422, 86 DTC 6184 (FCA); leave to appeal to SCC refused 70 NR 160 (taxpayer not allowed to deduct interest on money used to purchase shares after shares sold at loss); *The Queen v Bronfman Trust*, [1987] 1 SCR 32, [1987] 1 CTC 117, 87 DTC 5059 (SCC) (interest not deductible where principal borrowed to make capital distribution to trust beneficiary).

13 *ITA*, s 20.1(1).

- The property must have been disposed of at its fair market value.

iv. Accrued Interest

A taxpayer who purchases a debt obligation can generally deduct interest accrued on the debt to the date of the purchase. The deduction is restricted to the amount that is included as interest in computing income for the year. Any accrued interest paid to the vendor of the debt obligation is included in computing the vendor's income.[14] Alternatively, the purchasing taxpayer may choose to capitalize the interest.

v. Expenses of Issuing Debt

A taxpayer can deduct expenses incurred in borrowing money for the purpose of earning income from a business or property.[15] In the absence of specific authorization, financing expenses (which typically include legal and accounting fees, printing costs, commissions, etc.) would be caught by the prohibition against deducting expenses not directly related to the income-earning process.[16] However, financing expenses are deductible on a ratable basis over a five-year period.

vi. Lump-Sum Payments

Interest may be paid lump sum at the end of the term of a loan.[17]

vii. Capitalizing Interest

General Comment

A taxpayer may prefer not to write off their interest expense against current operations. For example, there may be little advantage in

14 *ITA*, s 20(14); IT-410R, "Debt Obligations — Accrued Interest on Transfer" (23 April 1993) archived by CRA. This rule only operates where there has been an assignment or transfer of title. Evidence of registration of title would likely be necessary; see *Hill v MNR*, [1981] CTC 2120, 81 DTC 167 (TRB); *Antosko v Canada*, [1994] 2 SCR 312, [1994] 2 CTC 25, 94 DTC 6314 (SCC).

15 *ITA*, s 20(1)(e).

16 *Montreal Light, Heat & Power Consol v MNR*, [1944] CTC 94, 2 DTC 654 (PC); see also *The Queen v Royal Trust Corp of Can*, [1983] CTC 159, 83 DTC 5172 (FCA) (payment was commission for services rendered therefore qualified as an eligible capital expenditure).

17 *Lomax v Dixon*, [1943] 1 KB 671 (CA).

taking a deduction for interest expense on money borrowed to construct an asset, if the asset is not currently producing income. The deduction of interest would merely create a loss that the taxpayer may not be able to use within the time limits allowed for carryover of losses.[18] In such circumstances, the taxpayer may prefer to treat the interest expense as part of the capital cost of the asset and write off the total cost of the asset at a later time when it begins to produce income. In other words, a taxpayer may treat interest costs as a capital expenditure, rather than as a current expense.

Depreciable Property

A taxpayer who acquires depreciable property with borrowed money can elect to capitalize related interest charges.[19] However, the taxpayer can capitalize only those costs that would *otherwise have been deductible* as interest expense or as an expense of borrowing money. Interest expense to earn exempt income is not deductible and may not be capitalized.

The taxpayer can elect for costs incurred in the year they acquired the property and also for costs incurred in the three immediately preceding taxation years. The extension to the three preceding years recognizes that large undertakings extend over many years, and that a taxpayer may incur interest on money borrowed before they can actually use that money for its intended purpose.

Election

The taxpayer must make the election for the taxation year in which they:

- *Acquire* the depreciable property,[20] or
- *Use* the money borrowed for exploration, development, or acquisition of property.[21]

---

18 See para 111(1)(a) (limitation period in respect of non-capital losses). This concern has become less significant now that the carry forward of losses has been extended to twenty years.

19 *ITA*, s 21. Special restrictions on "soft costs" are discussed below; see also s 18(3.1).

20 *ITA*, s 21(1).

21 *ITA*, s 21(2).

A taxpayer may not elect to capitalize interest in anticipation of the acquisition of depreciable property or in anticipation of the use of borrowed money for exploration or development. The taxpayer may only elect *after* they acquire the property or expend the funds. However, once the election is made, it is effective for borrowing costs and interest incurred in the election year and in the three preceding years.

A taxpayer may elect under section 21(1) only for the taxation year in which they acquire the depreciable property. Where the taxpayer is in the process of erecting a building or other structure, they are considered to have "acquired" the asset to the extent of the construction costs up to any given time. Hence, a taxpayer must file a separate election for each taxation year.

Amount Capitalized

The election to capitalize interest does not have to be in respect of the full amount of the costs of borrowing. A taxpayer may elect to capitalize only part of the interest charges and deduct the remainder as a current expense.

The portion of any capitalized interest is added to the capital cost of the depreciable property acquired. Thus, any capitalized interest can be written off through capital cost allowance charges in the future. The adjusted cost base of the property is also increased for the purpose of determining capital gains upon disposition of the property.[22]

Compound Interest

A taxpayer may also capitalize compound interest and the expense of raising money. For example, a taxpayer may pay a commitment fee to a financier before funds are advanced. The taxpayer can capitalize the commitment fee, or standby interest, as part of the cost of borrowed money.[23]

22 *ITA* at para 54: "adjusted cost base."

23 *Sherritt Gordon Mines Ltd v MNR*, [1968] CTC 262, 68 DTC 5180 (Ex Ct).

Chapter 9: Equity

A. OVERVIEW

Corporations present unique problems in law because of the special nature of separate corporate existence and limited liability to creditors. We have seen that the fundamental accounting equation distinguishes between debt and equity capital on the balance sheet. Hence, the equation, $A = L + E$, takes on special meaning in the context of corporate accounting. The equation can be restated as $E = A - L$, whereby E represents the theoretical residual amount to which the shareholders of the corporation are entitled after it discharges all of its liabilities from corporate assets.

The capital structure of an enterprise has two elements, debt and equity capital, each of which has distinct rights and obligations in the law. Thus, the characterization of capital as either debt or equity is important in corporate and tax law.

There are two significant legal restrictions on corporate capital:

1) Corporations can generally only issue shares for the consideration that they receive in payment for the shares. Most jurisdictions generally require a corporation to add the full amount of the consideration it receives for any shares that it issues to the appropriate

stated capital account.[1] This restriction is the prerequisite condition for limiting the personal liability of shareholders.

2) There are strict restrictions on a corporation's ability to distribute its assets to its shareholders.[2]

Each of these restrictions has important legal, financial, and tax consequences in corporate finance.

B. SHAREHOLDERS' EQUITY

Equity capital is divided into two broad categories: (1) share capital and (2) retained earnings.

The following is a partial balance sheet of our hypothetical company, Duggan Inc, as at 30 September.

Shareholders' Equity (thousands of dollars)	20-2 $	20-1 $
Class A shares:		
Authorized — unlimited		
Issued and outstanding	1,496	1,467
Retained earnings	34,094	30,339
Treasury shares, at cost	−18,456	−12,354
Total shareholders' equity	17,134	19,452
Total Liabilities & Shareholders' Equity	42,371	40,150

1. Share Capital

"Capital" means many things in finance. For example:

- Share capital contributed by the owners of the business;
- Loan capital provided by creditors of a business;

1 See, for example, *Canada Business Corporations Act*, RSC, 1985, c C-44 [*CBCA*], s 26(2); the Ontario *Business Corporations Act*, RSO 1990, c B16 [*OBCA*], s 24(2); and the Alberta *Business Corporations Act*, Alta Reg 118/200 [*ABCA*], s 28(2). There are limited exceptions for shares issued to non-arm's length person in certain types of tax transactions. See also *CBCA*, s 26(3), *OBCA*, s 24(3), and *ABCA*, s 28(3).

2 See, for example, *CBCA*, ss 34, 35, 36, 38, and 42.

- Retained earnings left in the business by the owners;
- Tangible capital, such as physical resources used in the business;
- Intangible capital, such as intellectual property in the form of patents, trademarks, goodwill, and trade names; or
- Working capital, the difference between current assets and current liabilities.

In financial statements, however, capital generally refers to the consideration that shareholders pay for their stock.

Corporate share capital is divided into classes according to their terms and conditions. In Canada, the term "preferred share" is a financial term, not a legal term. Duggan Inc has issued an outstanding $1,496,000 of Class A share capital as at 30 September 20-2.

Share capital has two characteristics. First, it represents the ownership interest in the corporation. The rights, restrictions, terms, and conditions attached to the shares determine the nature of the legal interest. In the absence of any special provisions, all shares of a corporation are presumed to be equal.[3]

Second, shareholders rank behind creditors in claims on the corporation's assets. Thus, shareholders bear the ultimate financial risk in corporate failures.

These two characteristics influence the corporate financial structure of enterprises. For purposes of corporate law, a corporation's share capital is its "stated capital," which has two distinct aspects:

1) Protection of creditors; and
2) Protection of shareholders.

A corporation's creditors look to its stated capital as a notional measure of its ability to pay its debts. To be sure, the ability to pay debts ultimately depends upon available cash. Hence, creditors have a legal interest in the capital structure of the corporation to which they loan money. They have a legitimate concern in ensuring that the corporation will not dissipate its capital through unauthorized corporate distributions.

---

3 See, for example, *CBCA*, s 24(3).

Stated capital also serves as a measure of limiting shareholder liability for corporate debts. Corporate statutes generally limit a shareholder's exposure for corporate liabilities to the shareholder's contributions to its stated capital.[4] Thus, accounting for capital is an important stewardship function.

Neither the *Canada Business Corporations Act* nor the *Business Corporations Act* of Ontario define "capital." Generally, capital refers to proceeds from the sale of capital stock and represents money that the purchaser pays for an undivided interest in the assets of the corporation. The owners' equity segment of the corporate balance sheet shows the nature and amount of stated capital. For example, Duggan Inc has issued $1,496,000 of Class A share capital as at 30 September 20-2. The amount in this account is determined by corporate law.

However, the term "capital" also has other meanings depending upon the context and the adjective by which one modifies it. For example, in corporate finance, "capital" sometimes describes all capital, whether from debt or equity. In accounting, we use the term "working capital" to denote the excess of current assets over current liabilities and "liquid capital" to describe cash and marketable securities. In corporate law, however, the term "capital" only describes the share capital of a corporation. Thus, we must be aware of the context in which we use the term "capital" in legal agreements.

2. Nature of Shares

A "share" is the proportional financial interest of a shareholder in a corporation. It measures the liability of the shareholder to outside interests and the size of their financial interest in the corporate undertaking.

A share is not a sum of money: it is an interest measured by a sum of money. Hence, in law, a share is a "chose in action" that forms a separate right of personal property that represents a fractional interest in the capital of the corporation.

A share is the bundle of rights contained in the share contract. Thus, a share is that fraction of the capital of a corporation that confers

---

4 See, for example, *CBCA*, s 45.

on its owner a proportional proprietary and residual interest in the corporation. In law, shareholders are not part owners of the assets of the undertaking. They merely share certain rights, such as the right to participate in profits and capital.

(a) Rights of Shares

Shares have three basic rights:[5]

1) The right to vote;
2) The right to participate in profits through dividends; and
3) The right to share in the property of the corporation upon its dissolution.

Under the *CBCA*, where there is only one class of shares, these three rights attach to each share. Under the *OBCA*, however, only the right to vote and the right to receive property upon dissolution automatically attach to a single class of shares. Unlike the *CBCA*, the *OBCA* does not address the right of a shareholder to receive dividends.

A corporation may issue more than one class of shares. If it does issue multiple classes, it must set out the rights, privileges, restrictions, and conditions that attach to each class of shares in its articles of incorporation. Hence, if a corporation issues more than one class of shares, it must ensure that it attaches each of the rights to at least one of the classes of shares. The equity section of the balance sheet should segregate each class of shares. The Notes to the financial statements should explain the rights of each class.

(b) Issuance of Share

i. No Par Value

Under the *CBCA* and most provincial corporate statutes, a corporation must issue its shares in registered form without nominal or par value. Shares are considered to be issued when the corporation satisfies all the formalities in respect of their issuance.

---

5 See, for example, *CBCA*, s 24(3).

Shares with nominal or par value issued prior to the enactment of the *CBCA* and the *OBCA* are deemed to be shares without nominal or par value.

A corporation issues a share in registered form if it satisfies one of two conditions: it names a person who is entitled to the share such that its transfer may be recorded on a securities register, or it bears a statement that it is in registered form.

ii. Par Value

Some jurisdictions still use par value to denominate the nominal value of a corporation's shares. Par value shares can mislead investors. The par value generally denotes the nominal value of shares at the time that the corporation initially creates the shares. For example, a company may have been created in 1900 with a share capital of $100,000 divided into 100,000 shares, each having a par value of $1. This information would appear on the balance sheet. Over time, however, the company may issue further capital as it requires additional financing. The corporation will issue its additional shares at their fair market value, which will generally be higher than the nominal or par value. For example, the company might issue an additional 100,000 shares in 2021 at $10 per share. In a par value jurisdiction, the balance sheet would show additional share capital of only $100,000 at $1 par value and $900,000 as "Contributed Surplus."

iii. Unlimited Number

In the absence of a specific restriction in its articles of incorporation, a corporation can issue an unlimited number of shares of each class. A corporation can set an upper limit, however, on the number of shares it will issue, even if its articles do not specify a limit. The financial statements should disclose any limits on the issuance of shares. Duggan Inc's Balance Sheet shows that there is no limit to the number of Class A shares that it can issue.

A corporation that restricts the number of shares it may issue may, at any time, by special resolution, amend its articles of incorporation to remove and/or amend the restriction. However, an amendment to a corporation's authorized capital entitles a shareholder of the corporation to dissent from the change and be paid out the fair value of their shares.

3. Limited Liability

Corporate shares are non-assessable against the corporation's shareholders.[6] Shareholders are not, *qua shareholders*, liable for the acts or default of the corporation. The equity segment of financial statements signifies the notional buffer that creditors have on the assets of the corporation. Thus, with limited exceptions, shareholders cannot be called upon to pay additional amounts either to the corporation or to its creditors.[7]

4. Full Consideration

A corporation may not issue its shares until it receives full consideration for them in the form of money, property, or past services.[8] If past services constitute the consideration for issued shares, the fair value of those services must not be less than the money the corporation would have received had it issued the shares for cash.[9]

A corporation may issue shares for non-cash property if its value is no less than the fair cash consideration that it would have received had it issued its shares for money.

The directors of a corporation determine the value of consideration that the corporation will receive in exchange for its shares (whether in the form of property or past services). They must ensure that this amount is not less than the cash equivalent that it would have otherwise received. In determining what constitutes a fair equivalent value for property or past services, directors may consider reasonable charges and any expenses of organization that are expected to benefit the

6 See, for example, *CBCA*, s 25(2).
7 See, for example, *CBCA*, s 45(1).
8 See, for example, *CBCA*, s 25(3).
9 See, for example, *CBCA*, s 25(4).

corporation. Directors may be personally liable for any shortfall of consideration.[10]

These rules essentially embody the principle that a corporation that issues its shares as a gratuity violates the rights of existing shareholders who do not consent and is a fraud upon subsequent shareholders and creditors who deal with it on the faith of its share capital.

5. Stated Capital

"Stated capital" is the amount of money that a shareholder commits to the corporation and, in most cases, represents the shareholder's maximum liability to corporate creditors. Thus, in a sense, it is the financial measure of the limited liability of shareholders and represents to creditors the amount of funds or assets that the shareholders *initially* invested in the corporation. It is also the springboard for determining the "paid-up capital" (PUC) of a corporation for tax purposes.

(a) Separate Accounts for Each Class

A corporation must maintain a separate stated capital account for each class and series of shares that it issues.[11] Generally, the stated capital account is credited with the *full* amount of any consideration that the corporation receives in respect of the particular shares. There are some exceptions (discussed below) to this rule in respect of non-arm's length transactions.

(b) Shares Issued for Property

A corporation may not issue shares in exchange for any property (or past service) that is valued at less than the amount the corporation would have received had the shares been issued for money. It can, however, issue shares for consideration of greater value than the cash equivalent of property or past services.

10 See, for example, *CBCA*, s 118(1).
11 See, for example, *CBCA*, s 26(1).

(c) Credit Full Consideration

Generally, a corporation must credit the *full* amount of the consideration that it receives to its stated capital account. A corporation cannot credit to a stated capital account an amount that is greater than the amount of the consideration that it receives for its shares. This rule also plays an important role in tax law because a corporation can generally pay back its PUC without tax cost to shareholders.

The general rule is that PUC for income tax purposes is calculated by reference to the rules of corporate law. In the absence of technical adjustments, we determine the PUC of a class of shares of a corporation by dividing the stated capital account for that class of shares by the number of issued shares of that class.

(d) Non-arm's-length Transactions

There are several exceptions to the general rule that a corporation must credit the full amount of consideration that it receives to its stated capital account. A corporation may add, to its stated capital account, an amount that is *less* than the consideration that it receives for its shares if it issues the shares:[12]

1) In exchange for property of a person who, immediately before the exchange, does not deal with the corporation at arm's length;
2) In exchange for shares of a body corporate that, immediately before the exchange or because of the exchange, does not deal with the issuing corporation at arm's length;
3) Pursuant to an amalgamation with another corporation; or
4) Pursuant to an "arrangement" that is, in effect, an amalgamation of the issuing corporation with another corporation.

This exception accommodates income tax and estate planning, particularly under section 84.1 of the *Income Tax Act*.[13]

A corporation may also add an amount *less* than the fair market value of property to its stated capital account in respect of arm's-length transactions if it, and all of the shareholders of the particular

12 See, for example, *CBCA*, s 26(3).
13 RSC, 1985, c 1 (5th Supp) [*ITA*].

class, consent.[14] Is such cases, the corporation does not prejudice its creditors or shareholders of its other classes.

In each of the above circumstances, the corporation may add either all or *some lesser part of* the consideration that it receives for its shares to the appropriate stated capital account. As already noted, it cannot add an amount that is greater than the amount it receives.

6. Stock Dividends & Stock Splits

Stock dividends and stock splits are distributions that a corporation pays by issuing its own fully paid shares to its existing shareholders. Corporations typically issue stock dividends and splits in order to give shareholders cosmetic evidence that their investments have grown. For example, a corporation might declare a 10 percent stock dividend and issue ten additional shares to a shareholder who owns 100 shares. The shareholder would end up with 110 shares. If the corporation declared a stock split of 3:2, the shareholder would end up with 150 shares.

Neither stock dividends nor stock splits involve any cash distributions to shareholders, and they do not involve any change to their proportionate ownership interests. They simply change the number of shares owned without any underlying economic change in the corporation's assets.

Example

Caroline owns 500 shares in Beta Limited, which has 50,000 issued and outstanding shares. If Beta declares a 200 percent stock dividend, Caroline will receive two new shares for each share that she owns. She will end up with 1,500 shares of Beta's 150,000 outstanding shares. Her proportionate share interest in the company remains 1 percent. Similarly, if Beta declares a stock split of 3:1, Caroline's shares will increase to 1500 shares out of a total share capital of 150,000. Once again, her economic interest remains 1 percent.

---

14 See, for example, *CBCA* at para 26(3)(a)(iii).

In theory, stock dividends and stock splits should not change the value of the issuing company or the price of the shareholder's shares.

Example

If, in the above example, each Beta share traded at $300 before the split, the company would have a theoretical value of $15,000,000. Caroline's pre-dividend shares would be worth $150,000. After the dividend, she would own 1,500 shares, which should now be worth $100 per share, for a total of $150,000 or 1 percent of Beta's total value. The same result would apply to a 3:1 stock split.

Why, then, do companies issue stock dividends and stock splits, if they do not change the underlying value of the shares or the overall economic value of the issuing company? Apart from their cosmetic value, stock dividends and stock splits reduce the value of each share and make them more attractive to individual investors who cannot afford to purchase the shares in even lots of 100. In the above example, an even lot of pre-split shares of 100 would cost $30,000, which would be beyond the reach of many retail investors who might be interested in acquiring some Beta shares. If the per share value is reduced to $100, an even lot would cost $10,000, which would reduce the commission on the transaction. As a result, companies split their shares to make them more affordable and marketable. However, this rationale becomes less significant as electronic trading commissions for retail investors have fallen to near zero.[15]

For corporate purposes, a corporation that pays a stock dividend must add the full financial equivalent of the declared amount of the dividend to the stated capital account of the class of shares on which it pays the dividend, Thus, the corporation merely capitalizes a portion of its retained earnings to its share capital for accounting purposes and there is no change in its overall shareholders' equity. No such adjustment is required for stock splits.

---

15 See, generally, Patrick McGeehan, "Stock Splits Feast on Bull Market" *Wall Street Journal* (5 February 1996) at C1 and John R Dorfman, "A Stock Split Can Be Tastier than a Banana Split for Investors" *Wall Street Journal* (15 August 1995) at C2.

7. Recapitalization

A recapitalization of shares is a slightly different method of achieving the same result as a stock dividend or stock split, but on a larger scale. In 1996, for example, shares of Berkshire Hathaway, which Warren Buffet bought for $16 per share in 1964, were trading at more than $30,000 per share, well above the reach of most retail investors. The company recapitalized its shares, which allowed shareholders to exchange each share for thirty shares of a new Class B stock. The economic impact of the recapitalization was, in effect, the same as a 30:1 stock split. The stock split again 50:1 on 21 January 2010, meaning that for each share of pre-split Berkshire B shares (BRK.B), the shareholder now owned fifty shares. For example, a 1,000-pre-split share position became a 50,000-share position following the split. The two recapitalizations converted each original share into 1,500 new shares. As at 6 July 2020, BRK.B traded at $182.64 per share and the original Class A shares (BRK.A) traded at $274,300.[16]

8. Reverse Stock Splits

Reverse stock splits *increase* the number of outstanding shares a company has (and decrease their price) by issuing more shares to current shareholders. In effect, reverse stock splits are the opposite of stock splits. After a reverse stock split, the price of each share rises but the total value of the company remains the same.

(a) Rationale

There are two main reasons for reverse stock splits. Stock exchange regulations may require delisting a company where its shares trade at less than $1 per share to prevent the company from becoming a "penny stock" on the exchange. For example, if a company's stock is trading at $0.65 per share and the requirements to be listed on the stock exchange specify that all stocks must be priced above $1, the corporation may implement a reverse stock split to avoid being delisted from the exchange. A *reverse*

16 NYSE quotation (6 July 2020).

stock split allows a company to combine a number of its outstanding shares to form one new share. In effect, a reverse stock split *decreases* the number of outstanding shares in the company. The terms "stock consolidation" or "share rollback" also describe reverse stock splits.

A reverse stock split will be expressed as a ratio, such as, for example, 1:2. This means that the shareholder will own one share for every two of the particular stock previously owned and the price per share will double. For example, on Friday, 8 May 2020, Aurora Cannabis, a Canada-based medical cannabis company, consolidated its common shares on the basis of 1:12. The shares then started trading on a post-consolidated basis as of 12 May 2020 at $ 9.68.[17]

A company may complete a reverse stock split because many mutual funds and institutional investors have rules against purchasing a stock with a price below a pre-defined minimum. A company looking to remain on the radar of large investors may increase its share price to maintain the minimum threshold set by these institutions.

Example

Tony owns 1,000 shares of Matilda Corporation Inc, which is currently trading at $0.50 per share. This means that the total value of Tony's shares is $500. Matilda implements a 1:2 reverse stock split. The 500 new shares would increase to $500. There is no change in the overall economic value of Tony's shares in Matilda.

There are some studies that suggest that investors like stock dividends and splits and that such stocks perform well after the dividend or split. Hence, some companies use them to promote the market price of their shares.[18]

(b) Accounting

Although there is no substantive economic difference between stock dividends and stock splits, they are treated differently for accounting purposes. If a corporation issues less than 25 percent of the total amount of the number of its outstanding shares to shareholders, the

17 NYSE quotation (12 May 2020).

18 See, for example, Jonathan Clements, "The Pros and Cons of Doing the Splits" *Wall Street Journal* (3 October 2000) at C1.

transaction is a stock dividend. If the issuance is for a greater proportion of the previously outstanding shares, the transaction is considered a stock split.[19]

For financial accounting purposes, generally accepted accounting principles (GAAP) requires that the corporation issuing a stock dividend transfer the appropriate amount from its retained earnings account to its share capital account.

This simply means that there is a transfer from one segment of the equity account (retained earnings) into another segment, but without any economic change in the overall shareholders' equity. A stock split does not require any adjustment. The company simply records the additional number of shares issued, but without any transfer from retained earnings to share capital.

Example

Assume that X Corporation Inc has 10,000,000 issued and outstanding common shares, which trade on the stock exchange at $20 per share. Hence, the nominal total value of the shares is $200,000,000. If the corporation issues a stock dividend of 10 percent, it will issue 1,000,000 shares, which will bring the total shares to 11,000,000. Under GAAP, X Corporation Inc would transfer $20,000,000 from its retained earnings to its common share capital account. The nominal total value of share capital is now $220,000,000. With 11,000,000 shares outstanding, the nominal value of each share is $220,000,000 / 11,000,000 — that is $20 per share.

This is the result one would intuitively expect as one cannot increase corporate value simply by issuing more paper and not bringing in any new assets.

9. Continuances

A corporation continued under either the *CBCA* or the *OBCA* may add to its stated capital accounts any consideration that it receives for

19 See, for example, ARB No 43, ch. 7 B, ¶10 (American Institute of Certified Public Accountants, 1953).

shares issued prior to its continuance. It also may, at any time, add to its stated capital account any amount credited to its retained earnings or other surplus accounts.

C. REDUCTION OF STATED CAPITAL

Corporate statutes strictly control adjustments, particularly downward adjustments, to stated capital. The *Income Tax Act* also stringently controls adjustments to the PUC of corporations.

The general rule is that a corporation may not reduce its stated capital. There are exceptions to this rule, but the exceptions apply only in narrowly circumscribed circumstances.

Generally, a corporation may reduce its stated capital only if it satisfies two financial requirements: the reduction must not impair either the solvency or liquidity of the corporation. Thus, a corporation may reduce its stated capital only if it is able to pay its obligations as they fall due and discharge its obligations to its shareholders and creditors.[20]

The stringency of the financial tests varies with the reason for the reduction of capital and the potential for harm to investors. The less the risk of harm and the lower the potential for abuse, the less stringent the test that the corporation must satisfy to reduce its stated capital.

1. Acquisition of a Corporation's Own Shares

Under the common law, a corporation could not reduce its capital except with judicial approval. Thus, a corporation could not purchase its own shares, since the purchase would be tantamount to a reduction of capital.

The common law rule is incorporated into both the *CBCA* and the *OBCA*, but with substantial exceptions. A corporation may reduce its capital if it protects the financial interests of its investors and creditors. We see, for example, that Duggan Inc has repurchased $18,456,000 of its shares, which show as treasury shares on its balance sheet as at 30 September 20-2.

---

20 See, for example, *CBCA*, ss 36(2) and 38(3).

(a) Financial Tests

Subject to restrictions in its articles of incorporation, a corporation may purchase its own shares if it does not have reasonable grounds for believing that the purchase will:

1) Render the corporation unable to pay its liabilities as they come due (the liquidity test); or
2) Cause the realizable value of its assets to be less than the aggregate of its liabilities and the stated capital of all of its classes of shares (the solvency test).

Thus, the corporation must satisfy two financial tests: it must be liquid *and* solvent after it purchases its shares.

We determine corporate liquidity from the financial statements in terms of current market values. Duggan Inc, for example, has cash, cash equivalents, marketable securities, and net accounts receivable of only $7,449,000 to pay for substantially higher current liabilities (see Chapter 7: The Balance Sheet: Assets).

Long-term solvency is more difficult to measure because, unlike historical cost accounting, we must determine solvency based on the net realizable value of assets.

(b) Liability

Directors of a corporation who authorize the purchase of its shares in contravention of the solvency and liquidity tests are jointly and severally liable to the corporation for the amount of the unauthorized disbursement of funds.[21]

A director who dissents from the resolution authorizing the purchase of shares is not liable if the director records their dissent at the meeting. If the director is not present at the meeting, they must notify the secretary of the corporation and record the dissent in the minutes of the meeting.[22]

A director can rely upon reports presented by professionals who are qualified to comment on matters requiring technical expertise.

---

21 See, for example, *CBCA*, s 118(2).

22 See, for example, *CBCA*, s 123(1).

A director who relies upon the report of an auditor, accountant, appraiser, or other professional qualified to make valuation judgments is not liable if the purchase of shares subsequently proves to contravene the statutory financial tests.

(c) Dissenting Shareholders

A corporation that purchases its own shares to satisfy a dissenting shareholder's claim pursuant to the appraisal remedy faces a less stringent financial test. For example, under a buy-out pursuant to the appraisal remedy, a corporation cannot purchase its own shares from a dissenting shareholder if the purchase would render the corporation unable to pay its obligations as they fall due (the liquidity test), or if the purchase reduces the realizable value of its assets to less than the value of its outstanding liabilities. In these circumstances, the corporation's stated capital is not considered in the solvency test. Thus, a corporation may reduce its stated capital to purchase its own shares if it does not impair its liquidity and solvency towards creditors.

2. Alternative Acquisition of Corporation's Own Shares

There are three additional circumstances in which a corporation may acquire its own shares by satisfying a somewhat less stringent financial test than those generally applicable. Subject to its Articles, a corporation may purchase its own shares to:[23]

1) Settle or compromise debts asserted by or against the corporation;
2) Eliminate fractional shares; or
3) Fulfil the terms of a non-assignable agreement under which the corporation has an option or is obligated to purchase shares owned by a director, officer, or employee of the corporation.

In any of these situations, the corporation may purchase its shares *unless*:

- There are reasonable grounds for believing that the purchase will render the corporation unable to pay its obligations as they fall due; or

---

23 See, for example, *CBCA*, s 35(1).

- The realizable value of the corporation's assets after the purchase will be less than the aggregate of its liabilities and the amount required to redeem all of its shares, the holders of which have the right to be paid *prior* to the holders of the shares to be purchased.

The second prong of the financial tests ensures that a corporation that purchases its own shares does not prejudice the rights of "senior" shareholders who have a higher-ranking claim to the assets of the corporation than the holders of the shares purchased. For example, the corporation cannot prejudice the rights of preferred shareholders by purchasing shares that rank lower in corporate rights.

3. Redemption of Shares

A "redeemable share" is a share that is redeemable at the option of either the corporation or the shareholder.[24] From a corporate creditor's perspective, share redemptions have the same economic effects as dividends, as both transactions transfer corporate assets to shareholders without any consideration. There are, however, stringent controls on share redemptions.

A corporation can redeem its shares only if it satisfies two financial tests:[25]

1) There are reasonable grounds for believing that the redemption will not render the corporation unable to pay its obligations as they fall due (liquidity test). Thus, the corporation must be liquid enough to pay its debts as they mature. Therefore, the working capital ratio is important, which we shall examine later in Chapter 15.
2) The realizable value of the corporation's assets after the redemption must not be less than the aggregate of its liabilities and the amount required to pay other shareholders who rate equally with, or have a higher claim than, the holders of the redeemed shares (solvency test). The concern here is to protect only those who have a claim equal to or higher than the shares redeemed.

24 See, for example, *CBCA*, s 2(1) "redeemable share."

25 See, for example, *CBCA*, s 36(1).

The financial tests are less stringent because the shares would have been issued on the basis that they were "redeemable," and this information is available to the public. Here too, unlike historical cost accounting, the solvency test requires an assessment of the corporate assets based on realizable market values.

In addition to the tax advantages (discussed below under *Tax Issues*), there are some other advantages to share redemptions. Redemptions reduce the number of outstanding shares and, if earnings remain the same, increase the earnings per share (EPS), which is an important metric in securities markets. Redemptions also create a demand for the shares in publicly traded markets and tend to support their market price.

4. Reduction of Stated Capital

When a corporation reduces its share capital, it must adjust the amount shown in its stated capital account. The amount of the adjustment depends upon the manner in which the corporation acquires its own shares. Where the reduction in the share capital of a corporation is pursuant to:[26]

- An acquisition of the corporation's own shares;
- A settlement or compromise of a claim asserted against the corporation;
- A plan to eliminate fractional shares;
- The terms of a non-assignable agreement under which the corporation was obliged to purchase shares owned by its directors, officers, or employees;
- A redemption of its shares;
- The enforcement of a lien against its shares;
- A transaction whereby a dissenting shareholder of the corporation exercised appraisal rights; or
- A court order relieving a shareholder from oppression by the corporation.

---

26 See, for example, *CBCA*, s 39(1).

The amount to be deducted from the stated capital account is calculated according to a formula that reduces the stated capital account by the *average* issue price of all of the shares of the particular class or series.

The formula reduces the stated capital account of the shares in proportion to the amount that was credited to the account when the shares were issued. The premium paid to a shareholder on the redemption of shares in any of the above listed circumstances is not deducted from the stated capital account.

In contrast, if a corporation compensates a shareholder for the purchase price of the shares because of its oppressive conduct, the reduction in the stated capital account is the full amount paid to the shareholder.[27] This amount will not necessarily coincide with the amount credited to the corporation's stated capital account when the shares were initially issued as the shareholder may have purchased the shares from another shareholder at a later date.

Where a corporation reduces its stated capital account pursuant to a special resolution, the amount specified in the resolution is the amount deducted from the appropriate stated capital account.

5. Conversion or Change of Shares

A "conversion" of shares from one class into another occurs pursuant to the terms and conditions of the shares as described in the Articles of Incorporation. Where a corporation converts shares from one class into another, it must adjust the stated capital accounts of both of the classes to reflect the conversion.[28]

Similarly, where a corporation changes shares from one class or series into shares of another class or series, the stated capital account of both classes or series must be adjusted. A "change" of shares from one class into another is usually pursuant to a subsequent amendment to the terms and conditions attached to the shares.

The stated capital account of the class from which the shares are converted is reduced by the amount derived from a formula. The

27 See, for example, *CBCA* at para 241(3)(g).

28 See, for example, *CBCA*, s 39(4).

stated capital account of the shares into which the shares are converted or changed is increased by an equivalent amount *plus* any additional consideration payable on the conversion or change of shares.

Where a corporation has two classes of shares with rights of conversion from one class into the other (that is, inter-convertible shares), the adjustment to the stated capital account upon the conversion of a share from one class to the other is equal to the weighted average of the stated capital accounts of both classes of shares.[29]

When shares of one class or series are converted or changed into shares of another class or series, the old shares (that is, the converted or changed shares) are considered to be issued shares of the class or series into which the shares have been converted or changed.

Thus, to the extent of the number of shares converted, the issued capital of the old class or series *automatically* becomes issued shares of the new class or series. The automatic conversion of shares from one class into another applies only to the *issued* shares and does not apply to any *unissued* shares. The articles must be amended to convert the unissued shares of the old class into unissued shares of the new class.

6. Effect of Change of Shares on Authorized Capital

There are circumstances where a corporation may wish to restrict the amount of share capital that it issues. Where a corporation limits the number of shares that it may issue by stipulating a maximum authorized capital, a conversion of shares from one class into another will have the effect of increasing the unissued but authorized shares of the old class by the number of shares converted or changed into shares of the new class.[30] In other words, the authorized share capital of the old class is restored by the number of shares converted or changed into the new class.

29 See, for example, *CBCA*, s 39(5).

30 See, for example, *CBCA*, s 39(10).

7. Cancellation of Shares

If its articles of incorporation do not limit the number of shares that a corporation may issue, any shares (or fractions of shares) that the corporation issues and later acquires are automatically cancelled. Where, however, the authorized share capital of a corporation is limited, any of its shares acquired by the corporation are restored to the status of authorized but unissued shares of the particular class. The rationale of these provisions is to prevent the corporation and its senior officials from manipulating the market in the corporation's shares or using corporate assets to acquire, or enhance, voting power.

8. Corporation Holding its Own Shares

The common law rule against corporations "trafficking" in their own shares also prohibited a corporation from holding its shares since the retention of the cancelled shares would be tantamount to a reduction of capital. The common law rule is entrenched in the *CBCA* and the *OBCA*. The general rule is that a corporation may not hold shares in itself; nor may it hold shares in its parent corporation. A parent corporation is specifically prohibited from issuing its shares to any of its subsidiaries.

Although there are exceptions to these rules, each exception is circumscribed by liquidity and solvency tests that are intended to protect the interests of investors and creditors.

D. TAX ASPECTS

The *Income Tax Act* operates on the basis of two fundamental principles of corporate share capital:

1) A corporation can return its share capital to shareholders on a tax-free basis; and
2) Dividends on shares are not deductible in computing income and are paid with after-tax dollars.

The tax rules in respect of equity capital invoke these two rules.

We measure a shareholder's proportional ownership of a corporation by the number of shares that they own. In corporate law, we refer to this as "stated capital." For tax purposes, the concept of stated capital translates into PUC. The PUC of a class of shares is equal to its stated capital, as adjusted for tax purposes.[31]

The adjustments to stated capital are designed to prevent a corporation using tax-deferred transactions to increase its PUC, which it can then distribute tax-free to its shareholders. Hence, the tax rules concerning PUC adjustments are, in effect, specific anti-avoidance provisions.

1. Paid-Up Capital

A fundamental principle of income tax law is that the levy is a tax on income, and not on capital. Thus, in corporate taxation, we distinguish between a corporation's income and its capital, which is known as paid-up capital (PUC) for tax purposes. PUC in tax law is initially analogous to the concept of "stated capital" in corporate law—it is the amount that a shareholder contributes, or is deemed to contribute, to the corporate capital.

The second basic principle is that repayments of capital in excess of its PUC are taxable to shareholders. Thus, PUC is the maximum amount of capital that a resident corporation can return to shareholders on a tax-free basis. The Act deems payments to shareholders in excess of the PUC of their shares to be income.[32]

We initially determine the PUC of a class of shares under the applicable corporate statute.[33] Hence, the concept of paid-up capital can vary between different corporate jurisdictions in Canada.

(a) Meaning of PU

The PUC of a share is a characteristic of, and specific to, the share—it does not attach to the shareholder. It does not change when one sells the share. PUC, which is initially equal to the corporation's stated

31 *ITA*, s 89(1) "paid-up capital."

32 See, for example, *ITA*, s 84.

33 *ITA*, s 89(1) "paid-up capital."

capital, is a point in time calculation, and can change through numerous corporate transactions.

Section 89(1) of the *Income Tax Act* provides that the PUC of a share equals the PUC of the class divided by the number of shares. Thus, we start with corporate stated capital, and then adjust the stated capital for tax purposes.[34] The PUC of a class is shared *pro rata* between all shareholders of the class. The PUC of a corporation equals the aggregate of the PUC of all classes of shares.

The PUC of a share is different from the adjusted cost base (ACB) of the share. PUC is an attribute of the share. ACB is unique to the shareholder and does not affect the corporation. Over time, the two will vary as shares are bought and sold, or the corporation issues new share capital.

Example

Assume that in Year 1, Susan subscribes for 100 Class A shares of a corporation for $100. Then the PUC of the Class A shares is $100, and the stated capital of each share is $1. Susan's ACB is $1 per share.

If in Year 4 the corporation issues an additional 200 Class A shares to Jack for $20,000, the total stated capital and PUC of Class A increases to $20,100. The PUC of each Class A share is now $67. Jack's ACB is $100 per share.

Thus, Susan would see the PUC of her shares increase by $66, which she can extract tax-free, leaving the other shareholder (Jack) with PUC reduced from $100 (his original investment) to $67 for each share. Jack loses $33 of tax-free basis per Class A share.

In these circumstances, a private corporation should use another class (say, Class B) to issue the additional 200 shares, so that each class has its own PUC, which reflects each shareholder's invested amount.

(b) Adjustments to Paid-Up Capital

The PUC of a share starts off equal to its stated capital for corporate purposes. However, as noted above, the two measures of capital can diverge because of adjustments for tax purposes.

---

34 See *ITA* at para 89(1)(b)(iii).

i. Hidden Trap

The difference between PUC and corporate stated capital can be a trap for anyone who relies solely on the corporation's financial statements to determine the PUC of shares. For example, where a corporation redeems its shares, any amount paid over PUC to the shareholder is a dividend.[35] Since PUC for tax purposes may be lower than stated capital for accounting purposes, what appears on the financial statements to be a tax-free return of stated capital may, for tax purposes, actually be a taxable dividend in the hands of the shareholder.

ii. Return of Capital

A return of capital by a corporation resident in Canada is a capital receipt. Since returns of PUC are not taxable, the Act contains a series of deeming rules, which circumscribe improper withdrawals of corporate capital. The purpose of the dividend rules is to curtail dividend stripping by deeming payments in excess of the PUC of shares to be taxable dividends.

Broadly speaking, the deeming rules apply to corporate distributions that are not a distribution of profits as a matter of corporate law. Under these rules, a distribution is deemed to be a dividend to the extent that the amount of the distribution exceeds the PUC in respect of the subject shares.

For example, the Act prevents a corporation from converting its retained earnings into PUC, as a preliminary step, and then returning the PUC to shareholders tax-free.[36] Section 84(1) provides that every increase in PUC, other than certain enumerated exceptions, is a *deemed dividend* to the shareholder. PUC increases resulting from the issuance of shares for fair market value consideration equal to the PUC increase are excluded from the deemed dividend rule because the transaction does not undermine the purpose of the rule.

---

35 *ITA*, s 84(3).

36 *ITA*, s 84(1).

Example

Assume that in Year 1, a corporation issues 100 Class A shares for $100. Then the PUC and the stated capital of each share is $1. If a shareholder sells one of the Class A shares for $150, the ACB of the share to the purchaser becomes $150, whereas its PUC of $100 stays with the share. Thus, the initial shareholder derives a gain of $50 because they sell for more than their cost, but the PUC (and stated capital) of the share remains constant. The new purchaser can extract only $100 tax-free even though they paid $150 for the share.

2. Increase in PUC

A corporation can increase its PUC by special resolution.[37] However, to prevent tax abuse of the tax-free status of PUC, section 84(1) deems a dividend to the shareholder to the extent of the increase, unless one of the exceptions applies. For example, "dividend" includes a stock dividend. Stock dividends are taxed as dividends.[38] The amount of the dividend is equal to the increase in PUC. Hence, there is no need to apply section 84(1) as the dividend is already taxable.

To prevent double taxation on the same economic gain, the amount of the dividend deemed under section 84(1) increases the ACB to the shareholder of the shares on which they receive the dividend.[39] There is no adjustment to the ACB of the shares if the deemed dividend is deductible under section 112(1) because there is no risk of double taxation of the same amount.

3. Redemption of Shares

Similarly, where a corporation redeems its shares, section 84(3) requires that the PUC of the class be reduced *pro rata* for the number of shares redeemed. There is a deemed dividend to the extent that the redemption proceeds exceed the PUC of the shares.

---

37 *ITA*.

38 *ITA*, s 248(1) "dividend" and "stock dividend."

39 *ITA*, at para 53(1)(b).

Example

Assume that the aggregate PUC in respect of Class A shares of corporation X Ltd is $100,000, and their aggregate redemption amount is $1,000,000. If X Ltd redeems the shares, there is a deemed dividend of $900,000 for the Class A shareholders.[40]

However, the redemption also triggers a disposition of the shares for proceeds of $1,000,000 at the same time as the deemed dividend. To avoid double taxation of the same amount, the shareholder's proceeds are reduced by the amount of the deemed dividend of $900,000 to a net value of $100,000. The net proceeds of disposition may give rise to a capital gain or loss depending upon the ACB of the shares.

4. Classes of Shares

Corporate statutes presume all shares to be equal and hold the same rights unless they expressly state otherwise. In order for shares to be considered to belong to different classes, they must, in substance, have different rights, conditions, privileges, or restrictions. As Dickson CJ, said in *McClurg v MNR*:

> In my view, a precondition to the derogation from the presumption of equality, both with respect to entitlement to dividends and other shareholder entitlements, is the division of shares into different "classes." The rationale for this rule can be traced to the principle that shareholder rights attach to the shares themselves and not to shareholders. The division of shares into separate classes, then, is the means by which shares (as opposed to shareholders) are distinguished, and in turn allows for the derogation from the presumption of equality.[41]

The stated capital and paid-up capital of shares of inter-convertible classes are determined as if they were combined in one class.[42]

40 *ITA*, s 84(3).

41 (1990), [1990] 3 SCR 1020, [1991] 1 CTC 169, 91 DTC 5001 at 5007 (SCC); see also *Int Power Co v McMaster Univ*, [1946] SCR 178 (SCC) [Que].

42 *CBCA*, s 39(5); *OBCA*, s 35(5).

5. Stock Dividends

Section 248(1) of the Act defines a stock dividend as payment in shares. Stock dividends are taxable as regular cash dividends to the shareholder.[43] Typically, distributions of stock dividends are prompted by a desire to ostensibly allocate retained earnings to shareholders, but without distributing cash.

Section 43(2) of the *CBCA* requires the "declared amount" of a stock dividend to be added to the stated capital of the class of shares on which the corporation pays the dividend.[44] The "declared amount" of a dividend is the amount declared by the directors in the corporation's resolutions.

Pursuant to section 26(2) of the *CBCA*, the "full amount" of the consideration for the stock dividend is its fair value. This amount is added to the stated capital and PUC of the shares. This view accords with the policy of the corporate and tax statutes. It is also in keeping with general commercial and accounting practices. For example, as the American Institute of Certified Public Accountants said:

> [A] stock dividend does not, in fact, give rise to any change whatsoever in either the corporation's assets or its respective shareholders' proportionate interests therein. However, it cannot fail to be recognized that, merely as a consequence of the expressed purpose of the transaction and its characterization as a *dividend* in related notices to shareholders and the public at large, many recipients of stock dividends look upon them as distributions of corporate earnings and usually in an amount equivalent to the fair value of the additional shares received. Furthermore, it is to be presumed that such views of recipients are materially strengthened in those instances, which are by far the most numerous, where the issuances are so small in comparison with the shares previously outstanding that they do not have any apparent effect upon the share market price and, consequently, the market value of the shares previously held remains substantially unchanged. The committee, therefore,

---

43 *ITA*, s 248(1).

44 See also *OBCA*, s 38(2).

> believes that where these circumstances exist the corporation should, in the public interest, account for the transaction by transferring from earned surplus to the category of permanent capitalization (represented by the capital stock and capital surplus accounts) an amount equal to the fair value of the additional shares issued.[45]

6. Conversion of Shares

Section 39(4) of the *CBCA* requires stated capital adjustments to be made on a conversion of shares from one class into another class.[46] The stated capital of the class from which one converts the shares is reduced by the appropriate percentage. The stated capital of the class into which the shares are converted is increased by a corresponding amount.

7. Adjusted Cost Base

The adjusted cost base (ACB) of property refers to the cost or "basis" of capital property for tax purposes. The concept is used to determine the capital gain or loss when one disposes of capital property.[47]

Cost includes all legal, accounting, and engineering costs incurred in acquiring the property. It also includes interest expenses incurred during construction of depreciable property[48] but not interest expenses incurred for holding the asset after its acquisition.

8. Deemed Dividends

Where a corporation redeems shares for an amount that exceeds their PUC, the excess is deemed to be a dividend.[49]

45 ARB 43, ch 7 (1953) (American Institute of Certified Public Accountants).
46 See also *OBCA*, s 35(4).
47 *ITA*, s 54.
48 *ITA*, s 21 and *Sherritt Gordon Mines Ltd v MNR*, 68 DTC 5180 (Exch Ct).
49 *ITA*, s 84(3).

Example

Assume that the stated capital and PUC of a share are $100 each and the shareholder's ACB is $150. If the corporation redeems the share for $180, the shareholder is deemed to receive a dividend of $80.

Cash paid on redemption	$180
Paid-up capital	$100
Deemed dividend	$80

Concurrently, the shareholder is deemed to dispose of their share and derive proceeds of disposition, which may trigger a capital gain. However, in order to prevent double taxation, the shareholder is allowed to reduce the proceeds of disposition by the amount of the previously taxable deemed dividend—in the above example, $80.

Cash paid on redemption	$180
Subtract: deemed dividend	$80
Proceeds of disposition	$100
Subtract: adjusted cost base	$150
Capital loss	-$50

Thus, the shareholder is taxable on a deemed dividend of $80, and, at the same time, suffers a capital loss of $50. Their net economic gain is $30, which equals the difference between their redemption price ($180) and the ACB ($150) of the shares.

However, the tax treatment of the dividend and capital loss is quite different from the economic gain on the sale. The shareholder obtains a tax credit on the dividend if the corporation that redeems the share is a Canadian corporation.[50] However, they may deduct only 50 percent of the capital loss of $50 for tax purposes, and then only against their capital gains. A "buck is not a buck" in Canadian tax law. Also, if the shareholder does not have any capital gains against which to offset the capital loss, the tax bite will exceed their economic gain.

---

50 *ITA*, s 121.

9. Losses Deemed Nil

The capital loss of $50 is deemed to be nil if the taxpayer is affiliated with the corporation immediately after the redemption. In such a case, we add the amount of the denied loss proportionately (based on relative FMV) to the ACB of any other shares that the shareholder owns. The purpose of this stop-loss rule is to prevent the shareholder from recognizing their loss in circumstances where they remain a part of an economic group of affiliated persons.[51]

51 *ITA*, s 40(3.6) and para 53(2)(f.2).

Chapter 10: The Income Statement

A. OVERVIEW

The income statement provides a measure of an enterprise's profitability and past performance. It is of interest to shareholders, potential investors, creditors, employees, and government agencies, and regulators, but for different reasons. Shareholders and investors want to know how well the enterprise performed but, even more importantly, how well they can expect it to perform in the future. Creditors are concerned with the security of their loans and the ability of the enterprise to repay them from earnings. Employees in profit sharing plans are interested in determining their share of the profits. The CRA is concerned with the amount that they can collect in taxes. Regulators, such as securities commissions, are concerned with fair disclosure of information in filings for the benefit of investors.

B. THE CONCEPT OF NET INCOME

"Income" is a measure of net gain over a period of time. Revenues increase economic resources resulting from the ordinary activities of an entity, such as for example, from the sale of goods, the rendering of services or the use by others of entity resources that yield rent, interest, royalties, or dividends.[1] Thus, we identify the amount of the gain or revenue and *relate* it to the appropriate time period when we should recognize it. Both of these aspects of measurement involve legal, economic, and accounting principles.

Equally important, we measure net gain by *matching* an entity's revenues against the expenses that it incurs to earn the revenues.[2] Expenses are decreases in economic resources, either by way of outflows or reductions of assets or incurrences of liabilities, resulting from an entity's ordinary revenue generating or service delivery activities.[3]

As we have seen,[4] generally accepted accounting principles (GAAP) provides guidelines to resolve issues that arise in measuring net income for operating results for a particular period when there are alternative methods. Hence, the matching process is as much art as it is science. For example, the Royal Bank of Canada's 2019 Annual Report contains the following statement in its MD&A statement regarding comparison of its financial results:

> We believe that certain non-GAAP measures described below are more reflective of our ongoing operating results and provide readers with a better understanding of management's perspective on our performance. These measures enhance the comparability of our financial performance for the year ended October 31, 2019 with the results from last year. *Non-GAAP measures do not have a standardized meaning under GAAP and may not be comparable to similar measures disclosed by other financial institutions* (emphasis added).[5]

Net income essentially comprises two components, revenue and expenses, during a period of time. The income statement matches revenues (R) and expenses (E) to determine net income over the given period. The investment community refers to net income as the

1 *CPA Canada Handbook — Accounting*, Chartered Professional Accountants of Canada (2018) [*Handbook*] at para 1000.32.

2 See Chapter 2 for a description of the matching process and the cash and accrual basis of accounting.

3 *Handbook* at para 1000.33

4 See Chapter 4, Accounting Principles.

5 *Royal Bank of Canada: Annual Report 2019*, online: https://annualreports.rbc.com/ar2019/site-content/uploads/2019/12/01-RBC_AR_2019_ENG.pdf at page 22.

"bottom line," which is the stepping stone to earnings per share (EPS) and the focus of the financial press. In addition, however, there is a great deal of additional information above the bottom line in the body of the statement that is of interest to users of financial statements and lawyers in litigation and commercial transactions.

The following are the Income Statements for the hypothetical company Duggan Inc for 20-2 and 20-1:

Income Statement for the Years Ended 30 September (in thousands of dollars)	**20-2** $	**20-1** $
Net sales	62,954	61,906
Cost of goods sold	29,890	29,877
Gross margin	33,064	32,029
Selling and administrative expenses	20,225	19,401
Other expenses	15	−368
Research and development costs	2,150	2,000
Income from operations	10,674	10,996
Interest expense	333	292
Net income before income taxes	10,341	10,704
Income taxes	3,534	3,876
Earnings before extraordinary items	6,807	6,828
Extraordinary items (net of tax benefits)	0	−2,516
Net income after income taxes	6,807	4,312

C. THE INCOME FORMULA

The income statement tells us how much revenue (R) an entity earned and the expenses (E) that it incurred in order to earn its income for the specified period. Thus, the formula for the income statement is simple:

$$\text{Net Income} = R - E.$$

All measurement of income or gain for commercial purposes begins with this basic formula. The essence of the formula is in matching revenues and expenses over a period of time, usually one year for most financial and regulatory purposes.

For tax purposes, the first step in the calculation of net profit is to look to accounting and commercial principles. In *Daley v MNR*, for example:

> the first inquiry whether a particular disbursement or expense is deductible should not be whether it is excluded from deduction by [paragraph 18(1)(a) or (b)] but rather whether its deduction is permissible by the ordinary principles of commercial trading or accepted business and accounting practice.[6]

However, there are subtle nuances of measurement in commercial transactions and in GAAP that warrant attention.

D. THE EXPANDED FORMULA

The income statement links successive balance sheets and explains how the company's equity changed during the period. Hence, the income statement is a bridge between successive balance sheets. For example, Duggan Inc's balance sheet tells us where the company stood as at 30 September 20-2 and the income statement tells us how the company moved from its financial status at the end of 20-1 to its position at the end of 20-2.

We can see the relationship between the income statement and the balance sheet in the expanded accounting equation:

A = L + E
A = L + [Capital + RE]
A = L + Capital + [Opening RE + Net Income − Dividends]
A = L + Capital + [Opening RE + (R − E) − Dividends]

E. STRUCTURE OF INCOME STATEMENT

The income statement starts with sales on the top line, that is, the income that an enterprise derives from the product or services that it sells in order to earn income. "Net sales" means gross sales minus

6 *Daley v MNR*, [1950] CTC 254 (Ex Ct) at 260.

any returns of product sold. In 20-2, Duggan Inc had net sales of $62,954,000.

Net revenue (in financial jargon, "top-line revenue") is a significant figure in determining "bottom-line" net income, which affects the stock price of publicly listed corporations. Hence, investment analysts and market watchers look for trends in "top-line revenue" in trying to predict the future of the company's bottom line and its stock price.

The next major item on the income statement is usually the cost of goods or services sold. This number represents the expense that is *directly* associated with creating the product or the service that the entity sells to its customers. The difference between net sales and cost of goods sold is gross margin or gross profit. In 20-2, Duggan Inc had a gross margin of $33,064,000.

Next, we deduct from the gross margin all of the other expenses that an enterprise incurs to earn its income. Typically, there will be operating expenses, such as selling and administrative expenses, salaries, benefits, rent, etc. In published financial statements, such as those of Duggan Inc, all of these expenses are grouped together under one title, "Selling and Administrative Expenses." The aggregation of all of these different operating expenses into one number is acceptable for public reporting purposes because companies do not want to disclose sensitive confidential information. However, management will have a much more detailed breakdown of each component for their analysis.

When the costs of sales, and of operating (O), financing (F), and tax expenses (T), are less than net sales, we have net income or net profit. When the costs of sales, and O, F, and T expenses exceed net sales, we have a net loss. Subtracting the O, F, and T expenses from the gross margin left Duggan Inc with a net profit of $6,807,000 for the year ended 30 September 20-2.

It is premature at this point to say whether the net profit of $6,807,000 was a satisfactory return for Duggan Inc in 20-2. In Chapter 15, Interpretation of Financial Statements, we review methods of analysis to determine the components and adequacy of an entity's return on equity (ROE).

The net income or net loss is added to the opening balance of retained earnings to determine how much better off an entity is at the end of a year as compared to the beginning. In Chapter 11, we see the Statement of Retained Earnings of Duggan Inc, where its net income of $6,807,000 is added to the opening retained earnings balance of $30,339,000.

From the net income figure, we can also determine the earnings per share (EPS) of publicly listed operations. EPS, an important determinant in stock market prices, tells us how much each share of stock earned during the past year. Some companies also use it to determine executive bonuses and in setting stock option prices for management and employees. Hence, once again, we recognize the temptation that management endures to boost EPS by overstating revenues or understating expenses. Accounting is the apple in the garden of business.

F. MEASUREMENT AND TIMING

Measurement and timing of income are actually two different concepts. There is, however, an inextricable relationship between the two. For example, suppose a business started up in 1900 and closed down in 2021. If all we need to know is the net income figure for the 121 years, there is no issue of timing. There are serious problems of timing, however, if we need to measure income for any one of the 121 years. In that case, we need to match revenues and expenses for each of the years.

Thus, we address three questions:

1) When does an entity earn its revenues?
2) When does it recognize the revenues in its financial statements?
3) What are the principles for matching revenues and expenses?

The allocation of revenues and expenses to time periods raises important questions of timing as to when we recognize revenues and charge expenses against those revenues. The matching process involves professional judgment. History teaches us that many accounting frauds involve a deliberate mismatching of revenues and expenses, usually to increase net income and, hence, stock prices. For example, in the 1990s, WorldCom treated USD$8 billion of expenses as capital assets, thereby overstating net income by an equivalent amount. The stock shot up and management got rich.

G. REVENUE RECOGNITION

The business cycle of an enterprise can be broken down into steps:

1) Injection of capital in cash or assets;
2) Acquisition of inventory of raw metal;
3) Fabrication of metal into an inventory;
4) Sales activity that results in orders for the product;
5) Delivery of product to customers;
6) Invoicing of customers; and
7) Collection of receivables and payment of invoices in cash.

1. General Rule

The principles of revenue recognition require that we identify the time when we should include an amount in revenue. Improper revenue recognition, or delaying the recognition of expenses, hurts investors and damages the integrity of the capital markets. In addition, such practices can hurt employees who participate in profit sharing or bonus arrangements.

There are two factors to consider: (1) the existence of a "realization event" and (2) the completion of the earnings process.

The fundamental principle is that a business should recognize revenue only when it *realizes* its revenue. This occurs when:

1) It has a *bona fide* exchange transaction; and
2) The earnings process from the exchange has been substantially completed.

In most cases, an enterprise recognizes revenue from sales transactions when the seller transfers to the buyer the significant risks and rewards of ownership and there is reasonable assurance of the price. Thus, there is objective evidence of the amount of revenues.

The second aspect of measurement is to identify the appropriate period in which we wish to recognize the gain. "Recognition" is the taking into account of an amount in computing income.

Absent the above two conditions, a business should not generally recognize revenue until the process is complete. In most circumstances, an enterprise will recognize its revenues upon completion of steps 5 and 6, which are usually merged, of the above business cycle.

Example

Assume that a manufacturing company, with a calendar year end, receives an order of $100,000 for custom furniture on 1 November 2020. The customer pays a deposit of $15,000. In order to process the order, the company purchases raw materials for $12,000 from Italy and begins the production process on 15 December when the materials arrive. The company completes production of the furniture on 30 December. The cost of labour and direct production overhead is $18,000. The company ships the furniture to its customer on 5 January 2021 at a cost of $1,500 and issues an invoice for $101,500 minus the deposit of $15,000 on the same day. The deposit of $15,000 would be recorded initially as "Deferred Revenues," which would show as a liability account in the financial statements for 2020. The revenue of $101,500 from the sale (including the $15,000 deposit) would be recognized in 2021, as would the cost of goods sold of $30,000 and shipping costs of $1,500.

To be sure, this principle of recognizing revenues at the time of sale and shipment does not make a great deal of difference in most cases, except at the end of the fiscal period. For example, it matters little to a company with a 31 December year-end whether it takes its revenue for July sales into account in July, August, or September when it collects its cash from sales. Since all of the revenue falls in the same accounting period, it matters little for measurement purposes so long as the revenue falls in the current year.

The principle, however, is critical at the company's fiscal year end. It makes a great deal of difference whether revenues from sales for merchandise shipped out in mid-December are taken into the current year's income or into the income of the year following. In this case, the timing of revenues affects the company's bottom-line profit for commercial purposes and the amount of tax payable in the current year. Thus, we should match revenues and related expenses in the same period.

Some authorities, such as the US Securities and Exchange Commission (SEC), have a longer list of conditions that an enterprise must satisfy before it can recognize revenue. A SEC staff study noted that an enterprise should recognize revenue only when:

1) There was evidence that persuasively demonstrated that an arrangement existed;
2) The enterprise had delivered the product or performed the services;
3) The arrangement provided for a fixed or determinable sale price; and
4) There was some reasonable assurance of collectability.

Thus, although an enterprise does not have to wait until it actually collects cash from the sale transaction, it should have reasonable assurance of ultimate collectability of the account. An account that is considered uncollectable *ab initio* can hardly be considered a sale.

2. Canadian GAAP

When does revenue qualify for inclusion in the income statement? Paragraph 3400.03(a) of Part II (Accounting Standards for Private Enterprises (ASPE)) of the *Handbook—Accounting* defines revenue as follows:

> Revenue is the inflow of cash, receivables or other consideration arising in the course of the ordinary activities of an enterprise, normally from the sale of goods, the rendering of services and the use by others of enterprise resources yielding interest, royalties and dividends. Revenue is net of items such as trade or volume discounts, returns and allowances, claims for damaged goods and certain excise and sales taxes. Excise and sales taxes to be netted against revenue would normally include those imposed at the time of sale and would normally exclude those imposed prior to the time of sale on either the goods or their constituents.

Paragraph 3400.05 of the *Handbook* states:

> In a transaction involving the sale of goods, performance should be regarded as having been achieved when the following conditions have been fulfilled:
>
> (a) the seller of the goods has transferred to the buyer the significant risks and rewards of ownership, in that all significant acts have been completed and the seller retains no continuing managerial involvement in, or effective control of, the goods transferred to a degree usually associated with ownership; *and*
>
> (b) reasonable assurance exists regarding the measurement of the consideration that will be derived from the sale of goods, and the extent to which goods may be returned.

In EIC-141 (17 December 2003), the *Handbook* accepted that US Securities and Exchange Commission Staff Accounting Bulletin #101 (SAB 101) is consistent with the *Handbook* section 3400. The EIC also indicates that securities regulators in Canada would look to SAB 101 when determining whether reporting issuers have complied with Canadian GAAP.

3. Professional Judgment

The decision to recognize or defer revenue is ultimately a matter of professional judgment based on an evaluation of all the underlying facts revealed in the course of an audit. To be sure, professional accountants may arrive at different conclusions. The important point is that they base their conclusions on the audited facts. Financial accounting is not a science. It addresses many questions to which the answers are uncertain and is a "process that involves continuous judgments and estimates."[7] Conservatism is a foundational principle of financial accounting, with its corollary that possible errors in measurement should be in the direction of understatement rather than overstatement of net income and net assets.[8]

GAAP principles may assist but they are not absolute. As the United States Supreme Court noted in its 1995 opinion in *Shalala v*

---

7 Robert S Kay & D Gerald Searfoss, eds, *Handbook of Accounting and Auditing*, 2d ed (Boston: Warren, Gorham & Lamont, 1989) at 7.

8 See, for example, *Thor Power Tool Co v Commissioner*, 439 US 522, 542 (1979).

Guernsey Memorial Hosp: "GAAP is not the lucid or encyclopaedic set of pre-existing rules it has been made out to be .... GAAP changes and, even at any one point, is often indeterminate."[9]

4. Accounting Manipulations

The convictions of Bernie Madoff, Garth Drabinsky, and Myron Gottlieb for accounting and financial fraud are stepping-stones in the long history of financial debacles. If there is a lesson in recent years of the high-profile trials involving Enron, WorldCom, Bre-X, Livent, Tyco, and Sino-Forest, it is that scoundrels are creative and can always find a way around the rules. Financial statement manipulation is not a novel phenomenon. History teaches us that bad financial statements and weak regulations are an intrinsic risk of publicly listed securities.

Accounting principles and auditing standards affect corporate behaviour. Profits from stock manipulation are powerful incentives. For example, the accounting manipulations in *SEC v WorldCom, Inc*[10] were so simple that a first-year accounting student would have picked them up: WorldCom re-characterized USD$12 billion of its expenses as assets, thereby inflating its current profits to boost the value of its stock.

The essential question is always the same: Are our standards ahead of the curve or merely responsive to events after the fact? New techniques of financial frauds are merely variations on old themes. They all have three ingredients: confidence, cooperative bookkeepers, and accounting respectability. Madoff set the record at USD$50 billion for his Ponzi fraud! He will not be the last.

H. VARIATIONS ON ACCRUAL

1. Installment Sales Method

Some businesses involve such unusual features that the standard accrual basis of accounting fails to achieve an appropriate matching of expenses and revenues. For example, some businesses involve a high

9 (93-1251), 514 US 87 (1995).
10 273 F Supp 2d 431 (SDNY 2003) [*WorldCom*].

volume of sales on terms that call for installment payments over an extended period of time. Such a business may have significant costs associated with the selling activity but, notionally, a large "profit margin" as judged by the difference between selling price and cost of sales.

The incidence of uncollectable accounts in such a business, however, is usually higher than for most other businesses. At best, the accounts are not "receivable" on a current basis, but are going to be received over a much longer period than is usual for businesses generally. This kind of business might adopt the installment method of accounting which does not recognize the accounts receivable in revenue. In effect, the business uses a hybrid accounting system, which recognizes all expenses except the cost of goods sold on an accrual basis, but recognizes revenue on a cash basis by ignoring its accounts receivable.

2. Completed Performance Method

Some businesses carry on long-term projects that may involve several years' work to complete. We use the completed performance method when performance of the service involves a number of steps, but completion of the final stage is so significant that revenue is not really "earned" until the final critical step. The classic case is law firms that undertake litigation on a contingency fee arrangement. There is no revenue until final judgment or settlement of the litigation.

3. Percentage of Completion Method

There are other exceptions for specific industries from the general rules of realization. For example, in long-term construction contracts where the time of delivery may stretch out for several years, it is acceptable to recognize revenue on the percentage of completion of the project. Waiting until the completion of the project would distort the financial picture if all of the revenues were lumped into the final year.

Example

A contracting company enters into a project in 2020 to build an Olympic Stadium, which is estimated to cost $60 million and take three years to complete. At the end of 2022, the project is 60 percent complete at a cost of $36 million. The company estimates on the basis of engineering reports that it will cost another $24 million in the next year to complete the project. The company may claim 60 percent of $60 million or $36 million as revenue in 2022. The company may claim the remaining $24 million in the following year assuming the project and costs remain on target.

I. CHANGES IN MARKET VALUE

Fair value accounting principles would recognize all the "paper" gains and losses in a year even though they are "unrealized." There are good reasons for not recognizing paper gains. Accountants, true to the axiom of their conservatism in estimating income, normally disregard such gains because they may prove illusory if values decline in a subsequent period. On the other hand, the failure to recognize paper gains, and recognition of the entire gain at the point of realization, gives rise to problems of "lumping" income. GAAP tries to steer between these objectives to produce a fair measure of income in the appropriate period. Under IFRS rules, however, there is a shift towards fair value accounting.

In certain circumstances and for certain assets, a company can record revenues based on a change in market value even in the absence of a market transaction. For example, businesses reporting under IFRS principles are now required to report certain marketable securities at their market value. This process of "marking to market" reports gains and losses on "trading securities" based on their market value fluctuations.

This variation from the historical cost principle reflects the relatively reliable market value of traded securities. However, the method has its critics, who argue that the method can produce "wild and capricious swings" in the bottom line. See, for example, Warren Buffet's 2018 annual reporting letter to shareholders of Berkshire Hathaway:[11]

11 Warren E Buffett, *To the Shareholders of Berkshire Hathaway Inc* (23 February 2019), online: Berkshire Hathaway Inc www.berkshirehathaway.com/letters/2018ltr.pdf.

Berkshire earned $4.0 billion in 2018 utilizing generally accepted accounting principles (commonly called "GAAP"). The components of that figure are $24.8 billion in operating earnings, a $3.0 billion non-cash loss from an impairment of intangible assets (arising almost entirely from our equity interest in Kraft Heinz), $2.8 billion in realized capital gains from the sale of investment securities and a $20.6 billion loss from a reduction in the amount of unrealized capital gains that existed in our investment holdings.

A new GAAP rule requires us to include that last item in earnings. As I emphasized in the 2017 annual report, neither Berkshire's Vice Chairman, Charlie Munger, nor I believe that rule to be sensible. Rather, both of us have consistently thought that at Berkshire this mark-to-market change would produce what I described as "wild and capricious swings in our bottom line."

The accuracy of that prediction can be suggested by our quarterly results during 2018. In the first and fourth quarters, we reported GAAP losses of $1.1 billion and $25.4 billion respectively. In the second and third quarters, we reported profits of $12 billion and $18.5 billion. In complete contrast to these gyrations, the many businesses that Berkshire owns delivered consistent and satisfactory operating earnings in all quarters.

For the year, those earnings exceeded their 2016 high of $17.6 billion by 41%. Wide swings in our quarterly GAAP earnings will inevitably continue. That's because our huge equity portfolio—valued at nearly $173 billion at the end of 2018—will often experience one-day price fluctuations of $2 billion or more, all of which the new rule says must be dropped immediately to our bottom line.

Indeed, in the fourth quarter, a period of high volatility in stock prices, we experienced several days with a "profit" or "loss" of more than $4 billion. Our advice? Focus on operating earnings, paying little attention to gains or losses of any variety. My saying that in no way diminishes the importance of our investments to Berkshire. Over time, Charlie and I expect them to deliver substantial gains, albeit with highly irregular timing.

J. CHANNEL STUFFING

Except for income tax purposes, most listed companies would prefer to increase their revenues in the current period and defer their expenses in order to enhance their stock prices and executive bonuses in the short run. Hence, the usual problem in respect of revenue recognition is acceleration of sales revenue rather than delay.

"Channel stuffing" is a way of accelerating revenue recognition for financial reporting purposes. Channel stuffing refers to the practice of a business using its bargaining power or other financial incentives to pressure its customers to order more goods than they want or need, so that the business can report additional revenues in the current period. The parties can agree that excess inventories may be returned after the year end to the supplier.

Bristol-Myers Squibb Co (BMS), a major drug company, used channel stuffing by providing financial incentives to its wholesalers to buy extra product to stockpile inventory that they did not need. BMS recorded the additional sales as current revenues and inflated its sales numbers by $2.5 billion between 1999 and 2001. This had the effect of inflating earnings by $900 million.[12]

The US Justice Department launched a criminal investigation. In 2005, BMS settled with the US Department of Justice and paid $300 million to a shareholders' restitution fund. The company also paid $150 million to settle the SEC's civil charges and $339 million to settle a class action lawsuit. Thus, the total bill to BMS was $800 million.

In addition, two of the company's executives were criminally indicted. The company itself agreed to a deferred prosecution agreement (DPA), under which it escaped criminal charges if it complied with all the terms and conditions of the agreement. The DPA purportedly penalized the corporation without excessive loss to the employees and shareholders. Nevertheless, BMS's actions were reflected in the company's stock price, thereby penalizing shareholders indirectly.

12 *United States v Bristol-Myers Squibb Company*, Plea Agreement (11 June 2007).

K. SOX

Given the importance of the capital markets in the United States, the response to the accounting misdeeds of the 1990s was swift and hard. Congress enacted the *Sarbanes-Oxley Act* (SOX) of 2002, section 307, which directs the SEC to establish rules requiring lawyers who practise before the commission to report evidence of financial frauds that may violate the securities laws or breach fiduciary duties to the appropriate corporate officer or body, including the audit committee or board of directors.[13]

Of course, lawyers often draft agreements that use "net income" in various provisions, such as employment contracts, collective bargaining agreements, partnership, and buy-sell agreements.

In *Margonis v Rossi*, for example, the court found a lawyer had demonstrated an "ineptness of language" by confusing "net income" and "gross income" in drafting a partnership agreement! [14]

L. RECOGNITION OF EXPENSES

The revenue principle tells us when we should recognize revenues in the income statement. The matching principle of accrual accounting tells us when we should recognize the corresponding expenses associated with earning the revenues.

1. The Matching Principle

Accrual and matching are closely related. The matching principle requires us to deduct expenses (E) in the same period in which they contribute to the earning of revenues (R). Hence, if we incur expenses in one time period but the expenses will benefit several periods, we allocate the expense in some reasonable manner between the various periods. This principle lies at the core of the income equation. "R"

13 The Act took its name from its two sponsors: Sen Paul S Sarbanes (D-Md) and Rep Michael G Oxley (R-Ohio).

14 116 Ill App 2d 234 (1969), 253 NE 2d 577.

and "E" in the formula must match each other. The "E" must track the "R" so that both match for accounting purposes.

The principles of accrual accounting are central to the matching of revenues and expenses. Accrual accounting requires that we recognize revenues in the period to which they relate, rather than when we collect the cash. Similarly, we recognize expenses in the period when we incur the expense, rather than when we pay for it.

For example, assume we purchase merchandise on 20 December of the current year and pay for it on 10 January of the following year. Accrual accounting requires us to recognize the purchase in the current year, even though we did not pay for it until the following year.

As we shall see below, recognizing expenses in the appropriate period depends upon the nature of the expense.

2. Expense Recognition

There are three basic rules for recognizing expenses:

1) Direct matching
2) Immediate write-off
3) Rational allocation

(a) Direct Matching

We use direct matching when costs can be directly related to revenues. For example, when an enterprise acquires goods for sale, the costs of acquiring the goods are parked in inventory until the enterprise sells the goods. At that time, the cost comes out of inventory and the business recognizes it as the cost of goods sold in generating the sales revenue. For example, in 20-2, Duggan Inc matched $28,890,000 as cost of goods sold against its net revenues of $62,954,000, to produce a gross margin of $33,064,000.

If we defer revenue recognition for any reason, the corresponding expenses should also be deferred and applied against future revenues.

(b) Immediate Write-Off

Certain expenses cannot be directly matched against specific revenues. These are general overhead expenses that provide economic benefits to the business but are too remote to connect directly to specific revenues.

For example, we recognize time-related expenses such as salaries and wages, utilities, interest, etc., at the end of the accounting period to which they relate. This is so even though we have not paid the expenses. Again, this may not make a great deal of difference to expenses we incur in the middle of an accounting period, but it can be important in terms of year-end accounting. Here also, accounting principles do not rely upon the outgoing of cash to determine when we take the expenditure into account in the financial books. The essential concept is matching the expense with revenues in the period in which we derive the benefit of the expense to earn the revenues.

Duggan Inc reported selling and administrative expenses of $20,225,000 in 20-2.

(c) Rational Allocation

Certain costs cannot be directly matched against revenues and are not eligible for immediate write-off as expenses during the current accounting period. These expenses provide a benefit to the business but over an extended period and, therefore, need to be allocated in some rational manner. For example, the cost of fixed assets, such as buildings, plant, and equipment, are initially capitalized and then written off as depreciation over the life of the assets.

Example

Assume that City Dairy Ltd delivers milk door to door and for this purpose requires 100 trucks that cost $6,000 each. The trucks will have a useful life of approximately five years and will be disposed of for $1,000 each at the end of that time. Thus, over the course of five years, each truck represents a $5,000 expense of City Dairy's business. If, however, City Dairy bought and expensed 100 trucks in its first business year, it would dramatically distort its income for the year by recognizing the entire cost of $600,000 as an expenditure for that year. We resolve this particular problem by depreciating the trucks to spread the cost over five years, recognizing $100,000 each year.

M. TAX ISSUES

Mismatching of revenues and expenses distorts the net income figure and can seriously mislead users of financial statements. For example, for tax purposes, mismatching can lead to tax deferral if we delay recognizing revenues or accelerate recognizing expenses. From a tax perspective, the most extreme scenario is one where the taxpayer delays recognizing revenues and concurrently accelerates the time when they charge off the expenses. This might occur, for example, if the taxpayer receives a lump sum for two years' rental that they do not recognize until the second year, but recognizes the rental expenses in the first year. Such mismatching would be wrong for both accounting and tax purposes.

Paragraph 12(1)(a) of the *Income Tax Act*[15] requires any amounts received in advance of the delivery of goods or services to be included in income. This is contrary to GAAP.

N. EXTRAORDINARY ITEMS

Since the income statement reports the result of operations of an enterprise for a *particular* period, each income statement in a series should present a fair picture for each period. This creates problems where the enterprise incurs a gain or loss attributable to past period operations. For example, a company may receive a settlement for a lawsuit that has been in the judicial system for several years, indeed, even decades. How should the settlement be reflected in the current year's income statement? There is no easy answer.

If the settlement is taken into the current year's income statement, it will affect the bottom line and could mislead investors evaluating the results from operations. Typically, in such cases there would be a special item for "extraordinary items" below the line for net income from operations, which should show the item net of tax effects, which

15 1985, c 1 (5th Supp).

can be expanded in the Notes. However, the entry would, nevertheless, affect the ultimate bottom line, which is the number that many investors and the financial press turn to in the income statement. See Duggan Inc's Income Statements for 20-2 and 20-1.

Alternatively, the enterprise might bypass the income statement entirely and record the settlement as "special items" or "prior period adjustments" in the Statement of Retained Earnings. That, however, would distort the prior series of income statements for the time span that the settlement represents.

Extraordinary items create special problems for lawyers who draft agreements that refer to "net income." They should stipulate the definition of net income and whether it is before or after special or extraordinary items. If the latter, they need to define "extraordinary items." Without further definition, the term "special" is particularly confusing.[16]

1. Canadian GAAP

GAAP defines "extraordinary items" as gains and losses from events or transactions, other than the sale, abandonment, or other disposal of a business segment, that qualify as:

1) unusual in nature; and
2) infrequent in occurrence.

"Unusual in nature" means there should be a high degree of abnormality about the event, which is not related to the enterprise's ordinary business activities. "Infrequent in occurrence" means the enterprise should not reasonably expect the event to recur in the foreseeable future.

The following are some examples of unusual or infrequent items:

- gains or losses from a lawsuit;
- losses or slowdown of operations due to natural disasters;
- restructuring costs;
- gains or losses from the sale of assets;

---

16 See, for example, Jesse Drucker, "Motorola's Profit: 'Special Again?'" *Wall Street Journal* (15 October 2002) at C1 (Motorola reported at least one "special" item, albeit not the same item, in fourteen consecutive earnings reports).

- costs associated with acquiring another business;
- losses from the early retirement of debt; and
- plant shutdown costs.

The difficulty in accounting is in identifying "extraordinary" and the appropriate form of its disclosure in the financial statements. Prior to 2015, the threshold for extraordinary items under GAAP was so high that only a few businesses reported them. Even events such as the 11 September 2001 terrorist attacks and the Japanese tsunami in 2011 did not qualify as extraordinary items! Would the 2020 COVID-19 pandemic, described as "unprecedented," qualify as "extraordinary" in accounting terms?

Former section 3480 of the *CICA Handbook* required the separate presentation of "extraordinary items," which were defined as items that were not expected to occur frequently over several years, that did not typify the normal business activities of the entity, and that did not depend primarily on decisions or determinations by management or owners.

However, the concept of "extraordinary items" is no longer relevant for accounting under Canadian GAAP. This harmonizes with reporting by publicly accountable enterprises because IFRSs do not recognize an extraordinary item classification.

FASB changed the GAAP rules in January 2015 and eliminated the concept of extraordinary items in an effort to reduce the cost and complexity of preparing financial statements. It is still necessary for companies to disclose infrequent and unusual events (such as losses from theft or early retirement of debt), but now without designating them as extraordinary.

Businesses and other organizations are now expected to report unusual or infrequent transactions either on the income statement or disclosed in their financial statement footnotes.

The IFRS does not have special distinctions for items of an operational nature that occur irregularly or infrequently. Instead, IFRS requires disclosure of all results as revenues, finance costs, post-tax gains or losses, or results from associates and joint ventures.

Disclosure for income or expenses of abnormal size or nature can be on the face of the income statement or in the Notes section of the report.

O. STATEMENT OF COMPREHENSIVE INCOME

A statement of comprehensive income is a financial statement that includes both standard income and other comprehensive income. It starts with a standard income statement, adds a section for other comprehensive income, then shows the total of both.

A statement of comprehensive income provides more detail about the company's financial situation than that found on a basic income statement. This more robust document is usually only used by larger corporations, especially those operating in more than one country. Most small corporations do not need a statement of comprehensive income. However, a growing business seeking new investors or operating in multiple countries may need one.

Under IFRS, a correct measure of periodic income should include items that are charged to reserves, gains, and losses on securities that are available for sale, foreign exchange gains and losses, and certain revaluation adjustments to property, plant, and equipment.

The underlying concept is that these items, although different from traditional income statement items, are appropriately characterized as "income" in a broad sense. For example, the aggregate periodic amount charged to or released from reserves is included along with "conventional" net income to arrive at "comprehensive income." Similarly, expenditures that are periodically charged to reserves are elements of income for the period even if they are of a different nature from conventional income. Thus, the theory is that an analysis of the results of the entity should include changes in such reserves.

As a minimum, the income statement should disclose the following amounts as line items:

- Revenue;
- Finance costs;
- Share of the profit or loss of joint ventures;

- Tax expenses;
- A single amount comprising the total of:
  - The post-tax profit or loss of discontinued operations; and
  - The post-tax gain or loss recognized on the measurement to fair value minus costs to sell, or on the disposal of the assets or disposal groups constituting a discontinued operation; and
- Net income.

Chapter 11: Statement of Retained Earnings

A. OVERVIEW

The equity portion of a corporate balance sheet comprises two principal components: share capital and retained earnings. A corporation's retained earnings are its accumulated income, net of dividends and other distributions to shareholders. If the balance is negative because of accumulated losses, the account is called "Accumulated Deficit," which appears in the equity segment of the balance sheet.

There are very few transactions recorded directly into the retained earnings account. Typically, the most common entry is a transfer of the corporation's net income for the year from the income summary account to the retained earnings.

The first important point to note is that retained earnings do not represent cash or any other specific assets. *Retained earnings* is simply a balancing account that derives from the fundamental balance sheet equation:

$$A = L + E$$

E (Equity) has two components:

$$E = \text{Capital} + \text{Retained Earnings.}$$

Retained earnings is the difference between assets and liabilities and capital:

$$RE = (A - L) - C$$

In effect, the retained earnings account is the history of the corporation's earnings since its inception. The number does not reflect the market value of the entity.

B. HYPOTHETICAL STATEMENT

The following are the comparative Retained Earnings for the hypothetical company, Duggan Inc, for the years ended 30 September 20-2 and 20-1.

Retained Earnings Statement for the Years Ended 30 September (in thousands of dollars)	**20-2** **$**	**20-1** **$**
Retained earnings beginning of the year	30,339	28,891
Net income	6,807	4,312
Dividends, declared and paid	3,052	2,864
Retained earnings end of year	**34,094**	**30,339**

For example, since Duggan Inc has net income of $6,807,000 after taxes, it will transfer that balance into the retained earnings account and close off the income summary for 20-2.

C. DIVIDENDS

A corporation may pay dividends in cash, property, or its own shares (stock). There are three critical dates for dividends:

1) "Declaration date," the date on which the corporation's board of directors authorizes the payment of the dividend and stipulates the amount payable;
2) "Date of record," the date on which shareholders' records are closed and the identity of shareholders entitled to receive the dividend is tabulated; and
3) "Date of payment," the date on which the corporation actually pays the dividend to shareholders as of the date of record.

For example, a corporation may declare a dividend of $1 per share on 1 April payable to shareholders of record as of 15 April, with actual payment on 30 April. Thus, a shareholder who owns the stock on the date of record (15 April) is entitled to the dividend of $1 per share. If the shareholder sells their stock after the date of record, the purchaser will purchase the stock "ex-dividend"—that is, without the dividend.

1. Cash Dividends

Dividends are discretionary and there is no obligation on a corporation to pay a dividend. The power to declare dividends is with the board of directors, who may not delegate the power.[1] A cash dividend is the amount that the corporation pays in cash as of the declaration date. Once declared, the dividend becomes a legal obligation and a liability and is recorded as "Dividends Payable" on the balance sheet.

2. Dividends in Kind

Dividends in kind are the same as cash dividends, except that the distribution occurs in identified property rather than in cash. For example, a corporation may declare a dividend in the form of shares of another company that it owns. The amount of the dividend is the fair market value of the property. The same rules apply as with cash dividends. There will be a declaration date, date of record, and date of payment.

3. Stock Dividends & Splits

A stock dividend is a special kind of dividend in kind that involves a distribution of additional shares of the corporation's *own* shares to shareholders in proportion to their existing shareholdings. The accounting for stock dividends depends upon whether the distribution is considered "small" or "large."

---

1 *CBCA* at para 115(1)(d).

With a small stock dividend, generally under 25 percent of the current outstanding shares, the company will capitalize retained earnings equal to the value of the dividend into share capital. For example, assume that a corporation declares a dividend of 200,000 shares that have a market value immediately before distribution of $10 per share. Prior to the distribution, the corporation has 2 million shares outstanding. The corporation will capitalize (transfer) $2 million from its retained earnings to its share capital account. After the distribution, the corporation will have 2,200,000 issued shares. Note, the corporation cannot ever do the reverse—that is, transfer share capital into retained earnings—because that would prejudice its creditors.

A large distribution of the corporation's shares is known as a "stock split." In the above example, the corporation might declare a stock split of 2:1, which would increase its issued shares to 4 million outstanding shares. A stock split does not require any capitalization of retained earnings into share capital. The shareholder simply receives (or sees recorded on the share register) additional certificates for each share that they own. Hence, in a 2:1 stock split, the market value of the shares will usually drop by 50 percent to reflect the fact that there are now twice the number of shares outstanding.

It merely involves a proportional change in the number of shares outstanding and their per share price on the market. Corporations often issue stock splits in order to bring down the market price of their shares to make them more attractive to retail investors. A stock split does not involve any change in the underlying financial structure of the corporation.

A reverse stock split is similar in principle, except that the number of shares outstanding is consolidated and reduced. In the above example, the corporation might decide to reduce the number of its outstanding shares by a ratio of 1:2, which would reduce the number of outstanding shares to 1 million. Typically, the market value of the shares should double to reflect the fact that there are now 50 percent fewer shares outstanding.

Once again, the transaction is entirely cosmetic and does not change the underlying financial structure of the corporation. Typically, a corporation will employ a reverse stock split to increase the market price of its shares to a "respectable" value that qualifies for investment by institutional investors or to satisfy minimum stock exchange values. For example, the New York Stock Exchange (NYSE) will not list a stock under $1.

D. PRIOR PERIOD ADJUSTMENTS

Businesses and other organizations are expected to report "extraordinary" or "unusual" either on the income statement or disclose them in their financial statement footnotes (see, Chapter 10, The Income Statement).

There are, however, other "unusual" items that crop up. To be sure, bookkeepers using computer software keep the financial records of a business enterprise accurate to the penny. Accountants use the bookkeeper's numbers to produce the enterprise's financial statements: the income statement, balance sheet and statement of cash flows. Hence, it is understandable that investors and non-accountants consider reported net profits—the "bottom line" of an income statement—to be the last word in financial reporting.

In fact, the net income figure is only an *estimate* of financial performance based upon many management decisions that involve judgment, selection of accounting principles, estimates, values, and forecasts of future and contingent events. In preparing financial statements, management sometimes opts for decisions that, with the benefit of hindsight, may require financial restatement.

A "restatement" is a revision of a previously issued financial statement to correct an error. A company must restate its financials when it determines that a previous statement contains "material" inaccuracy.

However, unlike "extraordinary" items, restatements for prior accounting period adjustments are recorded directly in retained earnings statement and are not included in the current time period's income statement.

E. MATERIALITY

There is minimal guidance in accounting in defining materiality. "Material" inaccuracies usually result from accounting mistakes, noncompliance with generally accepted accounting principles (GAAP), fraud, misrepresentation, or clerical errors, such as:

- Recognition errors (for example, when accounting for leases or reporting compensation expenses from backdated stock options);
- Income statement and balance sheet misclassifications (for instance, a company may need to shift cash flows between investing, financing and operating on the statement of cash flows);
- Mistakes reporting equity transactions (such as improper accounting for business combinations and convertible securities);
- Valuation errors related to common stock issuances; and
- Rules related to acquisitions, investments, revenue recognition, and tax accounting.

Management is responsible for determining whether a past error is "material" enough to require a restatement.

Restatements appear in many forms. The following is an example:

> "At the end of last year, the Company restated its sales and profits for the five years ended August 31, 2007, reducing revenues over the 5-year span by $234 million and net income by $325 million."

How, one may well ask, can a business reduce its net income by more than the amount that it reduces its sales revenues in the same period? The answer is obvious, but disturbing. Not only did the company *overstate* its revenues by $234 million during the five years, but it also *understated* its expenses by $91 million in the same period. The cumulative effect of the two caused the company's revised net profit to fall by $325 million.

Such news would generally be bad for investors who rely on published financials and the tax collector, since the company would presumably ask for a refund of its previously paid taxes.

The language of reporting restatements is an art, but must comply with legal disclosure requirements. In April 2007, for example, a listed NYSE company filed its quarterly report with the Securities & Exchange Commission (SEC) in which it restated its accounting for income taxes as follows:

> During the second quarter of 2007, the Company identified certain errors in its income tax accounting primarily relating to maintaining and tax effecting jurisdictional data and the classification of tax amounts in the Consolidated Balance Sheets. In addition, certain errors had been recorded and disclosed in the period in which they were identified rather than in the period in which they occurred since they were immaterial. While these errors are immaterial both individually and in the aggregate to our Consolidated Financial Statements, the Company has determined that these errors will become material to ... income from continuing operations upon completion of [certain transactions].[2]

The previous year, the company also disclosed that it might restate net income figures depending upon the results of continuing investigations:

> The Company and others have received various subpoenas and requests from the SEC ... and others seeking the production of voluminous documents in connection with various investigations into our governance, management, operations, accounting and related controls.... the Company cannot predict when these investigations will be completed, nor can the Company predict what the results of these investigations may be. It is possible that the Company will be required to pay material fines, consent to injunctions on future conduct, lose the ability to conduct business with government entities or instrumentalities ... or suffer other penalties, each of which could have a material adverse impact on the Company's business. It is not possible to estimate the amount of loss, or range of possible loss, if any, that might result from an adverse resolution of the matters.[3]

---

2 Tyco International Ltd report to the United Sates Securities and Exchange Commission, "Amendment No. 1 on Form 10-K/A to the Annual Report on Form 10-K for the fiscal year ended September 29, 2006" commission file number 001-13836 (20 April 2007), online: www.sec.gov/Archives/edgar/data/833444/000104746907003018/a2177192z10-ka.htm at i.

3 Tyco International Ltd report to the United Sates Securities and Exchange Commission, "Quarterly Report Pursuant to Section 13 or 15(d) of the Securities Exchange Act of 1934: For the Quarterly Period Ended December 30, 2005," commission file number 001-13836 (7 February 2006), online:

To be sure, regulatory and tax authorities clearly understand that net profit does not always mean "net profit." Thus, both the Canada Revenue Agency and the US Internal Revenue Service have formal mechanisms for revising annual profits and filing amended tax returns based upon subsequent information. There is, of course, a financial penalty if the taxpayer underestimated its tax payable in the earlier filing. More frequently, however, restatements of financial statements reduce—rather than increase—previously reported amounts of net income.

For example, in February 2019, Molson Coors Brewing Co restated its financials for fiscal years 2016 and 2017 after auditors found accounting errors for income taxes related to deferred tax liabilities. The company said that the errors originated from its acquisition of the remaining 58 percent stake in MillerCoors LLC in 2016, adding that its impact would not be material. After restating, the financial results for fiscal 2016 would reflect an increase in Molson Coors' deferred tax liabilities and deferred tax expenses by $399.1 million, which in turn would pull down its net income and earnings per share.

Restatements usually occur when the company's financial statements are subjected to a higher level of scrutiny such as, for example, when a private company converts from "compiled" financial statements to "audited" financial statements or when it decides to file for an initial public offering.

The number of financial statement restatements by public companies used to be reasonably small. For example, a 2003 study of financial restatements by companies that filed reports with the SEC in the United States showed that there were only 206 restatements of annual audited financial reports—approximately 2 percent of all reports filed. More recently, however, the number of financial restatements is increasing, particularly since the enactment of *Sarbanes Oxley* legislation (SOX)—which imposes severe sanctions against senior management responsible for financial statements.

---

www.sec.gov/Archives/edgar/data/833444/000110465906006605/a05-18471_110q.htm at 13–14.

The bottom line net income figure is only an *estimate* of financial performance based upon many decisions involving judgment, accounting principles, estimates, values, and forecasts. Thus, the last word in financial reporting is not always the last word.

F. APPROPRIATIONS

A company may appropriate or set aside an amount from its retained earnings for specified purposes. For example, a company may allocate an amount for future capital expenditures by taking the amount from retained earnings and putting the amount into an account entitled "Anticipated computer upgrades." There are no legal requirements for such allocations. They are cosmetic in that the amounts reduce retained earnings and, hence, the pressure for larger dividend payouts.

Chapter 12: Statement of Cash Flows

A. OVERVIEW

The statement of cash flows provides details of an entity's cash management, which is an important aspect of a business. In accrual accounting, income does not equal cash. The statement of cash flows is a supplementary source of information to the other financial statements and provides a different perspective.

A successful business that reports growing net income may, nevertheless, run into financial difficulties if it cannot collect its revenues or there is undue delay between the time of its sales and the time that it collects its cash. Similarly, businesses must be sensitive to their ability to pay their expenses as they become due. Even successful businesses can have liquidity problems in paying their accounts because of cash shortages.

By comparing an enterprise's current balance sheet with a previous balance sheet, we can obtain useful information about its cash flows.

B. COMPONENTS OF STATEMENT

The statement of cash flows essentially reconciles opening and closing cash (and cash equivalents) for the fiscal period covered in the Balance Sheet. However, unlike the income statement, which uses accrual accounting to record revenues and expenses, a cash flow statement classifies and reports transactions based upon actual cash receipts and disbursements.[1] The statement of cash flows is important because it is easy to measure and report cash transactions, which do not involve judgment calls on accruals and allocations of expenses to particular periods. Hence, absent outright fraud, it is an extremely accurate statement. Cash is always king!

The statement of cash flows is a "period statement" that covers the same time horizon as the income statement. Thus, the statement supplements the income statement and links the cash components of the balance sheet. It is the third dimension of financial statements.

The cash flow statement is divided into three segments:

1) Cash provided or used by Operations;
2) Cash provided or used by Investing Activities; and
3) Cash provided or used by Financing Activities.

Together, these three segments reconcile the cash balance between the opening and close of the fiscal period.

C. CASH FLOW STATEMENT OF HYPOTHETICAL COMPANY, DUGGAN INC

Duggan Inc's Cash Flows for the year ended 30 September 20-2	**Thousands of dollars ($)**
Operating Activities:	
Net income	6,807
Add: items not affecting cash:	
Depreciation	1,731
Deferred income taxes	43
	8,581
Accounts receivable	−177
Inventories	133
Prepaids and other assets	−10
Accounts payable and accrued liabilities	170

1 See Chapter 2 for the difference between cash basis and accrual accounting.

Duggan Inc's Cash Flows for the year ended 30 September 20-2	Thousands of dollars ($)
Income taxes	–575
	8,122
Investing Activities:	
Fixed and intangible asset additions	–3,542
	–3,542
Financing Activities:	
Long-term debt payable	2,120
Notes payable	1,710
Issuance of common shares	29
Purchase of treasury shares	–6,102
Cash dividends paid	–3,052
Non-pension benefits	433
	–4,862
Decrease in cash and cash equivalents	–282
Cash and cash equivalents beginning of 20-2	1,263
Cash and cash equivalents end of 20-2	**981**

We see that Duggan Inc started the year with $1,263,000 in cash and cash equivalents and ended with $981,000. How did that happen? The cash flow statement tells the story.

1. Cash from Operations

The first segment shows the cash inflows and outflows from the business's primary income-producing and operating activities. This is the cash that the business receives from sales of its products or services and cash that it pays out for the ordinary operating expenses that it incurs in earning its sales revenues.

The following are the typical sources of cash transactions:

1) Cash collected from customers, lessees, and licensees;
2) Interest and dividends received;
3) Other operating cash receipts;
4) Cash paid to employees and suppliers of goods and services;
5) Interest paid;

6) Income taxes paid; and
7) Other operating cash payments.

Duggan Inc generated $8,122,000 in cash from its operations in the year ended 30 September 20-2.

We saw earlier that we calculate net income on an accrual basis—that is, recording revenues recognized from consummated sales and expenses incurred to match the revenues, regardless of when the enterprise actually collects or pays cash.[2] Hence, the operations segment starts with the net income figure from the income statement.

Then it adjusts the net income to reflect only actual cash receipts and disbursements. Income does not equal cash. A business must calculate its income based upon accrual principles, recording revenues and expenses in the period that it makes its sales and not when it collects or pays out cash. The statement of cash flows is useful because it supplements the income statement by providing information about the sources of cash and where the business is expending cash.

The first adjustment is usually in respect of depreciation and amortization. Depreciation and amortization are non-cash expenses. The cash expenditure occurs when the company actually pays for its assets. Depreciation is merely the process of allocating the cost of the asset over its useful life. Thus, we add back any depreciation that the company charges on its income statement to its net income because it does not involve any cash disbursement in the relevant period.

Example

ABC Ltd acquires a building on 31 December 20-1 for $10 million. The company pays 20 percent in cash and assumes a mortgage for the balance. Thus, in 20-1, ABC Ltd has a cash outflow of $2 million (assuming it does not pay anything on the mortgage). Assuming the building has a useful life of forty years and no residual value, ABC Ltd might depreciate it $250,000 annually. In 20-2, ABC Ltd will have depreciation expense of $250,000, which it will add back to net income to determine cash flow. Adding back depreciation converts the accrual net income back to a cash figure.

---

2 See Chapter 2.

The next set of adjustments to the operations component deals with current assets and liabilities. Accounts receivable, accounts payable, and inventories are the three most common adjustments.

When a business increases its accounts receivable, it means that the business has sold more on credit. In order to convert the sales income back to cash income, we deduct the increase in accounts receivable to reflect the actual amount of cash collected from sales. Similarly, we adjust inventories and accounts payable for increases and decreases from the prior year end.

2. Investing Activities

The second segment in the cash flow statement is investing activities. This segment discloses how much cash the business received or expended from investing, as opposed to from its operating activities. For example, in 20-2, Duggan Inc spent $3,542,000 cash on capital and intangible assets. Hence, that number shows as a negative item in the cash flow statement. If the company had sold any capital assets during 20-2, it would have shown it as a source of cash from the sales.

3. Financing Activities

The third segment concerns financing activities, showing how much cash the business derives or expends from selling financial instruments or financing its operations. For example, we see that Duggan Inc obtained $2,120,000 by issuing long-term debt. The company also purchased its own shares for $6,102,000 and paid cash dividends of $3,052,000.

In the result, Duggan Inc's cash and cash equivalent investments were $981,000 at 30 September 20-2. This is exactly the same number that appears on the balance sheet ended 30 September 20-2: cash of $268,000 and cash equivalents of $713,000, for a total of $981,000.

D. ANALYSIS

The cash flow statement allows us to determine where the enterprise derives its cash by examining patterns of its sources and expenditures of cash. A pattern showing positive cash flows from business operations is a healthy sign that the enterprise can expand its operations, sustain its debt payments, and provide a return to its shareholders. Duggan Inc generated $8,122,000 from operations.

Negative cash flows from operations are a danger signal. Since the enterprise cannot cover its operating expenses, it will have to raise cash from other sources, such as selling assets, additional borrowings, or raising further equity from the shareholders.

1. Free Cash Flow

"Free cash flow" defines cash flow from operations minus:

- Capital expenditures for property, plant, and equipment;
- Amounts paid to acquire businesses;
- Investments in affiliated businesses; and
- Dividends paid.

The term should be defined in any agreements.

2. Cash Flow Yield

A company's cash flow yield is its free cash flow per share divided by its share price. Free cash flow is the amount of cash that the company has after it pays out all of its expenses and expenditures on capital assets (see Chapter 15, Interpreting Financial Statements).

Chapter 13: Notes to Financial Statements

A. OVERVIEW

A complete set of financial statements includes the Notes, which are a form of accounting footnotes that disclose additional information about the enterprise. The purpose of the Notes to the financial statements is to enhance our understanding of the statements and to provide context and some detail of accounting principles. The theory is that the Notes should communicate relevant information in a readable form to assist the user in analyzing the statements. Unfortunately, management sometimes uses the Notes to obfuscate, minimize, or bury important information.

The Notes to the financial statements are similar to footnotes in a legal document. They provide supplemental information to the reader of the statements and disclose management choices in selecting between alternative accounting principles and methodologies. Since accounting involves choices between alternative methods of revealing financial information, management should select the method that is most appropriate to its particular business and operations. The Notes describe the important accounting policies that management adopts and, where necessary, explain changes in such policies between successive financial statements.

The Notes contain information on aspects of business operations that cannot conveniently be disclosed in the body of the financial statements. For example, the Notes may contain detailed discussions about an entity's legal obligations under long-term leases, retirement plans, pension plans, and pending legal actions that may create liabilities in the future.

The Notes can also provide useful comparative data that is not in the body of the financial statements. For example, the Notes may reveal comparative figures for the entity's sales and net income over a period of ten years. This type of detailed financial information is particularly useful for financial analysts and regulatory bodies.

Finally, the Notes may contain a section on Management's Discussion and Analysis (MDA) of the entity and its financial operations. Regulatory bodies, such as the Ontario Securities Commission (OSC) and the Securities and Exchange Commission (SEC), require such disclosure in public filings.

To be sure, the Notes to the financial statements are fairly boring, often tedious, and frequently ignored. They are, however, an integral part of the financial statements. As Pete Seeger said, "Education is when you read the fine print, experience is what you get when you don't."[1] So it is with the Notes.

B. INCLUSIONS

Notes to financial statements will typically include the following:

- Significant accounting policies;
- Subsequent events;
- Contingencies;
- Related-party transactions;
- Principles and methods used in preparation;
- Explanations of significant items in the balance sheet, income statement, and cash flow statement; and
- Buried skeletons.

1 Valerie Strauss, "Pete Seeger: 'Do You know the Difference between Education and Experience?'" *Washington Post* (28 January 2014), online: www.washingtonpost.com/news/answer-sheet/wp/2014/01/28/pete-seeger-do-you-know-the-difference-between-education-and-experience.

C. ILLUSTRATIVE NOTES (CONDENSED)

The accompanying financial statements of Duggan Inc were prepared by management, which is responsible for the integrity and fairness of the information presented, including the many amounts that must of necessity be based on estimates and judgments. These financial statements were prepared in accordance with International Financial Reporting Standards as issued by the International Accounting Standards Board.

Financial information appearing throughout our Management's Discussion and Analysis is consistent with these financial statements. Our internal controls are designed to provide reasonable assurance that transactions are authorized, assets are safeguarded, and proper records are maintained. These controls include quality standards in hiring and training of employees, policies and procedures manuals, a corporate code of conduct, and accountability for performance within appropriate and well-defined areas of responsibility; comply with securities legislation and conflict of interest rules; and are monitored by an internal audit staff, which conducts periodic audits of all aspects of our operations.

The Board of Directors oversees management's responsibilities for financial reporting through an Audit Committee, which is composed entirely of independent directors. This committee reviews our financial statements and recommends them to the board for approval. Other key responsibilities of the Audit Committee include reviewing our existing internal control procedures and planned revisions to those procedures, and advising the directors on auditing matters and financial reporting issues.

Our auditors have full and unrestricted access to the Audit Committee to discuss their audit and related findings.

D. BASIS OF PREPARATION AND SIGNIFICANT ACCOUNTING POLICIES

These financial statements have been prepared in accordance with Canadian generally accepted accounting principles as set out in the

Handbook of the Chartered Professional Accountants.[2] In 2010, the *Handbook* was revised to incorporate International Financial Reporting Standards (IFRS), as issued by the International Accounting Standards Board (IASB) and require publicly accountable enterprises to issue financial reports based on such standards effective for fiscal periods beginning on or after 1 January 2011.

The significant accounting policies used in the preparation of these financial statements are summarized below. These accounting policies conform, in all material respects, to IFRS.

E. BASIS OF MEASUREMENT

The financial statements have been prepared under the historical cost accounting convention, except for the revaluation of certain financial instruments to fair value, including cash, cash equivalents, and investments.

F. USE OF ESTIMATES AND JUDGMENTS MADE BY MANAGEMENT

The preparation of financial statements requires management to make estimates and assumptions that affect the reported amounts of assets, liabilities, and disclosure of contingent assets, as well as liabilities at the date of the financial statements and the reported amounts of revenues and expenses during the reporting period. Actual results could differ from these estimates and changes in estimates are recorded in the reporting period in which they are determined.

Key areas where management has made difficult, complex, or subjective judgments in the process of applying the company's accounting policies, often as a result of matters that are inherently uncertain, include investment impairment, valuation techniques for fair value measurements of investments, and income taxes.

---

2 *CPA Canada Handbook — Accounting*, Chartered Professional Accountants of Canada (2018) [*Handbook*].

G. FINANCIAL INSTRUMENTS — RECOGNITION AND MEASUREMENT

The company's financial assets and liabilities are measured on the statement of financial position at fair value on initial recognition and are subsequently measured at fair value or amortized cost depending on their classification. Fair values of financial instruments are based, when possible, on quoted market prices in active markets using bid prices for financial assets and ask prices for financial liabilities, or, if necessary, on valuations using market inputs.

Cash and cash equivalents consist of cash on deposit and short-term investments that mature in three months or less from the date of acquisition. The net gain or loss recognized incorporates any dividend or interest earned on the financial asset.

H. FOREIGN CURRENCY TRANSLATION

The Canadian dollar is the functional and presentation currency of the company. Transactions in foreign currencies are translated into Canadian dollars at rates of exchange at the time of such transactions. Monetary assets and liabilities are translated at current rates of exchange, with all translation differences recognized in investment income in the current period. Non-monetary assets and liabilities are translated at the date the fair value is determined.

I. PROPERTY AND EQUIPMENT

Property and equipment are recorded in the statement of financial position at cost less accumulated amortization. Amortization is charged to operating expense on a straight-line basis over the estimated useful lives of the assets as follows:

Furniture and fixtures	5 years
Computer equipment	3 years
Computer software	1 to 3 years
Leasehold improvements	Term of lease

The company reviews its property and equipment and other non-financial assets for impairment losses whenever events or changes in circumstances indicate that the carrying amount may not be recoverable. An impairment loss is recognized for the amount by which the carrying amount of the asset exceeds its recoverable amount.

J. INCOME TAXES

Income tax expense is recognized in the statement of income and the statement of comprehensive income. Current tax is based on taxable income, which differs from net income as reported in the statement of income and statement of comprehensive income because of items of income or expense that are taxable or deductible in other years and items that are never taxable or deductible. Current tax includes any adjustments in respect of prior years.

Deferred tax assets are generally recognized for all deductible temporary income tax differences to the extent that it is probable that taxable profits will be available against which those deductible temporary differences can be used.

Deferred tax liabilities are generally recognized for all taxable temporary differences.

Deferred tax assets and liabilities are determined based on the enacted or substantively enacted tax laws and rates that are anticipated to apply in the period of realization. The measurement of deferred tax assets and liabilities uses the liability method, reflecting the tax consequences that would follow from the manner in which the company expects to recover or settle the carrying amount of the related assets and liabilities.

The carrying amount of the deferred tax asset is reduced to the extent that it is no longer probable that sufficient taxable profits will be available to allow all or part of the asset to be recovered.

Income tax assets and liabilities are offset when the income taxes are levied by the same taxation authority and there is a legally enforceable right to offset current tax assets with current tax liabilities.

K. FAIR VALUE MEASUREMENTS

The company is responsible for determining the value of its financial assets and liabilities carried at fair value. The company considers fair value to represent the amount of consideration that would be agreed upon in an arm's length transaction between knowledgeable and willing parties who are under no compulsion to act. The valuation process includes using market-driven fair value measurements from active markets where available, considering other observable and unobservable inputs, and employing valuation techniques that make use of current market data.

The company exercises considerable judgment in interpreting market data used to develop the estimates of fair value. Accordingly, the estimates presented in these financial statements are not necessarily indicative of the amounts that would be realized in a current market exchange.

L. INCOME TAXES

1. Income Tax Expense Recognized in the Statement of Income

The total income tax expense recognized in the statement of income is comprised as follows:

	20-2 ($)	20-1 ($)
Current tax:		
Expensed (recovered) during the year	3,752	3,923
Prior year adjustments	–12	8
Total current tax expense	3,740	3,931
Deferred tax:		
Origination and reversal of temporary differences	–333	–214
Changes in statutory tax rates	127	159
Total deferred tax expense	–206	55
Total income tax expense	**3,534**	**3,876**

2. Net Deferred Income Tax Asset

The company's net deferred income tax asset is the result of temporary differences between the carrying amounts of assets and liabilities for financial reporting purposes and the amounts used for income tax purposes. The sources of these temporary differences and the tax effects are as follows:

Thousands of dollars	20-2 ($)	20-1 ($)
Deferred tax assets:		
Property and equipment	755	622
Deferred tax liabilities:		
Investments	1,889	1,846

3. Capital Stock and Retained Earnings

Capital stock of the Company represents:

14,960 Class A Shares npv – authorized, issued, and paid.

Chapter 14: Reports on Financial Statements

A. OVERVIEW

Reports on financial statements are an integral part of their verification and accountability and the subject of many lawsuits. Even if not legally required, many businesses will prepare such statements for the purpose of assuring their proprietors and creditors of the propriety of the financials. Thus, we refer to such reports as "assurance reports."

Financial statements may be audited or unaudited. In either case, the auditor may express an opinion — unrestricted or restricted — on the statements. The degree to which readers of the statements can assure themselves of the integrity of the financial statements depends, in part, upon the nature of the report. Audits enhance the confidence of users of the financial statements. The auditors' report is a key communication item that, although brief, contains valuable information.

B. AUDITORS

An auditor is an independent person or entity called upon to review the enterprise, its processes, and its internal controls, for the purpose of expressing an opinion on the financial statements. Corporate and securities statutes require publicly held corporations to appoint auditors and file audited financial statements with the appropriate regulatory authorities.

For example, section 162 of the *Canada Business Corporations Act*[1] requires the shareholders of every distributing corporation to appoint an auditor at their first annual meeting of shareholders and at each successive annual meeting thereafter. Section 163 allows non-distributing corporations not to appoint an auditor. Section 167 of the *CBCA* allows a court to appoint and fix the remuneration of an auditor if the corporation does not have one and a shareholder applies to have one appointed.

The auditor has considerable statutory rights and powers. For example, they are entitled under *CBCA* section 168 to receive notice of every meeting of shareholders and to attend, at the expense of the corporation, at such meetings and be heard on matters relating to their duties. Any shareholder can give notice to the corporation and have the auditor attend at a shareholder meeting at the expense of the corporation.

Similarly, section 78(1) of the Ontario *Securities Act* requires every reporting issuer to file annually audited comparative financial statements within 140 days of the end of its financial year. Section 78(2) mandates that: "Every financial statement referred to in section (1) shall be accompanied by a report of the auditor of the reporting issuer or mutual fund prepared in accordance with the regulations."

C. ROLE OF AUDITOR VS LAWYER

There is an important difference between the role of the auditor and the role of a lawyer. Auditors are independent persons and can be required to report illegal acts to other regulators, such as securities commissions. A lawyer owes their primary duty of loyalty to the client and is expected to zealously represent the client. A lawyer's communications on legal advice to their client are strictly privileged and protected from non-disclosure.

---

1 RSC, 1985, c C-44 [*CBCA*].

D. TYPES OF REPORTS

There are three types of reports on financial statements:

1) Audit reports;
2) Review engagements; and
3) Notice to reader.

We describe briefly the nature of these reports and the degree to which one can prudently rely upon them in analyzing financial statements.

E. AUDIT REPORTS

The overall objective of the auditor conducting an audit is to obtain reasonable assurance that the financial statements as a whole are free from material misstatement.

However, the first point to note is that the financial statements belong to management. The auditor merely reports on management's financial statements and renders an opinion thereon. The auditor's report belongs to the auditor. This is made quite clear in the general representation letter that management signs for the auditors and in the body of the report itself (see below).

1. General Representation Letter

The following is an example of a general representation letter that an auditor would usually expect from the client:

> Dear . . .
>
> In connection with your audit of the financial statements of Duggan Inc as of 30 September 20-2 and for the year then ended, for the purpose of expressing an opinion as to whether the financial statements present fairly, in all material respects, the financial position, results of operations, and changes in financial position of Duggan Inc in conformity with IFRS and Canadian generally accepted accounting principles, we confirm, to the best of our knowledge and belief, the following representations made to you during your audit:

1. We are responsible for the fair presentation in the financial statements of financial position, results of operations, and changes in financial position in conformity with generally accepted accounting principles.
2. We have made available to you all financial records and related data.
3. There have been no:
   (a) Irregularities involving management or employees who have significant roles in the internal control structure.
   (b) Irregularities involving other employees that could have a material effect on the financial statements.
   (c) Communications from regulatory agencies concerning non-compliance with, or deficiencies in, financial reporting practices that could have a material effect on the financial statements.
4. We have no plans or intentions that may materially affect the carrying value or classification of assets and liabilities.
5. The following have been disclosed to you and properly recorded or disclosed in the financial statements:
   (a) Related-party transactions and related amounts receivable or payable, including sales, purchases, loans, transfers, leasing arrangements, and guarantees.
   (b) Arrangements with financial institutions involving restrictions on cash balances and line-of-credit or similar arrangements.
   (c) Agreements to repurchase assets previously sold.
   (d) All financial instruments, including those with off-balance-sheet risk (such as swaps, forwards, and futures), as required under generally accepted accounting principles.
   (e) The nature of our operations, that the preparation of financial statements requires the use of estimates, and, when applicable, specific information regarding significant estimates embodied in the financial statements.
6. There are no:
   (a) Violations or possible violations of laws or regulations (other than those previously disclosed) whose effects should

be considered for disclosure in the financial statements or as a basis for recording a loss contingency.

(b) Other material liabilities or gain or loss contingencies that are required to be accrued or disclosed.

7. There are no unasserted claims or assessments that our lawyers have advised us are probable of assertion and must be disclosed.
8. The accounting records underlying the financial statements accurately and fairly reflect, in reasonable detail, the transactions of the company.
9. Duggan Inc has satisfactory title to all owned assets, and there are no liens or encumbrances on such assets nor has any asset been pledged.
10. Provision has been made for any material loss to be sustained in the fulfilment of, or from inability to fulfil, any commitments.
11. We have complied with all aspects of contractual agreements that would have a material effect on the financial statements in the event of noncompliance.
12. No events have occurred subsequent to the balance sheet date that would require adjustment to, or disclosure in, the financial statements.

Per: ....

Chief Executive Officer

Chief Financial Officer

Duggan Inc

As one can see from the above, the auditor disclaims responsibility for most irregularities that might be present in the client's business and financial information. As we shall see in Chapter 16, Accounting and Law, Canadian courts severely restrict the scope of auditors' liability to shareholders and investors who may rely upon the audited financial statements.[2] The theory in tort law is that the auditor owes its duty of care to the corporation and not to its shareholders and potential investors and that extending this duty would expand potential liability to an indeterminate class for an indeterminate amount.

2 *Hercules Managements Ltd v Ernst Young*, [1997] 2 SCR 165 [*Hercules*].

2. Structure of Audit Report

There is a clear distinction between ownership of the financial statements and the report thereon. The financial statements belong to the company. Management selects the accounting principles from amongst the alternatives that it considers acceptable to use in its financial statements. In addition, management also decides how the enterprise will report events where there is no specific rule. The auditor conducts their audit and reports on the financial statements on the basis of the above representations and choices by management.

The auditors' report comprises five segments, all of which appear on one page. The five components are as follows:

1) Addressee;
2) Scope of opinion;
3) Generally accepted auditing standards;
4) Opinion; and
5) Date of report.

The one-page report contains a lot of information. Although the opinion paragraph is the most important in the report, each of the above five components warrants attention. All of the paragraphs preceding the opinion are essentially exoneration clauses crafted to protect the audit firm.

3. Example of Clean Opinion

The following is the standard form of auditors' report.

> To the Shareholders of Duggan Inc,
>
> We have audited the accompanying financial statements of Duggan Inc, which comprise the statements of financial position as at 30 September 20-2 and 20-1, and the statements of income, comprehensive income, changes in equity, and cash flows for the years ended 30 September 20-2 and 20-1 and a summary of significant accounting policies and other explanatory information.

Management's Responsibility for the Financial Statements
Management is responsible for the preparation and fair presentation of these financial statements in accordance with International Financial Reporting Standards, and for such internal control as management determines is necessary to enable the preparation of financial statements that are free from material misstatement, whether due to fraud or error.

Auditor's Responsibility
Our responsibility is to express an opinion on these financial statements based on our audits. We conducted our audits in accordance with Canadian generally accepted auditing standards and IFRS. Those standards require that we comply with ethical requirements and plan and perform the audit to obtain reasonable assurance about whether the financial statements are free from material misstatement.

An audit involves performing procedures to obtain audit evidence about the amounts and disclosures in the financial statements. The procedures selected depend on the auditor's judgment, including the assessment of the risks of material misstatement of the financial statements, whether due to fraud or error. In making those risk assessments, the auditor considers internal control relevant to the entity's preparation and fair presentation of the financial statements in order to design audit procedures that are appropriate in the circumstances, but not for the purpose of expressing an opinion on the effectiveness of the entity's internal control. An audit also includes evaluating the appropriateness of accounting policies used and the reasonableness of accounting estimates made by management, as well as evaluating the overall presentation of the financial statements.

We believe that the audit evidence we have obtained in our audits is sufficient and appropriate to provide a basis for our audit opinion.

Opinion
In our opinion, the financial statements present fairly, in all material respects, the financial position of Duggan Inc as at 30 September 20-2 and 20-1, and its financial performance its cash flows for the years ended 30 September 20-2 and 20-1 in accordance

with Canadian generally accepted accounting principles and International Financial Reporting Standards.

Chartered Professional Accountants
Licensed Public Accountants
10 November 20-2

The first point to observe is the boilerplate language of the standard form audit report and the opinion.

Second, the auditor is not an insurer and their report does not constitute a guarantee of absolute accuracy. Hence, it is important to understand the limitations of the auditors' report and the degree to which one may rely upon it.

Third, the management representation letter that Duggan Inc signed illustrates the types of representations that companies make to their auditors. The representation letter covers various aspects of the corporation's financial and business operations. It is a comprehensive document of exonerations that audit firms insist upon before signing off on any opinion.

An audit firm will rely upon the general representation letter as its first line of defence in any litigation against the audit firm. Note, particularly, that the responsibility for the fair presentation of the financial statements in compliance with GAAP and IFRS is squarely on the shoulders of the company. Management will certify that the financial statements include amounts based on its best estimates and judgment. Thus, we repeat: accounting is as much art as it is a science.

Fourth, management also certifies that it maintains a system of internal accounting controls to provide reasonable assurance that assets are safeguarded and that transactions are authorized, recorded and reported properly. Further, that the internal audit department reviews these accounting controls on an ongoing basis and reports its findings and recommendations to management and the Audit, Finance, and Risk Management Committee of the Board of Directors.

(a) Addressee

The report starts out by identifying the party to whom it is addressed. In the case of Duggan Inc, it clearly states that it is addressed to the shareholders of the company. In theory, identification of the addressee determines the scope of the audit firm's liability. It is clear that the auditor is the auditor for the shareholders.

Unfortunately, the Supreme Court's decision in *Hercules* severely limited the liability of auditors to shareholders on policy grounds. The decision protects auditors at the expense of investors. As the events of 1990 through 2020 show, however, it is the investors, employees, and creditors who bear the ultimate financial brunt of auditor protection policies.

(b) Scope

The next segment identifies the scope of the auditors' opinion. The scope paragraph states:

> We have audited the balance sheets of Duggan Inc (the Company) as at 30 September 20-2 and 20-1, and the statements of income, retained earnings (deficit), and cash flows then ended. These financial statements are the responsibility of the Company's management. Our responsibility is to express an opinion on these financial statements based on our audit.

Note again, the clear and unequivocal statement that the auditor makes in placing the responsibility for the financial statements on the shoulders of corporate management.

(c) Generally Accepted Auditing Standards (GAAS)

GAAS defines the scope of the report, which states:

> We conducted our audits in accordance with Canadian generally accepted auditing standards. Those statements require that we plan and perform an audit to obtain reasonable assurance whether the financial statements are free of material misstatement. An audit includes examining, on a test basis, evidence supporting the amounts and disclosures in the financial statements. An audit also includes assessment of the accounting principles used and significant estimates made by management, as well as evaluating the overall financial statement presentation.

The quality and integrity of the auditors' opinion depends upon the scope of the work that they perform in order to arrive at the opinion.

The objective of an audit is to obtain *reasonable* assurance whether the financial statements are free of *material* misstatement. Having identified the party to whom the opinion is addressed, and the scope of the work performed, the auditor's report will provide an opinion.

(d) Opinion

Clean audit opinions are terse boilerplate statements. The following is a typical clean, unqualified (unmodified) opinion:

> In our opinion, these financial statements present fairly, in all material respects, the financial position of the Company as at 30 September 20-2 and 20-1, and the results of its operations and its cash flows for the year then ended in accordance with Canadian GAAP and International Financial Reporting Standards.

This is the gold-plated opinion that management wants. Anything less can have severe consequences for the enterprise, particularly if it is a listed company. Note the key terms in the opinion: "present fairly" and "in all material respects." The audit report is not a guarantee; it merely assures fair presentation.

(e) Date of Report

The date of the report serves several purposes. First, it tells us how relevant the report is by identifying the time that has lapsed since the auditor issued it. A stale-dated report is less relevant for analysis. Second, the date tells us the effective date for disclosure of contingent liabilities—that is, liabilities that potentially exist between the year-end of the financial statements and the disclosure date of the audit report. In the case of Duggan Inc, for example, the auditors' report is dated 10 November 20-2. This means that all contingent liabilities between 30 September and 10 November 20-2 must be disclosed in the Notes to the financial statements. Third, the date effectively frames the time limits of liability for the report.

4. Qualified Opinions

Where the auditor gives a qualified (modified) opinion, they will state any scope limitations and disclaimers on particular aspects of the financial statements. The auditor may also address concerns with the "going concern" assumption. In addition to the clean opinion, here are three other types of opinions:

1) Qualified (Modified);
2) Adverse; and
3) Disclaimed.

(a) Qualified Reports

As its name implies, a qualified (modified) report limits some aspects of the audit opinion and is less than an unqualified opinion. The auditor will express a qualified opinion when, having obtained sufficient appropriate audit evidence, they conclude that there are material misstatements, but that they are not pervasive. Hence, it will say that "except for" or "with the exception of" the reservation, the financial statements are fair. For example, the auditor could not observe the physical counting of inventories or there is a departure from GAAP.

A qualified report will start with the same introductory paragraph as in a clean audit opinion but will go on to disclose the nature of the qualification by saying:

> Except as discussed in the following paragraph, we conducted our audit in accordance with Canadian generally accepted auditing standards . . .
>
> In our opinion, *except for* the effects of (reason for the reservation) discussed in the preceding paragraph, these financial statements present fairly, etc.

One must review carefully the reservation and qualification. It may pertain to a relatively minor issue, such as a minor and immaterial departure from GAAP, or a substantial and significant aspect of the corporation's operations, such as non-observation of inventory counts where inventory is a material component of the balance sheet. If there are several minor qualifications and reservations, their cumulative effect may render the entire report unreliable and the auditor may render an adverse opinion or decline to give one at all.

(b) Adverse Opinion

An adverse opinion states that the financial statements do not present fairly the financial position, results of operations, or cash flows of the entity in conformity with GAAP. For example:

> The Company does not provide for income taxes with respect to differences between financial income and taxable income for income tax purposes and does not provide for deferred income taxes. . . .
>
> In our opinion, because of the matters discussed in the preceding paragraphs, the financial statements referred to above do not present fairly in conformity with Canadian generally accepted accounting principles.

An adverse opinion virtually destroys a listed company's ability to raise capital or borrow money in the public markets. As a practical matter, the enterprise will do almost anything to prevent the auditor from issuing an adverse opinion. However, this is where the client can put economic pressure on the auditor to refrain from issuing an adverse opinion (see, for example, the Enron debacle in Chapter 16, Accounting and the Law).

(c) Disclaimer of Opinion

A disclaimer of opinion states that the auditor does not express an opinion on the financial statements of the Company because the audit was not of sufficient scope to allow the auditor to form an opinion. For example:

> The Company did not make a physical count of its inventory stated in the financial statements and did not have adequate records to apply other auditing procedures to satisfy us as to inventory quantities.

F. REVIEW ENGAGEMENTS

Going down the hierarchy of auditors' reports, the next rung on the ladder is the review engagement. A review engagement limits the scope and work of the auditor. Private unlisted companies do not generally require full scale audits, which are time consuming and expensive. The managers of a private company are usually quite familiar with its finances and can dispense with a full audit. The auditor will describe the limits of the engagement as follows:

> We have reviewed the balance sheet of "X" Company as at December 20-2 and the statements of income, retained earnings, and changes in financial position for the year then ended. Our review was made in accordance with generally accepted standards for review engagements and accordingly consisted primarily of enquiry, analytical procedures and discussion related to information supplied to us by the Company.

Review engagements typically do not require testing of the corporation's financial records but rely on enquiry, analysis of procedures, and discussions with management.

The auditor will disclaim any audit opinion by stating:

> A review does not constitute an audit and consequently we do not express an audit opinion on these financial statements.

Despite the reservations, review engagements do have some value in that they provide a form of negative assurance to the reader, such as:

> Based upon our review, nothing has come to our attention that causes us to believe that these financial statements are not, in all material respects, in accordance with generally accepted accounting principles.

Thus, unlike qualified opinions, which provide positive assurance that the statements are prepared in accordance with GAAP and IFRS and present fairly the financial state of affairs, a review engagement tells us that the auditor did not see anything unfavourable in the limited work that they performed on the corporation's books and records.

G. NOTICE TO READER REPORTS

"Compilations" are at the bottom of the hierarchy of opinions. In a compilation, the accountant prepares, or helps to prepare, financial statements based on the client's records and representations. A compilation does not require any audit and does not meet even with the limited aspects of review engagements. Compilations are simply a simulation of data with a notice to the reader, such as:

> We have compiled the balance sheet of "X" Company as at 31 December 20-2 and the statements of income, retained earnings and changes in financial position for the period then ended from information provided by management. We have not audited, reviewed, or otherwise attempted to verify the accuracy or completeness of such information. Readers are cautioned that these statements may not be appropriate for their purpose.

Notice to reader statements following a compilation engagement are of minimal value to persons who are outsiders of the corporation. Thus, notice to reader statements for external users are sometimes characterized as "burn before you read" statements. They may, however, have some value to the owners of a business who are actively involved in, and have substantial knowledge of, the business and its financial position and who do not need an expensive audit opinion.

H. RECENT DEVELOPMENTS

Traditional audit reports are brief boilerplate documents that cast minimal light on issues of interest to most users. The IAASB published "Invitation to Comment: Improving the Audit Report" (June 2012) that suggested various improvements and enhancements.[3]

---

3 "Invitation to Comment: Improving the Auditor's Report" *IAASB* (June 2012), online: International Federation of Accountants www.ifac.org/system/files/publications/files/Auditor%20Reporting%20At%20a%20Glance%20June%20 2012%20-%20final.pdf

The first is that the opinion should be the first paragraph of the auditors' report. This is hardly a radical proposal, since it is the most important part of the report.

Another option that faces opposition from the large audit firms is a proposal to highlight "auditor commentary" and outstanding litigation, valuation of financial instruments and internal control, and management's assessment of the going concern assumption. A less than complete endorsement, for example, of the going concern assumption may well be the catalyst that drives a company under and exposes the audit firm to litigation. Audit firms do not want to take on the added risk of lawsuits.

I. PROBLEM AREAS

1. Write-Downs

Write-downs occur when the costs and values of property diverge, and current values fall below cost. Thus, conservatism requires that we write down the assets on the financial statements. For example, the traditional view in accounting is that long-lived assets, such as property, plant, and equipment, should be recorded at cost minus accumulated depreciation, unless they are permanently impaired and their value has declined below net book value. In such circumstances, a company may reduce its long-lived assets to their fair market value by taking a charge against earnings so as to reflect the lower and more conservative value. However, the difficulty with write-downs is in determining when the company should employ them and the effect that doing so will have on earnings, stock prices, and stock options.

Nortel was a classic example of delusion and despair in recognizing its financial picture. Nortel's operating profit for fiscal year 2000 was USD$1.73 billion. The CEO of the company, John Roth, said on 25 June 2000 that Nortel was "firing on all cylinders."[4] The *Globe and*

---

4 Duff McDonald, "The Black Watch" *National Post Business* (July 2004) 36, online: Duff McDonald: A Collection of my Work https://duffmcdonald.wordpress.com/2004/07/01; see also Theresa Tedesco, "Nortel Trial to Open Old Wounds" *Financial Post* (14 January 2012), online: https://business.financialpost.com/technology/nortel-trial-to-open-old-wounds.

Mail reported Roth as commenting: "It isn't that Nortel is overvalued, its maybe that everything else is undervalued."[5]

By 17 November 2000, Nortel's shares had plunged by 8.9 percent on rumours that it was losing business to rivals. Nortel called the claim "nonsense." In a speech to the Canadian Club on 19 February 2001, Roth said: "We don't have any control over the stock prices. We are just running a terrific business here." On 21 April 2001, Roth went on to say: "I'm not going to pretend we grew efficiently. You don't grow that fast in elegant fashion." By 15 June 2001, Nortel's tone had deteriorated from exuberance to despair when Roth said: "We have had better times. Is this the end? God, we sure hope so, this is a brutal experience."

Nortel's financial profile had changed remarkably from a year earlier. The company had an operating loss of USD$1.5 billion and total losses of USD$19.2 billion. It took restructuring charges of $12.3 billion, $2 billion in amortization charges, and $959 million on receivables, inventory, and investments. It spent $830 million on 20,000 job cuts and announced 10,000 more job cuts to come in the future.

In 2012, three of its senior executives were charged with fraud and accounting manipulation ("earnings management") to perk up their bonuses and went on trial in the Superior Court of Ontario. They were acquitted on the basis of GAAP.[6]

2. Restructuring Charges

"Restructuring" is one of those fluid accounting terms that covers a multitude of events and changes in business operations, some of which are voluntary, while others are imposed. Restructuring charges are

---

5 Margaret Wente, "John Roth, Speed Junkie" *Globe and Mail* (20 February 2001), online: www.theglobeandmail.com/news/national/john-roth-speed-junkie/article759729.

6 See "Nortel Fraud Trial Begins" *The Record* (16 January 2012), *Canada.com*, online: www.therecord.com/business/2012/01/16/nortel-fraud-trial-begins.html; and James Bagnall, "Top Brass at Nortel Found Not Guilty as Judge Dismisses Charges Against ex-CEO Frank Dunn, ex-CFO Douglas Beatty and ex-Controller Michael Gollogly" (14 January 2013), online: https://o.canada.com/news/top-brass-at-nortel.

write-downs that clean up the balance sheet and can improve future earnings. They also remove redundant assets from the balance sheet.

Restructuring charges or write-downs generally arise when corporations write off excessive goodwill resulting from extravagant acquisitions at inflated prices. For example, in 2013, Barrick Gold Corp, the world's biggest gold miner, wrote down USD$4.2 billion, most of which related to its copper mine in Zambia.[7]

Restructuring charges can also accumulate and have dramatic effects on the financial statements. For example, restructuring charges for American Telephone & Telegraph from 1986 to 1996 amounted to USD$14.2 billion, which exceeded its total net income of USD$10.3 billion during those years.[8]

3. Goodwill

Goodwill is the premium that a company pays over the fair value of assets that it purchases from another company. The premium that the purchaser pays is supposed to reflect the anticipated "superior earnings" from the assets acquired. For example, if a purchaser company buys another company that has assets with a fair value of $10 million, but is willing to pay $13 million for the assets, the premium is presumably attributable to the perceived superior earning power that the purchaser anticipates it will generate from the assets. For accounting purposes, the premium of $3 million is reported as purchased "goodwill," a loose term that describes factors that will generate superior earnings attributable to customer relationships, good labour union relationships and contracts, supplier reliability, or lucrative government licences.

During boom times, companies can use their inflated stock to buy other companies, often at substantial premiums. When lean times follow the boom, companies may be stuck with over-inflated assets

7 "Barrick Gold Posts Loss After Writedowns on Assets in Zambia, Pakistan" *Dawn* (14 February 2013), online: www.dawn.com/news/786062.

8 "American Telephone & Telegraph Reports Earnings for Qtr to Sept 30" *New York Times* (23 October 1992), online: www.nytimes.com/1992/10/23/business/american-telephone-telegraph-reports-earnings-for-qtr-to-sept-30.html.

on their books, which are typically buried in their goodwill account. Where goodwill is substantially impaired, companies will write-down the account to reflect the reduced values.

We saw this in 2002 following the technology bust. JDS Uniphase, for example, wrote down USD$56.15 billion on assets that it had previously acquired at inflated prices. AOL Time Warner took write-downs in 2002 of USD$99.7 billion, which was an all-time record at that time. The company acknowledged substantial and permanent impairment of its assets. The total impact on profits from technology companies' write-downs in 2002 was estimated to be USD$235 billion.

The net effect of corporate write-downs is to leave a cleaner and more conservative balance sheet going forward. Of course, from the investor's perspective write-downs can be either good news or bad news. They are good news if the investor purchases after the write-down; they are bad news if the investor went in before the write-downs when asset values were inflated.

4. Stock Options

Stock options are contracts that give the holder the option to purchase shares at predetermined prices. The holder will exercise this option only if the stock is above the price at which they can buy. Option values rise as the price of the underlying stock increases.

One of the main propellants behind stock prices is anticipated earnings. As earnings increase, stock prices will generally react favourably and increase as well. Stock prices are the principal impetus behind stock option plans, which management typically reserves for employees and senior officers. Hence, there is a direct relationship between earnings and stock option prices, which is a powerful incentive for corporate management to "improve" earnings, by either increasing revenues or decreasing expenses.

During the Internet boom in 2000, investors focused more on revenues that technology companies earned and not as much on "bottom line" earnings. As stock prices increased, so did the value of stock options. In fact, a very large number of Internet companies never had any earnings at all. Nevertheless, they hyped up their stock options.

There are various methods for determining the fair value of stock options, but none of them are entirely appropriate for stock market and accounting purposes. The Black-Scholes formula, for example, is not ideally suited for accounting purposes. It is designed essentially for determining values in short-term trading. Thus, the formula makes options on highly volatile stocks unduly valuable.

The discretion to use "fair value" opens up the potential for manipulation of values. Some companies simply ignore the cost of stock options and consider them to be "free compensation" notwithstanding their dilutive effect on future share values. Others backdated their options retroactively to take advantage of hindsight practice, which is akin to placing a bet on a horse after the race is over. The 2002 technology bust and scandals associated with fictional stock option prices produced some reforms. The accounting rules were changed to account for stock options as expenses.

5. Pensions

The stock market boom of the 2000s also enabled companies to look at their pension surpluses and take some surpluses into income, in order to bolster the latter. With the market bust, pension shortfalls became the norm and there were (and are) continuing deficiencies in many defined benefit plans. Air Canada, for example, had a major pension shortfall that caused the company to seek bankruptcy protection.

6. Accounting Jargon

Accounting is the language that we use to communicate financial information. Thus, terms such as "revenues," "expenses," "capital assets," "capital expenditures," and "accrual and cash basis" have a special meaning in the context of accounting and financial statements. If accounting is the language of communication, it can also be an instrument of obfuscation. Here are some jargon phrases and practices that should be viewed with caution.

(a) "Accelerating the booking of contracts"

Loosely translated, this means that the company is recognizing revenue early by signing and recognizing contracts that may not generate the revenues until sometime in the future.

(b) "Premature revenue recognition"

This is another phrase that simply says that the company did not adhere to GAAP and recognized its revenues before its sales were completed or when the customer still had options to terminate, void, or delay the sale.

(c) "Aggressive accounting"

This phrase can cover a multitude of circumstances when management prepares its financial statements and stretches accounting principles to their limits. Management may do this to inflate revenues or decrease expenses. This includes aggressive restructuring overcharges to "clean up" the balance sheet by giving it a "big bath" through enormous write-downs or write-offs.[9] By lumping losses into one quarter, the enterprise can remove the drag on future earnings and improve its financial picture.[10]

(d) "Income smoothing"

The objective here is to smooth income between successive financial periods to show a steady increase and to conceal volatility in earnings. Stock markets react favourably to consistently increasing earnings, rather than erratic fluctuations. By adjusting accounting entries, a company can level out the troughs and pare down the peaks in earnings to produce a nice steady earnings per share graph.

(e) "Options selected with some hindsight"

This innocuous phrase refers to the practice of backdating options to a favourable price after the trigger date of option execution has passed.

---

9 For examples, see Martin Peers & Julia Angwin, "AOL Reports Record Annual Loss and Says Ted Turner Will Resign" *Wall Street Journal* (30 January 2003) at A1.

10 See Roger Lowenstein, "Did AOL Succeed in Spinning the Street" *Wall Street Journal* (7 November 1996) at C1.

It is a form of contractual retroactivity with the benefit of hindsight. In horse racing, it would be comparable to betting on Secretariat in the Kentucky Derby after the race was over.[11] Bookmakers do not pay on such bets. Corporate management may, however, do so with the shareholders' money! Securities regulators frown on such activities.

(f) "Earnings management"

This term refers to the game of "nods and winks" among market participants of manipulating revenues and expenses to meet earnings expectations of a smooth earnings path to desired goals—generally to enhance stock prices and executive compensation. As Arthur Levitt, former Chairman of the SEC, observed: [12]

> While the problem of earnings management is not new, it has swelled in a market that is unforgiving of companies that miss their estimates. I recently read of one major U.S. company, that failed to meet its so-called "numbers" by one penny and lost more than six percent of its stock value in one day. . . .
>
> I believe that almost everyone in the financial community shares responsibility for fostering a climate in which earnings management is on the rise and the quality of financial reporting is on the decline. Corporate management isn't operating in a vacuum. In fact, the different pressures and expectations placed by, and on, various participants in the financial community appear to be almost self-perpetuating.

(g) "Cookie jar reserves"

This practice refers to building up excess reserves through unrealistic assumptions about future liabilities, such as sales returns, loan losses,

---

11 The 1973 Kentucky Derby was the 99th running of the Kentucky Derby at Churchill Downs in Louisville, Kentucky. *Secretariat* won the Derby in a record time of 1: 59 2/5, 2 1/2 lengths ahead of Sham, while Our Native finished in third position. Of the thirteen horses that entered and started the race, all horses completed the event.

12 Arthur Levitt (Chairman, SEC), "The Numbers Game," speech at NYU Center for Law and Business (28 September 1998), online: www.sec.gov/news/speech/speecharchive/1998/spch220.txt.

or warranty costs. Management can draw upon these reserves in bad times to smooth earnings (see *Earnings Management* above).

(h) "Materiality"

The concept of materiality, generally at the root of most accounting-based litigation, allows for flexible financial reporting under GAAP by recording errors below a threshold amount, meaning that they are then excused as not materially affecting the bottom line.

J. AUDIT INQUIRY LETTERS

Audit inquiry letters pose particular difficulties for companies because they create a conflict between the auditor's desire to disclose relevant contingencies and litigation risks and the lawyer's desire to protect confidential information on behalf of their clients.

A lawyer cannot disclose confidential information without the consent of their client. If the lawyer discloses with the client's consent, the information may lose its solicitor-client privilege. There is no comparable accountant-client privilege.

Law firms regularly receive inquiry letters from accountants asking whether the lawyer (or law firm) is aware of any outstanding claims against a particular client. Such letters should be carefully managed to ensure that confidentiality and privilege are not compromised in any reply, which should be addressed to the client and not the audit firm.

K. WHISTLEBLOWING

Ralph Nader described whistleblowing as "an act of a man or a woman who, believing in the public interest overrides the interest of the organization he serves, publicly blows the whistle if the organization is involved in corrupt, illegal, fraudulent or harmful activity."[13] The *Ontario Securities Act* provides financial incentives for whistleblowing.[14]

13 Ralph Nader, "Publisher's Preface" in Ralph Nader, Peter J Petkas & Kate Blackwell, eds, *Whistle Blowing* (New York: Grossman Publishers, 1972) vii at vii.

14 See OSC Policy 15-601, "Whistleblower Program" (as amended October 2018).

A whistleblower can be an individual, or a group of individuals acting jointly, who:

- are aware of, or suspect, a violation of Ontario securities law; and
- voluntarily come forward and report that information.

Potential whistleblowers may include employees, former employees, suppliers, contractors, clients, and others.

Even individuals or groups of individuals who are involved in the misconduct can be whistleblowers and may still be eligible for a whistleblower award.

1. Ineligible Whistleblowers

Lawyers are not eligible for whistle blowing rewards. Section 15 of the OSC Policy lists, *inter alia*, persons who are *not eligible* for whistle-blowing rewards:

(c) those who obtained information in connection with providing legal services to, or conducting the legal representation of, a client that is, or that employs, the subject of the whistleblower submission, unless disclosure of that information would otherwise be permitted by a lawyer under applicable provincial or territorial bar or law society rules, or the equivalent rules applicable in another jurisdiction;

(d) those who obtained information in connection with providing legal services to, or conducting the legal representation of, an employer that is, or that employs, the subject of the whistle-blower submission, unless disclosure of that information would otherwise be permitted by a lawyer under applicable provincial or territorial bar or law society rules, or the equivalent rules applicable in another jurisdiction;

(e) those who obtained information in connection with providing internal audit or external assurance services to, or conducting an internal or financial audit of, a client or employer that is, or that employs, the subject of the whistleblower submission, unless disclosure of that information would otherwise be permitted by an auditor under the applicable rules of professional conduct;

(f) those who obtained information while conducting an inquiry or investigation into possible violations of law by a client or employer that is, or that employs, the subject of the whistleblower submission;

(g) those who were directors or officers of the entity that is, or that employs, the subject of the whistleblower submission at the time the information was acquired.

Chapter 15: Interpretation of Financial Statements

A. OVERVIEW

We have seen that there are four basic financial statements:

- The balance sheet;
- The income statement;
- The statement of owners' equity; and
- The statement of cash flows.

We need all four statements for the purpose of corporate analysis. A missing statement is a red flag.

We use the information in these four statements to analyze the enterprise's past economic performance, compliance with legal stewardship, and fiduciary requirements, and for predicting its future prospects. Different users will focus on different measures of past performance. For example, creditors will focus on the enterprise's ability to repay its debts, investors will look to predict future performance of its common stock, and regulators will use the information for regulatory compliance. Lawyers use financial statements in drafting contracts and loan agreements and specify yardsticks for performance.

Financial analysts and advisors are an important constituency interested in corporate statements. They pore over the statements to detect future trends and report their findings to investors, private clients, and investment media. Indeed, some specialized television channels, such as CNBC, do little else other than analyze financial information, economic trends, and the general business environment for their investor-oriented audiences.

Lawyers who are responsible for their clients' corporate transactions and agreements that contain financial covenants and restrictions are also interested in financial statements. Lawyers acting for creditors, partners, joint ventures, trustee stakeholders, or labour unions look at the financial statements to ensure that they comply with the terms of agreements.

Of course, management is interested in all aspects and perspectives of financial statements, past, present, and future. They must ensure that the statements properly report information as part of their custodial and fiduciary responsibilities to the corporation and that the enterprise complies with all of its legal covenants and contractual arrangements with creditors and regulators. Management must also make decisions about the direction in which it should steer the corporation in order to maximize its return on equity (ROE) to create wealth for its shareholders

B. MEASURING FINANCIAL SUCCESS

From a shareholder's or owner's perspective, the primary objective of a business is to maximize its ROE and control risk, both of which require reliable tools of measurement to facilitate analysis. Absolute numbers are not very helpful in financial analysis because they do not account for the size and scope of the enterprise's operations. For example, absolute numbers mean little if we are comparing IBM with a small start-up technology company. Ratios are a better tool to analyze businesses of varying sizes.

Ratios use a common denominator to measure status or performance. For example, if one company earns $100 million in sales and another $10 million in sales, but both earn $5 million in net income, we must adjust for relative size of the businesses. One has a rate of return of 5 percent on sales; the other a return of 50 percent. By reducing the numbers to a common ratio, such as, for example, net income as a percentage of sales, we obtain a more meaningful snapshot of the two companies than we would by looking at their absolute numbers.

However, we must be careful with numbers analysis. There is a psychological tendency to draw comfort from numbers. There is also a danger in interpreting numbers as absolutes. There is no predetermined "good" ratio for financial analysis. Each situation requires contextual analysis of the particular business, its environment, its stage of development, and the economic climate at the particular time. Thus, properly used, a ratio is an analytical tool for financial interpretation and not an end in itself.

Ratio analysis plays different roles depending upon the purpose for which one engages in it. In a legal document, such as a bond indenture or loan contract, a covenant on a particular ratio (for example, working capital) is an absolute requirement that the borrower must comply with to avoid legal sanctions. Thus, the question that we ask is whether the borrower has complied with the covenant in the lending document. We do not enquire whether the ratio, *per se*, is good, bad, or indifferent. In contract law, ratios play a rigid role to measure compliance. In financial analysis, however, ratios are a predictive tool.

C. RETURN ON EQUITY (ROE)

ROE is the starting point of all ratios in "for profit" companies. A business corporation exists to make a profit for its shareholders. Thus, for a shareholder, ROE is the critical performance indicator of the corporation's success. As a general rule: High ROE means "come play"; Low ROE suggests "stay away."

The formula for ROE is simple.

ROE = Net Income/Shareholders' Equity

Although ROE appears as a single number, it is actually the product of three separate components:

1) Profit margin (Net income/Sales);
2) Asset turnover (Sales/Assets); and
3) Leverage (Assets/Equity).

If we multiply the three components, we obtain the return on equity. This is the classic Dupont formula:

(Net Income/Sales) × (Sales/Assets) × (Assets/Equity)

When expressed as a percentage, it gives us the overall return on the shareholders' investment. For example, our hypothetical company, Duggan Inc has net income of $6,807 and equity of $17,134. Hence, its ROE equals:[1]

$6,807/$17,134 = 40%

In order to determine whether Duggan's ROE is good or poor, we must compare the percentage return with comparable returns from competitors in the same industry in the same period.

A high return on equity means that the enterprise is making good use of its current and retained earnings, which will ultimately reflect in share values.

We should also look at ROE in the context of past performance and general trends and satisfy ourselves that the return is indicative of normal returns and is not distorted by unique or non-recurring or "extraordinary" events. Hence, we must be satisfied that the net income figure properly reflects the income of the enterprise and that it has not been boosted by accounting manipulations, such as earnings management.

D. FINANCIAL RATIOS

With one important exception, corporate financial statements do not usually show financial ratios. We must calculate these ratios from the data in the statements. There are four broad groupings of financial ratios, each of which measures different aspects of operations:

1) Profitability ratios;
2) Liquidity ratios;
3) Solvency ratios; and
4) Activity ratios.

---

1 See chapters 6 and 10.

1. Profitability Ratios

Profitability ratios assess the financial profitability of an enterprise. Typically, they measure earnings per share, profit margins, return on assets, and return on equity.

(a) Earnings per Share

"Earnings per share" (EPS), or earnings yield, is the one ratio that companies disclose in the body of their financial statements, usually at the bottom of the Income Statement. EPS is probably the most used financial tool in analyzing and predicting corporate performance. The number tells us how much money each share earns.

Basic EPS, or net income per common share, are earnings attributable to the residual owners of the enterprise, the common stockholders. It is calculated by dividing net income minus any preferred stock dividends by the weighted average number of shares of common stock outstanding for the year. This measures the profitability of the enterprise. Duggan Inc's EPS in 20-2 was $6,807/1,482 or $4.59. In other words, for every dollar of common stock, Duggan's shareholders earned $4.59. The higher the EPS, the greater the corporation's rate of return.

The earnings attributable to common stock is net income for the year less any dividends and accumulations of dividends, if any, on preferred shares. The ratio measures the amount of earnings left for the residual owners of the corporation who invested in its common stock. Thus, it is the amount of earnings for a particular year that is allocable to each share of the corporation's residual security interest—the common shares of the corporation.

There are, however, various other forms of EPS. EPS can be affected by changes in the number of common shares outstanding—for example, through stock splits and stock consolidations (reverse splits). These require further analysis.

i. Dilution of Shares

Even more significant than the basic EPS of a corporation is its diluted EPS. Diluted EPS considers the dilutive effect of issuing additional shares through stock options, warrants, or other agreements that require the company to issue additional shares in the future. The denominator is the fully diluted number of shares.

Basic EPS may also be adjusted for extraordinary items, changes in accounting principles, or gains or losses on the disposal of a business. In such cases, there may be several EPS calculations and amounts disclosed on the income statement.

ii. Convertible Securities

In considering EPS, one must also consider the effect of convertible securities and their potential dilutive effect on earnings. Thus, we can report EPS on an "if converted" basis—that is, assuming that the convertibles are actually converted into common stock.

There are two effects to the "if converted" calculation of EPS. First, the number of common shares outstanding is deemed to increase. Thus, the denominator increases. Second, we must adjust the earnings in the numerator by assuming that there will be no priority payment of interest or preferred cumulative dividends if the convertibles are converted into common stock. The numerator will therefore also increase.

If the combined effect of these two adjustments increases the EPS, the convertible securities are anti-dilutive, and they are not deemed to be converted in calculating EPS. If the conversion is dilutive, the diluted EPS should be disclosed.

iii. Preferred Dividends

We must also adjust EPS for dividends on senior stock. For example, if a corporation has a net income of $2 million and 200,000 shares outstanding all year, the EPS is $10 per share.

However, if the corporation also has cumulative preferred shares outstanding, we deduct the amount attributable to the preferred shares before calculating the EPS per common share. For example, if the corporation has 30,000 preferred shares with a dividend of $8 per share, we would subtract the $240,000 in preferred dividends (whether paid or accumulated) from the $2 million net income. Then, the remaining $1,760,000 of net income available to the common shares would provide an EPS of only $8.80 for common stockholders.

iv. Weighted Average

The denominator in the EPS calculation is the weighted average of common charges outstanding during the year. For example, if a corporation has 80,000 shares outstanding on 1 January, the beginning of its fiscal year, and issues 20,000 additional common shares on 1 October of the year, the weighted average of shares outstanding for the calendar year is 85,000—that is, 80,000 for the year plus 5,000 for one quarter.

Example

Assume that ABC Ltd has a calendar fiscal year with net income of $12,500,000. The company has a capital structure as follows:

- 100,000 Preferred shares with a cumulative dividend of $7 per share
- 100,000 Common shares outstanding at its year-end (20,000 shares issued on 1 October)

Net income		$12,500,000
100,000 preferred shares	$7 dividend per share	$700,000
Net income available for common shares		$11,800,000
Common shares outstanding:		
During entire year — 80,000	$80,000	
For 25% of the year — 20,000	$5,000	
Weighted average for year	$85,000	
Earnings per common share (EPS)		$139

(b) Limitations of EPS

EPS is a convenient figure and, hence, used extensively in financial markets. The risk is that focusing on a single figure may detract from other economic indicators, such as inclusions and adjustments to the net income figure over several years. Hence, it should be used cautiously in time series analysis of corporate performance. Cash earned per share is less susceptible to accounting adjustments and manipulation.

(c) Price/Earnings Ratio

The price to earnings ratio (P/E) is probably the single most important measure of stock price valuation and the one that most analysts and investors follow.

What does the P/E ratio tell us? When one buys corporate stock, one is, in effect, buying the corporation's future earnings, which is a surrogate for its ROE. The P/E ratio is a measure of the amount that one is willing to pay for those earnings in the future.

Example

Assume that ABC Ltd's EPS is $139 a share, and one is willing to purchase the share for $2100.

EPS	$139
Cost price per share	$2,085
P/E ratio	15
Implied rate of return (100/15)	6.67%

In this case, its P/E ratio is 15. This means that one is willing to pay fifteen times the company's current earnings for the shares. Stated another way, if earnings and stock prices remained constant, it would take fifteen years to recover the cost of ABC Ltd's shares through corporate earnings. This implies an annual rate of return of 6.7 percent if earnings remain constant.

The P/E ratio is important because it allows us to compare companies, industries, countries, and indices using a common yardstick. For example, we know that investors are willing to pay a higher multiple for technology companies than they are for utilities. This is entirely reasonable because technology is a growth industry, whereas utilities are stable earners. Thus, a growth investor might be willing to pay more (and risk more) for a growing company than for a stable company. In contrast, an income investor might prefer a stable and boring (but less risky) utility company with steady cash flow and dividends.

As valuable as the P/E ratio is, it has its limitations and we should interpret it with care. The classic P/E is a measure of *past* earnings compared to current stock prices. It tells us about the relationship between last year's earnings and today's stock price. This information is useful but can be misleading. If the company has taken a substantial write-off or recorded an unusual one-time gain in the preceding year, the earnings may not reflect a typical pattern that is useful for predicting future values. In 2008 and 2009, for example, during the financial crisis, many companies, especially financial institutions, took large write-offs and provided substantial reserves against future losses. All of this had the effect of reducing current earnings and enlarging P/E ratios. The backward-looking P/E ratio is not useful in these circumstances for predicting future earnings.

The forward P/E ratio is a more useful number for financial analysis. The earnings in the ratio are the expected future earnings of the company. Since a stock investor purchases future earnings, this is a more meaningful number. It tells us how much an investor is willing to pay for stock ownership in the future.

Example

Assume the EPS of ABC Ltd in the above example is expected to be $160 next year and the stock trades at $2,085. The P/E ratio drops to 13, and the yield on the investment increases to 7.7 percent. This presents a different picture from the backward-looking P/E. If the market continues to support a P/E of 15, it is possible that the stock may rise to $2,400.

EPS	$160
Cost price per share	$2,085
P/E ratio	13
Implied rate of return (100/15)	7.7%

To be sure, the prospective P/E ratio is more difficult to estimate because, by definition, it involves predicting earnings. Hence, we do not have the benefit of hindsight as we have in the case of the backward-looking P/E ratio. However, for analytical purposes, we trade off historical precision for relevance of information in predicting the future.

(d) Stock Splits

The PE multiple for a stock adjusts for stock splits. For example, assume that a company with 100,000 shares outstanding has an EPS of $2 and trades at $10 per share. The PE is 5. If it increases the number of shares outstanding through a 2:1 stock split, it will have 200,000 shares outstanding after the split, which will reduce its EPS to $1 per share. In these circumstances, the price of the stock should, in theory, fall to $5 per share after the split. The PE multiple remains 5.

EPS is reduced by one-half because there are double the number of outstanding shares. The drop in the EPS from $2 to $1 is not meaningful in and of itself. All that has happened is that the number of outstanding shares has increased from 100,000 to 200,000 and, therefore, net income is being divided by a larger figure. Each shareholder now owns two shares for every one share that they owned previously. The stockholder's *pro rata* share of corporate earnings is exactly the same. A stockholder who owned one share trading at $10 now owns two shares trading at $5 per share.

Example

Assume that a corporation has net income as follows and splits its common share 3:1. Jane Doe owns 5,000 shares. Then:

	Year 1 ($)	**Year 2 ($)**
Net income	15,000,000	15,000,000
Weighted average common shares outstanding	2,000,000	
EPS	7.50	
Weighted average common shares outstanding		6,000,000
EPS		2.50
Jane Doe's investment of 5,000 shares	**37,500**	**37,500**

(e) Reverse Stock Splits

Conversely, a company can increase its EPS by doing a reverse stock split or stock consolidation. For example, a company with 90,000 outstanding shares can consolidate its outstanding shares 1:3 and reduce the number of shares outstanding to 30,000. The number of outstanding shares is now that much lower, so the EPS of the company will increase proportionately if net income remains at the same level.

Example

Assume that a corporation has net income as follows and reverse splits its common share 3:1. Kathy owns 6,000 shares. Then:

	Year 1 ($)	Year 2 ($)
Net income	15,000,000	15,000,000
Weighted average common shares outstanding	3,000,000	
EPS	5	
Weighted average common shares outstanding		1,000,000
EPS		15
Jane Doe's investment of 6,000 shares	**30,000**	**30,000**

(f) **Profit Margins**

The profitability of a business depends, in part, upon its profit margin. The business may have a high or low profit margin depending upon the industry within which it operates and the segment of that industry that it occupies. We measure the profitability of a business by comparing its profits to sales, investment, and the market price of its shares.

There are actually three measures of profitability: gross profit, net profit, and net return on common equity. The most commonly used is net profit margin, which is net income before taxes as a percentage of sales:

Net Income before taxes/Sales

In Duggan Inc, for example:

$10,341/$62,954 = 16%

It is not possible to generalize about profit margins. The profit margin tells us how much of its sales dollars the enterprise keeps. However, a business may have a high profit margin but a low turnover of assets (for example, a high-end restaurant). Another business may be equally profitable by maintaining a low profit margin with a high turnover of assets (for example, a fast-food restaurant, such as McDonalds). Thus, although profit margin is a very useful figure, it is only the starting point in analyzing an enterprise's profitability.

There are many competitive and industry reasons that determine a company's profit margin. Businesses in highly competitive industries must maintain a profit margin commensurate with their competitors. Excessively high margins will drive away customers to competitors.

In monopolies and oligopolies, companies can maintain higher profit margins than in competitive industries. For example, a liquor licensing board that has a monopoly over all liquor, beer, and wine sales can set a high profit margin and not be concerned about its competitors going elsewhere to purchase their supplies. There is nowhere else to go except into the underground economy. Hence, governments like liquor monopolies because they provide a steady and predictable source of revenue from a captive market. During the COVID-19 pandemic, for example, Ontario locked down most businesses for health reasons but the LCBOs remained open.

Profit margin is determined by numerous factors, all the way from the top of the income statement (the top line) down to the bottom (the bottom line). An increase or decrease in any of the items in the income statement will ultimately affect the profit margin.

Profit margins are only one indicator of overall profitability. One is tempted to think that the higher the profit margin, the better off the company. In fact, low profit margins can also be very good if the company's turnover is high. For example, a company with $100 per unit profit margin that turns over its assets only once has a profitability of $100. In contrast, another company with a lower profit margin of $50 that can turn over its assets three times will earn $150. Apple Inc, for example, is a classic case of high gross margins in a highly competitive industry.

We see this also in the restaurant business. Some restaurants are high-end establishments with large profit margins on food and liquor. Patrons who go to such establishments usually stay for quite a while. Dinner guests, for example, may stay for a couple of hours or more. The restaurant's nightly turnover of tables may be only 1.5 or 2 sittings. In contrast, a lower-end fast-food service will have lower profit margins, but high turnover. The classic case is McDonalds, which may have ten or more sittings during the evening dinner hour. It can afford to earn less on each sale because it makes more sales to increase net earnings.

(g) Financial Yields

"Yield" is an important measurement for evaluating business enterprises in the private, for-profit sector. There are, however, many different aspects of yield and each of them looks at financial results from a different perspective. In combination, they are valuable tools of analysis.

(h) Dividend Yield

Dividend yield is the easiest of financial yields to understand. It is simply a company's annual dividend payout divided by its stock price. For example, if Company A pays an annual dividend of $2 per share and its stock is trading at $40, the dividend yield is 5 percent. Dividend yield tells us how much income an investor can expect to earn annually from their stock if the dividend remains constant.

A company's yield varies inversely to its stock price. As the price of stock goes up, the yield of its dividend will fall. In the above example, if Company A's stock price goes up to $50 and it maintains its payout at $2 per share, the yield falls to 4 percent. Conversely, as stock prices fall, yields go up.

Yields vary between industries and over time. We evaluate the dividend yield of stock by comparing it with the comparable yield on government bonds. However, not everyone is enamoured by dividend yields. Warren Buffett, for example, has never paid a dividend on his Berkshire Hathaway stock since it went public in 1985.[2] Nevertheless, the stock has done very well, giving its owners large capital gains.

Taxes are also a significant factor in evaluating dividend yields and capital gains. Not all investment dollars are equal. The Canadian income tax system, for example, taxes dividends, capital gains, and

---

2 See Warren Buffett's (Chairman) 2018 annual letter to shareholders of Berkshire Hathaway, Chapter 2.

interest income at different rates. At the top marginal rate of tax, for example, dividends are taxed at approximately 39 or 47 percent, capital gains at 27 percent, and interest at 54 percent (Ontario, 2019).[3] Thus, in comparing the yield on investments, it is important to consider the net after-tax yield, which is the amount that the investor actually keeps after paying the government its share in taxes.

(i) Earnings Yield

We can also look at a company's performance by measuring its earnings yield against the payout yield of its dividends. Earnings yield is the company's annual earnings divided by its share price, also known as earning per share (EPS). For example, if Company B has EPS of $5 per share and its stock is trading at $60, the earnings yield is 8.3 percent.

Earnings yield tells us how well the company is doing, regardless of its payout ratio. Berkshire Hathaway, for example, has a high earnings yield, but pays out no dividends. In these circumstances, investors must make their decisions based upon their particular requirements and other economic considerations. For example, an income investor may prefer stock with a high dividend yield because of their cash requirements. A younger and more aggressive investor may prefer zero dividend yield and invest for longer-term capital gains. In Canada, the income investor would be taxed at approximately 39 percent on eligible dividends from public companies. In contrast, the growth investor would eventually be taxed at 27 percent on capital gains, but only when they dispose, or are deemed to dispose, of the stock. Thus, in addition to the differential tax rates that apply, there is also the deferral value in the time value of money (see Chapter 5, Time Value of Money).

(j) Cash Flow Yield

A company's financial statements are prepared using accrual accounting principles. Accrual accounting requires a company to recognize its revenues and expenses when it earns them or incurs its costs, regardless of when it actually collects or pays out cash. For example,

3 *Income Tax Act*, RSC, 1985, c 1.

if a company sells $100 of merchandise on ninety days credit, it will recognize its sales revenue of $100 immediately even though it may not collect its accounts receivable for ninety days.

Cash flow measures the actual amount of cash that a company receives or pays out in the course of its operations. Cash measurement is, of course, much more certain than income measured on accrual principles. Hence, cash flow is considered a more reliable indicator of corporate operations. At the end of the day, a company pays dividends from its cash. Hence, cash flow is an important measure of the safety of future dividends.

A company's cash flow yield is its free cash flow per share divided by its share price. Free cash flow is the amount of cash that the company has after it pays out all of its expenses and expenditures on capital assets.

(k) Bond Yields

Bond yields are more complicated calculations.[4] Bond yield refers to the amount that an investor can expect to earn on their investment in a bond over its term. An investor's bond yield to maturity comprises two components: periodic interest payments and the capital gain or loss when they redeem the bond.

In the simplest case, where an investor buys a bond at par, the yield to maturity is equal to the coupon rate on the bond. For example, if an investor buys a $1,000 bond at its face value when it is initially issued and the bond pays 6 percent interest annually, the yield to maturity is 6 percent. Thus, the yield is equal to the coupon interest rate on the bond without any capital gain or loss on maturity.

Where an investor purchases a bond at a price above or below its par value, the yield to maturity will be made up of the interest components and the capital gain or loss. In the preceding example, if the investor purchased the bond at $950, the yield to maturity would be made up of the 6 percent ($60) annual coupon interest rate and the capital gain of $50, upon maturity. The capital gain is the

4 See Chapter 8, Liabilities.

difference between the investor's cost of $950 and the redemption price of $1,000 at par.

As with the earnings yield on stock, the maturity yield on bonds fluctuates. Bond yields move inversely to bond prices. As interest rates rise, the capital value of the bond will fall in order to maintain parity between the bond's coupon rate and market rates of interest. Similarly, when interest rates fall, the capital value of bonds will increase in order to equalize the effective yield on the bond coupon with current market interest rates. As bond yields fluctuate, stock investors also make decisions to rationalize stock earnings yields with bond yields.

(I) Price to Book Value

The price to book value ratio is a conservative measure of the relationship between the price of shares and the book value of its assets minus liabilities of a company. Stated another way, the price to book value looks at the relationship between stock prices and the company's equity, which is assets minus liabilities, which are valued on a hybrid of historical costs and fair value.

2. Liquidity Ratios

The balance sheet provides a lot of useful information concerning an enterprise's financial liquidity, solvency, leverage, and debt to equity relationships. Each ratio provides us with a different snapshot of the enterprise's financial standing.

Liquidity ratios measure the ability of a company to satisfy its financial obligations in a timely manner. Thus, these ratios measure liquidity, as opposed to long-term solvency. Liquidity ratios supplement information provided by the cash flow statement.

There are several liquidity ratios, but the two most commonly used ones are:

1) Current (working capital) ratio; and
2) Quick ratio.

(a) Current Ratio

The current ratio is calculated as:

Current Assets/Current Liabilities

Current assets include cash (and cash equivalents), accounts receivable, marketable securities, inventory, and short-term prepayments. Depending on a company's industry, there may be a time lag between the manufacture of a product into inventory, which will become accounts receivable when sold, and its ultimate conversion into collected cash. The time lag from inventory to cash may be 120 days or longer.

Current liabilities include accounts payable, accrued liabilities, and other short-term liabilities that will come due during the year.

Duggan Inc's current ratio is:

$12,451/$12,146 = 1:1

Thus, Duggan has just about enough current assets to be able to pay for its current obligations as they become due. The margin of safety is minimal. Any downturn in Duggan's cash collection from its business operations may cause financial stress. For example, Duggan may have to resort to short-term borrowing or credit facilities to cover its current liabilities.

A more conservative assessment of Duggan Inc's current assets would exclude its deferred tax assets, as they can be delayed for tax adjustments in the future.

The conventional view is that a working capital ratio of 2:1 is "good" because there is ample safety margin. In fact, there is no such thing as "good" in evaluating ratios. Much depends upon the nature of the business and its industry, access to credit lines, predictability, and stability of cash flows. Safety margin comes at a price: current assets reduce risk but produce minimal (if any) income.

(b) The Quick Ratio

The quick ratio is a more stringent measure of liquidity than the current ratio. The quick ratio is:

Monetary Assets/Current Liabilities

Monetary assets include cash, cash equivalents, marketable securities, and net accounts receivable. These assets are the most easily and quickly convertible into cash. Receivables can usually be turned into cash within thirty to sixty days. Hence, we sometimes refer to the quick ratio as an "acid test," because it tells us how quickly a company can meet its obligations without having to sell its inventory and, then, collect its receivables.

Monetary assets exclude inventory and prepaid expenses. (*Note*: prepaid expenses do not convert into cash but are amounts that the company pays in advance and represent an outflow of cash.)

Duggan's quick ratio is:

$7,449/$12,146 = 0.6

The ratio is on the low side. A ratio of 1:1 would be more conservative in most cases.

3. Solvency Ratios

Solvency ratios measure financial leverage, that is, the manner in which a corporation uses debt to finance its capital structure. Thus, solvency ratios focus on a longer term than liquidity ratios.

A company can improve its ROE by using debt capital if it earns more from the debt than its cost. For example, if a company can borrow at 6 percent interest and use the money to earn 10 percent, it will enhance its net income by the amount of the spread (net of taxes) between its borrowing cost and the earnings rate. The reverse is also true. A company with interest costs that are higher than its earnings rate will diminish its ROE. Debt also increases risk. Thus, a firm must balance the benefits of leverage against risk.

(a) Debt/Equity Ratio

The debt/equity ratio is the standard measure of leverage. The ratio measures the relative use of debt and equity in a company's capital structure. The formula for the debt/equity ratio is:

Long-Term Debt/Equity

Duggan Inc's debt/equity ratio is:

$13,091/$17,134 = 0.8:1

Thus, debt represents 43 percent of the company's overall financial structure. Too much debt can be risky, particularly if earnings are not stable and predictable. There is no absolute measure of the right amount of debt for an enterprise. Much depends upon the stability of earnings. Utilities, for example, can carry a lot of debt because their earnings are stable and predictable, and some are monopolies. Too little debt can lead to lost financial opportunities.

(b) Return on Capital

A company's return on capital is:

Net Income/Total Capital

A company with strong earnings can have a low return on capital if it carries a high level of debt. Both short- and long-term debt can be used to leverage earnings if the cost of capital is less than the rate of earnings. There are variations of the debt/equity ratio depending upon how one measures "debt." Some analysts include all debt; others include only long-term debt. Since the working-capital ratio measures the ability of a company to pay its short-term debt, it is usually more meaningful to measure only long-term debt when measuring leverage.

(c) Financial Leverage

Another way to measure leverage is to see how much of the total assets of a company are financed through equity. The financial leverage ratio is:

Total Assets/Equity

In the case of Duggan Inc, for example, the financial leverage is:

$42,371/$17,134 = 2.47

Thus, the company has 2.5 times as much in assets as its owner's equity; the remainder is financed by debt.

(d) Times Interest Earned

Times interest earned, or interest coverage, is a way to measure solvency that is of particular interest to the company's long-term creditors. The ratio measures the degree of safety that the creditors have from the earnings of the company.

Times interest earned is:

(Net Income before Interest + Taxes)/Interest Expense

Duggan Inc's interest coverage is:

$10,674/$333 = 32

Duggan's creditors are very well secured by its earnings. The company is earning thirty-two times what it needs to pay its creditors.

Stated another way, interest coverage tells us how much a company's income can deteriorate without prejudicing the creditors or putting them at risk. (*Note*: we add back taxes to the net income because interest is a deductible expense for tax purposes. Thus, taxes do not affect the company's ability to pay interest.)

(e) Preferred Dividends

There are other variations on interest coverage and solvency measures. Some analysts, for example, will add dividends on preferred shares to the interest expense in the denominator. Although preferred share dividends are not fixed legal obligations, they represent, in a business sense, obligations that a company will not want to default on. Hence, from a business perspective, interest expense and preferred share dividends are both "fixed" obligations.

4. Activity Ratios

Activity ratios measure a firm's efficiency in utilizing its assets. We measure activity by comparing the relationship between two connected and relevant numbers to see how effectively or efficiently the business is operating. As a group, we refer to these as "turnover" ratios.

(a) Asset Turnover

The broadest turnover ratio is that of the company's total assets, usually at the average of the opening and the closing balance of assets. This ratio measures how efficiently the company uses its total assets. The formula for asset turnover is:

Sales Revenue/Average Assets

The average of Duggan Inc's assets for 20-2 and 20-1 is $41,261. Hence, its asset turnover is:

$62,954/$41,261 = 1.53

The higher the asset turnover, the more efficiently the business is using its assets to generate sales. If a company can use a small base of assets to generate large volume of profitable sales, it will be operating efficiently.

(b) Accounts Receivable Turnover

Accounts receivable turnover measures the receivables that a company carries in relation to its sales. The formula for receivables turnover is:

Sales Revenue/Average Receivables

Duggan's average *net* receivables for 20-2 and 20-1 are $5,280.

Hence, Duggan's accounts receivable turnover is:

$62,954/$5,280 = 11.9

The higher the receivables turnover, the better the company is in terms of converting its sales into cash. A short period for outstanding accounts receivable is in the company's interest as it does not have to tie up its capital but can use it in its business operations. For example, a receivables turnover of 10 implies that the accounts receivable is outstanding for 10 percent of the year—that is, thirty-six days.

As an absolute number, the number of days outstanding is not particularly helpful. We must compare the number with the actual terms of sale to see whether the company is performing efficiently. For example, if the terms of sale are thirty days for net payment, then thirty-six days of actual outstanding receivables reflects well on the company's sales and credit operations. If the terms of sale are net ten days, the thirty-six days of outstanding receivables indicates a cash collection problem.

(c) Inventory Turnover

Another way to measure the efficiency of asset usage is inventory turnover, which measures the amount of inventory through the volume of goods produced and sold. The formula for inventory turnover is:

Cost of Goods Sold/Average Inventory

Duggan's average inventory for 20-2 and 20-1 is $4,098

Hence, Duggan's inventory turnover is:

29,890/4,098 = 7.3

This ratio tells us how quickly an enterprise is consuming its inventory. The higher the ratio, the faster the consumption of inventory. A high turnover ratio implies that the company does not have its capital tied up in inventory for a long time. For example, an inventory turnover of 15 implies that the business holds its inventory for approximately twenty-four days of sales.

E. SUMMARY

1. Users of Financial Statements

Bankers	Assess viability for loans. Evaluate cash flow and ability to repay loans.
Shareholders	Determine ability of enterprise to maintain profits. Decide whether to maintain, sell, or purchase equity in company.
Managers	Assess if bonus is owing to them and evaluation of basis of performance and profits.
Employees	Assess company's performance, in which they have invested, and amount of bonus, if any.
Suppliers	Assess ability of company to pay its debts.
CRA	Determine whether company has complied with tax laws in preparation of its tax financial statements.
Potential investors	Assess current situation and predict future cash flows, rate of return on investment, and price-earnings multiple in context of market conditions.

2. Summary of Financial Statement Ratios

	Profitability Ratios		
1	Return on equity (ROE)	Net income/Equity	Is the starting point of all ratios and is a measure of overall performance of the enterprise.
2	Return on assets (ROA)	Net income/Total assets	Measures net profit margin as a function of asset turnover.
3	Profit margin (PM)	Net income/Sales	Measures amount of ***after-tax*** income as a percentage of sales
4	Gross profit margin (GPM)	Gross profit/Sales	Measures relationship between sales prices and cost of goods sold
5	Earnings per share (EPS)	(Net income — Pref. dividend)/# of common shares	Measures earnings for common shareholders.
6	Cash flow per common share	CFFO — Preferred stock dividend preferences/ Weighted average common shares o/s	Measures how much cash the enterprise generated for every outstanding common share outstanding.
	Liquidity Ratios	Important in corporate law restrictions on distributions.	
7	Current ratio (CR)	Current assets/Current liabilities	Measures liquidity of company to pay its current liabilities. Shows coverage for every dollar of current liabilities.
8	Quick ratio (QR)	Cash and liquid assets/Current liabilities	Stringent test of company's liquidity to pay current liabilities.

9	Cash interest coverage	Cash flow from operations before interest and taxes (CFFO)/Interest expense	Measures ability to pay interest on debt from operations.
	Solvency Ratios	Important in corporate law restrictions on distributions.	
10	Debt to asset ratio (DA)	Total debt/Total assets	Measures extent to which creditors are cushioned against potential decrease in asset values.
11	Debt to equity (DE)	Total debt/Total equity	For every $ of shareholder equity, the $ contributed by creditors. This ratio indicates financial leverage (FL).
12	Times interest earned (TIE)	EBIT/Interest expense	Measures ability of business to generate sufficient earnings to pay its interest on debt. Measure of safety net for creditors.
13	Financial leverage	Assets/Equity	The larger this ratio, the more the company has been financed with debt
	Activity Ratios	Evaluate corporate management.	
14	Inventory turnover (ITO)	Cost of goods sold/Inventory	Low value indicates slow-moving inventory. Very high ratio indicates possibility of inventory shortages.
15	Average collection period of receivables (ACP)	Accounts receivable/Average daily sales	Average daily sales equal total sales divided by 365 days.
16	Average payment period of accounts payable	Accounts payable/Average daily purchases	Measures ability of entity to pay its short term (current) debt.
17	Fixed asset utilization	Sales/Net fixed assets	Measures income-generating ability of investment in fixed assets.

18	Income tax rate (ITR)	Income tax expense/EBT	EBT is earnings before taxes. Measures the effective tax rate paid.
	Value Ratios		
19	Book Value	Common shareholders'/equity/Common shares outstanding	Measures book value of each common share. Every common share outstanding has a book value of $XX based on financial statement values, which may be historical and fair values.
20	ROE = PM×AT×FL	Dupont Formula	Breaks down ROE into its component contributors.
21	Dividend payout ratio (DP)	Dividends per share/EPS	Shows percentage of earnings distributed as dividends
22	Cash dividend coverage	CFFO/Total cash dividends	Ability to sustain dividends from operations after payment of taxes and interest.
23	Cash quality of income	CFFO/Net income	How readily enterprise converts net income into cash. Low number suggests net income significantly exceeds cash flow.
24	Dividend yield (YLD)	Dividends per share/Common share price	Measures return via dividends relative to share price.
25	Price-earnings ratio	Market price per share/EPS	Measures return on investment based on stock price. For every $ of EPS, the multiple in market price.

Chapter 16: Accounting and Law

A. OVERVIEW

Accountants and auditors can be liable to users of financial statements. Liability may be in contract, tort, securities, or tax law. The scope and extent of their liability depends upon the branch of law, the particular users of the financial statements, the nature of the claims, statutory structures, and public policy considerations.

Although public accountants perform a wide variety of services for their clients, their primary function, and the one that most frequently gets them into legal trouble, is auditing financial statements. Accountants are the traditional target in business lawsuits. This is because most business failures, whether of public or private companies, involve some aspect of their financials. The plaintiff might complain that the statements were prepared without adequate care in the audit process or that the auditors misapplied GAAP or IFRS. The plaintiff may allege that the statements are misleading, whether innocently or fraudulently, and caused the plaintiff (or class of plaintiffs) financial harm.

However, there is another more practical reason why accountants are often in the crosshairs of plaintiffs' lawyers. Accounting firms do not like to be dragged into court, where litigation can extend for years and attract attention in the business press. In many cases, it is the insurance coverage that attracts plaintiffs' lawyers, like bees to honey. Thus, accountants and accounting firms are amenable to settlement, if the settlement is within their professional insurance limits, and their legal fees are insured. In the final analysis, it is the insurance company that loses. However, it makes up its losses through increased premiums and tax write-offs. Ultimately, taxpayers bear the settlement costs.

For example, in the 1990s, the "Big Five" (originally the "Big Eight" and now reduced to the "Big Four") faced more than USD$30 billion in legal actions against them. Laventhol & Horwarth, the seventh largest accounting firm at the time, declared bankruptcy in 1990 because it could not meet its liability claims. In four years, the "Big Six" (as they then became) paid out USD$1.7 billion in securities fraud cases.

The current debacle of financial statement manipulation is merely a variation on old themes. Accounting and auditing standards induce behavioural responses from the users of financial statements. The essential question is whether the standards are ahead of the creativity of enterprising manipulators and financial regulators.

Although accounting fraud is sometimes a problem in the securities markets, the more significant risk of financial misstatement is auditor bias. This risk arises when the auditor of a company also advises on consulting matters, which puts pressure on the auditor to accommodate the client on its financial statements or risk losing the lucrative consulting or tax work. This creates a conflict between the self-interest of the audit firm and the public interest of investors.

Ultimately, the integrity of the financial markets depends upon the unbiased authentication of public financial information and fair audit opinions. This requires regulatory and judicial rules that discourage, and penalize, inappropriate financial reporting.

B. THE ENRON DEBACLE

The Enron scandal represented the most serious consequences ever visited upon an accounting firm and its ultimate demise. The scandal, which destroyed a reputable accounting firm, illustrates the magnitude of financial problems in the capital markets, and the human and financial tragedy that results from inadequate auditing and financial reporting.

Enron, an energy company, was formed in 1985 after merging Houston Natural Gas and InterNorth. Enron's original accounting in its natural gas business was quite simple. In each time period, the company listed actual costs of supplying the gas and actual revenues received from selling it.

However, under new executive leadership of Jeffrey Skilling, the company adopted mark-to-market accounting,

> claiming that it would represent "true economic value." . . . Mark-to-market accounting requires that once a long-term contract has been signed, income is estimated as the present value of net future cash flow. Often, the viability of these contracts and their related costs were difficult to estimate. Owing to the large discrepancies between reported profits and cash, investors were typically given false or misleading reports.[1]

For example:

> For one contract, in July 2000, Enron and Blockbuster Video signed a 20-year agreement to introduce on-demand entertainment to various U.S. cities by year's end. After several pilot projects, Enron claimed estimated profits of more than $110 million from the deal, even though analysts questioned the technical viability and market demand of the service. When the network failed to work, Blockbuster withdrew from the contract. Enron continued to claim future profits, even though the deal resulted in a loss.[2]

The company used special purpose entities (SPEs) to hide billions of dollars of debt off its balance sheet. A SPE is a fenced organization having limited pre-defined purposes and a legal personality that are essentially limited partnerships created with outside parties. Companies typically use SPEs to isolate the corporate entity from financial risk. Enron abused the practice by using SPEs as dump sites for its troubled assets. Transferring those assets to SPEs meant that they

1 "Enron Scandal" *Wikipedia*, online: https://en.wikipedia.org/wiki/Enron_scandal.
2 *Ibid.*

were kept off Enron's financials, making its losses look less severe than they really were.

Enron's Chief Financial Officer (Andrew Fastow) and other executives misled Enron's board of directors and the audit committee on its high-risk accounting practices and also pressured its auditors, Arthur Andersen LLP, to ignore the issues.

As the boom years came to an end, Enron faced increased competition in the energy-trading business and the company's profits shrank rapidly:

> [T]he company's stock price, which achieved a high of US$90.75 per share in mid-2000, plummeted to less than $1 by the end of November 2001. The U.S. Securities and Exchange Commission (SEC) began an investigation ... and on December 2, 2001, Enron filed for bankruptcy under Chapter 11 of the United States Bankruptcy Code. Enron's $63.4 billion in assets made it the largest corporate bankruptcy in U.S. history until the WorldCom scandal the next year.[3]

Throughout the years, Arthur Andersen LLP had served not only as Enron's auditor but also as a consultant for the company. During the fall of Enron, Andersen instructed its employees to destroy documents relating to Enron after they learned they would soon be investigated by the SEC. Andersen was charged on 6 March 2002 for obstructing justice. The firm was convicted of illegally destroying documents relevant to the SEC investigation, fined USD$500,000, and put on probation for five years. The conviction destroyed Andersen's reputation. Andersen was also barred from auditing public companies, which, effectively, closed the firm.

The conviction was overturned three years later by the United States Supreme Court. In a unanimous decision, the Supreme Court held that the jury had been improperly instructed at trial, which allowed them to convict Andersen without proof that the firm knew it had broken the law, or that there had been a link to any official proceeding

---

3 *Ibid.*

that prohibited the destruction of documents. Chief Justice William Rehnquist, who wrote the opinion for the court, said that the instructions were so vague that they "simply failed to convey the requisite consciousness of wrongdoing. Indeed, it is striking how little culpability the instructions required." Rehnquist CJ also expressed grave skepticism at the government's definition of "corrupt persuasion"—persuasion with an improper purpose even without knowing an act is unlawful.[4]

However, the decision came too late to save the firm.[5] The damage had been done and Andersen was destroyed. Thousands lost their jobs and there were lawsuits against the firm seeking $25 billion from Enron's investors and former employees.

Many executives at Enron were indicted for a variety of charges and some were later sentenced to prison. Enron employees and shareholders received limited returns in lawsuits, despite losing billions in pensions and stock prices.

As a consequence of the Enron and other (for example, Tyco International plc, and WorldCom) scandals, which shattered investor confidence in the trustworthiness of corporate financial statements, the United States enacted new regulations and legislation in 2002 to expand the accuracy of financial reporting for public companies. One piece of legislation, the *Sarbanes-Oxley Act*, known as SOX, increased penalties for destroying, altering, or fabricating records in federal investigations or for attempting to defraud shareholders.[6] SOX also increased the accountability of auditing firms to remain unbiased and independent of their clients.

---

4 *Arthur Andersen LLP v United States*, 544 US 696 (2005).

5 See James Kelly, "The Power of an Indictment and the Demise of Arthur Andersen" (2006) 48 *South Texas Law Review* 509; Ellen S Podgor, "The Impact of Criminal Sanctions on Corporate Misconduct" (2007) 2 *Journal of Business & Technology Law* 119; and KR Taylor, "The Obstruction of Justice Nexus Requirement after *Arthur Andersen* and Sarbanes–Oxley" (2008) 93 *Cornell Law Review* 401.

6 The Act took its name from its two sponsors: Paul S Sarbanes (D-Md) and Michael G Oxley (R-Ohio).

C. SOX (2002)

Section 302 of SOX mandates that senior corporate officers personally certify in writing that the company's financial statements "comply with SEC disclosure requirements and fairly present in all material aspects the operations and financial condition of the issuer." Officers who sign off on financial statements that they know to be inaccurate are subject to criminal penalties, including prison terms.

Section 404 requires that management and auditors establish internal controls and reporting methods to ensure the adequacy of those controls.

Section 802 contains three rules that affect recordkeeping. The first deals with destruction and falsification of records. The second strictly defines the retention period for storing records. The third outlines the specific business records that companies need to store, which includes electronic communications.

D. ARCHIMEDES, A SCIENTIFIC FRAUD AUDITOR

As we shall see below, auditors often invoke science to detect fraud. In the first century BCE, for example, Archimedes uncovered a fraud in the manufacture of a golden crown commissioned by Hiero II. According to the legend, Hiero II of Syracuse asked Archimedes to determine if a crown he had ordered was really made of gold. He suspected it was made of a cheaper metal. Suspecting that the goldsmith might have replaced some of the gold given to him by an equal weight of silver, Hiero asked Archimedes to determine whether the wreath was pure gold. Because the wreath was a holy object dedicated to the gods, Archimedes could not disturb the wreath in any way.

Archimedes happened to go for a bath, and, on getting into the tub, he noted that the more his body sank into it, the more water ran out over the tub. He realized that he could measure how much water the crown would displace, and thus calculate its mass. The mass of the crown could then be compared to the mass of an equal volume of pure gold, and if the numbers did not match, then the goldsmith had lied. According to legend, he jumped out of the tub and rushed home naked, crying with a loud voice that he had found what he was seeking: in Greek, "Eureka, eureka."

E. SELECTED ACCOUNTING SCANDALS

Financial statements are an intrinsic risk in the securities markets. The risk derives from two separate sources: behavioural responses to inadequate accounting standards and auditor bias in opining on financial statements. The history of securities fraud is long and reveals the innovative skills of those who engage in financial statement manipulations. There follows a sample of some of the schemes.

1. The South Sea Bubble

The South Sea Bubble scandal marks a watershed event in British economic history. The scandal had features that became common to many subsequent scandals and set the regulatory agenda for many decades. In 1720, the House of Lords passed the South Sea Bill, which allowed the South Sea Company "a monopoly in trade with South America. The company underwrote the English National Debt . . . on a promise of 5% interest from the Government."[7]

There was rampant speculation and the country's economy seemed to boom, until the "bubble" burst. The stocks crashed and investors went bankrupt, leading to suicides and lost savings in all walks of life, including among the Clergy, Bishops, Gentry, Porters, and ladies' maids. Across the board, the country "suffered a catastrophic loss of money and property."[8]

Investors were misled, politicians bribed, and the promoters paid dividends out of capital. Even as brilliant a scientist as Sir Isaac Newton was taken in and lost a fortune. He is reputed to have commented: *"I can calculate the movement of stars, but not the madness of men."*

---

7 Ellen Castelow, "The South Sea Bubble," *Historic UK: The History and Heritage Accomodation Guide*, online: www.historic-uk.com/HistoryUK/HistoryofEngland/South-Sea-Bubble.

8 *Ibid.*

2. The Great Crash (1929)

American fraudsters also played their role in exploiting flexible accounting rules. In drafting the *Securities Act* of 1933, the first legislation to control securities manipulations, legislators attributed the overvaluation of stocks prior to the Great Crash in 1929 to accounting valuation rules. The main Stock Exchanges, in conjunction with the American Institute of Public Accountants, issued guidelines requiring audited financial statements.

However, the 1933 Act was only the first stage of further regulatory tightening, which continues to this day. See, for example, the Enron scandal (October 2001), which eventually led to the bankruptcy of the Enron Corporation, an American energy company based in Houston, Texas, and the unfortunate *de facto* dissolution of Arthur Andersen, one of the most respected accountancy partnerships. In addition to being the largest bankruptcy reorganization in American history at that time, Enron was cited as the biggest audit failure.

3. McKesson & Robbins

McKesson & Robbins (M&R) was a diversified pharmaceutical company in the United States that constructed a Canadian operation with fictitious assets totalling $17 million. One of the greatest accounting frauds of the late 1930s, the M&R case illustrates management's response to auditing standards and the changes that followed the debacle.

The case involved Philip Musica, a high school dropout, twice convicted of commercial fraud for which he did time in prison. However, upon his release from prison in 1924, Musica reincarnated himself as F Donald Coster. He then conferred upon himself two advanced degrees, a MD, and a PhD. In order to assume the appropriate aura of respectability, he announced that his two doctorates were from Heidelberg University, the most elite educational institution in Germany at the time. Coster then acquired M&R, became its president, and embarked upon a massive fraud that lasted for twelve years until 1937.

Coster's fraud was conceptually simple. He wanted to make the company look successful and profit from its publicly listed shares. To do so, he formed a Canadian company and purchased five manual typewriters, which he used to create a fictitious financial empire. He typed out purchase orders, sales invoices, and shipping documents, each always on a different typewriter. The company showed substantial fictitious inventories and accounts receivable on its balance sheet. Coster told the auditors that M&R did not have physical possession of the goods because vendors kept the goods in their own warehouses for direct shipment to customers. M&R issued cheques to the vendors, purportedly for payment of the goods. However, Coster intercepted the cheques.

Of course, M&R had to comply with the legal formalities of preparing financial statements and making them appear respectable. Coster retained one of the most respectable accounting firms of the day, Price Waterhouse (PW), to audit it. PW filed a "clean" audit report.[9] As a director of the company later testified at trial: "I just took it that when you put *PW* on the bottom of a statement, it was sterling silver, and everything went."[10] The markets bought the fiction.

Coster and his cohorts absconded with $2.8 million. He never stood trial for the fraud as he committed suicide before the authorities could indict him.

The auditing standards of the day did not require auditors to "kick the tires" by physically examining inventories or confirming accounts receivables to validate financial statements. Thus, Coster managed to conceal his fraud for twelve years, always showing substantial inventories and accounts receivable from ever increasing sales.

The bubble ultimately burst. An SEC investigation highlighted PW's failure to detect the fraud. At the SEC's prodding, the accounting

---

9 See Chapter 14, Reports on Financial Statements, for the meaning of "clean" audit report.

10 William E Bealing, Mark W Dirsmith & Timothy Fogarty, "Early Regulatory Actions by the SEC: An Institutional Theory Perspective on the Dramaturgy of Political Exchanges" (1996) 21:4 *Accounting, Organizations and Society* 317, online: www.sciencedirect.com/science/article/pii/0361368295000240 (citing a 1982 Brief at 140); William E Bealing & Edward Pitingolo, "Same Song, Same Dance: Evidence of Patterns in Securities and Exchange Commission Funding" (2015) 6:2 *Review of Business and Finance Studies* 1, online: www.theibfr2.com/RePEc/ibf/rbfstu/rbfs-v6n2-2015/RBFS-V6N2-2015-1.pdf.

profession changed its audit standards to require physical inspection of all material inventories stated on the financial statements. The new standards governed receivables and inventory verification, audit reports, and appointments, but limited responsibility to detect fraud and manipulation (SEC release ASR No 19).

4. Great Salad Oil Swindle

The problems of inventory manipulation did not disappear with the new standard of physical observation of inventories as we see in the Great Salad Oil Swindle. Anthony "Tino" DeAngelis controlled Allied Crude Vegetable Oil and Refining Corp (Allied). Pursuant to the new auditing standards of physical inventory observation, the auditors physically examined Allied's barrels of oil to confirm that they existed. However, like Archimedes, Tino understood physics. He falsified his inventory records to create phantom amounts of salad oil by filling the oil barrels with 90 percent water and floating 10 percent of oil on the top. A superficial physical examination of the barrels showed that each contained oil. Allied also reported owning more holding tanks than actually existed. As the auditors moved from tank to tank, company employees moved behind them and repainted the numbers on the tanks that the auditors had previously examined. Hence, not only did the auditors count water as oil, but they counted the same water as oil more than once! The plan worked, until an astute auditor put a dipstick into one of the barrels to check the oil.[11]

5. Crazy Eddie Inc

The Crazy Eddie Inc story had a novel twist on conventional white-collar fraud, inventory manipulation, and public offerings. Crazy Eddie

11 "Salad Oil Scandal" *Wikipedia*, online: https://en.wikipedia.org/wiki/Salad_Oil_Scandal; Bryan Taylor, "How the Salad Oil Swindle of 1963 Nearly Crippled the NYSE" *Warren Buffet Tracker*, online: warrenbuffetttracker.com/stocks/how-the-salad-oil; Bryan Taylor, "The Fiftieth Anniversary of JFK and the Great Salad Oil Swindle" *GLocal Financial Data* blog (19 November 2013), online: www.globalfinancialdata.com/the-fiftieth.

Inc operated a chain of consumer electronic stores. Eddie Antar served as an officer, director, and employee of the corporation. The frauds, which spanned eighteen years, involved three phases.

Phase 1:1969–1979	Antar and his associates skimmed and under-reported income, which amounted to tax fraud.
Phase 2:1980–1984	Antar gradually reduced his income skimming in order to increase the company's profit growth in preparation for the company's initial public offering.
Phase 3:1984–1987	As a public company, Crazy Eddie *overstated* its income to help insiders dump stock at inflated prices, using a variety of fraudulent mechanisms, such as overstating inventory assets to inflate reported profits. The company inflated its 1985 profits by USD$2 million. The fraudulent schemes turned a substantial loss into a $20.6 million profit.

Even by criminal fraud standards, the Crazy Eddie Inc case was novel in that Antar stole less each year by skimming, and paid more in taxes, all with the objective of committing a bigger fraud in the securities markets. Securities fraud was more profitable than merely skimming cash sales, tax evasion, and paying employees "off the books." Antar anticipated getting a "bigger bang for the buck" by inflating earnings as a public company.

Antar understood the workings of the public securities markets as, indeed, he should have, having passed the CPA examination with a 90 percent average and scoring in the top 1 percent in the country. As he explained the math for those uninitiated in securities valuation:

> When a public company reports a profit, those earnings are divided by each share of common stock outstanding to compute earnings per share (EPS). If a company reports a $1 million profit and has 1 million shares outstanding, its EPS is $1 per share [see Chapter 15, Interpretation of Financial Statements].
>
> A public company's stock trades at a multiple of earnings known as the "price earnings ratio" (P/E ratio). Hence, if the stock trades at $30 per share, its P/E ratio is 30.
>
> If the company's management could inflate its earnings by $1 million or $1 per share, it would report earnings of $2 million, or

$2 EPS. Assuming the P/E ratio remains at 30, if the earnings were now $2 per share, the price per share would increase to $60. The company's market capitalization would increase by $30 million ($30 price per share × one million shares outstanding = $30 million). All things being equal, inflating earnings by only $1 million or $1 per share would add $30 million to the company's market cap. Insiders can then pocket $30 per share of ill-gotten gains.

The Antar family owned all of the shares of the company before it went public. The math was simple. A small one-million-dollar deception would multiply into $30 million of fictitious wealth! By comparison, assuming a 30 percent tax rate, skimming one million dollars from cash sales would only save about $300,000 of income taxes. Securities fraud offered a higher rate of return than mere tax evasion! Furthermore, faster growing companies are often rewarded with higher P/E ratios by the stock market, which translates into even higher stock prices, demonstrating the importance of proper allocation of fraud-tainted funds.

Hence, Antar had to stop the illegal skimming of cash sales before Crazy Eddie's IPO. As a public company, Crazy Eddie would need to report growing profits, so investors would be willing to pay higher prices for its stock. So, ironically, to prepare for their infamous future as a public company, Crazy Eddie had to "legitimize" its business by "going legit" before it could go criminal.[12]

F. PRINCIPLES OF LIABILITY

There are various types of reports on financial statements, each of which specifies the nature and extent of work done by the auditors, the standards applied, and the assurance given (see Chapter 14, Reports on Financial Statements). Liability for each of these types of

12 Sam Antar, "Crazy Eddie Fraud" *White Collar Fraud*, online: https://whitecollarfraud.com/crazy-eddie/crazy-eddie-fraud/; see also "Crazy Eddie, Inc. Financial Fraud Case Essay" *Academiscope*, online: www.academicscope.com/crazy-eddie-inc-financial-fraud-case-essay.

reports also varies. The less intense the involvement of the auditor in preparing the report, the higher the threshold for legal liability.

Audit reports affect confidence. They alert the reader to the degree of confidence or reliance that they can place on the financial statements. They are the centrepiece of the financial communication process. Although they are short, they contain valuable information. The auditors' report is the basis of liability for public accountants.

1. Scope of Engagement

The first consideration in determining liability is the scope of the task for which the business retains the auditor. The auditors' potential liability is highest when the auditor is retained for a complete unrestricted audit. Potential exposure diminishes as the terms of engagement reduces the scope of the work that the auditor is asked to perform.

For example, the objective of an audit engagement is to enable the independent professional public accountant to issue an opinion on the fairness of the financial statements. A clean audit opinion provides reasonable assurance that the financial statements are free of material misstatement and are in accordance with Canadian accounting and auditing standards. In contrast, a "review engagement" entails less detailed examination and no testing of financial transactions, and is cheaper than an audit. It is basically enquiry, analysis of procedures, and discussions with management. Hence, the accountant's exposure to liability is lower than for a complete audit with an unqualified (unmodified) assurance opinion.

2. Causation of Damage

To establish liability and collect damages from an accountant, the plaintiff must prove that the auditor's negligence or intentional misconduct caused the financial damage. The plaintiff must also establish that they are within the class of persons who warrant protection from the auditor's negligence that results from the audit.

3. Duty of Care

There are two preliminary issues to decide in accounting malpractice litigation:

1) Did the accountant owe the plaintiff or class of plaintiffs a duty of care in the preparation of an independent audit of the client's financial statements? and
2) Did the accountant breach the appropriate standard of care in conducting the independent audit?

These are fundamental and basic questions of tort liability.

However, they have a slightly different hue in cases involving accounting malpractice. Clients commission audits for a variety of purposes. Some must be audited. For example, public companies must be audited under statutory and regulatory requirements of the *Canada Business Corporations Act*[13]and the *Ontario Securities Act*. Others request audits to establish their financial credibility with lenders and government agencies, such as the Canada Revenue Agency and regulatory rate setting commissions. Indeed, a so-called clean opinion from one of the "Big Four" accounting firms is often the *sine qua non* for admission into the capital markets.

Fraudsters also understand the value of audited financial statements and will rely on the stamp of approval of one of the "Big Four" to perpetrate securities frauds in the public markets. See, for example, the statements of the director of McKesson & Robbins, "I just took it that when you put *PW* on the bottom of a statement, it was sterling silver, and everything went,"[14] and of Sino-Forest Corporation (Sino-Forest).[15]

---

13 RSC, 1985, c C-44 [*CBCA*], Part XIV, Financial Disclosure.

14 Bealing, Dirsmith & Fogarty, above note 10; Bealing & Pitingolo, above note 10.

15 *Sino-Forest Corporation*, listed on the TSE, claimed to be one of the leading commercial forest plantation operators in the People's Republic of China. In 2011, the company was accused of fraud and investigated by the Royal Canadian Mounted Police and the Ontario Securities Commission. Six years later, on 13 July 2017, the OSC released its decision finding that Sino-Forest and four individuals, including former CEO Allen Chan, committed fraud: *Sino-Forest Corporation (Re)*, 2018 ONSEC 37.

4. Privity of Relationship

To whom does the auditor owes the duty of care? In *Ultramares Corporation v Touche*,[16] for example, Touche Niven gave Fred Stern and Company "clean opinion." The auditors knew that the accounts when certified would be used to raise money and for that purpose it supplied thirty-two certified and serially numbered copies as counterpart originals. The auditors failed to discover that management had falsified entries to overstate accounts receivable. On the faith of one of the certified copies, the plaintiff, Ultramares, lent Fred Stern and Company money. The balance sheet showed a net worth of USD$1 million. In fact, the company was insolvent. The plaintiff made three unsecured loans totalling $165,000 to the company, which declared bankruptcy in a year later. Ultramares sued Touche Niven for the amount of the Stern debt, declaring that a careful audit would have shown Stern to be insolvent.

The auditors had failed to follow paper trails to "off-the-books" transactions that, if properly analyzed, would have revealed the company's impecunious situation.[17] In what is considered to be the seminal opinion on auditor malpractice, Chief Judge Cardozo reversed the jury verdict:

> The auditor in *Ultramares* knew the company was in need of capital and that its audit opinion would be displayed to third parties "as the basis of financial dealings." The Plaintiff's name, however, was not mentioned to the auditor, nor was the auditor told about any actual or proposed credit or investment transactions in which its audit opinion would be presented to a third party.[18]

The court found that the auditor owed no duty to the third party creditor for an "erroneous opinion." Chief Judge Cardozo narrowed the scope of the duty of care:

---

16 174 NE 441 (1932) [*Ultramares*].

17 Ironically, it was the same error that led to the eventual bankruptcy of Enron, which transferred part of its troubled operations to so-called special purpose entities (SPEs), essentially limited partnerships created with outside parties.

18 *Ultramares Corp v Touche*, 174 NE 441, 255 NY 170.

> If liability for negligence exists, a thoughtless slip or blunder, the failure to detect a theft or forgery beneath the cover of deceptive entries, may expose accountants to a liability in an indeterminate amount for an indeterminate time to an indeterminate class. The hazards of a business conducted on these terms are so extreme as to enkindle doubt whether a flaw may not exist in the implication of a duty that exposes to these consequences.[19]

Chief Judge Cardozo did not exonerate auditors from liability to third parties for fraud, but merely for "honest blunder." Thus, the decision narrowed the class of persons to whom accountants owe a duty of care because of public policy considerations.

The essential issue is whether the auditor has sufficient nexus with the third party to constitute a relationship approaching privity. This is essentially a question of fact. The auditor's liability to a client with whom they have a contract is clear if the auditor breaches the standard of care in providing services. The client and the auditor are in a relationship of privity.

The more difficult question is determining the standard of auditor liability to third parties. As one moves away from privity of contract to privity of relationship, the line for liability becomes obscure. In *Credit Alliance v Arthur Andersen & Co*,[20] for example, the New York Court of Appeals restated the American law of liability as follows:

> Before accountants may be held liable in negligence to non-contractual parties who rely to their detriment on inaccurate financial reports, certain prerequisites must be satisfied: (1) the accountant must have been aware that the financial reports were to be used for a particular purpose or purposes; (2) in the furtherance of which a known party or parties was intended to rely; and (3) there must have been some conduct on the part of the accountants linking

---

19 *Ultramares Corp v Touche*, 174 NE 441 (NY 1931) New York Court of Appeals.

20 *Credit Alliance Corp v Arthur Andersen & Co*, 65 NY 2d 536, 483 NE 2d 110, 493 NYS 2d 435, 198.

them to that party or parties, which evinces the accountants' understanding of what that party or parties' reliance.[21]

Thus, the essential question is whether accountants should be subject to liability to third persons (persons not in contractual relationships with the auditor) on the same basis as all other tortfeasors or whether they should enjoy special protection from the doctrine of foreseeability on public policy ground.

5. Foreseeability and Duty of Care

Ultramares is an "anachronistic protection" of accountants, which was decided in 1932, in the midst of the Depression following the Great Crash of 1929. In a 1983 law review article, Howard Weiner J wrote that "accountant liability based on foreseeable injury would serve the dual functions of compensation for injury and deterrence of negligent conduct."[22] Other judges have said that it is a just and rational judicial policy that the same criteria govern the imposition of negligence liability, regardless of the context in which it arises. As Lucas CJ said in *Bily v Arthur Young & Company*, "the accountant, the investor, and the general public will in the long run benefit when the liability of the certified public accountant for negligent misrepresentation is measured by the foreseeability standard."[23]

There is really no reason to distinguish accountants from other professionals and suppliers of services and goods to the public. To be sure, the public policy limitation protects accountants. However, the rule impairs the potential deterrent effect of liability based on negligent conduct. As Weiner J said:

---

21 Per Judge Jasen, Credit *Alliance Corp v Arthur Andersen & Co*, 65 NY 2d 536, 483 NE 2d 110, 493 NYS 2d 435, 1985.

22 Howard Weiner, "Common Law Liability of the Certified Public Accountant for Negligent Misrepresentation" (1983) 20:2 *San Diego Law Review* 233 at 263.

23 *Bily v Arthur Young & Co* (1992), 11 Cal Rptr 2d 51, 3 Cal 4th 370, 834 P 2d 745, opinion by Lucas CJ, with Panelli, Arabian, Baxter, and George JJ, concurring. (Separate dissenting opinion by Kennard J, with Mosk J concurring.)

The imposition of a duty to foreseeable users may cause accounting firms to engage in more thorough reviews. This might be setting up stricter standards and applying closer supervision, which should tend to reduce the number of instances in which liability would ensue. Much of the additional cost incurred because of more thorough auditing review or increased insurance premiums would be borne by the business entity and its stockholders or its customers.

G. NEGLIGENT MISREPRESENTATION

In *Hercules Managements Ltd v Ernst Young*,[24] the Supreme Court of Canada followed Cardozo CJ's reasoning and limited the scope of auditors' liability to shareholders, investors, and other potential users of financial statements. The plaintiffs were two shareholders of two companies that carried on business of lending and investing money on the security of real property mortgages. The defendant Ernst & Young, a firm of public accountants, performed the annual audits of the financial statements of the two companies and provided their reports to the companies' shareholders. The two companies went into receivership. The plaintiffs, who had relied on the auditors' reports, suffered damages on account of their investments in the companies. They alleged that the audit reports were negligently prepared.

Once again, the principal issue was the scope of the duty of care in cases involving negligent misrepresentation. The Court reiterated the two-part test that the House of Lords had used earlier in *Anns v Merton London Borough Council*:

> First one has to ask whether, as between the alleged wrongdoer and the person who has suffered damage there is a sufficient relationship of proximity or neighbourhood such that, in the reasonable contemplation of the former, carelessness on his part may be likely to cause damage to the latter n which case a prima facie duty of care arises. Secondly, if the first question is answered affirmatively, it is necessary to consider whether there are any considerations which ought to negative, or to reduce or limit the scope of the duty or

24 [1997] 2 SCR 165 [*Hercules*].

> the class of person to whom it is owed, or the damages to which a breach of it may give rise.[25]

"Proximity" is simply an alternative articulation of the "duty of care" test that Lord Atkin first developed in *Donoghue v Stevenson*. Professor Fleming called proximity a "vacuous test."[26]

Negligent misrepresentation actions differ from physical damage cases. In physical damage cases, the reasonableness of the plaintiff's expectations is not really an issue. Where there is a duty of care, injury is sufficient to support an action. In negligent misrepresentation actions, however, the plaintiff relies on detrimental reliance on the negligent statement. The general framework set out in *Anns v London Borough of Merton*, and later refined in *Cooper v Hobart*,[27] applies in cases of pure economic loss arising from an auditor's negligent misrepresentation or performance of a service. In these circumstances, the reliance must be reasonable and is not taken for granted.

1. Policy Considerations

It is in respect of the reasonableness of the reliance that public policy considerations may override the simple "duty of care." Thus, policy considerations are an additional burden on a plaintiff in negligent misrepresentation actions. As LaForest J said in *Hercules*:

> Plainly stated, adding further requirements to the duty of care test provides a means by which policy concerns that are extrinsic to simple justice that are, nevertheless, fundamentally important, may be taken into account in assessing whether the defendant should be compelled to compensate the plaintiff for losses suffered. In other

25 [1978] AC 728 (HL) [*Anns*]. See also *Scott Group Ltd v McFarlane*, [1978] 1 NZLR 553 (auditors' liability for negligently prepared audit reports), in which the *Anns* test was adopted and applied by a majority of the New Zealand Court of Appeal.

26 John G Fleming, "The Negligent Auditor and Shareholders" (1990) 106 *Law Quarterly Review* 349; Werner Lorenz & Basil Markesinis, "Solicitors' Liability Towards Third Parties: Back Into the Troubled Waters of the Contract/Tort Divide" (1993) 56 *Modern Law Review* 558, online: https://onlinelibrary.wiley.com/doi/pdf/10.1111/j.1468-2230.1993.tb01886.x.

27 2001 SCC 79, [2001] 3 SCR 537.

> words, these further requirements serve a policy-based limiting function with respect to the ambit of the duty of care in negligent misrepresentation actions.[28]

Ultimately, all policy making is a compromise between competing values. The Supreme Court of Canada considered the competing values in *Hercules*, balancing the interests of the auditors against the interests of individual shareholders. The Court went with the auditors, whose interests prevail in their role as auditors of corporations under statutory requirements.

There are many people who rely upon audit reports in making decisions. Shareholders, creditors, potential investors, financial analysts, and financial planners all use audit reports in various decisions that rely on financial statements to be fairly presented and in accordance with sound accounting principles. At the very least, it is entirely reasonable for users to expect that the auditors' opinion on the financial statements that they *present fairly* the results of operations is a stamp of their approval. Indeed, the "Big Four" accounting firms realize their brand value and market their signature on financial statements. Users of financial statements treat their signature at the bottom of the audit opinion as the hallmark of probity. Should auditors, who benefit from such reverence from the business and investment community, be accountable in law for their audit opinions? If so, to whom and under what circumstances?

There are conflicting and competing interests in determining the scope of auditor liability. Since, ultimately, all rules are behavioural, broad-based liability for negligent misrepresentation to users who rely on financial statements would deter negligent conduct. As liability costs go up, the auditor would become more self-conscious that their professional liability insurance costs would also go up. As insurance premiums escalate for liability insurance, the cost of audit services would increase and, eventually, get passed on to the ultimate consumer, which includes investors.

In *Hercules*, however, the Supreme Court considered that the deterrence of negligent conduct was outweighed by "socially undesirable

---

28 At para 28.

consequences" that would flow from imposing indeterminate liability on auditors: once again, the spectre of "liability in an indeterminate amount for an indeterminate time to an indeterminate class."[29]

Thus, despite the interest that the plaintiffs had as individual shareholders in the defendant company, the Supreme Court restricted the scope of auditors' liability to their statutory mandate, which was to report to the corporation and the collectivity of shareholders, but not to any individual shareholders who made personal investment decisions based on the audit report. Relying on the corporate doctrine that the duty that auditors owe is to the corporation, a separate fictional legal entity, and not to the shareholders personally, the Supreme Court restricted the scope of the potential liability of auditors. As Lord Oliver said in *Caparo* (quoted with approval by the Supreme Court of Canada):

> My Lords, the primary purpose of the statutory requirement that a company's accounts shall be audited annually is almost self-evident. . . . The management is confided to a board of directors which operates in a fiduciary capacity and is answerable to and removable by the shareholders who can act, if they act at all, only collectively and only through the medium of a general meeting. Hence the legislative provisions requiring the board annually to give an account of its stewardship to a general meeting of the shareholders. . . . It is the auditors' function to ensure, so far as possible, that the financial information as to the company's affairs prepared by the directors accurately reflects the company's position in order first, to protect the company itself from the consequences of undetected errors, or, possibly wrongdoing. And, second, to provide shareholders with reliable intelligence for the purpose of enabling them to scrutinize the conduct of the company's affairs and to exercise their collective powers to reward or control or remove those to whom that conduct has been confided.[30]

Similarly, in *Roman Corp Ltd*, Farley J stated:

---

29 At para 33.

30 *Caparo Industries plc v Dickman*, [1990] 1 All ER 568.

> As a matter of law, the only purpose for which the shareholders receive an auditor's report is to provide the shareholders with information for the purpose of overseeing the management and affairs of the corporation and not for the purpose of guiding personal investment decisions or personal speculation with a view to profit.[31]

This is a narrow view of the role of investors in the capital markets. Thus, we emphasize the responsibility of the auditor to the corporation and the "collectivity" of shareholders, but not to individual shareholders, who use the audit information in making personal investment decisions. This, despite the fact that it is the shareholders who finance the corporation with risk capital! Financial statements, preferably audited, are the first step in financial analysis by investors and analysts and ensure the integrity of the capital markets.

Most shareholders' meetings are in fact perfunctory, superficial and pithy, programmed to a script. Retail investors are not usually well informed and have limited understanding of financial statements. The real financial analysis is done by professionals who scour the financial statements, the audit report, the notes to the financial statements (which under IFRS are voluminous), and the more detailed information usually provided to securities regulators in quarterly and annual filings. How effective is their analysis? In 2008, the Congressional Budget Office of the United States reported that Americans lost over USD$2 trillion in accumulated retirement assets in their 401(k) accounts, pensions, and other traditional retirement savings during the preceding fifteen months. Absent accountability of auditors to investors, we can expect more of the same in the future.

2. *Deloitte & Touche v Livent Inc*

In cases of pure economic loss arising from negligent misrepresentation or performance of a service, there are two factors in the proximity analysis: the defendant's undertaking and the plaintiff's reliance. Where the defendant undertakes to provide a representation or service

31 *Roman Corp Ltd v Peat Marwick Thorne* (1992), 1992 CanLII 7404 (ON SC), 11 OR (3d) 248; *Roman Corp v Peat Marwick Thorne* (1993), 12 BLR (2d) 10.

in circumstances that invite the plaintiff's reasonable reliance, the defendant becomes obligated to take reasonable care and the plaintiff has a right to rely on the defendant's undertaking. Any reliance on the part of the plaintiff that falls outside of the scope of the defendant's undertaking necessarily falls outside the scope of the proximate relationship and, therefore, of the defendant's duty of care.

Livent Inc was a publicly listed company that produced and staged performances in theatres that it owned in Canada and the United States. Livent's directors fraudulently manipulated the company's financial records to make it look more successful than it really was. Deloitte was Livent's auditor.

Deloitte never uncovered the fraud. In August 1997, however, Deloitte identified irregularities in the reporting of profit from an asset sale. Deloitte did not resign. Instead, for the purpose of helping Livent to solicit further investment from a public offering, Deloitte provided a "comfort letter" and helped prepare, and approved, a press release, which misrepresented the basis for the reporting of the profit. It also prepared Livent's 1997 audit, which it finalized in April 1998. Livent filed for insolvency protection in November 1998. It sold its assets and went into receivership. Livent sued Deloitte in tort and contract.[32]

The purpose of the auditor's undertaking is critical to determining the existence and scope of any duty of care in cases of negligent misrepresentation or performance of a service. Where a duty of care arises in respect of an auditor's representation or services, the scope of the duty is limited to the *purpose* for which the auditor undertakes to provide the representation or services. Hence, an auditor will not be liable where a corporate client detrimentally relies on the auditor's representation or services for any purpose other than that for which the auditor undertook to act. The Court said:

> Any reliance on the part of the plaintiff which falls outside of the scope of the defendant's undertaking of responsibility—that is, of the purpose for which the representation was made or the service was undertaken—necessarily falls outside the scope of the proximate relationship and, therefore, of the defendant's duty of care.

32 *Deloitte & Touche v Livent Inc (Receiver of)*, 2017 SCC 63.

> Simply put, Deloitte never undertook, in preparing the Comfort Letter, to assist Livent's shareholders in overseeing management; it cannot therefore be held liable for failing to take reasonable care to assist such oversight. And, given that Livent had no right to rely on Deloitte's representations for a purpose other than that for which Deloitte undertook to act, Livent's reliance was neither reasonable nor reasonably foreseeable.[33]

However, having dismissed the comfort letter portion of Livent's claim, the majority went on to find that the auditor was nonetheless liable for Livent's losses arising from the negligently prepared 1997 statutory audit. Livent had detrimentally relied on the 1997 statutory audit for one of its intended purposes, namely, to provide its shareholders with reliable information so that they could oversee the conduct of management.

Hence, the resulting losses were reasonably foreseeable and therefore recoverable.

33 *Ibid* at para 31.

Chapter 17: Law and Accounting

A. OVERVIEW

Accounting deals with measurement and summarization of financial transactions according to generally accepted accounting principles and concepts. Finance is essentially corporate law that concerns the creation and valuation of financial instruments, such as stocks, bonds, and derivatives. Thus, both accounting and finance are important for lawyers when they advise on commercial transactions, family law, public securities, and litigation, such as in:

- Business contracts;
  - Buyout clauses in buy-sell agreements;
  - Partnership agreements;
  - Purchase-sale of assets;
  - Purchase-sale of shares;
  - Joint ventures
- Employment Contracts;
- Tort litigation;
- Supply contracts;
- Minutes of settlement in litigation;
- Employment agreements; and
- Marriage contracts.

B. BUSINESS CONTRACTS

The most common scenario where lawyers encounter accounting and finance issues is in litigation over agreements where the parties interpret basic concepts and financial terminology, such as "book value," "net profits," and "income," differently. In such cases, lawyers must either negotiate a settlement of the dispute or have a court adjudicate if negotiations are unsuccessful.

In some cases, the courts defer to GAAP and rely upon the accounting profession's understanding of these terms. In others, however, the courts reject GAAP and insert their own interpretation of the words. As the cases that follow show, interpretation of accounting terminology often arises in corporate agreements involving buyout clauses and in incentive compensation agreements for key employees. Most of the problems can be resolved at the drafting stage by using conventional terminology and defining the meaning of terms in the contract.

Even simple words can lead to misunderstanding and litigation. In *Piedmont Publishing Company (A Corporation) et al v Mary Pickford Rogers et al,*[1] for example, Mary Pickford Rogers (star of silent pictures) and Piedmont were rival applicants for a licence from the Federal Communications Commission (FCC) for a television station in Winston-Salem, North Carolina, where Piedmont also owned and published two newspapers and a radio broadcasting station. Piedmont and Pickford decided to pool their interests and organized a new company, Triangle Broadcasting Corporation (Triangle) in North Carolina to apply for the licence. The parties knew that the FCC would grant only one licence, and that a contest for it might take so long that a television station already licensed in Winston-Salem might capture the television audience. Triangle was awarded the licence and an exclusive local contract with National Broadcasting Company (NBC).

The parties signed an agreement in New York on 25 May 1953 under which Piedmont subscribed for 1,000 shares of Triangle's stock, for USD$100,000. Pickford subscribed for 500 shares, for which she

1 Civ No 24268 Second Dist, Div One June 19, 1961 [*Piedmont*].

paid USD$50,000. Thus, Piedmont owned two-thirds and Pickford one-third of Triangle's stock.

The contract contained a buyout clause, which gave Piedmont an option to purchase Pickford's stock at the end of any of Triangle's fiscal years in 1956, 1957, 1958, and 1959. The formula to be used by Triangle's "regularly employed independent certified public accountants" to determine the purchase price for the stock was as follows:[2]

> An amount per share of stock equal to the *sum* of the two following items, divided by the number of outstanding shares of the corporation:
>
> 1. an amount equal to the *total* book value at the beginning of any such period of Triangle's common stock adjusted to reflect an annual depreciation and obsolescence charge of not over 10% against such tangible assets as have been depreciated on the books of Triangle at a higher rate; *and*
> 2. an amount determined by multiplying the average net annual profits of Triangle by five.

The multiplier was to decline over the four years. The multiplier for 1956 was five. If the option had been exercised in 1957, it would have been four; in 1958, three; and in 1959, two.

Piedmont exercised its option on 20 July 1956. The independent public accountants valued Triangle at USD$1,270,548, which made the Pickford's one-third interest worth USD$423,516. The option price was approximately USD$86,000. The market value of Triangle did not include goodwill in "total book value" in the formula.

Goodwill would be the fair market value of the telecasting licence, the fair market value of the television station as its listening audience grew in numbers, the value of its advertising contracts, and the fair market value of contracts with NBC. Pickford rejected the offer and the parties ended up in court.

What did the word "total" add to the meaning of "total book value"? The court concluded that by adding the word "total" to "book value," the parties meant to include the value of Triangle's intangible

2 Per Drapeu J, pro tem.

assets, including the goodwill (licence to telecast, the advertising value of the station, and Triangle's contract with NBC). The court interpreted "total book value" to mean "fair value":

> We do not believe that gentlemen in control of Piedmont's policies, with their standing in their community and state, meant to use an accounting method that would cut down the fair value of Ms. Pickford's stock, if they exercise their option. We think, rather, they intended to pay her a fair price for her participation in securing the television license and in making the television station an outstanding success.
>
> Sounder and safer principles of equity and fair dealing dictate the conclusion that when the contract was made everyone intended to include the value of the goodwill of the television station . . . in computing the price of the Pickford stock when the time came for Piedmont to exercise its option; or if Piedmont did not exercise its option, the price Ms. Pickford was to pay if she exercised her option.[3]

Under general accounting principles, only *purchased* goodwill is reflected on the balance sheet. Otherwise, goodwill is not included as an asset and does not affect "book value." However, the court rejected general accounting principles as determining what the parties *intended* when they entered into the contract, saying that the issue is one of law and fact and is not to be determined solely on principles of accounting.

Of course, the entire dispute could have been avoided if the lawyers had used the traditional and accepted accounting terminology, "book value," if that was what they intended. Alternatively, if they intended to deviate from the accounting principle by including goodwill in the formula, the agreement could have defined "total book value" in the contract to include goodwill. The solution would have been simple if only the lawyers had considered their use of accounting terminology in the agreement.

3 *Piedmont*, above note 1 at 188–89 (Cal App 2nd).

C. EMPLOYMENT CONTRACTS

Executive compensation policies for key employees based upon generally accepted accounting principles (GAAP) can, and usually will, affect management's behaviour. Since the measurement of profit is as much a question of timing as it is of valuation, management has an incentive, in most cases, to accelerate the recognition of profit. It is only in rare cases that it will be advantageous to delay the recognition of revenues and profits. Ultimately, the incentive effect depends on the wording of the employment contract.

The term "net profit" appears frequently in employment contracts of managers, executives, and chief executive officers of corporations. Net profit is essentially an accounting concept that derives from the principles of bookkeeping applied in the preparation of the income statement.

Net profit of a business derives from amounts that the entity receives, or has receivable, in the form of cash or its equivalent from completed sales minus net of all current expenses. The difference between the cost price and the market price of unsold goods (inventory) is not profit in a going concern. Inventory is an asset or resource that the business will realize in a future fiscal period.

Profits include only realized profits and not potential profits. In *Jennery v Olmstead*,[4] for example, Justice Peckham said:

> The profits are, as I have said, the amount of money received by the bank from its investments, by way of interest, over and above the amount of interest it has to pay its depositors, together with the amount of any money it had received by sale of property over and above its cost to the bank. If such a sale had been made, then a profit had arisen, but if not, then no profit had accrued simply from the fact that the property, if sold, would have resulted in a profit.

The term "profit" is inherently a *net* concept, the difference between income and expenses. In contrast, "income" means what comes in or

4 36 Hun (NY) 536.

has been earned as a receivable or cash. Thus, income is inherently a gross concept.

We derive the meaning of "net profits" in a contract from the words of the contract, and such conduct of the parties as is warranted in interpreting the contract. Without further elaboration, net profits do not include estimated or "*pro forma*" profits, or earnings never received or entered upon the books of the corporation. Thus, without receipt or the equivalent, profits do not legally exist.[5]

The measurement of "net profit" or its equivalent, "net income," involves two components, valuation of the transaction through objective evidence and timing. Thus, we answer two questions:

1) How much to record? And
2) In which fiscal period should we record the transaction?

These questions are particularly important in contracts that contain bonus or profit-sharing clauses if the employees' employment contract is terminated or comes to an end.

In *Tooey*, for example, the employee (plaintiff) was employed as the manager of the paper and wooden ware department of the defendant company. His contract provided for a salary of USD$150 per month "and 25 percent of the net profits of this department up to December 31, 1916 . . . the division of the profits to be made in January 1916 and January 1917." The plaintiff received his normal salary and also the net profits on sales made and delivered to the defendant's customers up to 31 December 1916, when the contract was terminated.

The corporation would record its sales only when it shipped its merchandise to customers. The plaintiff claimed additional bonus based upon sales of merchandise that were made prior to 31 December 1916 but had not been shipped by year end, and were subject to cancellation. The plaintiff wanted to accelerate revenue recognition prior to shipment of merchandise, which would offend the revenue recognition principle.

The court rejected the plaintiff's claim based upon both accounting principles, which the court described as "practical bookkeeping,"

5 *Tooey v CL Percival Co*, 192 Iowa 267, 182 NW 403 [*Tooey*].

and the legal definition of net profits. It is a well-established rule of law that, in all cases in which the terms of the contract or the language employed raise a question of doubtful construction and it appears that the parties have practically interpreted their contract, the courts will follow that practical construction. The court reached the same conclusion based on the practical construction that the parties themselves had put upon the terms of their contract.

D. NEGLIGENT MISREPRESENTATION

Negligent misrepresentation of financial statements is an actionable tort. A successful claim for negligent misrepresentation has five requirements:

1) A duty of care based on a "special relationship" between the parties;
2) Misrepresentation of fact;
3) Negligence by the representor in making the misrepresentation;
4) Reasonable reliance by the representee on the misrepresentation; and
5) Damages to the representee by the reliance.[6]

Note that some Securities Acts have a less stringent statutory civil liability provision for auditors, whereby a plaintiff does not have to establish that the auditor owed a duty of care, that there was reliance on the auditor's report, or that the auditor was negligent (although the auditor may have a due diligence defence), but merely that the report contained a misrepresentation.

Where an auditor issues an unqualified (unmodified) audit opinion on financial statements, the opinion will typically be in a standard form, such as:

> In our opinion, these financial statements present fairly in all material respects, the financial position of the company as at . . . and the results of its operations and for the years ended . . . in

6 *Queen v Cognos Inc*, [1993] 1SCR 87 at 110.

accordance with Canadian generally accepted accounting principles applied on a consistent basis.

The essential element of this opinion is that the financial statements must "present fairly" and be in accordance with GAAP. Problems arise where the statements are materially misleading but still in accordance with accounting principles or where GAAPs are evolving.

In *Kripps et al v Touche Ross*,[7] for example, the plaintiffs were investors who purchased debentures from a mortgage corporation that had issued a prospectus containing financial statements and an audit opinion certified by the defendant accounting firm, Touche Ross. The mortgage corporation disclosed in its notes to the financial statements that it "capitalized" accrued interest on mortgages in default if the company's management believed those amounts to be adequately secured. The uncollected interest was included in the corporation's income and added to the principal of the mortgage. The trial judge found that the company policy with respect to capitalizing unpaid interest was consistent with GAAP during the relevant period. The trial judge also found that the amount of the mortgages in default was material information that had not been adequately disclosed and that would have given the investors a better understanding of the risks involved.

However, although capitalizing unpaid interest was part of GAAP at the time, Touche prepared its auditor's report when the accounting profession had begun to recognize the inherent failings in this approach. The CICA (now CPA Canada) began to recognize that failing to disclose the explicit amount of unpaid interest made it difficult for financial statements to fulfil the broad aim of presenting fairly the financial position of the company, and that GAAP had to be changed so as to fulfil the broader aim of fair presentation.

GAAP may be the auditor's guide to forming their opinion, but they were retained to form an opinion on the *fairness* of the financial statements, and not merely on their conformity to GAAP. The Court of Appeal held that the auditor's opinion that "financial statements present fairly the financial position of the company in accordance

7 (1997) Court of Appeal for British Columbia, docket CA019919 (1997 0425) [*Kripps*].

with general accepted accounting principles" was ambiguous. It was neither a clear statement of opinion by the professional auditor that the financial statements presented the position of the company fairly, nor an assertion that the financial statements were in accordance with GAAP.

GAAP is only a tool to achieve fair representation and not an end in and of itself:

> Given the aim in auditing, the understanding of audits that those who might rely on them have on them, and that auditors know of this understanding, auditors cannot hide behind the qualifications of their reports ('according to GAAP') where the financial statements nevertheless misrepresent the financial position of the company. This does not open the floodgates to liability for auditors.[8]

The test, however, should be applied deferentially to professional practices and standards and only in those circumstances "if a standard practice fails to adopt obvious and reasonable precautions which are readily apparent to the ordinary finder of fact."[9] However, ultimately, the selection of the appropriate standard of care is a question of law.[10]

E. INCOME TAX

1. Accounting Period

The *Income Tax Act* prescribes a calendar year for individuals as their reporting period. Corporations are allowed to choose their own fiscal periods.[11] This division of a business into arbitrary segments gives rise to problems of accurate income calculation. A taxpayer's lifetime is similarly segmented into annual periods and this segmentation also gives rise to some special problems.

Partnerships and sole proprietorships do not have a separate legal personality and are not taxpayers as such. The income from such

---

8 *Ibid* at 36–37.

9 *Ter Neuzen v Korn* (1995), 11 BCLR (3d) 201 (SCC).

10 *CNR v Vincent*, [1979] 1 SCR 364; see also *Wade v CNR*, [1978] 1 SCR 1064.

11 *Income Tax Act*, RSC, 1985, c 1 (5th Supp) [*ITA*], ss 249(1) and 249.1.

businesses must be reported by the partners or the proprietor in their personal capacity. The business may, however, use a fiscal period that is different from the calendar year. Thus, taxpayers must apply appropriate measurements of net income for each fiscal period.

2. Accounting Methods

(a) General Comment

Although employees must report their income according to the cash basis of accounting, businesses are generally required to use the accrual method. The accrual method is considered particularly appropriate for a trading business.[12] There are, however, other methods of accounting that may be more appropriate for some businesses, particularly businesses with peculiar or unique cash flow patterns.

(b) Installment Sales

For tax accounting, an installment sales business may adopt a variation of the accrual method. The installment method of accounting, for example, is considered appropriate for a taxpayer whose business involves installment sales that require a small down payment with the balance due over an extended period.[13]

(c) Completed Contract

Under the completed contract method, the taxpayer defers recognition of all expenses and all revenues, in respect of long-term contracts, until the contract is complete.[14] The completed contract method of accounting has been rejected for tax purposes, although it might be an appropriate accounting method.

(d) Cash Method

Income from office or employment is usually reported on a cash basis. This is confirmed by the use of the words "received" and "enjoyed" in sections 5 and 6 of the *Income Tax Act*.

---

12 *Ken Steeves Sales Ltd v MNR*, [1955] CTC 47 (Ex Ct).

13 *MNR v Publishers Guild of Canada Ltd* (1957), 57 DTC 1017 (Ex Ct).

14 *Wilson & Wilson Ltd*, [1960] CTC 1 (Ex Ct).

The decision to allow certain taxpayers to use the cash method of accounting is based primarily on a concern for administrative convenience. It would be quite difficult, if not impossible, for millions of employees to prepare their annual income tax returns on an accrual basis of accounting (see the following section). The accrual basis requires at least some rudimentary knowledge of accounting principles (realization, timing, etc.) that is beyond the inclination or interest of most non-accountants.

Accrual basis statements also require careful auditing by the tax authorities. Since employee income tax returns represent approximately 80 percent of all filed tax returns, mandatory accrual basis returns from all taxpayers would place an intolerable burden on the Canada Revenue Agency's (CRA) resources. The incremental auditing and accounting fees that taxpayers and the CRA incurred as a result of accrual accounting would not be justified by the marginal improvement in the accuracy of annual net income calculations.

There is an important exception from the accrual method for farmers and fishers, who are specifically authorized to use the cash basis method of accounting.[15] The theoretical justification for this particular variation is that, in most circumstances, the distortion of net income is minimal when the cash basis method is used and, hence, justifiable in that it is easier for these taxpayers to maintain cash basis books of account.

More pragmatically, it would be politically inconvenient to withdraw a tax concession that has been made available to farmers for so long. If anything, the pull is in the opposite direction. Until 1980, only farmers could use the cash basis of accounting. In that year the legislation extended the cash basis of accounting to fishers, a practice that the CRA had administratively tolerated for many years prior.

In determining income for tax purposes under the cash method, an individual must include not only the cash that they receive in the year, but also any other payments that they constructively receive. Thus, the cash method of accounting includes both actual and constructive receipts in income. The essence of the constructive receipt

15 *ITA*, s 28.

doctrine is that an individual cannot postpone recognizing income simply by failing to exercise their power to collect it. For example, although an individual can delay actual payment beyond the year end, they cannot avoid including an amount in income merely by waiting until the next year to pick up their paycheque.

The distinction between the two situations is subtle but significant. In the first case, the taxpayer does not have the power to cash, or otherwise control, the cheque because they do not receive it until after the year end. In the second case, the taxpayer constructively possesses the cheque, but chooses not to exercise their power of possession in order to delay including the amount in income.

These distinctions are particularly important in closely held corporations. Where an owner-manager of a corporation performs services for the corporation, they are entitled to payment for services. Although the owner has discretion as to the timing of the payment, the salary is not considered to be paid until they have the corporation's cheque in their possession. Thus, merely because the owner controls the timing of the cheque does not mean that payment to them is accelerated to a point in time before the corporation actually issues the cheque.

To be sure, this allows owner-managers of corporations some flexibility in arranging their annual compensation through salary and bonuses. Depending upon the prevailing rates of tax for a particular year, an owner can elect to accelerate or defer salary payments in order to maximize their after-tax returns. This form of tax avoidance is a small price to pay for what would otherwise become an impossibly complex accounting system for employees.

Similarly, the owner-manager may choose to forgo some or all of their salary in a year. The amount forgone, however, is not imputed to the individual merely because they were entitled to the amount. We do not impute taxable salaries to controlling shareholders.

(e) Accrual Method

In contrast with the requirement of cash basis accounting for employment income, taxpayers must report business and property income on an accrual basis. The *Income Tax Act* does not specifically stipulate a particular method for calculating business or property income.

Section 9 only says that a taxpayer's income from a business or property is their profit therefrom. In law, however, the term "profit" means profit calculated in accordance with commercial practice, and commercial practice favours accrual accounting for most businesses. Hence, the Act indirectly endorses the requirement to adhere to GAAP in most cases. Ultimately, however, the meaning of "profit" in section 9 is a question of law.

(f) Holdbacks

In applying the accrual basis of accounting, the time of sale of goods and services is usually the most convenient time to recognize revenue. The time of sale is not, however, the only time for revenue recognition. Certain businesses may deviate from the norm and recognize revenue at some other time. For example, contractors (persons engaged in the construction of buildings, roads, dams, bridges, and similar structures) can, by administrative grace, defer recognition of their income until such time as "holdback payments" become legally receivable.[16] This rule varies from the usual accrual accounting test, which does not use legal entitlement as the determining criterion for recognizing revenue. Contractors may, however, also accelerate the recognition of profit by bringing into income amounts that may not be legally receivable by virtue of a mechanics' lien or similar statute.

3. Generally Accepted Accounting Principles

The Act determines income from business or property by reference to section 9(1):

> Subject to this Part, a taxpayer's income for a taxation year from a business or property is the taxpayer's profit from that business or property for that year.

At one time there was a tentative proposal to incorporate in the Act a general statement to the effect that business profits should be calculated according to GAAP. The proposal was never implemented

16 CRA IT-92R2, *Income of Contractors*, 1 January 1995 (archived).

because of the difficulty in establishing just what GAAP means in all cases. The absence of a statutory provision requiring the computation of profits according to GAAP did not, however, inhibit the development of a similar doctrine in case law. Indeed, if anything, we have arrived at virtually the same result through judicial decisions.

Although there may be disagreement among accountants concerning the best practice in respect of certain matters, it is now well established that, as a starting point, section 9 imports into the Act the standard accounting methods used in the business world. President Thorson dealt with this matter in *Imperial Oil v MNR*,[17] in *Daley v MNR*,[18] and in *Royal Trust Co v MNR*.[19] In this last case, dealing with the deductibility of a claimed expenditure, he said:

> [I]t may be stated categorically that . . . the first matter to be determined . . . is whether it was made or incurred by the taxpayer in accordance with the ordinary principles of commercial trading or well accepted principles of business practice.[20]

The important point, however, is that the determination of net profit is a question of law and not a matter of GAAP.[21] Although a court may look at the treatment of particular items by reference to GAAP, these principles at best only represent some of the guidelines for preparing financial statements. GAAP may influence the calculation of income, but only on a case-by-case basis.[22] GAAP may well be influential in determining what is deductible, but they are not the operative legal criteria.

(a) Tax Profits

What is the relationship between accounting profit and profit as determined for income tax purposes? For tax purposes, the starting point

17 [1947] CTC 353 (Ex Ct).

18 [1950] CTC 254, 4 DTC 877 (Ex Ct).

19 [1957] CTC 32, 57 DTC 1055 (Ex Ct) (ordinary principles of commercial trading and business practice are the normal rule for measuring income).

20 *Ibid* at 1060 (DTC).

21 *Symes v Canada*, [1993] 4 SCR 695; *Neonex International Ltd v Canada* [1978] CTC 485 (FCA).

22 *Canderel Ltd v Canada*, [1998] 1 SCR 147.

requires an examination of generally accepted commercial practice. Is a particular expenditure deductible in computing income according to the rules of general commercial and accounting practice? Or is a particular receipt included in computing income according to commercial rules? Once we answer these preliminary questions, other factors may come into play in determining the appropriate tax treatment.

Take depreciation as an example. The general commercial and accounting rule is that, in calculating net income, a reasonable amount of depreciation can be deducted from revenues. Indeed, commercial practice recognizes many different methods of calculating depreciation (for example, straight-line, declining balance, sum of the years, etc.). Provided that the method is acceptable, and the amount is reasonable, depreciation expense is a deductible expense in determining net income for financial statement purposes.

The Act, however, *specifically* prohibits a deduction for depreciation, obsolescence or depletion. Hence, a taxpayer cannot deduct such expenses in calculating profit for tax purposes.[23] In lieu of depreciation, the Act allows a deduction for capital cost allowance (CCA) in an amount that may or may not be related to accounting depreciation.[24] Thus, tax profits and accounting income may be substantially different.

(b) Reserves and Allowances

Accountants sometimes prefer to anticipate certain contingencies by setting up an allowance that has the effect of reducing income in the current period. The Act seriously inhibits this conservative and quite normal accounting practice by denying, as a deduction, "an amount transferred or credited to a reserve, contingent account or sinking fund except as expressly permitted by this Part."[25] Instead, the Act sets out a specific and rigid regime in respect of accounting for reserves.[26] Thus, once again, we see that there can be a significant difference between accounting and taxable income.

---

23 *ITA* at para 18(1)(b).

24 *ITA* at para 20(1)(a).

25 *ITA* at para 18(1)(e).

26 See, for example, *ITA* at paras 20(1)(l), (l.1), (m), (m.1), and (n).

(c) Depreciation

At one time, depreciation expense was recognized as a legitimate deduction for tax purposes, subject to showing a sound accounting basis for the deduction. It is indisputable that most capital assets should be depreciated over time and with use, but the amount of depreciation and the rate at which it occurs are frequently quite speculative. To control the speculations, and to minimize disputes, the Act details a rigid CCA system, which imposes limits on the amount of depreciation deductible in calculating income for tax purposes.

Although, in general, CCA rates are designed to be reasonably realistic, the system is Procrustean. There is no attempt to guarantee that the rates for tax purposes conform to depreciation recognized for accounting purposes. The rates are the same for all taxpayers, although their depreciation may differ greatly. Thus, income for tax purposes can differ quite significantly from income reported to shareholders or creditors. There is nothing unusual or improper in this.

(d) Inventory

A major component of the expenses of some businesses is the cost of goods sold. To calculate the cost of goods sold, a business must establish its inventory of goods on hand at its year end, and then determine its value. There are a number of accounting approaches to inventory valuation. One method that is commonly used by accountants for financial statement purposes, the last-in, first-out (LIFO) method, has been judicially rejected for tax purposes as being inappropriate.[27] Here once again, the use of one method for accounting and another for tax purposes can cause a significant difference in the final net income figure.

---

27 *MNR v Anaconda American Brass Ltd*, [1956] 2 WLR 31 (PC on appeal from SCC) [*Anaconda*].

4. Conformity of Accounting Methods

A taxpayer's income for a taxation year from a business or property is the profit therefrom for the year.[28]

The term "profit" means net profit. In the absence of any specific proscription, profit is determined according to commercial and generally accepted accounting principles. Hence, absent an express or implicit statutory or judicial proscription against the use of a particular accounting method, a taxpayer may determine income for tax purposes according to any appropriate accounting method. President Thorson explained the rule in *MNR v Publishers Guild of Canada Ltd*:[29]

> If the law does not prohibit the use of a particular system of accounting then the opinion of accountancy experts that it is an accepted system and is appropriate to the taxpayer's business and most nearly accurately reflects his income position should prevail with the Court if the reasons for the opinion commend themselves to it.

Similarly, in *Silverman v MNR*:[30]

> [T]he statute does not define what is to be taken as the profit from a business, nor does it describe how or by what method such profit is to be computed, though it does contain provisions to which, for income tax purposes, any method is subject . . . .
>
> [T]he method must be one which accurately reflects the result of the year's operation, and where two different methods, either of which may be acceptable for business purposes, differ in their results, for income tax purposes the appropriate method is that which most accurately shows the profit from the year's operations.

As noted above, the measure of profit is a question of law.

A taxpayer can use one generally accepted accounting method for financial statement purposes and another for income tax purposes. In the absence of any statutory requirement that a taxpayer use the same method of accounting to calculate income for both tax and

28 *ITA*, s 9(1).

29 *MNR v Publishers Guild of Canada Ltd* (1957), 57 DTC 1017 (Ex Ct).

30 *Silverman v MNR* (1960), 60 DTC 5032 at 5034–35 (FCA).

financial statement purposes, a taxpayer can select the most appropriate method of accounting for tax purposes.

The purpose for which we calculate income determines the appropriate method of accounting. An accounting method that is suitable for one purpose is not necessarily also the appropriate measure of income for tax purposes.[31]

What is appropriate for tax purposes? The general rule is to apply that principle or method that provides the "proper picture" of net income. In MacGuigan J's words:

> [I]t would be undesirable to establish an absolute requirement that there must always be conformity between financial statements and tax returns and I am satisfied that the cases do not do so. *The approved principle* is that whichever method presents the "truer picture" of a taxpayer's revenue, which more fairly and accurately portrays income, and which "matches" revenue and expenditure, if one method does, is the one that must be followed.[32]

It is not always easy to apply the rule that a taxpayer may adopt whichever accounting method presents the "truer picture" of revenues and expenses. There are cases where a particular accounting principle presents a truer picture for income statement purposes at the expense of some accuracy or relevance in the balance sheet. In other cases, the adoption of a particular accounting method more accurately summarizes a taxpayer's closing balances while sacrificing accuracy on the income statement.

A classic example of the conflict between income statement and balance sheet values is seen in accounting for inventory values. Under LIFO method of inventory accounting, the cost of goods most recently purchased or acquired is the cost that is assigned to the cost of goods sold. Hence, the inventory on hand at the end of an accounting period is valued at the cost that was attributed to the inventory at the beginning of the period (first-in, still here). Any increases in quantity during a period are valued at the cost prevailing

31 *Friedberg v Canada*, [1993] 4 SCR 285.

32 *West Kootenay Power & Light Co v MNR* (1991), 92 DTC 6023 (FCA).

during the time the accumulations are deemed to have occurred. Any decreases in quantities are considered to have first reduced the most recent accumulations.

Under the first-in, first-out (FIFO) method, the process is reversed: the cost of goods first acquired is assigned to the first goods sold. The closing inventory comprises the cost of the most recent purchases (last-in, still here).

The use of the FIFO method of accounting for the flow of inventory costs tends to overstate net income during inflationary periods and more accurately reflect the current value of closing inventory on the balance sheet. In contrast, the LIFO method more realistically measures "real" net income, while sacrificing some accuracy in year-end balance sheet values.

Most accountants and business people would argue that the use of LIFO for inventory accounting during inflationary periods results in a more meaningful and truer picture of business income during inflationary periods. However, in *Anaconda*, the Privy Council rejected the use of the LIFO method of inventory valuation for tax purposes.

The *Handbook* states the principle as follows:[33]

> The method selected for determining cost should be one which results in the fairest matching of costs against revenues regardless of whether or not the method corresponds to the physical flow of goods.

Anaconda was an unfortunate decision based upon a misunderstanding of accounting methods. The decision rests on two notions: 1) the physical flow of inventory determines values; and 2) the potential for creation of hidden reserves. Both premises are fundamentally flawed. The determination of cost does not depend upon the physical flow of goods but on the fairest matching of revenues and expenses. The fairest matching of costs against revenues is, presumably, also the method which presents the truer picture of income for tax purposes. Thus, the question is: which method of accounting produces the best

33 See also the virtually identical language of the American Institute of Chartered Public Accountants (AICPA), ARB No 43, ch 4.

and fairest picture of annual profits? Equally, the hidden reserve argument ignores the primary purpose that the method serves, namely, the determination of a fair measure of an enterprise's annual income.

5. Non-arm's-length Transactions

The Act contains stringent anti-avoidance rules to govern transfers of property between persons who do not deal with each other at arm's length. The purpose of these rules is to discourage taxpayers who have close social, family, or economic relationships with each other from artificially avoiding tax through the manipulation of transaction values.

Related persons are deemed not to deal with each other at arm's length.[34] It is a question of fact whether unrelated persons deal with each other at arm's length. Parties are not considered to be dealing with each other at arm's length if one person dictates the terms of the bargain on both sides of a transaction.[35]

---

34 *ITA*, s 251.

35 *Swiss Bank Corp v MNR*, [1971] CTC 427 (Ex Ct), aff'd (1972), ([1974] SCR 1144; *Millward v MNR*, [1986] 2 CTC 423 (FCTD) (members of a law firm who dealt with each other at less than commercial rates of interest were not at arm's length).

Chapter 18: Investment and Retirement Planning

A. OVERVIEW

Most people understand the value of contributing to retirement accounts during their productive years of gainful employment and then living off the accumulated nest egg after they retire. Certainly, the government's tax policies encourage deferring current income until retirement. There is a good reason for this: for most Canadians the Canada Pension Plan (CPP), Old Age Security (OAS) and the Guaranteed Income Supplement (GIS) are insufficient support in retirement years.

The evidence is alarming. More than half of Canadians live from pay cheque to pay cheque and are not prepared for any unforeseen financial crisis, such as Covid-19 in 2020. One-third of Canadians are "asset poor" with their wealth in housing but with little income. Ten million Canadians have no workplace retirement plans, and 40 percent have no retirement savings. The median retirement savings of near-retirement individuals is $3,000!

B. WHY PLAN FOR RETIREMENT?

As the above financial profile of Canadians shows, there are several reasons to plan for retirement. The first, and perhaps most obvious, is that, with good medical care, we are fortunate to be living healthier and longer lives. In 2020, the current average life expectancy of Canadians at birth is 82.52 years.

The second is that government support payments are not nearly sufficient to sustain retirement and, given the state of government finances and debt, are unlikely to improve. While government payments such as CPP and OAS are helpful, they are not nearly enough to meet retirement needs, so we need to supplement them with additional sources of income.

Third, private pension plans are not nearly as generous as they once were and are being cut back. Changes in employer pensions from Defined Benefit Pension Plans, which are the responsibility of the employer, to Defined Contribution Pension Plans, which are the responsibility of the employee, mean that individuals will require a much higher level of private savings in the future.

Hence, unless one is on a government or public service indexed pension plan, it is incumbent upon us to plan for our later years. The good news is that we are more likely to live longer, but that means we will also need more savings for our later years.

C. BASIC CONCEPTS OF RETIREMENT PLANNING

There are three basic concepts in retirement planning:

1) the time value of money (see Chapter 5);
2) inflation risk; and
3) the income tax cost of investments.

The government has an important role in all three of these segments. The time value of money depends upon interest rates, which central banks (such as the Bank of Canada or, in the United States, the Federal Reserve) set to control inflation and employment. Of course, the government has exclusive control of tax rates on investment income.

1. Time Value of Money

We start with the time value of money in retirement planning. There are two dimensions of time to consider in planning: future and present.

Given a sum of money, we can determine its value at some future date if we know the rate of compound interest at which we can invest it. Conversely, if we know that we will receive a sum of money in the future, we can determine its present value today if we know the compound rate at which it is, or can be, invested. Thus, all money is related to time. Money has no value other than in the context of time. [1]

Example

Assume that Sacha, who is 35, wants to plan for his retirement, which he expects will be when he is 65. He wants to make annual payments into his retirement fund so that he can withdraw $60,000 annually for 20 years during his retirement, starting one year after he retires. Assuming an 8 percent interest rate, compounded annually (ignoring taxes), Sacha needs to make annual payments of $5,201 into his savings fund.

Years	Interest Rate (%)	PV of $1 Ordinary Annuity (Table 5.3)	FV of $1 Annuity (Table 5.4)	Withdrawal/ Payment ($)	PV ($)	FV ($)
20	8	9.82		60,000 p.a.	589,200	
30	8		113.2832	589,200/113.2832 = 5,201 p.a.		589,200

The *present value* of the $60,000 annual withdrawal is equal to $589,200, which equals (with rounding) the *future value* of annual contributions of $5,201.

Now, assume that the rate of interest is only 4 percent and Sacha still wants an annual retirement withdrawal of $60,000 in 30 years. Then:

1 See Chapter 5 for discussion of time values.

Years	Interest Rate (%)	PV of $1 Ordinary Annuity (Table 5.3)	FV of $1 Annuity (Table 5.4)	Withdrawal/ Payment ($)	PV ($)	FV ($)
20	4	13.6		60,000 p.a.	816,000	
30	4		56.0849	816,000/56.0849 = 14,549 p.a.		816,000

As one might intuitively expect, the *present value* of the $60,000 annual withdrawal requires a higher amount, $816,000, of savings. Hence, annual contributions must increase to $14,549 to achieve the same retirement goals.

There are two factors at play here:

- The rate of interest, and
- The length of time to save and accumulate retirement funds.

The higher the rate of interest and the longer the investment horizon, the larger the value of compounded growth and, hence, the lower the rate of annual savings required. Individuals cannot directly control prevailing rates of interest, which the market determines according to government policies. However, they can control the length of their savings horizon to accumulate and compound savings growth. The lesson is simple: start saving as early as reasonably possible to maximize future values.

There is a third component of retirement planning that requires a review of savings in the context of current tax rates. An investor's rate of return only has meaning net of tax. That is, how much does the government allow one to keep invested net of tax. As we shall see below, choice of an appropriate tax efficient vehicle is an important element in retirement planning because it affects the net rate at which we compound savings.

2. Inflation Risk

Inflation is the silent killer that erodes the time value of money. Inflation is beyond the control of individuals, but they must take it into account in their investment decisions. Hence, we must think of rates of return on money in real rather than nominal terms.

Example

Assume an investment of $1,000 earns a compound rate of return of 6 percent per year. After ten years, the investment will grow to $1,790. If we assume an annual inflation rate of 3 percent, the real value of the investment will be $1,340. Inflation erodes $450 of the investment value in ten years (see Table 5.1).

D. THE ROLE OF INCOME TAX

The first step in understanding retirement planning is to appreciate the role of the Canadian marginal income tax rate structure that applies to individuals.

1. Marginal Tax Rates

The marginal tax rate is the rate of tax that applies to the *top dollar* of an individual's taxable income. As marginal rates rise, the total tax payable increases by a rate that is more than proportional to the increase in income.

The following are the five *federal* marginal rates on taxable income for individuals in 2020:

Federal tax rates (%) as of 31 March 2020	Tax Brackets (lower) ($)	Tax Brackets (upper) ($)
15.0	Up to 48,535	
20.5	48,536	97,069
26.0	97,070	150,473
29.0	150,474	214,368
33.0	214,369	And over

The federal tax brackets are indexed each year by an inflation factor, which is based on the change in the average federal inflation rate over the twelve-month period ending September 30 of the previous year compared to the change in the rate for the same period of the year prior. The federal inflation factor is 1.9 percent for 2020.

We see that the rate of tax increases as taxable income rises. The rates start at 15 percent, and then rise in steps to 20.5 percent, 26 percent, 29 percent, and, finally, 33 percent. An individual pays tax on the first bracket of income at 15 percent, 20.5 percent on the second bracket, 26 percent on the third bracket, 29 percent on the fourth bracket, and 33 percent on the fifth bracket. An individual's marginal rate is the rate that applies to their highest tax bracket.

The marginal rate is the key to tax planning because we measure the amount of tax payable or benefit resulting from a decision or change of financial circumstances. For example, in decisions involving retirement plans, choices buy or lease, and agreements to enter into new contracts or pay damages to exit an old one, we calculate the tax cost or benefit at the margin for engaging in the transaction. Each dollar by which an individual reduces their income saves tax at their marginal rate.

Example

If Harry earns $30,000 taxable income, he would calculate his basic *federal* tax at a marginal rate of 15 percent. In contrast, if Janice earns taxable income of $300,000, she would have a 2020 federal marginal rate of 33 percent. However, the 33 percent applies only on her income over $214,369, which is the threshold amount for the top marginal rate.

Thus, marginal rates reflect the tax cost or tax benefit of the *next dollar* transaction, which is what investors should focus on in retirement planning.

Example

An individual with a 33 percent marginal rate will save $6,600 tax if they contribute $20,000 to a tax-sheltered plan and reduce their current taxable income by that amount. If their marginal rate upon retirement is lower (say 26 percent), they will be taxed at the lower rate on their income. Hence, assuming tax rates remain the same, they will save 7 percent in tax in the long run because of the decline in their current versus retirement marginal rates. They will also defer their current tax liability to a later date, which will add to their tax savings in the long run. For example, each $1 savings at 7 percent will be worth $7.61 in thirty years (see Chapter 5 on the time value of money and deferral).

The progressive marginal rate structure is an incentive for high rate individuals to shift their income to members of their family with lower rates. For example, if Jane has a *federal* marginal rate of 33 percent and her spouse (Michel) has a rate of 20.5 percent, she has an economic incentive to move some of her investments to him in order to take advantage of his lower tax rate. Overall, the family will be better off if Michel is taxed on the investment income at the lower tax rate.

As one might expect, the *Income Tax Act* has a complex maze of rules that address income shifting. Some of the rules allow income shifting to reduce taxes, such as spousal RRSPs and pension income.[2] Others penalize income shifting, such as income attribution on property transferred between spouses and minors.[3] Hidden in the maze of rules are swamps that impose specific and general penalties.[4] Hence, before shifting investments and income, one must first navigate the maze carefully to avoid unpleasant surprises and tax assessments. Litigation with the CRA is a long and expensive process, where six years is considered fast track. It takes the CRA eighteen to twenty-four months to respond to a Notice of Objection. Hence, litigation costs can easily erase any perceived tax savings.

2. Average Rates

The average tax rate tells us the rate payable on the taxpayer's *entire* income. Hence, it measures the total tax burden of the taxpayer. We obtain the "average rate" of tax by dividing the total tax payable by the tax base. If Jane earns $25,000 and pays $3,750 tax, her average tax rate is 15 percent. This is the rate that people implicitly refer to

---

2 See, for example, *Income Tax Act*, RSC, 1985, c 1 (5th Supp) [*ITA*], s 146(5.1) for contributions to spousal RRSPs.

3 See, for example, *ITA*, ss 74.1(1) & (2).

4 See, for example, *ITA*, ss 74.5(11) and 245.

when they complain that their taxes are too high, or that their neighbour's taxes are too low.

The average rate is the *weighted* average of all of the individual's marginal tax rates. Hence, an individual's average rate of tax is always lower than their marginal rate.

Example

The average federal tax rate of an individual who earns taxable income of $30,000 is $4,500, 15 percent. In this case, the average and the marginal rates are equal because only one federal marginal rate (15 percent) applies to all of the income. However, if Janice earned taxable income of $250,000 in 2020, she would pay federal tax (excluding CPP) of $58,138. Her average federal tax rate is approximately 23 percent—that is, 10 percent lower than her federal marginal rate of 33 percent. The same principle applies if we factor in provincial taxes.

3. Tax Deferral

As a general rule, income is taxable only when we "realize" the income.[5] The realization concept affects the timing of any tax payable on a transaction and, in certain circumstances, allows taxpayers to defer their tax liabilities. Hence, the realization principle performs the lead role in many tax strategies that benefit from tax deferral.

Apart from certain events such as death, we can generally control when we will recognize income from appreciated property. However, tax deferral costs the treasury. Hence, the government controls deferral through complex rules (discussed below).

E. STATUTORY TAX SHELTERS

In addition to raising revenues, the government uses the *Income Tax Act* as a tool of social engineering. Hence, there are several investment plans, which are essentially legislated tax shelters, which individuals

5 Special rules apply upon the death of an individual. See, for example, *ITA*, s 70.

can use for retirement planning. Most of them are based on the time value of money and tax deferral.

Each of the plans has its own technical rules that govern contributions, time limits, mode of taxation, and rules for the withdrawal of funds. However, the rules attempt to harmonize equal access to the plans and provide flexibility. As all of the plans are deferral tax shelters that cost the government in lost revenues, there are stringent limits on contributions, generally 18 percent of earned income up to phased-in dollar limits.

1. Registered Pension Plans (RPPs)

There are two principal types of pension plans:

1) Defined benefit plans; and
2) Money purchase plans.

The major difference between the two is the mode of funding and the calculation of pension benefits under the plans.

(a) Defined Benefit Plans

Under a defined benefit plan (DBP), the benefit paid to each employee is *defined* as a percentage of the employee's earnings, usually in the last years of their employment. The employer must pay the benefit from the plan, regardless of its cost or investment experience. Hence, the employer bears the risk of the DBP.

The employer can deduct its contributions into the plan, which must be registered with the CRA, if an actuary certifies them to be necessary to fund the accruing benefits. The contributions are not taxable to the employee as a current benefit.[6]

The employee's contributions into the plan are deductible but are subject to a maximum. The maximum tax-assisted benefit that a DBP can provide is 2 percent per year of the employee's average best three years of remuneration multiplied by the number of years of

---

6 *ITA* at para 6(1)(a).

pensionable service. There is also a phased-in dollar limit. The maximum tax-assisted benefit for 2020 is $3,092.22.

The employee is taxable when they receive their pension out of the plan, which is usually upon retirement.[7] Special rules apply if they withdraw their pension before retirement.

(b) Money Purchase Plans

Under a money purchase plan (MPP), also known as a defined contribution plan (DCP), the plan defines the *contributions* of the employer and the employee, rather than defining the benefit from the plan.

The ultimate value of the benefit from a DCP is determined upon retirement by purchasing an annuity with the contributions into the plan plus its investment earnings. Thus, the payout from the DCP depends upon market performance during the tenure of the individual's employment. The maximum tax-assisted benefit for 2020 is $27,830.

2. Deferred Profit-Sharing Plans

There are two sources of contributions to a deferred profit-sharing plan (DPSP):[8]

1) Employer payments; and
2) Reallocated forfeited amounts.

Only the employer may contribute to the plan for the employee. The employee cannot contribute to a DPSP.

The amount is based upon the profits of the business. However, employer contributions and any forfeited amounts allocated to an employee during the year cannot exceed the *lesser* of:[9]

- 18 percent of an employee's compensation for the year; or
- A dollar limit equal to half of the money purchase plan limit.

The overall limit in 2020 is $13,915.

---

7 *ITA* at para. 56(1)(a).
8 *ITA*, s 147.
9 *ITA*, s 147(5.1).

The funds must vest irrevocably in the employee after two years of employment and the plan may invest in the employer's equity shares if they qualify. However, an employer cannot deduct contributions for a beneficiary who is related to the employer.[10]

The employer's contributions into a DPSP are not taxable as a benefit to the employee.[11] The DPSP is not taxable on its income.[12]

3. Registered Retirement Savings Plans

A "registered" retirement savings plan (RRSP) is a tax shelter that allows individuals to reduce their current taxes and can also reduce tax on the ultimate payout upon retirement. "Registered" means that the plan is a trust registered with the CRA and that complies with the technical requirements of the Act.[13]

Although RRSPs are primarily retirement vehicles, they can also be used for any other savings purpose, such as financing a home, providing for education, or simply deferring payment of current income taxes. Hence, they are efficient tax shelters.

(a) Basic Concept

Although the technical rules governing RRSPs are detailed and complex, their basic concept is simple. They allow individuals to contribute a portion of their "earned income" to a trust registered as a RRSP with the CRA.

There are three principal advantages to RRSPs:

1) Contributions into the plan are deductible within limits;
2) Income and capital gains retained in the plan are not taxable on a current basis; and
3) Taxes on proceeds from the RRSP can be further deferred (in part) through investment in another vehicle, a Registered Retirement Income Fund (RRIF).

10 *ITA* at para 147(2)(k.2).
11 *ITA* at para 6(1)(a).
12 *ITA*, s 147(7).
13 See, generally, *ITA* s 146.

Unlike other sources of income that are usually taxable when earned, investment income in an RRSP is taxable only when one withdraws it from the plan. Hence, RRSPs allow income compounding and tax deferral within the plan.

Example

Contribution room for the year	$10,000
Amount contributed to RRSP	$10,000
Individual's federal marginal tax rate	33%
Federal tax savings from contribution	$3,300

In this example, the individual gets a refund and saves $3,300 by making a $10,000 contribution into the plan. Hence, the net cost of their contribution is only $6,700. However, the entire $10,000 in the plan will earn investment income on a compounded tax-free basis. The individual can use the $3,300 refund for next year's contribution into the plan or pay down any loan if they borrowed the funds to contribute to their RRSP.

(b) Interest on Borrowed Money

Interest on money borrowed to make contributions into RRSPs is not deductible for tax purposes, as the money is used to earn income that is exempt from tax.[14]

(c) Investments Within RRSPs

Funds within an RRSP may be invested in a variety of vehicles, such as savings accounts, guaranteed investment certificates (GICs), bonds, mortgage loans, mutual funds, exchange traded funds, income trusts, or corporate shares.[15] Any income or capital gains that the plan earns is not taxable while it remains within the plan, but will ultimately be taxable when withdrawn from the plan. Hence, the plan benefits from tax deferral, which is a significant form of saving.

14 *ITA* at para 18(11)(b).

15 *ITA* at para 146(1) "qualified investment."

(d) Types of RRSPs

There are two basic types of plans:

- Financial institution plans; and
- Self-administered plans.

Although the rules governing RRSP trusts are detailed and complex, an individual can open an account quite easily with any bank, trust company, insurance company, credit union, or investment advisor, which will look after all the technical details. The application requires one to fill out a form and contribute the money into the plan. The institution provides a tax receipt, which the taxpayer files with their tax return.

The financial institution and its investment advisors will select the investments for the individual's particular plan. Investment management fees are typically charged against the underlying investment funds, rather than the RRSP.

Alternatively, an individual can set up a self-administered fund with most financial institutions and direct the investment portfolio within a broad range of permitted qualified investments, such as publicly traded equities, debt securities, mutual funds, and treasury bills. A trustee will hold the RRSP investments.

The individual is responsible for payment of any administration charges of the RRSP. However, they may not deduct any fees paid in respect of the plan.[16]

(e) Contribution Limits

Since RRSPs are tax saving trusts, the government controls and limits the amounts that can be contributed or withdrawn from them. There are three limits on the amount that an individual may contribute in any year to an RRSP:

1) Dollar limit.
    - This limit is indexed annually. The maximum RRSP deduction limit is $27,230 in 2020 and $27,830 in 2021.[17]

---

16 *ITA* at para 18(1)(u).

17 Without considering any RRSP carry-forward contribution room.

2) Earned income limit.
   - This limit is 18 percent of "earned income." The maximum in 2020 is $151,777.
3) Pension adjustment (PA).

A taxpayer's PA, which is essentially the value of other tax-sheltered benefits that they accrue in the previous year through their employer's registered pension plan (RPP) and deferred profit-sharing plan (DPSP), reduces their earned income limit for the current year. The PA reduction prevents doubling up of the amounts that can be deferred though multiple tax-sheltered programs. The employer reports the employee's PA on a T4 slip.

Example

Assume an individual earns $72,000 in the year and has a PA of $11,960. Then:

Earned income for the year	$72,000
Earned income limit of 18%	$12,960
Subtract: PA reported	$11,960
Net contribution limit for RRSP for the year	$1,000

The CRA checks the deduction against its pension file to determine if the amount contributed is deductible.[18]

(f) Unused Contribution Amounts

An individual may carry forward and deduct any amounts of unused contributions since 1991 to future years and add the amount to their contribution limit.[19] For example, assume a taxpayer's RRSP contribution limit for 2019 was $20,000 and they contributed only $17,000 for the year. Then they may carry forward the unused balance of $3,000 and apply it in future years.

18 *ITA*, s 146(5).

19 *ITA*, s 146(1).

(g) Earned Income

"Earned income" of an individual who was resident in Canada throughout the year includes most forms of active income, such as income from:[20]

- An office or employment;
- Business;
- Rental of property;
- Support payments;
- Supplementary unemployment benefits;
- Net research grants; and
- Disability pension receipts.

However, earned income does *not* include:

- Pension benefits;
- Retiring allowances;
- EI benefits;
- Amounts paid out of an RRSP;
- Investment income; and
- Taxable capital gains.

(h) Contributions of Property

An individual can contribute certain types of property, such as shares or mutual fund units, into a self-administered RRSP and deduct the fair market value of the property from their income. The amount deductible is subject to the normal contribution limits. However, any capital gain on the disposition of the property to the RRSP is taxable and any loss is deemed to be nil and not deductible for tax purposes.[21]

(i) Spousal RRSPs

A spousal RRSP is a plan under which the taxpayer's spouse is the annuitant. This allows spouses to income split and reduce their marginal rates of tax. Any property contributed to a spousal RRSP is the

---

20 *ITA*, s 146(1) "earned income."

21 *ITA* at para 40(2)(g)(iv).

property of the recipient annuitant and will affect division of property upon matrimonial breakdown.

An individual can contribute to their spousal RRSP and deduct the contribution from their income. This is an advantage if the contributing individual has the higher marginal tax rate in the family. The benefit of such a plan is that the proceeds from withdrawal of funds will be taxable to the lower income spouse who, presumably, will have a lower marginal rate of tax upon retirement. Hence, it is a form of income splitting.[22]

Overall contribution limits apply. An individual's contributions to both their own and their spousal plan are restricted in total to the contributor's limits.

Anti-avoidance rules apply if funds from a spousal RRSP are withdrawn within three years of a contribution. All premiums paid into the spousal RRSP within the three-year period are included in the contributor's income even if the premiums were not deducted or deductible in the three years.[23] Further, it does not matter whether the funds are withdrawn from the same plan as was most recently contributed into or some other plan. This rule does not apply if the parties separate because of matrimonial breakdown.

(j) Withdrawals Before Retirement

The primary purpose of RRSPs is to encourage Canadians to set aside money for retirement. However, individuals may terminate their RRSPs at any time and withdraw some or all of the accumulated funds prior to retirement. The *gross* amount of funds withdrawn is taxable as income.[24] Payments to residents are subject to withholding of tax at source under Reg 103(4) of the *ITA*.

However, there are also two programs that allow for early withdrawals from an RRSP with easier conditions and limited tax deferral.

---

22 *ITA*, s 146(5.1).

23 *ITA*, s 146(8.3).

24 *ITA*, s 146(8).

(k) Home Buyers' Plan (HBP)

The HBP allows a first-time home buyer to use up to $35,000 of RRSP savings ($70,000 for a couple) to help finance a down payment to buy or build a principal residence.[25] In effect, an individual can borrow from their RRSP to build or purchase their first home.

The individual must have a written agreement before the withdrawal to buy or build the qualifying home. The first-time home buyer restriction does not apply if the individual is going to build a home for a related person with a disability.

There are no immediate tax consequences for funds withdrawn from an HBP and the withdrawal is not included in the individual's income. There is no withholding tax (use form T1036).[26]

However, the individual must repay the funds to the RRSP on a non-deductible basis within a fifteen-year period. The minimum annual repayment is $35,000/15 or $2,333. The repayment period begins in the second calendar year following the calendar year of the withdrawal. Failure to repay the annual minimum amount will result in the unpaid portion being considered taxable income for that year.[27] For example, if the individual repays only $1,000 in a year, $1,333 will be added to income in that year. Although there are no immediate adverse tax consequences from the withdrawal of funds, the RRSP will lose the benefit of tax-free compounding during the period that the funds are not repaid into the plan.

An individual can participate in the HBP even if they do not meet the first-time home buyer requirement, provided that they live separate and apart from their spouse or common-law partner for a period of at least ninety days as a result of a breakdown in their marriage or common-law partnership. In these circumstances, the individual can withdraw funds under the HBP if they live separate and apart from their spouse or common-law partner at the time of the withdrawal and began to live separate and apart in the year in which they withdrew the funds, or any time in the four preceding years.

25 *ITA*, s 146.01 "regular eligible amount."

26 Excluded withdrawal under *ITA*, s 146(8).

27 *ITA*, s 146.01(4).

However, the individual will not be able to withdraw funds under the HBP if they had a principal place of residence that is a home owned and occupied by their *new* spouse or common-law partner.[28] In these circumstances, the individual must dispose of their previous principal place of residence no later than two years after the end of the year in which the HBP withdrawal is made.

The requirement to dispose of the previous principal place of residence is waived if they buy out the share of the residence owned by their spouse or common-law partner. The rule that individuals may not acquire the home more than thirty days before making the HBP withdrawal is also waived.

(l) Lifelong Learning Plan

An individual may withdraw up to $10,000 annually (maximum $20,000) (unindexed) from their RRSP to pay for full-time education or training for themself or their spouse at a designated educational institution.[29]

Contributions are repayable to the plan in ten equal annual installments following the last year that the student was enrolled in the institution on a full-time basis. The repayments are not deductible but merely replenish the RRSP. Any unpaid amounts are taxable income for the year.

(m) Other Withdrawals

It is possible to withdraw funds from an RRSP for other reasons as well. However, "non-qualified" withdrawals are taxable income and subject to withholding tax, which the financial institution will deduct immediately.

(n) Withdrawals Upon Retirement

An individual can contribute into their RRSP up to December 31 of the year in which they turn seventy-one years. Thereafter, the individual has three options. They can either:

---

28 *ITA*, s 146.01(2.1) (effective 2020).

29 *ITA*, ss 146.02 and 118.6(1).

1) Convert the RRSP into a RRIF (not taxable);
2) Purchase an annuity (not taxed); or
3) Withdraw the funds from the RRSP (taxable and subject to withholding).

A RRIF is essentially a modified extension of an RRSP that allows further deferral of taxes, but subject to new rules concerning minimum annual withdrawals (see below).

A fixed-term annuity provides benefits up to age ninety, or if the spouse is younger than the annuitant and the parties elect until the younger reaches age ninety.

A life annuity provides benefits during the individual's life, or during the lives of the annuitant and their spouse.

4. Registered Retirement Income Fund (RRIF)

A RRIF is essentially a tax-shelter vehicle that individuals can use to further defer taxes after they are compelled to collapse their RRSP at age seventy-one. As with RRSPs, a RRIF is a registered trust arrangement between an individual and a financial institution, such as an insurance company, trust company, bank, or credit union. The CRA registers RRIFs.[30]

An individual can transfer property to a RRIF from an RRSP, a RPP, a SPP, or another RRIF.

(a) Creating a RRIF

An individual may create a RRIF, or multiple RRIFs, at any time before the end of the year in which she reaches age 71. Hence, a RRIF is useful in planning for early retirement. Individuals can self-direct their RRIFs if they prefer to manage their own investment portfolio with a variety of different types of qualified investments.[31]

30 *ITA*, s 146.3(1) "registered retirement income fund."

31 *ITA* at para 146.3(1) "qualified investments."

(b) Minimum Withdrawals

A unique feature of RRIFs is that, beginning in the calendar year following the year in which they set up the plans, the annuitant must withdraw a *minimum* amount *annually* from each plan. Of course, since all withdrawn amounts are taxable in the year, the individual can always withdraw more than the specified minimum amount. Thus, a RRIF is essentially a deferral vehicle within controlled parameters.

The minimum withdrawal rate is based on a complicated formula depending on the annuitant's age, starting at age seventy-one (see §146.3(1) "minimum amount" and Reg 7308(4) of the *ITA*). Before age seventy-one, the withdrawal factor is 1/(9-Y). At age 94 and after, the annual factor for withdrawal is 20 percent of the remaining balance. Hence, the payout period under an individual's RRIF is a diminishing amount for their entire life.

As with lump-sum RRSP withdrawals, amounts in excess of the minimum amount are subject to withholding tax and are taxable.[32]

Because of the annual minimum withdrawal requirement, it is prudent to have at least some of the RRIF's assets in liquid investments. If an individual's spouse is younger than them, they can elect to have the minimum withdrawal amount determined by the spouse's age, which will result in a lower amount being taken out and taxed.

(c) Lump-Sum Direct Transfers

The Act permits various rollovers from tax-deferred plans into other plans. For example, an individual can transfer a lump-sum payout from a Registered Pension Plan (RPP) or Deferred Profit-sharing Plan (DPSP) on a tax-free basis if the amount is paid directly into another RPP or an RRSP under which the individual is the annuitant. Similarly, tax may be deferred if there is a lump sum paid out of an unmatured RRSP to an RPP, another RRSP, or a RRIF. In effect, these are all rollover provisions for tax sheltered retirement investments with tax deferral advantages. Taxes are generally payable only when the annuitant withdraws money from the plans.[33]

---

32 See *ITA*, Regs 103(4) and (6).

33 *ITA*, s 147.3

(d) Death

A qualified beneficiary of a deceased annuitant who receives an amount from an RRIF upon the death of the annuitant can transfer the funds directly or indirectly to their RRSP or RRIF or buy an eligible annuity.

5. Tax-Free Savings Account (TFSA)

A TFSA is also a tax deferral vehicle but with a difference. Unlike an RRSP, contributions to a TFSA are *not* deductible for income tax purposes. However, any amount contributed, as well as any income earned in the account, generally accumulates tax-free and withdrawals from the account are not taxable.

A RRIF can be set up by individuals who are eighteen and older if they have a social insurance number. Administrative or other fees in relation to a TFSA and any interest on money borrowed to contribute to a TFSA are not tax deductible.

(a) Opening a TFSA

As with RRSPs and RRIFs, a TFSA is a trust arrangement between an individual and a financial institution, such as an insurance company, trust company, bank, or credit union, which will register the TFSA with the CRA. A TFSA can be self-administered or managed by the financial institution.

(b) Contribution Room

The TFSA contribution room is made up of the total of the following:

- The TFSA's annual dollar limit;
- Any unused TFSA contribution room from previous years; and
- Any withdrawals made from the TFSA in the previous year.

The annual contribution limit for 2020 is $6,000. However, an individual can deposit any past unused contributions since 2009, when the program started. The annual contribution limits were as follows:

Years	Annual Limit ($)
2009–2012	5,000 per year
2013–2014	5,500 per year
2015	10,000
2016–2018	5,500 per year
2019	6,000
2020	6,000

The TFSA annual room limit is indexed to inflation and rounded to the nearest $500.

(c) Qualified Investments

As with all tax shelters, there are a wide variety of qualified investments, including money, guaranteed investment certificates (GICs), government and corporate bonds, mutual funds, and securities listed on a designated stock exchange. These types of investments are generally similar to those that qualify for RRSPs.[34]

(d) Matrimonial Breakdown

Upon the breakdown of their marriage or common-law partnership, an annuitant can transfer payments to their spouse if the transfer is pursuant to a decree, order, or judgment of a court, or under a written agreement relating to a division of property in settlement of rights arising from the breakdown of their relationship and the parties are living separate and apart at the time of the transfer. However, the transfer must be completed by a financial institution.

6. Retiring Allowances

(a) What is a Retiring Allowance (RA)?

A retiring allowance is an amount that an individual (or, after their death, a dependant or legal representative) receives:[35]

---

34 See generally, Income Tax Folio S3-F10-C1, Qualified Investments - RRSPs, RESPs, RRIFs, RDSPs, and TFSAs.

35 *ITA* at para 248(1) "retiring allowance." See also Income Tax Folio S2-F1-C2.

- Upon or after retirement for the individual's service from an office or employment in recognition of long service; or
- In respect of a loss of an office or employment, regardless of whether it is payable on account or in lieu of damages or pursuant to an order or judgment of a competent tribunal.

A retiring allowance does *not* include a superannuation or pension benefit, an amount received as a consequence of the death of an employee, or benefits from certain counselling services.[36]

(b) Essential Tests

A retiring allowance includes a wrongful dismissal award, severance payment, or a termination payment.[37] There are two essential tests to determine whether an amount is an RA:

1) But for the loss of employment, would the individual have received the payment? [*No*]; and
2) Was the purpose of the payment to compensate for the loss of employment? [*Yes*]

A settlement for personal injury, moral damages, or human rights complaint is not taxable if there is clear evidence in the settlement agreement of the nature of the claim being compensated. The evidence must show a clear connection to such injuries that are separate from loss of employment. Hence, it is important that the language of the settlement agreement or court judgment is clear and unequivocal to avoid CRA harassment.

Damages for breach of an employment contract before it begins are also not taxable.[38] Similarly, damages for the tort of inducing a breach of contract are not taxable.[39]

---

36 *ITA* at para 6(1)(a)(iv).

37 See *Naraine*, 2015 TCC 104; *Putland*, 2009 TCC 349.

38 *Schwartz*, [1996] 1 CTC 303 (SCC).

39 *Ahmad*, [2002] 4 CTC 2497 (TCC).

(c) Taxation

Retiring allowances are taxable in the year the individual receives payment and are subject to lump-sum withholding.[40] The employer is required to report the amount on a T4 slip.[41]

F. INVESTMENT INCOME

1. Income by Source

The quintessential characteristic of Canadian income tax law is that we are taxed based on the source of income. The *Income Tax Act* divides income into five principal types, each of which is a source of income. The named sources are office, employment, business, property, and capital gains. Each source is taxed according to different rules and, often, at different rates. There are also certain other specified sources in section 56.

The salient characteristic of the source structure is that the various sources of income cannot be commingled. Income from each source remains within its own silo and according to the special rules that apply to that particular source.

Hence, the first principle of investment planning is that all dollars are not equal in tax law. "A buck is not a buck" for tax purposes. Each source and type of income is taxable at different rates and at different times. Some are not taxable at all. The following is a sampling of the top marginal tax rates applicable in 2019 to different sources of investment income, which we will explore in greater detail below.

1 July 2019	Interest Income (%)	Capital Gains (%)	Eligible Dividends (%)	Non-eligible Dividends (%)
Federal	33.0	16.50	24.81	27.57
Alberta	48.00	24.00	31.71	42.31
Nova Scotia	54.00	27.00	41.58	48.28
Ontario	53.53	26.76	39.34	47.40

40 *ITA* at paras 56(1)(a)(ii) and 153(1)(c).

41 *ITA*, Reg 200.

In tax planning we need to consider both the source of income and the entity in which we should hold the source for maximum return.

2. Interest Income

Interest is payment for the use of money over time. Thus, in commercial terms, interest is the "rental" charge for the use of someone else's money. We determine interest by reference to a principal sum of money or an obligation to pay money.[42] As we see in the above table, interest is the highest rate. The combined federal and provincial marginal rate on interest income at the top generally exceeds 50 percent. In Ontario, for example, an individual in the top bracket (income over $214,369) pays tax on interest at 53.53 percent, which means that the individual retains only 46.47 cents on every dollar of their income. In Nova Scotia the rate is 54 percent. Hence the rationale for protecting as much interest income as possible in tax shelters.

(a) Basic Rule

The basic rule is that an individual is taxable on interest income that they receive, or that is receivable, in the year (depending on the method regularly followed in computing income) to the extent that the interest was not included in computing the taxpayer's income for a preceding taxation year.[43]

The rule would appear to allow a taxpayer to include interest in income on either a cash or accrual basis. However, there are other provisions that effectively require taxpayers to account for the majority of interest receipts on an accrual basis.[44]

42 *Ref re s 6 of Farm Security Act 1944 of Sask*, [1947] SCR 394 at 411; affd [1949] AC 110 (PC); *The Queen v Melford Dev Inc*, [1982] 2 SCR 504, [1982] CTC 330, 82 DTC 6281 (SCC); see also, *Halsbury's Laws of England*, 4th ed, vol 32 (London: Butterworths, 1980) at 53, where "interest" is defined as "the return or compensation for the use or retention by one person of a sum of money belonging to or owed to another. Interest accrues from day to day even if payable only at intervals." The CRA generally accepts these criteria in defining interest. See IT-533 (31 October 2003) at para 1.

43 *ITA* at para 12(1)(c).

44 See for example, *ITA*, s 12(4).

i. Investment Contracts

There are special restrictions in respect of "investment contracts." An investment contract is a debt, such as a note, bond, debenture, or guaranteed investment certificate. This is a fairly comprehensive list.

Income from "investment contracts" must be reported on an annual basis, regardless whether or not the income has been paid out in the year.[45] Individuals generally cannot defer including interest from investments in their income for longer than a year.[46] This rule prevents prolonged deferral of tax on investment income.

However, investment contracts do *not* include the following:[47]

- Salary deferral arrangements;
- Income bonds and debentures;
- Retirement compensation arrangements;
- Employee benefit plans;
- Small business development bonds;
- Small business bonds; or
- Debt obligations in respect of which investment income is otherwise included in income at least annually.

ii. Consistent Reporting

A taxpayer who selects a particular method of reporting interest income for a particular property must conform to that method from year to year.

iii. Blended Payments

A blended payment is a composite in which interest and principal are blended into one amount.[48] Whether a payment is blended is a question of fact that depends upon the terms of the contract, the course of the negotiation between the parties, and, of particular importance, the price at which the property is sold.

---

45 *ITA*, s 12(4).
46 *ITA*, s 12(4).
47 *ITA*, s 12(4).
48 See, generally, IT-265R3 "Payments of Income and Capital Combined" (7 October 1991) (now archived by the CRA as being out of date).

An issuer can blend interest and principal by issuing a bond at a discount and redeeming it at its face value upon maturity. For example, Treasury Bills typically do not stipulate any interest rate or amount on their face. The government issues them at a discount from their face value. The discount rate is a direct function of the prevailing interest rate. The economic substance of the bills is that, in effect, their redemption value comprises both principal and interest. Hence, for tax purposes, we must break down the payment on maturity into its interest (income) and principal (capital) components.[49]

iv. Zero Coupon Bonds

A "zero coupon" bond is an extreme discount bond that is sold without any coupons attached. Also known as "strip bonds," these are long-term bonds where the interest is paid as part of the redemption proceeds upon maturity. Until that time, there is no interest payable on the bond. The difference between the cost of the bond and its maturity value represents the present value of the accumulated interest income compounded on an annual basis[50] (see Chapter 5 for determining the present value of a bond).

v. Rates of Tax

Interest income is taxable at the ordinary or general rates applicable to individuals (see federal marginal tax rates, above). In 2019, the top *federal* marginal rate of tax is 33 percent on income above $214,369. Combined with provincial rates, the top rate is much higher. For example, 53.53 percent (Ontario); 48 percent (Alberta); 54 percent (Nova Scotia). These punitive rates apply to top rate individuals who earn interest income.

Hence, for retirement planning, it is advantageous to place interest-bearing debt instruments and zero-coupon bonds in tax sheltered vehicles, such as RRSPs, RRIFs, or TFSAs, in order to maximize their tax deferral benefits.

---

49 *O'Neil v MNR* (1991), 91 DTC 692 (TCC); see also *Beck v Lord Howard de Walden*, [1940] TR 143; *Lomax v Peter Dixon & Sons Ltd*, [1943] 1 KB 671.

50 See *ITA*, Reg 7000, "Prescribed Debt Obligations."

3. Dividends

The tax payable on dividends depends upon several factors:

- The type of corporation;
- The residence of the corporation;
- The source of its income; and
- The status of the recipient.

Taxable dividends from Canadian sources are taxed at lower rates than income interest and foreign dividends. As we see from the above table, for example, a Canadian dividend may be taxable anywhere from 24.81 percent to 48.28 percent depending on the individual's province of residence and the type of dividend.

Dividends from non-resident corporations could be taxable at the top marginal rate applicable to interest income, which in Ontario, for example, is 53.53 percent. Hence, it is imperative for retirement planning to place dividend paying stocks in the appropriate vehicle to maximize returns.

(a) Nature of Dividends

A dividend is essentially a pro rata distribution of a portion of a corporation's retained earnings to its shareholders.[51] The board of directors determines the amount, date of record, and date of payment of the dividend. Only shareholders who own the stock on the ex-dividend date are eligible to receive declared dividends. For tax purposes, corporations pay dividends with after-tax dollars.

(b) Types of Dividends

Dividends may be paid out in cash, in additional stock, in kind, or as capital dividends. All dividends, other than capital dividends, are taxable as income, but according to a myriad of technical rules.[52]

---

51 See *ITA*, s 248(1), *Marshall*, 2011 TCC 497 at para 16, and *Moose Jaw Flying Club*, [1949] CTC 279 (Ex Ct).

52 *ITA* at para 89(1) "taxable dividend" and s 83(2).

A taxable dividend is any dividend *other than* a tax-free capital dividend. A dividend in kind is equal to its fair market value.[53]

A stock dividend is simply the amount of retained earnings that are capitalized into share capital. It represents the transformation of one type of equity capital (retained earnings) into another type (share capital). There is no increase in the total equity capital of the corporation. Hence, a stock dividend does not have any real effect in accounting or economic terms. However, for tax purposes, stock dividends are taxable dividends.[54]

(c) Taxable Dividends

The basic rule is that an individual is taxable on dividends from resident and non-resident corporations.[55] However, there are special rules for individuals, which affect the net tax costs of dividends, and these are critical in planning investments and retirement.

There are two broad categories of taxable dividends: "eligible" and "ordinary" dividends. The latter are also sometimes referred to as "non-eligible" dividends. The language of the two types of dividends is counter-intuitive and confusing:

- An eligible dividend is one that a corporation pays from income that is *not eligible* for the small business deduction.
- An ordinary or ineligible dividend is one that a corporation pays from income that is eligible for the small business deduction.

In the top marginal bracket, the federal rate on ineligible dividends is 24.81 percent, whereas it is 27.57 percent on eligible dividends. The rates are higher with provincial taxes. In Ontario, for example, eligible dividends are taxable at 39.34 percent and ineligible dividends at 47.40 percent. The rates differ because corporations pay tax at different rates and, hence, their dividends are paid from different pools of income, which bear different federal and provincial taxes. However, the income tax system integrates the taxes payable by corporations at different rates with the tax that individuals pay on their dividends.

53 *ITA*, s 52(2); *Rezayat*, 2011 TCC 286.

54 *ITA*, s 248(1) "dividend."

55 *ITA* at paras 12(1)(j) and (k).

(d) Tax Integration

The theoretical concept of "tax integration" is simple: An individual should pay the same amount of tax on their dividend income, regardless whether they earn the income personally or indirectly through a corporation. We attempt to achieve this objective by mathematically synchronizing the underlying tax that the corporation pays with the tax that an individual shareholder will pay on their dividends from the corporation.

This requires two mathematical adjustments. First, the individual must include in their income the cash value of the dividend plus an amount that *notionally* reflects the underlying corporate tax that the corporation *theoretically* paid on the income from which it pays the dividend. We call this the dividend "gross-up," which, in theory, makes the amount included in the individual's income equal to the corporation's pre-tax income.[56]

The second mathematical adjustment gives the individual a federal tax credit that is equal to the *theoretical* amount of the corporate tax that the corporation previously paid. This is known as the "dividend tax credit" (DTC).[57]

Since corporations pay tax on their business income at varying rates, the mathematical adjustments differ depending on the source of the dividend income and rely on assumptions about prevailing corporate and individual tax rates. They also assume that the corporation actually paid corporate tax, which may or may not be the case. For example, a corporation with fast depreciation write-offs or special incentive credits may not pay any tax in a particular year. However, for the purposes of taxing the dividends, the Act assumes that the corporation paid tax on the underlying income and gives the individual a tax credit.

With perfect integration, the underlying corporate tax is essentially a form of withholding tax, which the corporation pays on behalf of its shareholders. The individual reclaims the corporate tax paid through the DTC when the corporation pays them a dividend. Hence, in a sense, the corporate tax resembles the withholding tax on

56 *ITA*, s 82(1).

57 *ITA*, s 121.

an employee's salary and wages. Provincial taxes are added and credited on top of the federal tax.

i. Dividend Gross-Up

The dividend gross-up requires individuals who receive a dividend from a corporation to add a notional amount to their actual dividend.[58] In theory, the gross-up is intended to equal the amount of underlying income tax that the corporation paid on the income from which it paid the dividend. The amount of the gross-up depends upon the type of corporation and the source of its business income. For example, if a corporation pays tax at 20 percent, grossing-up its after-tax income by 25 percent brings the income up to the corporation's *pre-tax* income.

Corporate business income	$100
Corporate tax @ 20%	$20
After-tax income	$80
Gross-up @ 25%	$20
Grossed-up amount	$100

Thus, in effect, the gross-up is the reciprocal of the reciprocal, which gets us back to where we started, which is equal to the payer corporation's pre-tax income.

ii. Dividend Tax Credit (DTC)

The federal DTC refunds a portion of the dividend gross-up.[59] The amount of the DTC also depends upon the type of corporation paying the dividend and the source of its business income.

iii. Theoretical Example of Integration

The following is a simple theoretical example of tax integration. Assume that *Alpha Ltd* pays Jane a dividend of $800 after it paid federal and provincial taxes of 20 percent on its business income of $1,000. We assume that Jane has a 50 percent marginal tax rate. If we

58 *ITA* at para 82(1)(b).
59 *ITA*, s 121.

gross up Jane's dividend of $800 by 25 percent, it will equal Alpha's *pre-tax* corporate business income of $1,000. Then:

Tax payable by Alpha Ltd:	$
Net business income before tax	**1000**
Corporate taxes @ 20%	200
Net income after tax	800
Tax payable by Jane:	
Dividend from *Alpha*	800
Gross-up by 25%	200
Taxable amount of dividend (equals corporate pre-tax income)	**1000**
Tax payable @ 50%	500
Dividend tax credit (equal to corporate tax)	200
Net tax payable by Jane	300
Total tax payable by corporation and individual	500

In this example, we assume that both federal *and* provincial taxes exactly equal the total tax that Jane would have paid on $1,000 of income at 50 percent if she earned the income directly instead of through a corporation. The gross-up restores the taxable amount of the dividend to the corporation's pre-tax income, and the DTC equals the corporation's tax. This is the theoretically perfect integration model.

However, corporations pay taxes at different rates and the provinces impose their taxes at different rates. Hence, we adapt the mathematical adjustments to account for various rates.

In general terms, Canadian-controlled private corporations (CCPCs) pay a lower rate of tax on their active business income (ABI). Public corporations pay tax at a higher rate. The underlying principle of integration is the same for both types of corporations, but the math is different to account for the different rates of corporate tax.

iv. CCPCs

In 2020, the federal tax rate on CCPCs is 9 percent on the first $500,000 of active business income. For purposes of integration, we *assume* an average provincial corporate tax rate of 4.03 percent. Hence, the combined corporate tax rate is 13.04 percent. The gross-up factor is 15 percent, which brings the income inclusion up to the theoretical pre-tax corporate income (15⁄115).

The federal DTC is 9⁄13 of the gross-up, which is the *theoretical* amount of the *federal* tax that the corporation paid. Each province then provides a DTC that approximately equals the remaining 4⁄13 of the gross-up. Hence, in theory, we refund the full gross-up and achieve perfect integration of corporate and shareholder taxes.

v. Theoretical Example (CCPC)

The following theoretical example illustrates the concept of integration for CCPCs in 2020. Assume a CCPC earns $1,000 active business income (ABI), pays a combined federal and provincial tax of 13.04 percent (9 percent federal and 4.04 percent provincial), and pays out all of its after-tax income to an individual with a 50 percent marginal rate of tax. Then:

Corporate Tax on ABI of CCPC:	($)
Corporate business income	1000
Tax rate (13.04%)	130
Net after-tax income	870
Shareholder's Tax:	
Dividend	870
Gross-up (15%) [§ 82(1)(b)(i)]	130
Taxable amount (equals corporate pre-tax income)	1000
Combined personal tax @ 50%	500
Federal DTC (9/13×$130)	-90
Provincial DTC (4/13×$130)	-40
Net personal tax	370
After-tax cash available to shareholder	500
If Income Earned Personally:	
Active business income	1,000
Personal tax @ 50%	500
After-tax cash available	500

The individual retains the same amount of after-tax income ($500) whether they earn the business income personally or through a corporation. Hence, in theory, perfect integration of corporate and personal taxes.

vi. Public Corporations

We also integrate dividends from public corporations with shareholder taxes. However, because of different tax rates that apply to public corporations, the mathematics of the adjustments are necessarily different.

For public corporations, we assume a combined corporate tax rate of 27.5 percent, a gross-up of 38 percent, and a federal DTC for "eligible dividends" of 6⁄11 and provincial DTC of 5⁄11.

vii. Theoretical Example (Public Corporation)

The following theoretical example illustrates the concept of integration for public corporations paying eligible dividends in 2020. Assume the corporation earns $1,000 business income, pays a combined federal and provincial tax of 27.5 percent (15 percent federal and 12.5 percent provincial), and pays out all of its after-tax income to an individual with a 50 percent marginal rate of tax. Then:

Corporate Tax:	$
Corporate business income	1000
Tax rate (27.5%)	275
Net after-tax income	725
Shareholder's Tax:	
Dividend	725
Gross-up (38%) [§82(1)(b)(ii)]	275
Taxable amount (equals corporate pre-tax income)	1000
Combined personal tax @ 50%	500
Federal DTC (6/11×$275)	–150
Provincial DTC (5/11×$275)	–125
Net personal tax	225
After-tax cash available to shareholder	500
If Income Earned Personally:	
Business income	1,000
Personal tax @ 50%	500
After-tax cash available	500

Once again, the individual has the same amount of after-tax income ($500) whether they earn the business income personally or as a dividend from a public corporation. Hence, once again, perfect integration of corporate and personal taxes, in theory.

Although a simple concept in theory, we do not achieve perfect integration of corporate and shareholder taxes because there are fourteen tax jurisdictions in Canada, and each sets its own corporate and personal tax rates. The top combined marginal rates for individuals vary 44.5 percent (Nunavut) to 53.53 percent (Ontario) and corporate rates also vary. For example, in 2019:

Jurisdiction	Corporate Tax Rate (%)
Federal	15.0
British Columbia	12.0
Ontario	11.5
Nova Scotia	16.0

Hence, the model is not perfect. Nevertheless, despite the variation in provincial corporate rates, there is substantial harmony in respect of dividends from Canadian resident corporations.

viii. Non-resident Corporations

Dividends from non-resident corporations are not eligible for a DTC and are taxable at full rates equivalent to the rates applicable to interest income (see above). This is an important consideration in determining where one should hold shares of non-resident corporations, such as shares listed on US stock exchanges.

4. Capital Gains

"Capital gains" are a separate source of income, which we calculate according with a distinct set of rules. There are two particular rules in respect of capital gains, one of which is an advantage for investors and the other a disadvantage.

First, generally, a taxpayer needs to include only 50 percent of capital gains in income and may deduct 50 percent of capital losses.[60] Thus, strictly speaking, there is no separate tax on capital gains. Capital gains merely expand or contract the taxable base to which we apply the normal tax rates. However, for planning purposes, given the lower *effective* tax rate on capital gains, they are an important consideration in retirement planning.

In 2020, for example, the top marginal effective federal, provincial, and territorial rates on investment income were as follows:

	Interest	Capital Gains	Eligible Dividends	Non-Eligible Dividends
Federal	**33.00**	**16.50**	**24.81**	**25.57**
Alberta	48.00	24.00	31.71	42.31
British Columbia	49.80	24.90	31.44	44.64
Manitoba	50.40	25.20	37.78	46.67
New Brunswick	53.30	26.65	33.51	47.75
Nfld & Lab	41.30	25.65	42.61	44.59
NWT	47.05	23.53	28.33	36.82
Nova Scotia	54.00	27.00	41.58	48.28
Nunavut	44.50	22.25	33.08	37.79
Ontario	53.53	26.76	39.34	47.40
PEI	51.37	25.69	34.22	45.22
Quebec	53.31	26.65	40.00	46.25
Saskatchewan	47.50	23.75	29.64	40.37
Yukon	48.00	24.00	28.93	42.17

We see that capital gains are generally taxable at an effective rate of one-half of interest income. The disparity in rates of tax on sources of investment income is a key consideration in determining whether to place investments in tax shelters or hold them personally.

The second rule is that capital losses are generally deductible only against capital gains. One cannot use any excess of capital losses over capital gains to reduce income from other sources.[61] This too is an important consideration in planning when to dispose of assets to

60 *ITA*, s 38.

61 See *ITA* at paras 3(d)–(f).

recognize gains and losses. There is an exception to this rule: business investment capital losses can be applied against "ordinary" income.

The effect of this silo structure is to treat capital gains and losses as income from a distinct and separate source.

(a) What Is a Capital Gain?

Generally speaking, capital gains and losses result from the disposition of capital properties acquired for investment purposes. The purpose test depends upon the taxpayer's intentions in acquiring the asset. In contrast, a taxpayer acquires income assets with the intention of speculation or resale. This distinction is simple to state but can be difficult to apply, particularly in the context of real estate. For most investors, other than speculators and day traders, however, investments in stocks, bonds, and securities will be treated as capital properties.

(b) Computation of Capital Gain

A capital gain from a disposition of capital property is the difference between the proceeds of disposition (POD) that one receives from the property and the sum of its adjusted cost base (ACB) and the expenses of disposition:[62]

Capital Gain = POD – (ACB + Expenses)

Generally, "proceeds of disposition" means selling price and "adjusted cost base" means the cost of property.

Example

Assume a taxpayer sells a capital property for $10,000. He purchased the asset for $6,000. He incurs expenses of $800 in selling the property.

Then:		
Selling price		$10,000
Subtract: Cost (ACB)	$6,000	
Selling expenses	$800	($6,800)
Capital gain		$3,200

62 *ITA* at para 40(1)(a).

The taxpayer's taxable capital gain is $1,600, that is, the capital gain times the inclusion rate of 50 percent ($3,200 × ½).

Conversely, a taxpayer's capital loss from a disposition of property is the amount by which the "adjusted cost base" and selling expenses exceed the "proceeds of disposition."[63]

Example

Assume: T sells a capital property that cost $16,000 for cash proceeds of $2,000 and incurs $80 as expenses of sale.

Then:	$	$
Proceeds of Sale		2,000
Subtract: Cost (ACB)	16,000	
Selling expenses	80	(16,080)
Capital gain		(14,080)

T's allowable capital loss is $7,040, that is, the capital loss times the inclusion rate ($14,080 × ½).

Transfers of property to or by a trust (including transfers to an RRSP, DPSP, EPSP, or RRIF, even if the transfer does not involve a change of beneficial ownership) are dispositions of property and should be carefully timed.

(c) Superficial Losses

An individual is not allowed to claim a "superficial loss."[64] A superficial loss arises when an individual, or certain affiliated parties,[65] disposes of property and replaces it with "substituted property" within a period of sixty-one days.[66] This is an anti-avoidance rule that prevents individuals from claiming paper losses for tax purposes.

For the purpose of this rule, the sixty-one–day period commences thirty days before, and ends thirty days after, the day that the taxpayer disposes of the property. This rule also applies to property that certain

63 *ITA* at para 40(1)(b).
64 *ITA* at para 40(2)(g)(i).
65 *ITA*, s 251.1(1).
66 *ITA*, s 54 "superficial loss."

affiliated persons may acquire during the sixty-one days. For example, it applies to property acquired by the individual, their spouse or common law partner, and controlled corporations.

The taxpayer can, however, increase the cost base of the "substituted property" by the amount of their superficial loss.[67] Consequently, when the taxpayer disposes of the "substituted property," they can reduce any gain on the property. Alternatively, the taxpayer can increase the actual loss by the amount of their superficial loss.

(d) Capital Gains Exemption

Every individual is allowed a "capital gains exemption" of $866,912 (2019), indexed annually, on the equivalent of capital gains when they dispose of "qualified small business corporation shares" (QSBC).[68] This exemption is shared with the farming/fishing property capital gains exemption, which is $1,000,000.

5. Annuities

We saw in Chapter 5 that we can measure the time value of money in two ways: the future value of a present sum of money or the present value of a future sum. The present value of an annuity is equal to the sum of the present values of a series of payments discounted at the appropriate rate of interest. Conversely, we can also think of the present value as a lump-sum amount invested now at compound interest that will permit a series of equal withdrawals at regular intervals and end up with nothing after the final withdrawal.

Example

Assume a simple annuity pays $1,000 per year at *year-end* for each of ten years. If the compound rate of interest is 10 percent per year, we can discount the series of $1,000 payments to their present value by adding the present values of each payment from Table 5.2 as follows.

67 *ITA* at para 53(1)(f).
68 *ITA*, s 110.6.

Years (*n*)	Rate (*r*) @ 10%
1	.91
2	.83
3	.75
4	.68
5	.62
6	.56
7	.51
8	.47
9	.42
10	.39
Total (rounded)	6.14

Thus, the present value of the ten equal payments of $1,000 at 10 percent is $6,140.

We arrive at the same conclusion by looking at Table 5.3 to determine the present value of an annuity of $1 received at the end of ten years. Looking at the 10 percent column and reading down to year 10, we see that the present value factor of a $1 annuity is 6.14. Hence, the present value of a $1,000 annuity is $6,140.

We can also check the above calculation using simple arithmetic.

Example

Assume that we deposit $6,140 in a savings account that pays 10 percent per year and we make $1,000 withdrawals at the end of each year. The ten-year profile of the account would be as follows:

Year (*n*)	Opening Balance (*P*)	Add: Annual Interest (*r*) 10%	Subtract: Withdrawals	Closing Balance
1	$6,140	$614	$1,000	$5,754
2	$5,754	$575	$1,000	$5,329
3	$5,329	$533	$1,000	$4,862
4	$4,862	$486	$1,000	$4,348
5	$4,348	$435	$1,000	$3,783
6	$3,783	$378	$1,000	$3,161

Year (*n*)	Opening Balance (*P*)	Add: Annual Interest (*r*) 10%	Subtract: Withdrawals	Closing Balance
7	$3,161	$316	$1,000	$$2,477
8	$2,477	$248	$1,000	1,725
9	$1,725	$173	$1,000	$898
10	$898	$90	$1,000	$0

We add the annual interest on the principal amount remaining at the end of each year and deduct the annual withdrawal of $1,000 annuity, which exhausts the entire amount by the end of year 10. The closing balance of $0 is rounded because we are working with only two decimal places.

(a) Rate of Increase of Annuities

The present value of an annuity will increase as duration lengthens, but at a decreasing rate. For example, the present value of an annuity of $1 at 5 percent in ten years is $7.72, but in twenty years it is $12.5 and in forty years $17.2. For fifty years, the present value is only $18.3. Hence, two-thirds of the value of the 50-year annuity is added in the first 20 years.

(b) Perpetuities

Annuities usually have a limited and finite duration. A perpetuity is a special form of annuity that promises to pay a certain periodic sum forever. For an annuity to continue forever, the investor may withdraw only the interest earned and not any of the principal. A pure perpetuity is a theoretical ideal that is useful in valuing a business. However, in reality, the closest thing to a perpetuity is land, because it offers a perpetual potential income stream.

Under a discounted present value model, a perpetuity has finite value because the payments that will be made far in the future have such minuscule values that their sum is considered finite. For example, look at the value of $1 at 20 percent in fifty years in Table 5.2. A dollar receivable in fifty years is worth only .000109 today. In other words, working with two decimal places, a dollar is worth zero today. Hence, the paradox of the tired walker who gets halfway to their ultimate destination each hour. They never overshoot their destination, no matter how long they walk, even though they make real progress each hour.

i. Present Value of Perpetuity

The present value of a perpetuity is the amount of money that one would pay lump sum today in order to produce an annual yield equal to the appropriate rate of interest without eroding capital. For example, in order to obtain a dollar in perpetuity at an interest rate of 10 percent, we would need to put \$10 on deposit to produce the requisite flow of income if payments were made at the end of each year. Thus, the present value of a \$1 a year perpetuity is worth \$10 today.

To generalize:

$$\text{Value (V)} \times r = \text{PMT}$$
$$\text{Thus, V} = \text{PMT}/r$$

Where:

V = Value of a perpetuity
r = Market rate of interest
PMT = Perpetual payment

Example

Assume that Sue wants to make sure that she has \$100,000 per year in annual income upon her retirement without eroding capital. Assuming a 5 percent rate of interest, how much must Sue have in her retirement fund to guarantee \$100,000 in annual income. Then:

$$\begin{aligned} .05X &= \$100{,}000 \\ X &= \$100{,}000/.05 \\ X &= \$2{,}000{,}000 \end{aligned}$$

Hence, Sue will need a fund of \$2,000,000 to guarantee \$100,000 annual income.

ii. Tax Considerations

The government has its hand in every investor's pocket. It is sheer folly to plan for retirement without considering the impact of the government's tax bite, which will reduce the net investment return on all taxable investments.

Example

Assume that in the above example, Sue wants to make sure that she has $100,000 per year in net annual income after taxes upon her retirement. Assuming a 5 percent rate of interest, Sue must have $3,333,333 in her retirement fund to guarantee $100,000 in net after tax annual income if her tax rate is 40 percent. Then:

Gross interest = 5%
Tax rate = 40%
Net interest = 3%
.03X = $100,000
X = $100,000/.03
X = $3,333,333

Sue will need a fund of $3,333,333 to guarantee $100,000 net after tax annual income in perpetuity without eroding capital.

iii. Tax-Free or Taxable Accounts

We can use annuity values to plan for retirement in tax-free or taxable accounts. Understandably, the amount invested will grow faster in a tax-free account because the net interest reinvested is greater. This is an important principle in retirement and estate planning using tax shelters.

Example

Suppose that Sacha (age 35) invests $5,000 at the *end* of each year (ordinary annuity) at 10 percent in a tax-free account, such as an RRSP or TFSA. Table 5.4 provides a factor of 164.49 for 30 years. His tax-free account will grow to $822,450 by the time he is 65 years of age.

If, instead, he has a personal tax rate of 40 percent and invests the same amount for 30 years, he will accumulate only $493,470 because his reinvestment is only $3,000 net of tax. Hence, rates of return on investments only have meaning after considering the tax bite on earnings. Tax deferral is tax saved.

Appendix A: Time Value Tables

Compound Amount of $1: Amount to Which $1 Now Will Grow by End of Specified Year at Compounded Interest

Year	3%	4%	5%	6%	7%	8%	10%	12%	15%	20%
1	1.03	1.04	1.05	1.06	1.07	1.08	1.10	1.12	1.15	1.20
2	1.06	1.08	1.10	1.12	1.14	**1.17**	1.21	1.25	1.32	1.44
3	1.09	1.12	1.16	1.19	1.23	1.26	1.33	1.40	1.52	1.73
4	1.13	1.17	1.22	1.26	1.31	1.36	**1.46**	1.57	1.74	2.07
5	1.16	1.22	1.28	1.34	1.40	1.47	1.61	1.76	2.01	2.49
6	1.19	1.27	1.34	1.41	1.50	1.59	1.77	1.97	2.31	2.99
7	1.23	1.32	1.41	1.50	1.61	1.71	1.94	2.21	2.66	3.58
8	1.27	1.37	1.48	1.59	1.72	1.85	2.14	2.48	3.05	4.30
9	1.30	1.42	1.55	1.68	1.84	**2.00**	2.35	2.77	3.52	5.16
10	1.34	1.48	1.63	**1.79**	1.97	2.16	**2.59**	3.11	4.05	6.19
11	1.38	1.54	1.71	1.89	2.10	2.33	2.85	3.48	4.66	7.43
12	1.43	1.60	1.80	**2.01**	2.25	2.52	3.13	3.90	5.30	8.92
13	1.47	1.67	1.89	2.13	2.41	2.72	3.45	4.36	6.10	10.7
14	1.51	1.73	1.98	2.26	2.58	2.94	3.79	4.89	7.00	12.8
15	1.56	1.80	2.08	2.39	2.76	3.17	4.17	5.47	8.13	15.4
16	1.60	1.87	2.18	2.54	2.95	3.43	4.59	6.13	9.40	18.5
17	1.65	1.95	2.29	2.69	3.16	3.70	5.05	6.87	10.6	22.2
18	1.70	2.03	2.41	2.85	3.38	4.00	5.55	7.70	12.5	26.6
19	1.75	2.11	2.53	3.02	3.62	4.32	6.11	8.61	14.0	31.9
20	1.81	2.19	2.65	3.20	3.87	**4.66**	6.72	9.65	16.1	38.3
25	2.09	2.67	3.39	4.29	5.43	6.85	10.8	17.0	32.9	95.4
30	2.43	3.24	4.32	5.74	**7.61**	10.0	17.4	30.0	66.2	237
40	3.26	**4.80**	7.04	10.3	15.0	21.7	45.3	**93.1**	**267.0**	**1470**
50	4.38	7.11	11.5	18.4	29.5	46.9	117	289	1080	9100

Present Value of $1: What a Dollar at End of Specified Future Year Is Worth Today										
Year	3%	4%	5%	6%	7%	8%	10%	12%	15%	20%
1	.971	.962	.952	.943	.935	.926	.909	.893	.870	.833
2	.943	.925	.907	.890	.873	.857	.826	.797	.756	.694
3	.915	.890	.864	.839	.816	.794	.751	.711	.658	.578
4	.889	.855	.823	.792	.763	.735	.683	.636	.572	.482
5	.863	.823	.784	.747	.713	.681	.620	.567	.497	.402
6	.838	.790	.746	.705	.666	.630	.564	.507	.432	.335
7	.813	.760	.711	.665	.623	.583	.513	.452	.376	.279
8	.789	.731	.677	.627	.582	.540	.466	.404	.326	.233
9	.766	.703	.645	.591	.544	.500	.424	.360	.284	.194
10	.744	.676	.614	.558	**.508**	.463	.385	.322	.247	.162
11	.722	.650	.585	.526	.475	.429	.350	.287	.215	.134
12	.701	.625	.557	.497	.444	.397	.318	.257	.187	.112
13	.681	.601	.530	.468	.415	.368	.289	.229	.162	.0935
14	.661	.577	.505	.442	.388	.340	.263	.204	.141	.0779
15	.642	.555	.481	.417	.362	.315	.239	.183	.122	.0649
16	.623	.534	.458	.393	.339	.292	.217	.163	.107	.0541
17	.605	.513	.436	.371	.317	.270	.197	.146	.093	.0451
18	.587	.494	.416	.350	.296	.250	.179	.130	.0808	.0376
19	.570	.475	.396	.330	.277	.232	.163	.116	.0703	.0313
20	.554	.456	.377	.311	.258	.215	.148	.104	.0611	.0261
25	.478	.375	.295	.232	.184	.146	.0923	.0588	.0304	.0105
30	.412	.308	.231	.174	.131	.0994	.0573	.0334	.0151	.00421
40	.307	.208	.142	.0972	.067	.0460	.0221	.0107	.00373	.000680
50	.228	.141	.087	.0543	.034	.0213	.00852	.00346	.000922	.000109

Present Value of Annuity of $1, Received at End of Each Year

Year	3%	4%	5%	6%	7%	8%	10%	12%	15%	20%
1	0.971	0.960	0.952	0.943	0.935	0.926	0.909	0.890	0.870	0.833
2	1.91	1.89	1.86	1.83	1.81	1.78	1.73	1.69	1.63	1.53
3	2.53	2.78	2.72	2.67	2.62	2.58	2.45	2.40	2.28	2.11
4	3.72	3.63	3.55	3.46	3.39	3.31	3.16	3.04	2.86	2.59
5	4.58	4.45	4.33	**4.21**	**4.10**	3.99	**3.79**	**3.60**	3.35	2.99
6	5.42	**5.24**	5.08	4.91	4.77	4.62	**4.35**	4.11	3.78	3.33
7	6.23	6.00	5.79	5.58	5.39	5.21	4.89	4.56	4.16	3.60
8	7.02	6.73	6.46	6.20	5.97	5.75	5.33	4.97	4.49	3.84
9	7.79	7.44	7.11	6.80	6.52	6.25	5.75	5.33	4.78	4.03
10	8.53	8.11	7.72	7.36	7.02	6.71	**6.14**	5.65	5.02	4.19
11	9.25	8.76	8.31	7.88	7.50	7.14	6.49	5.94	5.23	4.33
12	9.95	9.39	8.86	8.38	7.94	7.54	6.81	6.19	5.41	4.44
13	10.6	9.99	9.39	8.85	8.36	7.90	7.10	6.42	5.65	4.53
14	11.3	10.6	9.90	9.29	8.75	8.24	7.36	6.63	5.76	4.61
15	11.9	11.1	10.4	9.71	9.11	8.56	7.60	6.81	5.87	4.68
16	12.6	11.6	10.8	10.1	9.45	8.85	7.82	6.97	5.96	4.73
17	13.2	12.2	11.3	10.4	9.76	9.12	8.02	7.12	6.03	4.77
18	13.8	12.7	11.7	10.8	10.1	9.37	8.20	7.25	6.10	4.81
19	14.3	13.1	12.1	11.1	10.3	9.60	8.36	7.37	6.17	4.84
20	14.9	**13.6**	12.5	11.4	10.6	**9.82**	8.51	7.47	6.23	4.87
25	17.4	15.6	14.1	12.8	11.7	10.7	9.08	7.84	6.46	4.95
30	19.6	17.3	15.4	13.5	12.4	11.3	9.43	8.06	6.57	4.98
40	23.1	19.8	17.2	15.0	13.3	11.9	9.78	8.24	6.64	5.00
50	25.7	21.5	18.3	15.8	13.8	12.2	9.91	8.30	6.66	5.00

Future Value of an Annuity

n/i	1%	2%	3%	4%	5%	6%	7%
1	1.0000	1.0000	1.0000	1.0000	1.0000	1.0000	1.0000
2	2.0100	2.0200	2.0300	2.0400	2.0500	2.0600	2.0700
3	3.0301	3.0604	3.0909	3.1216	3.1525	3.1836	3.2149
4	4.0604	4.1216	4.1836	4.2465	4.3101	4.3746	4.4399
5	5.1010	5.2040	5.3091	5.4163	5.5256	5.6371	5.7507
6	6.1520	6.3081	6.4684	6.6330	6.8019	6.9753	7.1533
7	7.2135	7.4343	7.6625	7.8983	8.1420	8.3938	8.6540
8	8.2857	8.5830	8.8923	9.2142	9.5491	9.8975	10.2598
9	9.3685	9.7546	10.1591	10.5828	11.0266	11.4913	11.9780
10	10.4622	10.9497	11.4639	12.0061	12.5779	13.1808	13.8164
11	11.5668	12.1687	12.8078	13.4864	14.2068	14.9716	15.7836
12	12.6825	13.4121	14.1920	15.0258	15.9171	16.8699	17.8885
13	13.8093	14.6803	15.6178	16.6268	17.7130	18.8821	20.1406
14	14.9474	15.9739	17.0863	18.2919	19.5986	21.0151	22.5505
15	16.0969	17.2934	18.5989	20.0236	21.5786	23.2760	25.1290
16	17.2579	18.6393	20.1569	21.8245	23.6575	25.6725	27.8881
17	18.4304	20.0121	21.7616	23.6975	25.8404	28.2129	30.8402
18	19.6147	21.4123	23.4144	25.6454	28.1324	30.9057	33.9990
19	20.8109	22.8406	25.1169	27.6712	30.5390	33.7600	37.3790
20	22.0190	24.2974	26.8704	29.7781	33.0660	36.7856	40.9955
21	23.2392	25.7833	28.6765	31.9692	35.7193	39.9927	44.8652
22	24.4716	27.2990	30.5368	34.2480	38.5052	43.3923	49.0057
23	25.7163	28.8450	32.4529	36.6179	41.4305	46.9958	53.4361
24	26.9735	30.4219	34.4265	39.0826	44.5020	50.8156	58.1767
25	28.2432	32.0303	36.4593	41.6459	47.7271	54.8645	63.2490
26	29.5256	33.6709	38.5530	44.3117	51.1135	59.1564	68.6765
27	30.8209	35.3443	40.7096	47.0842	54.6691	63.7058	74.4838
28	32.1291	37.0512	42.9309	49.9676	58.4026	68.5281	80.6977
29	33.4504	38.7922	45.2189	52.9663	62.3227	73.6398	87.3465
30	34.7849	40.5681	47.5754	56.0849	66.4388	79.0582	94.4608

8%	9%	10%	11%	12%	13%	14%	15%
1.0000	1.0000	1.0000	1.0000	1.0000	1.0000	1.0000	1.0000
2.0800	2.0900	2.1000	2.1100	2.1200	2.1300	2.1400	2.1500
3.2464	3.2781	3.3100	3.3421	3.3744	3.4069	3.4396	3.4725
4.5061	4.5731	4.6410	4.7097	4.7793	4.8498	4.9211	4.9934
5.8666	5.9847	6.1051	6.2278	6.3528	6.4803	6.6101	6.7424
7.3359	7.5233	7.7156	7.9129	8.1152	8.3227	8.5355	8.7537
8.9228	9.2004	9.4872	9.7833	10.0890	10.4047	10.7305	11.0668
10.6366	11.0285	11.4359	11.8594	12.2997	12.7573	13.2328	13.7268
12.4876	13.0210	13.5795	14.1640	14.7757	15.4157	16.0853	16.7858
14.4866	15.1929	15.9374	16.7220	17.5487	18.4197	19.3373	20.3037
16.6455	17.5603	18.5312	19.5614	20.6546	21.8143	23.0445	24.3493
18.9771	20.1407	21.3843	22.7132	24.1331	25.6502	27.2707	29.0017
21.4953	22.9534	24.5227	26.2116	28.0291	29.9847	32.0887	34.3519
24.2149	26.0192	27.9750	30.0949	32.3926	34.8827	37.5811	40.5047
27.1521	29.3609	31.7725	34.4054	37.2797	40.4175	43.8424	47.5804
30.3243	33.0034	35.9497	39.1899	42.7533	46.6717	50.9804	55.7175
33.7502	36.9737	40.5447	44.5008	48.8837	53.7391	59.1176	65.0751
37.4502	41.3013	45.5992	50.3959	55.7497	61.7251	68.3941	75.8364
41.4463	46.0185	51.1591	56.9395	63.4397	70.7494	78.9692	88.2118
45.7620	51.1601	57.2750	64.2028	72.0524	80.9468	91.0249	102.4436
50.4229	56.7645	64.0025	72.2651	81.6987	92.4699	104.7684	118.8101
55.4568	62.8733	71.4027	81.2143	92.5026	105.4910	120.4360	137.6316
60.8933	69.5319	79.5430	91.1479	104.6029	120.2048	138.2970	159.2764
66.7648	76.7898	88.4973	102.1742	118.1552	136.8315	158.6586	184.1678
73.1059	84.7009	98.3471	114.4133	133.3339	155.6196	181.8708	212.7930
79.9544	93.3240	109.1818	127.9988	150.3339	176.8501	208.3327	245.7120
87.3508	102.7231	121.0999	143.0786	169.3740	200.8406	238.4993	283.5688
95.3388	112.9682	134.2099	159.8173	190.6989	227.9499	272.8892	327.1041
103.9659	124.1354	148.6309	178.3972	214.5828	258.5834	312.0937	377.1697
113.2832	136.3075	164.4940	199.0209	241.3327	293.1992	356.7868	434.7451

Appendix B: Duggan Inc

A. BALANCE SHEET

Balance Sheet as at 30 September (thousands of dollars)	**20–2** $	**20–1** $
Assets		
Current Assets:		
Cash	268	561
Cash equivalents	713	702
Marketable securities	1,100	1,000
Accounts receivable	5,835	5,621
Allowance for doubtful accounts	–467	–430
Inventories	4,031	4,164
Deferred tax assets	755	662
Prepaid expenses	216	86
Total current assets	**12,451**	**12,366**
Fixed Assets:		
Land	406	405
Buildings	10,657	10,212
Machinery & equipment	28,576	26,294
Leasehold improvements	3,086	3,026
Accumulated depreciation	–15,041	–13,310
Capital assets (net)	27,684	26,627
Intangible Assets:	1,287	533
Other Assets:		
Accrued benefits	949	624
Total Assets	**42,371**	**40,150**

Liabilities (thousands of dollars)	**20–2** $	**20–1** $
Current Liabilities:		
Current portion of long-term debt	210	157
Notes payable	3,672	1,962
Accounts payable	3,088	3,138
Accrued Liabilities:		
Income taxes	659	1,041
Salaries & wages	765	780
Advertising & promotion	2,338	2,280
Deferred revenue	1,414	1,352
Total current liabilities	**12,146**	**10,710**
Long-term Liabilities:		
Long-term debt	5,216	3,149
Non-pension post-retirement benefits	4,509	4,076
Deferred income taxes	1,889	1,846
Capital leases	1,477	917
Total long-term liabilities	**13,091**	**9,988**
Total Liabilities	**25,237**	**20,698**

Shareholders' Equity (thousands of dollars)	**20–2** $	**20–1** $
Class A shares:		
Authorized – unlimited		
Issued and outstanding	1,496	1,467
Retained earnings	34,094	30,339
Treasury shares, at cost	–18,456	–12,354
Total shareholders' equity	**17,134**	**19,452**
Total Liabilities & Shareholders' Equity	**42,371**	**40,150**

B. INCOME STATEMENT

Income Statement for the Years Ended 30 September	**20–2**	**20–1**
(in thousands of dollars)	$	$
Net sales	62,954	61,906
Cost of goods sold	29,890	29,877
Gross margin	33,064	32,029
Selling and administrative expenses	20,225	19,401
Other expenses	15	-368
Research and development costs	2,150	2,000
Income from operations	10,674	10,996
Interest expense	333	292
Net income before income taxes	10,341	10,704
Income taxes	3,534	3,876
Earnings before extraordinary items	6,807	6,828
Extraordinary items (net of tax benefits)	0	-2,516
Net income after income taxes	**6,807**	**4,312**

C. CASH FLOW STATEMENT

Duggan Inc's Cash Flows for the year ended 30 September 20-2	**Thousands of dollars ($)**
Operating Activities:	
Net income	6,807
Add: items not affecting cash:	
Depreciation	1,731
Deferred income taxes	43
	8,581
Accounts receivable	–177
Inventories	133
Prepaids and other assets	–10
Accounts payable and accrued liabilities	170
Income taxes	–575
	8,122
Investing Activities:	
Fixed and intangible asset additions	–3,542
	–3,542
Financing Activities:	
Long–term debt payable	2,120
Notes payable	1,710
Issuance of common shares	29
Purchase of treasury shares	–6,102
Cash dividends paid	–3,052
Non–pension benefits	433
	–4,862
Decrease in cash and cash equivalents	–282
Cash and cash equivalents beginning of 20–2	1,263
Cash and cash equivalents end of 20–2	**981**

Glossary

Accelerated Amortization
A method of allocating costs against income that records a greater portion of the total cost in the earlier years of an asset's life, and a lower portion in later years. For example: declining balance amortization allocates more in the earlier years than does the straight-line method.

Account
A record of an asset, liability, owners' equity, revenue, or expense in which an enterprise records transactions, accruals, and adjustments, generally in the local currency of the country.

Account Aging
Usually refers to the methods of tracking past due accounts in accounts receivable based on the dates the charges were incurred. Account aging can also be used in accounts payable, to a lesser degree, to monitor payment history to suppliers.

Accountant's Opinion
A signed statement regarding the financial status of an entity from an independent public accountant after examination of that entity's records and accounts.

Accounting Entity
The enterprise for which the accounting is being done. The entity may be a single legal corporation or other organization, an economic unit without legal standing (such as a proprietorship), or a group of corporations with connected ownership for which consolidated financial statements are prepared.

Accounting Policies
The accounting methods chosen by a company to recognize economic events on an accrual basis and to report the financial position and results of operations.

Accounting Principles
See Generally Accepted Accounting Principles (GAAP).

Accounts Payable
Liabilities representing amounts owed to short-term trade creditors. An account payable for the debtor is an account receivable for the creditor.

Accounts Receivable
A current asset representing amounts owed by debtors (usually customers) for services performed or merchandise sold on credit.

Accounts Receivable Financing
A secured short-term loan that involves either the assignment or factoring of receivable.

Accretion
The adjustment of the difference between the price of a bond purchased at an original discount and the par value of the bond.

Accrual Basis of Accounting (Accrual Accounting)
Wherein revenue and expenses are recorded in the period in which they are earned or incurred regardless of whether cash is received or disbursed in that period.

Accrual Income
The result of subtracting expenses from revenue(s) when both kinds of accounts are calculated by accrual accounting.

Accrued Assets
Assets from revenues earned but not yet received.

Accrued Expenses
Expenses incurred during an accounting period for which payment is postponed.

Accrued Income
Income earned during a fiscal period but not paid by the end of the period.

Accrued Interest
Interest earned but not yet received.

Accrued Liability
Liabilities that are incurred, but for which payment is not yet made, during a given accounting period.

Accumulated Amortization
The cumulative charges against the intangible assets of a company over the expected useful life of the assets.

Accumulated Amortization (Depreciation)
A balance sheet account that accumulates total amortization expense (for intangible assets) or depreciation expense (for fixed assets) over a number of years.

Accumulated Depreciation
The cumulative charges against the fixed assets of a company for wear and tear or obsolescence.

Acid-Test Ratio
See Quick Ratio.

Acquisition
One company taking over controlling interest in another company.

Adjusted Present Value (APV)
Base case net present value of a project's operating cash flows plus present value of any financing benefits.

Adjusted Trial Balance
The list of accounts prepared after all the accrual accounting adjustments and corrections have been made and so representing the final account balances used in preparing the financial statements.

Allocating, Allocation
Spreading the impact of an event out over time, as in amortization of an asset's cost over its useful life or recognition of revenue for a long-term contract over several periods.

Allowance for Doubtful Accounts
The estimated amount of accounts receivable that will not be collected (which are "doubtful"). The allowance, which is a contra account to accounts receivable, is used in order to recognize the bad debts expense related to such doubtful accounts but without removing those accounts from the books because the firm will still try to collect the amounts owing.

Alpha
The measurement of returns from an investment in excess of market returns. It represents the amount expected from fundamental causes, e.g., the growth rate in earnings per share.

Amalgamations
Combinations of firms that have been joined by merger, consolidation, or acquisition.

American Options
A call or put option that can be exercised on or before its expiration date.

Amortization Expense
The expense recorded to recognize asset amortization.

Annual Report
The document provided annually to the shareholders by the officers of a company, including the financial statements, the notes to the financial statements, the auditor's report, and reports from the company's board of directors and management.

Annuity
A level stream of cash flows for a fixed period of time.

Annuity Due
Annuity contract specification of payments at the beginning of each period.

Arm's Length
Arm's length refers to the proximity of the relationship between taxpayers. Persons who are related to each other are considered to be non-arm's length with each other. An arm's length price is a price charged in similar transactions between unrelated parties.

Arm's Length Principle
A fundamental principle of international tax law is that entities should transact with each other on open market terms even if they are related parties.

Articles of Association
Regulations for governing the rights and duties of the members of a company among themselves. Articles (also Bylaws in some jurisdictions) deal with internal matters such as general meetings, appointment of directors, issue and transfer of shares, dividends, accounts and audits.

Asset
Anything owned by an individual or a business, which has commercial or exchange value. Assets may consist of specific property or claims against others, in contrast to obligations due others. *See also* Liabilities.

Asset Earning Power
A common profitability measure used to determine the profitability of a business by taking its total earnings before taxes and dividing that by total assets.

Asset Turnover Ratio
A general measure of a firm's ability to generate sales in relation to total assets. Used to compare firms within specific industry groups and in

conjunction with other operating ratios to determine the effective employment of assets.

Asset Valuation
Determination of the amounts to be used for assets on the balance sheet.

Assumed Cost Flow
The practice in inventory accounting of determining the cost of inventories purchased at varying unit costs by assuming a specific order in which the inventory will be taken to have flowed into and out of the country.

AT
The total assets turnover ratio.

Audit
The inspection of the accounting records and procedures of a business, government unit, or other reporting entity by an accountant for the purpose of verifying the accuracy and completeness of the records.

Audit Committee
A committee of a corporation's board of directors, usually composed largely or entirely of directors not also having management positions, which reviews the company's accounting statements and communicates directly with the external auditor.

Auditor
The person or firm who performs an audit for the purpose of preparing a report on the credibility of the financial statements; also called the external auditor.

Auditor's Report (or Auditors' Report)
The document accompanying the financial statements that expresses the auditor's opinion on the fairness of the financial statements.

Average Interest Rate
An average calculated by dividing interest expense by total liabilities.

Average Tax Rate
Total taxes paid divided by total taxable income.

Bad Debt
An open account balance or loan receivable that has proven to be uncollectible and is written off.

Bad Debts Expense
An expense account that results from the reduction in carrying value of those accounts receivable that have been projected to be uncollectible or doubtful.

Balance Sheet
An itemized statement that lists the total assets and the total liabilities of a given business to portray its net equity at a given moment of time. Also called a Statement of Financial Position.

Balance Sheet Equation
Assets = Liabilities + Owners' Equity.

Basis
That figure or value that is the starting point in computing gain or loss, depreciation, depletion, and amortization of a company.

Basis Points
The smallest measure used in quoting interest rates and yields on bills, notes, and bonds. One basis point is equal to one one-hundredth of one percent.

Bearer Form
Bond issued without record of the owner's name; payment is made to whoever holds the bond.

Bearer Share Certificate
A negotiable share certificate filled out in the name of "bearer" and not to a particular person or organization.

Betterment
An expenditure to improve an asset's value to the business, more than just repairs and maintenance.

Bid
(1) The price at which a market maker will buy shares; (2) An approach made by one company wishing to purchase the entire share capital of another company.

Billings
Sales for which invoicing has been issued.

Blind Trust
A trust in which the trustees are enjoined from providing any information to the beneficiaries about the administration of assets of the trust.

Blue Chip
Term for the most prestigious industrial shares. Originally an American term derived from the colour of the highest value poker chip.

Board of Directors
The senior level of management, representing and directly responsible to the owners (shareholders).

Bond
A debt security issued by a government or company. Short-term bonds mature in less than one year; medium-term bonds mature in two to ten years; and long-term bonds mature in more than ten years.

Bond Covenant
Agreements within a bond that can either be negative or positive. A negative bond covenant is one that prevents certain activities unless agreed to by the bondholders.

Bonded Warehouse
A warehouse authorized by customs officials for the storage of goods on which payment of duty is deferred until the goods are removed.

Book Cost
Normally the cost at the time an asset is purchased or realized, i.e., the total amount paid to acquire an asset.

Bookkeeping
The process of recording, classifying, and summarizing transactions in a business's books of account (accounting records).

Books
Colloquial term for the accounting records, including computerized records, left over from the time when the records were written in bound books.

Book-to-Market
The ratio of the firm's book equity to market equity.

Book Value
(1) The original purchase price of an investment; (2) A business's historical cost of assets minus liabilities.

Book Value per Share
Total shareholders' equity divided by the number of shares issued.

Bottom Line
Net Income after taxes.

Bottom Up
A concept of analyzing a subject, such as costs or revenue, starting from the lowest level working towards the top.

Branch
A branch of an enterprise is a business carried on through a fixed place of business, which is also referred to as a permanent establishment. A branch is not separately incorporated.

Break-Even
For accounting purposes, the sales level that results in zero project net income.

Break-Even Analysis
An analysis method used to determine the number of jobs or products that need to be sold to reach a break-even point in a business.

Break-Even Point
The volume point at which revenues and costs are equal; a combination of sales and costs that will yield a no profit/no loss operation.

Bull Market
One in which "bulls" prosper; that is, a rising market.

Business Combination
A merger of separate corporations or an acquisition of control of one corporation by another, in which the corporations become a single economic entity.

Business Entity
A selection of the legal form under which a business is to operate: sole proprietorship, general partnership, corporation, or limited liability company.

Call
The amount due to be paid to a company by the purchase of new or partly paid shares.

Call Option
The right to buy stock or shares at an agreed price at a future date. The opposite of a Put Option.

Call Premium
Amount by which the call price exceeds the par value of the bond.

Call Protected
Bond during a period in which it cannot be redeemed by the issuer.

Call Provision
Agreement giving the corporation the option to repurchase the bond at a specified price before maturity.

***Canada Business Corporations Act* (CBCA)**
The federal corporations' statute that provides the authority for the incorporation of federally incorporated companies in Canada and generally sets the requirements for their activities.

Canada Yield Curve
A plot of the yields on Government of Canada bonds relative to maturity.

C&F (Cost & Freight)
Includes all shipping costs except insurance. The buyer is responsible for insurance.

C&I (Cost & Insurance)
"C&I" means that the cost of the product and insurance are included in the quoted price. The cost of shipping would be borne by the buyer.

Capital
In finance, capital is money and other property of a corporation or other enterprise used in transacting the business; the owner's contribution to or interest in a business (the equity). It is often used specifically to refer to the equity of unincorporated businesses (proprietorships and partnerships).

Capital Asset
A long-term asset that is not purchased or sold in the normal course of business. Generally, it includes fixed assets, e.g., land, buildings, furniture, equipment, and fixtures.

Capital Cost Allowance (CCA)
A method of depreciation prescribed by tax law. The CCA method allows the government to categorize business-related property into classes and then control the rates at which the various classes are depreciated. Businesses can deduct up to a fixed percentage of the depreciated cost each year.

Capital Expenditure
The amount used during a particular period to acquire or improve long-term assets such as property, plant, or equipment.

Capital Gain (Loss)
The difference between the cost of an investment and its selling price.

Capital Gains Tax
A tax levied on the profits from the sale of capital assets or the deemed sale of capital assets. Usually, only a portion (e.g. 50 percent) of the gain is taxable.

Capitalization Rate ("Cap Rate")
The rate of return a property will produce on the owner's investment, usually stated as a rate of interest or discount rate used to convert a series of future payments into a single "present value."

Capitalized Costs
Costs that have been included with an asset on the balance sheet instead of being deducted as expenses on the income statement.

Capital Lease
A lease obligation that has to be capitalized on the balance sheet. A capital lease has the economic character of asset ownership.

Capital Markets
Markets in which financial instruments such as shares and bonds are traded.

Capital Stock
The ownership shares of a corporation authorized by its articles of incorporation, including preferred and common stock.

Capital Structure
The mix of debt and equity maintained by a firm.

Carrying Value ("Book Value")
A company's total assets minus intangible assets and liabilities, such as debt.

Cash
Currency and coin on hand, balances in bank accounts, and other highly liquid assets.

Cash and Equivalents
Cash and near-cash assets minus near-cash liabilities: cash equivalent assets minus cash equivalent liabilities.

Cash Basis of Accounting
The accounting basis in which revenue and expenses are recorded in the period they are actually received or expended in cash.

Cash Break-Even
The sales level where operating cash flow is equal to zero.

Cash Budget
A forecast of cash receipts and disbursements for the next planning period.

Cash Cycle
The time between cash disbursement and cash collection.

Cash Debt Coverage Ratio
The ratio of net cash provided by operating activities to average total liabilities, called the cash debt coverage ratio, is a cash-basis measure of solvency.

Cash Disbursements
Cash payouts, by cheque, currency, or direct deductions from the bank account.

Cash Equivalent Assets
A term used to describe cash plus very liquid bank deposits and similar assets that can be converted into cash on demand.

Cash Equivalent Liabilities
Liabilities that are payable on demand and so represent a reduction in the liquidity otherwise apparent from the amount of cash.

Cash Flow
The inflows of cash (cash receipts) and outflows of cash (cash disbursements) over a period.

Cash Flow Analysis
A method of accounting analysis directed at understanding the enterprise's cash inflows, outflows, and resulting balances in the Cash Flow Statement.

Cash Flow from Operations
The sum of all the individual operating activity cash flow line items, minus cash realized from the sale of extraordinary items, e.g., fixed assets.

Cash Flow Statement
A statement that explains the changes in cash (and equivalent) balances during a fiscal period. Also referred to as "Statement of changes in financial position (SCFP)," "Funds statement," or "Statement of cash flows."

Cash Income
Cash receipts minus cash disbursements, or that subset of both that relates to day-to-day operations.

Certified Financial Statements
Financial statements that have undergone a formal audit by a licensed public accountant and usually contain statements of opinion or certification.

CFO
Acronym for Chief Financial Officer.

Chattel Mortgage Contract
A credit contract used for the purchase of equipment where the purchaser receives title of the equipment upon delivery but the creditor holds a mortgage claim against it.

CPA Handbook
The authoritative source of financial accounting standards in Canada.

CIF (Cost, Insurance, and Freight)
A shipment where all shipping costs are paid by the exporter, including insurance.

Clean Opinion
An external auditor's report which states the auditor's opinion that the financial statements are fairly presented. Indicates the auditor found no problems.

Collateral
Assets used as security for the extension of a loan.

Collection Period
Used to appraise accounts receivable (AR). Ratio measures the length of time it takes to convert average sales into cash.

Commercial Paper
Short-term obligations with maturities ranging from 2 to 270 days issued by corporations, banks, or other borrowers to investors who have temporarily idle cash on hand. Commercial paper is usually unsecured and discounted.

Common Share
A security that represents part ownership in a company.

Common-Size Financial Statements
A technique of analyzing financial statements in which income statement figures are expressed in percentages of revenue and balance sheet accounts are expressed in percentages of total assets.

Common Size Percentages
In the income statement, each common size percentage is the field amount expressed as a percentage of net revenues. In the balance sheet, each common size percentage is the amount in the category as a percentage of total assets.

Comparability
Information that enables users to identify similarities in and differences between two sets of economic phenomena, such as two different years of a company's financial statements.

Compilation
The presentation of financial statement information by the entity without the accountant's assurance as to conformity with generally accepted accounting principles (GAAP).

Completed Contract
A method of revenue recognition for long-term contracts in which the revenue is not reported on the income statement until the contract has been completed.

Compounding
The process of accumulating and reinvesting interest in an investment over time to earn even more interest.

Compound Interest
Interest earned on both the initial principal and the interest reinvested from prior periods.

Conservatism, Conservative
A prudent reaction to uncertainty to ensure that risks inherent in business situations are adequately considered — often phrased as "anticipate possible losses but not possible gains."

Consideration
The money value of a transaction (number of shares multiplied by the price) before adding commission, stamp duty, etc.

Consignment
When goods are offered for sale on behalf of another without the seller actually purchasing or taking title to the goods.

Consistency
Treatment of like transactions in the same way in consecutive periods so that financial statements will be comparable. The reporting policy implying that procedures, once adopted, should be followed from period to period by a company.

Consistency Principle
Requires accountants to apply the same methods and procedures from period to period.

Consol
A perpetual bond.

Consolidated Financial Statements
Consolidation is a method of preparing financial statements for a group of corporations linked by ownership as if they were a single corporation. Consolidated financial statements recognize that the separate legal entities are components of one economic unit.

Contingency
An economic event (especially a negative one) that is in the process of occurring and so is not yet resolved. Examples: pending or threatened litigation; threat of expropriation of assets; guarantees of the indebtedness of others; possible liabilities arising from discounted bills of exchange or promissory notes.

Contingent Liability
A liability that is dependent upon uncertain events that may occur in the future.

Contributed Surplus
The difference between the legal par value (or Stated value) of a share and the cash or other consideration received by the company when the share was issued. Does not apply to no-par shares.

Contribution Margin (CM)
The difference between sales and the variable costs of the product or service, also called marginal income.

Convertible
A bond or share that can be changed into another kind of security, usually a preferred share that can be converted into a common share.

Conversion Price
The dollar amount of a bond's par value that is exchangeable for one share of stock.

Conversion Ratio
The number of shares per $1,000 bond received for conversion into stock.

Conversion Value
The value of a convertible bond if it was immediately converted into common stock.

Convertible Bond
A bond that can be exchanged for a fixed number of shares of stock for a specified amount of time.

Convertible Debenture
A debenture that can be exchanged for common shares at a specified rate and date.

Convertible Preferred Share
A share that can be exchanged for common shares at a specified rate and date.

Copyright
A form of legal protection used to safeguard original literary works, performing arts, sound recordings, visual arts, original software code, and renewals.

Corporate Group
A group of corporations linked by common or mutual ownership.

Corporation
A legal entity with or without share capital, legally separate from those who own it or work as a part of it.

Cost
The amount of money that must be paid to take ownership of something; expense or purchase price.

Cost Allocation
Spreading the cost of an asset out over the periods in which it is useful.

Cost Basis
In securities, is the purchase price after commissions or other expenses. Used to calculate capital gains or losses when the security is eventually sold.

Cost Flow Assumption
An assumption made about the order in which units of inventory move into and out of an enterprise, used to compute inventory asset value and cost of goods sold in cases where the order of flow is not or cannot be identified. Possible assumptions include FIFO, LIFO, and weighted average.

Cost of Capital
(1) The cost of raising debt or equity funds (e.g., the cost of borrowed funds is mostly the interest to be paid to the lender); (2) The rate of return that a business could earn if it chose other investments with the equivalent risks.

Cost of Debt
The return that lenders require on the firm's debt.

Cost of Equity
The return that equity investors require on their investment in the firm.

Cost of Goods Sold (COGS)
A figure representing the cost of buying raw material and producing finished goods.

Cost-of-Living Lease
A lease where yearly increases are tied to the cost of living index.

Cost Principle
The use of the historical cost of assets to value them on the balance sheet.

Coupon
(1) On bearer stocks, the detachable part of the certificate exchangeable for dividends; (2) On bonds and debentures, the stated interest payments (e.g., 10 percent coupon pays interest of 10 percent per year).

Coupon Rate
The annual coupon divided by the face value of a bond.

Covenants

A promise by the firm, included in the debt contract, to perform certain acts. A restrictive covenant imposes constraints on the firm to protect the interests of the debt-holder.

Cover

The total net profit a company has available for distribution as dividend, divided by the amount paid, gives the number of times that the dividend is covered.

Cum

Latin for "with," used in the abbreviations Cum Cap, Cum Div, Cum Rights, and so on, to indicate that the buyer of a security is entitled to participate in the forthcoming capitalization issue, dividend, or rights issue.

Cumulative Voting

Procedure where a shareholder may cast all votes for one member of the board of directors.

Current Assets

Cash and other assets such as temporary investments, inventory, receivables, and current prepayments that are realizable or will be consumed within the normal operating cycle of an enterprise (usually one year).

Current Cash Debt Ratio

Measures ability to pay current liabilities in given year with cash derived from operating activities. Calculated using net cash from operating activities divided by average current liabilities.

Current Liabilities

Debts or estimated claims on the resources of a firm that are expected to be paid within the normal operating cycle of an enterprise (usually one year).

Current Ratio

A comparison of current assets to current liabilities.

Current (or Market) Value

The estimated sale value of an asset, settlement value of a debt, or trading value of an equity share.

Current Value Accounting

A proposed accounting method that would use current or market values to value assets and liabilities and to calculate income.

Cut Off

The end of a fiscal period and the procedures used to ensure accuracy in measuring phenomena up to that date.

Date of Payment
Date on the dividend cheques.

Date of Record
Date on which holders of record are designated to receive a dividend.

Days Inventory
Shows the average length of time items are in inventory.

Days' Sales in Receivables
The ratio of accounts receivable to the daily sales, expressed in number of days' sales represented by accounts receivable.

DCF
See Discounted Cash Flows, another phrase for "present value" analysis of future cash flows.

Debenture
A loan raised by a company paying a fixed rate of interest, usually with a maturity of ten years or more, and secured on the general, rather than specific, assets of the company.

Debt
An obligation to make a future payment in return for a benefit already received.

Debt Capacity
The ability to borrow to increase firm value.

Debt Covenant
One of many terms used to describe rules governing the loans that a company has outstanding. Other related phrases would be "loan terms," "credit agreement," "loan agreement."

Debt Financing
Raising money through selling bonds, notes, or mortgages, or borrowing directly from financial institutions.

Debt Ratio
Measures the percent of total funds provided by creditors.

Debt to Assets Ratio
Total liabilities divided by total assets.

Debt to Equity Ratio
Total liabilities divided by total equity. Measures the risk of the firm's capital structure in terms of amounts of capital contributed by creditors and that contributed by owners.

Debt to Total Assets Ratio
Measures the percentage of assets financed by all terms of debt, includes both current and long term debt.

Declaration Date
Date on which the board of directors passes a resolution to pay a dividend.

Declining Balance Amortization
An accelerated amortization (depreciation) method in which the annual amortization (depreciation) expense is calculated as a fixed percentage of the book value of the asset, which declines over time as amortization is deducted.

Deferral Method
Accounting for future income tax expenses incurred by present activities, now largely replaced by future income tax liability estimates.

Deferred
In accounting, is any account where the asset or liability is not realized until a future date. Examples: annuities, charges, taxes, income.

Deferred Asset
An amount owed to an entity that is not expected to be received by that entity within one year from the date of the balance sheet.

Deferred Call
Call provision prohibiting the company from redeeming the bond before a certain date.

Deferred Charge
A non-current prepaid expense, in which the costs of issuing bonds, incorporation costs, or other expenditures benefiting several future periods are shown as non-current assets. Usually amortized to expense over several periods or otherwise charged to expenses in some future period.

Deferred Income Tax (Expense and Liability)
An expense account and corresponding liability intended to recognize the future tax consequences of income reported on the current income statement but not to be reported on the tax return until a future period. Now largely replaced by future income tax liability estimates.

Deferred Revenue
A liability account used for customer deposits or other cash receipts prior to the completion of the sale.

Deficit
Negative retained earnings and sometimes also used to refer to negative earnings.

Delta
In securities trading, the relationship between an option price and the underlying futures contract or stock price.

De minimus
De minimis non curat lex (Latin), a common law principle whereby judges will not sit in judgment of extremely minor transgressions of the law. Essentially: "The law does not concern itself with trifles."

Depletion
An amortization (depreciation) method used for physically wasting assets, such as natural resources.

Depreciation
The recognition of the expense due to use of the fixed tangible assets such as, for example, trucks, buildings, or plant.

Derivative
A transaction or contract whose value derives from the value of underlying assets such as stock, bonds, mortgages, market indices, or foreign currencies.

Derivative Securities
Securities whose returns depend on the price of an underlying asset and that allow market participants to offset the exposure of their cash market positions.

Diluted Earnings per Share
Earnings per share, including common stock, preferred stock, unexercised stock options, and some convertible debt.

Dilution
Loss in existing shareholders' value, in either ownership, market value, book value, or EPS.

Diminishing Balance
Declining Balance Amortization.

Direct Cost
That portion of cost that is directly expended in providing a product or service for sale and is included in the calculation of cost of goods sold, e.g., labour and inventory.

Direct Expense
That portion of expense that is directly expended in providing a product or service for sale and is included in the calculation of cost of goods sold, e.g., labour and inventory.

Disbursement
The paying out of money to satisfy a debt or an expense.

Disclosure
Provision of information about economic events beyond that included in the financial statement figures, usually in the Notes to the financial statements.

Disclosure Principle
States that any and all information that affects the full understanding of a company's financial statements should be included with the financial statements.

Discount
(1) Calculate the present value of some future amount; (2) When the market price of a newly issued security is lower than the issue price. If it is higher, the difference is called the premium.

Discounted Cash Flow
A valuation method best used to evaluate a business established for the purpose of fulfilling a specific project, in certain startups and other companies where cash flow is more important than net income, and when a certain time frame is set where an investor wishes to see their investment returned over a specific period of time.

Discounted Cash Flow (DCF) Valuation
The process of valuing an investment by discounting its future cash flows.

Discounted Earnings
Determines the value of a business based on the present value of projected future earnings, discounted by the required rate of return (capitalization rate).

Discounted Payback Period
The length of time required for an investment's discounted cash flows to equal its initial cost.

Discount Note
Debt security that is sold at less than face value and matures at face value. A treasury bill is an example of a discount note.

Discount on Bonds
Arises when bonds are issued at a price below their legal face value, such as a $100 bond being issued for $95 cash, indicating a $5 discount.

Discount Rate
The rate used to calculate the present value of future cash flows.

Discretionary Expenses
Expenses that depend on management's discretion rather than on the necessities of producing, selling, or shipping goods and services. Examples: donations, political contributions, some maintenance and warranty costs, and bonuses not specifically called for in employment contracts.

Discretionary Income
The amount of a company's income available for spending after the essentials have been met.

Distributions
Payments from fund or corporate cash flow (e.g., payment of a mutual fund's income to its unit holders). May include dividends from earnings, capital gains from sale of portfolio holdings and return of capital.

Dividend(s)
"Dividends" refer to income from shares or other corporate rights (other than debt-claims) that participate in profits. In general terms, dividend income is attributable to the ownership of shares or other units of equity ownership carrying a right to participate in profits.

Dividend Capitalization
Since most closely held companies do not pay dividends, when using dividend capitalization valuators must first determine dividend paying capacity of a business.

Dividend Capture
A strategy in which an investor purchases securities to own them on the day of record and then quickly sells them; designed to attain dividends but avoid the risk of a lengthy hold.

Dividend Growth Model
Model that determines the current price of a stock as its future dividend period, divided by the discount rate minus the dividend growth rate.

Dividend Payout Ratio
A measure of the percentage of earnings paid out in dividends; computed by dividing cash dividends by the net income available to each class of stock.

Dividend Yield
A stock's cash dividend divided by its current price.

Dollar Value LIFO
A method of expressing the value of an inventory in monetary values rather than units.

Dollar-Weighted Rate of Return
The interest rate that makes the present value of the cash flows from all the sub-periods in an evaluation period plus the terminal market value of the portfolio equal to the initial market value of the portfolio; also called the internal rate of return.

Doomsday Ratio
Related to the quick (acid test) ratio in that it is a conservative approach to debt coverage. The doomsday ratio only considers the cash on hand when evaluating if an entity can cover their current liabilities.

Double-Entry Accounting (DEB)
A system of recording transactions in a way that maintains the equality of the accounting equation. The accounting technique records each transaction as both a credit and a debit.

Dr
An ancient Italian abbreviation for the Italian word "debare," meaning "debit."

Dun
When you importune a debtor for payment; a dunning letter.

E&OE
A British acronym that stands for "Errors and Omissions Excepted." E&OE is a legal disclaimer that notifies the reader that, without prejudice, the content and/or validity of the subject data may change without notice.

Earned Income
That income realized by the provisioning of goods and services.

Earning Power
Earnings before interest and taxes (EBIT) divided by total assets.

Earnings
A common synonym for net income.

Earnings Management
Choosing accounting methods and/or making business deals with the specific objective of altering the size, trend, or interpretation of the company's earnings (net income).

Earnings per Share (EPS)
Net income minus any cash dividends to preferred stock, divided by the average number of common (voting) shares outstanding. This ratio is used to allow the owner of the shares to relate the corporation's earning power to the size of their investment.

Earnings Retention
The proportion of net income that is not paid in dividends.

EBITDA
Earnings Before Interest, Taxes, Depreciation, and Amortization, but after all product/service, sales, and overhead (SG&A) costs are accounted for. Sometimes referred to as operating profit.

EBITDARM
An acronym for Earnings Before Interest, Taxes, Depreciation, Amortization, Rent, and Management fees.

Economic Book Value
Allows for a book value analysis that adjusts the assets to their market value. This valuation allows valuation of goodwill, real estate, inventories, and other assets at their market value.

Economic Entity
The financial accounting definition of an enterprise, used to determine what is to be included in transactions and in the financial statements.

Effective Annual Rate (EAR)
The interest rate expressed as if it were compounded once per year.

Effective Income Tax Rate
The income tax rate the company appears to incur, as deduced from the financial statements.

Effective Interest Rate
The cost of credit on a yearly basis expressed as a percentage. Includes up-front costs paid to obtain the loan, and is, therefore, usually a higher amount than the interest rate stipulated in the note.

Employee Deductions
Amounts an employer is required to deduct from an employee's pay and remit to someone else on behalf of the employee. Examples: income tax, pension contributions, union dues, and other amounts the employee wants to or has to pay before receiving the net pay that is left over.

Encumbered
When an asset is owned by one party subject to the legal claims of another party.

Entity Assumption
The assumption that financial statements are prepared for an entity that is separate and distinct from its owners.

Entity Concept
The concept that financial accounting and reporting relates only to the activities of a specific business entity and not to the activities of the owners of that entity.

Equity
Normally, ownership or percentage of ownership in a company or items of value. Equity equals the net assets or residual interest of an owner or shareholder (Assets = Liabilities + Equity, or restated as Equity = Assets – Liabilities).

Equity Accounting
The practice of showing in a company's accounts the share of undistributed profits of another company in which it holds equity ownership (usually below 50 percent).

Equity Basis
A method of accounting for intercorporate investments usually used when a company owns between 20 percent and 50 percent of another company. The investment is carried at cost, and any profit or loss, multiplied by the percentage ownership of the owned company, is added to or deducted from the investment. Any dividends received are deducted from the investment.

Equity Capital
Capital raised by an entity through the sale of common shares.

Equity Financing
A method of an entity obtaining funds by issuing either common or preferred stock, or both.

Equity Options
Encompass a class of options giving the purchaser the right but not the obligation to buy or sell an individual share, a basket of shares, or an equity index at a predetermined price on or before a fixed date.

Equity-to-Asset Ratio
Expresses the proportion of total assets financed by the owner's equity capital. It is the reciprocal of the debt-to-asset ratio.

Ex
Latin for "without," the opposite of Cum. Used to indicate that the buyer is not entitled to participate in whatever forthcoming event is specified, for example, Ex Cap, Ex Dividend, and Ex Rights.

Ex-Dividend Date
Date before the date of record, establishing those individuals entitled to a dividend.

Exercise Price
The fixed price at which an option holder has the right to buy, in the case of a call option, or to sell, in the case of a put option, the financial instrument covered by the option.

Exercising the Option
The act of buying or selling the underlying asset via the option contract.

Expense
The cost of assets used and/or obligations created in generating revenue, whether or not paid for in cash in the period they appear on the Income statement.

Expense Recognition
Incorporating measures of expenses incurred into the measurement of income by entering into the accounts the amount of expense determined, according to the firm's accounting policies, to be attributable to the current period.

Expensing
Classifying an expenditure or promised expenditure (accrual) as an expense rather than an asset. Opposite of capitalization.

Expiration Date
The last day on which an option can be exercised.

Ex Rights
Period when stock is selling without a recently declared right, normally beginning four business days before the holder-of-record date.

External Audit
The audit conducted by an External Auditor.

External Auditor
An independent outside auditor appointed to review the financial statements.

Extraordinary Items
Gains and losses that arise out of situations that are not normal to the operations of a firm, not under the control of management, and not expected to recur regularly in the future.

Face Value
The principal amount of a bond that is repaid at the end of the term. The expression "par value" is often used interchangeably.

Factoring
The practice of buying debt at a discount.

Fair Market Value
A value or price determined by an unrelated buyer and seller who are separate and acting rationally in their own self-interest. Historical cost is assumed to have been the fair market value of an asset when it was acquired.

Fairness
The opinion paragraph of the auditor's report states that the financial statements "present fairly ... in accordance with generally accepted accounting principles."

Fictitious Name
Often referred to as a DBA, "Doing Business As," a fictitious name is frequently used by sole proprietors or partnerships to provide a name, other than those of the owners or partners, under which the business will operate.

FIFO (First-In, First-Out)
An inventory cost flow assumption whereby the first goods purchased are assumed to be the first goods sold so that the ending inventory consists of the most recently purchased goods.

Final Dividend
The dividend paid by a company at the end of its financial year, recommended by the directors not authorized by the shareholders at the company's annual general meeting.

Financial Accounting Standards Board (FASB)
A US body responsible for setting the standards that financial reporting must follow. The Canadian counterpart is the Chartered Professional Accountants (CPAs).

Financial Analysis
Analysis of a company's financial statement, usually by accountants or financial analysts.

Financial Assets
Near-cash assets such as traded shares, bonds, some kinds of loans, and accounts receivable, especially as would be held by financial institutions such as banks.

Financial Break-Even
The sales level that results in a zero NPV.

Financial Instruments
Debts, shares, foreign exchange contracts, and other financial obligations and assets, many of which are traded on Stock markets and other Capital markets.

Financial Lease
Typically, a longer-term, fully amortized lease under which the lessee is responsible for upkeep. Usually not cancellable without penalty.

Financial Performance
The enterprise's ability to generate new resources from day-to-day operations over a period of time, via dealing with customers, employees, and suppliers. Measured by the net income figure in the income statement and the cash from operations figure in the cash flow statement, as well as by the details of both statements.

Financial Position
The enterprise's set of assets, liabilities, and owners' equity at a point in time. Measured by the balance sheet; also called the statement of financial position.

Financial Ratios
Relationships determined from a firm's financial information and used for comparison purposes.

Financial Reporting
Use of Financial statements and Disclosure to report to people outside the enterprise on its Financial performance and Financial position.

Financial Results
Usually refers to the summary financial results provided in compliance to the GAAP guidelines. They can cover any period(s), but usually cover either single month, quarter, or annual periods.

Financial Statements
The reports, for people external to the enterprise but also of interest to management, referred to in the definition of accounting, which generally comprise a balance sheet, income statement, statement of retained earnings, cash flow statement, and the Notes to these statements.

First-In, First-Out
See FIFO.

Fiscal Period
The period (usually a year, a quarter, or a month) over which performance (net income) is measured and at the end of which the corporation's position (balance sheet) is determined.

Fiscal Year
The declared accounting year for a company, but it is not necessarily in conformance to a calendar year (January through December). However, it does cover twelve months, fifty-two weeks, 365 days.

Five Cs of Credit
Five basic credit factors: character, capacity, capital, collateral, and conditions.

Fixed Assets
Those assets of a permanent nature required for the normal conduct of a business, which will not normally be converted into cash during the ensuing fiscal period.

Fixed Assets (Net)
All property, plant, leasehold improvements, and equipment, net of accumulated depreciation or depletion.

Fixed Assets (Net)/Net Worth
Measures liquidity by comparing "fixed" assets with "fixed" capital. A lower ratio indicates proportionately smaller investment and a better "cushion" for creditors in case of liquidation.

Fixed Asset Turnover
Measures management's ability to generate revenues from investments in fixed assets.

Fixed Costs
Costs that do not change when the quantity of output changes during a particular time period. Examples: rent, property taxes, and interest expense. Contrast to Variable Costs.

Fixed Expenses
Expenses that remain the same regardless of production or sales volume, i.e., do not fluctuate with sales volume. Contrast with Variable Expenses.

Fixed Overhead
Costs like rent, utilities, basic telephone, loan payments, etc., that stay the same whether sales go up or down. Variable overhead, on the other hand, are those costs which vary directly with production.

Flat Interest

Refers to charging interest on the full original loan amount, rather than on the declining balance. With group based loans, for example, a common "interest rate" is "3 percent per month, flat, for four months." This means that a $100 principal amount lent is multiplied by 3 percent, and then by four months, to come up with $12 in interest. Thus, $112 would be repaid over four months in equal installments.

Flat Lease

A lease where the cost is fixed for a specific period of time.

Flow-through Share

A flow-through share is available to mining and petroleum companies to facilitate financing their exploration and development activities. Investors receive an equity interest in the company and income tax deductions associated with new expenditures incurred by the company on exploration and development.

FOB (Free on Board)

For example, "*FOB New York*" is where the importer would pay all costs for shipping from one point (New York) on to the final destination.

Forensic Accounting

Provides for an accounting analysis that is suitable to a court of law which will form the basis for discussion, debate, and ultimately dispute resolution. Forensic accounting encompasses investigative accounting and litigation support.

Free Cash Flow

Net income plus non-cash charges to income, specifically depreciation and amortization minus capital expenditures, to sustain the basic business. Free cash flow is another name for cash flow from assets.

Full Disclosure

Generally, the requirement to disclose all relevant or material facts to a transaction.

Fund Accounting

A kind of accounting used by governments and other non-business organizations to segregate groups of assets, liabilities, some forms of equity, revenues, and expenditures, in accordance with the purpose for which the funds were obtained.

Future Income Tax

Income tax expected to be paid in future years based on business events and income tax calculations done up to the present. The liability and associated expense are calculated by the Liability method, which estimates the likely future tax payments directly. Sometimes replaces the deferral method and its Deferred Income Tax.

Future Value
The amount of money that an investment made today (the Present Value) will grow to by some future date.

Gain(s)
Usually refers to the profit (proceeds minus book value) obtained from the disposition of assets (or liabilities) not normally disposed of in the daily course of business, such as from selling land, buildings, or other non-current assets, or from refinancing debt.

Gain (Loss) on Sale
A gain on sale occurs when a company receives a larger amount of proceeds for an asset than its book value.

G&A
Usually refers to the indirect overhead costs contained within the General and Administrative expense/cost categories.

Gearing
A company's debts expressed as a percentage of its equity capital. High gearing means that debts are high in relation to assets.

Gearing Ratio
Measures the percentage of capital employed that is financed by debt and long term financing.

Generally Accepted Accounting Principles (GAAP)
Principles and methods of accounting that have the general support of standard-setting bodies, general practice, texts, and other sources. These are the common set of standards and procedures by which financial statements should be prepared.

Generally Accepted Auditing Standards (GAAS)
Broad rules and guidelines for auditing set down by the the Chartered Professional Accounts (CPAs) of Canada.

General Partnership
One or more partners who are jointly and severally responsible or liable for the debts of the partnership.

Going Concern
A fundamental assumption in financial accounting that a firm will be financially viable and remain in business long enough to see all of its current plans carried out.

Goodwill
The difference between the price paid for a group of assets and the sum of their apparent fair (market) values. Arises when a bundle of assets or a whole company is acquired and when the difference is positive.

Grossing Up
(1) Calculating the amount that would be required in the case of an investment subject to tax, to equal the income from that investment as if it were not subject to tax; (2) Tax credits are normally given by deduction from tax that is calculated on the amount of income received grossed-up for underlying tax, or the tax credit itself. For example, in Canada, the federal Dividend Tax Credit (DTC) provides a tax credit based on the grossed-up value of dividends from Canadian companies.

Gross Margin or Gross Profit
Revenue minus cost of goods sold expense (i.e., net sales minus cost of sales).

Gross Margin Ratio or Gross Profit Ratio
Equals (revenue – cost of goods sold) / revenue.

Gross Profit Margin on Sales (GPM)
The gross profit margin gives an indication on whether the average markup on goods and services is sufficient to cover expenses and make a profit. GPM shows the relationship between sales and the direct cost of products/services sold.

Gross Receipts
The total amount received prior to the deduction of any allowances, discounts, credits, etc.

Gross Sales
The total revenue at invoice value prior to any discounts or allowances.

Growing Perpetuity
A constant stream of cash flows without end that is expected to rise indefinitely.

Hard Costs
The purchase price of actual assets.

Historical Cost
The dollar value of a transaction on the date it happens, normally maintained in the accounting records from then on because of accounting's reliance on transactions as the basis for recording events. The cost, or historical cost, of an asset is the dollar amount paid for it or promised to be paid as of the date the asset was acquired.

Historical Cost Accounting
An accounting principle requiring all financial statement items to be based on original cost.

Holder-of-Record Date
The date on which existing shareholders on company records are designated as the recipients of stock rights.

Horizontal Financial Analysis
Allows comparison of one company's ratios to the ratios of other companies as well as to average industrial ratios and internal industrial deviation of these ratios.

Hurdle Rate
A term used in the budgeting of capital expenditures meaning the required rate of return in a discounted cash flow analysis. If the *expected rate of return* on an investment is below the hurdle rate, the project is not undertaken.

Identifiable Assets and Liabilities
Those assets and liabilities of a business that can be disposed of without disposing of the entire business. Includes both tangible and intangible assets.

Income
The money and other benefits net of certain expenses flowing to individuals, firms, and other groups in the economy.

Income before Tax
An amount equal to revenue plus other income minus all other ordinary expenses except income tax.

Income Capitalization
First determine the capitalization rate — a rate of return required to take on the risk of operating the business (the riskier the business, the higher the required return). Earnings are then divided by that capitalization rate.

Income Smoothing
The "manipulation" of net income so that the year-to-year variations in reported income are reduced.

Income Statement
See Profit and Loss Statement.

Income Tax
Tax assessed on income, according to laws about the computation of income for tax purposes.

Income Tax Allocation
The attempt to allocate income tax expense to the appropriate year or activity to which it applies even if it is paid in another year or in aggregate across activities.

Incremental Cash Flows
The difference between a firm's future cash flows with a project and without the project.

Indenture
A contract signed by a borrower and lender under which the borrower undertakes to meet certain conditions, such as keeping the working capital ratio above a specified amount, violation of which would give the lender the right to ask for immediate repayment of the loan or to take other action.

Indirect Cost
That portion of cost that is indirectly expended in providing a product or service for sale (cannot be traced to a given cost object in an economically feasible manner) and is included in the calculation of cost of goods sold. Examples: rent, utilities, equipment maintenance, etc.

Inflation
An increase in the general price level of goods and services; alternatively, a decrease in the purchasing power of the dollar or other currency.

Inflation Accounting
A system of accounting which, unlike *historical cost accounting*, takes into account changing prices.

Inflation Premium
The portion of a nominal interest rate that represents compensation for expected future inflation.

Insolvency
Occurs when a business is unable to pay debts as they fall due.

Installment Sale
Selling property and receiving the sales price over a series of payments, instead of all at once at the close of the sale, is an installment sale.

Intangible Asset
An asset that is not physical in nature. Examples: copyrights, patents, intellectual property, or purchased goodwill.

Interest
The amount charged by a lender for the use of borrowed money.

Interest Coverage Ratio
Usually calculated as (income before interest expense + income tax) / interest expense.

Interest Expense
The cost of borrowing funds in the current period. It is shown as a financial expense item within the income statement.

Interest on Interest
Interest earned on the reinvestment of previous interest payments. See Compound Interest.

Internal Auditor
An auditor who works for the enterprise and thus verifies information for management's use and to help the enterprise perform better.

Internal Control
Methods of providing physical security and management control over an enterprise's cash, inventories, and other assets.

Internal Rate of Return (IRR)
Also called the dollar-weighted rate of return; the interest rate that makes the present value of the cash flows from all the sub-periods in an evaluation period plus the terminal market value of the portfolio equal to the initial market value of the portfolio.

International Accounting Standards Committee (IASC)
A committee made up of representatives of more than fifty countries that sets international accounting standards.

Intrinsic Value
The lower bound of an option's value, or what the option would be worth if it were about to expire.

Inventory(ies)
The goods purchased or manufactured by a company for sale, resale, or further use in operations, including finished goods, goods in process, raw materials, and supplies.

Inventory Costing
Comprises various methods of determining the cost of inventory for balance sheet valuation purposes and of valuing cost of goods sold. The more common methods are FIFO, LIFO, and Weighted average.

Inventory Turnover
A ratio that shows how many times the inventory of a firm is sold and replaced over a specific period. Calculated as the cost of goods sold / average inventory assets.

Inventory Valuation
The process of determining the amount at which inventory is shown on the balance sheet, normally the lower of cost or market.

Investment Income
The income received from investment in securities and property. Examples: rent from property, dividends from shares in corporations, and interest from bonds, guaranteed-investment certificates, bank accounts, certificates of deposit, treasury bills.

Invoice
Bill for goods or services provided by the seller to the purchaser.

Joint Stock Company
A company that has some features of a corporation and some features of a partnership. This type of company has access to the liquidity and financial reserves of stock markets as a corporation, however, as in a partnership; the stockholders are liable for company debts and have additional restrictions of a partnership.

Journal
In accounting transactions, is where transactions are recorded as they occur.

Journal Entry
A record of a transaction or accrual adjustment that lists the accounts affected and in which the total of the debits equals the total of the credits.

Lease
A contract requiring the user of an asset to pay the owner of the asset a predetermined fee for the use of the asset.

Leasehold Improvements
Those repairs and/or improvements, usually prior to occupancy, made to a leased facility by the lessee. The cost is then added to fixed assets and amortized over the life of the lease.

Ledger
Any book or electronic record that summarizes the transactions from the "books of original entry" in the form of accounts.

Legal Entity
A person or organization that has the legal standing to enter into contracts and may be sued for failure to perform as agreed in the contract.

Lessee
The user of an asset in a leasing agreement. Lessee makes payments to lessor.

Lessor
The owner of an asset in a leasing agreement. Lessor receives payments from the lessee.

Letter to the Shareholders
Part of the Annual report; a letter from senior management to the shareholders, summarizing major decisions and strategies, commenting on the company's performance for the year, and usually looking ahead to future performance.

Leverage
Value of property rising or falling at a proportionally greater amount than comparable investments. Example: an option has high leverage relative to the underlying stock because a small price change in the stock may result in a relatively large increase or decrease in the value of the option.

Leverage Analysis
Study of the financial statements and corporate financial structure in order to determine how, and how well, the company is making use of leverage.

Leveraged Lease
A financial lease where the lessor borrows a substantial fraction of the cost of the leased asset.

Leverage Ratios
Measures the relative contribution of stockholders and creditors, and of the firm's ability to pay financing charges. Value of firm's debt to the total value of the firm.

Leverage Return
The portion of the return on equity that is due to earning more return on borrowed funds than it costs in interest to borrow them.

Liability
In accounting, a loan, expense, or any other form of claim on the assets of an entity that must be paid or otherwise honoured by that entity. The debt may be legally existing or estimated via accrual accounting techniques.

Liability Method
A method of Income Tax Allocation in which the impact of Future Income Tax is estimated according to what is expected to be paid rather than according to past timing differences as done in Deferred Income Tax accounting.

LIFO (Last-In, First-Out)
A cost flow assumption that is the opposite of FIFO. "Last in, first out" assumes that the units sold are from the most recent purchases and thus bases cost of goods sold on the most recent purchases and ending inventory on the oldest purchases.

LIFO Reserve
The difference between the ending inventory under LIFO and FIFO (or other method that might be chosen).

Limited Partner
A partner in a venture who has no management authority and whose liability is restricted to the amount of their investment.

Liquidating Dividends
Dividends paid by a corporation that is in the process of liquidation/ bankruptcy.

Liquidation
Termination of the firm as a going concern.

Liquidation Value
Liquidation value uses the value of the assets at liquidation, which is often less than market and sometimes book. Liabilities are deducted from the liquidation value of the assets to determine the liquidation value of the business.

Liquidity
A company's ability to meet current obligations with cash or other assets that can be quickly converted to cash.

Listed Company
A company that has obtained permission for its shares to be admitted to the Stock Exchange's Official List. See also Public Company.

Loan Covenant
A legally enforceable promise or restriction in a mortgage.

Loans from Shareholder(s)
Informal loans to the corporation by shareholders(s), who therefore act as creditors as well as owners. It is most common in private company corporations.

Long-Lived Assets
Usually those assets that are not consumed during the normal course of business, Examples: land, buildings and equipment, etc.

Long-Term Debt
All senior debt, including bonds, debentures, bank debt, mortgages, deferred portions of long term debt, and capital lease obligations.

Long-Term Debt to Equity Ratio
[Long-term loans + mortgages + bonds + similar long-term debts] / total equity.

Long-Term Liabilities
Liabilities of a business that are due in more than one year.

Loss(es)
Usually refers to the case of a negative return (proceeds being less than book value) obtained from the disposition of assets (or liabilities) not normally disposed of in the daily course of business, such as from selling land, buildings or other non-current assets, or from refinancing debt.

Loss Carry-Overs
Business or investment losses that are incurred in one year that may be used as a deduction from taxable income in another year.

Loss on Sale
Selling a non-current asset for less than its Book Value.

Lower of Cost or Market
A method of valuing items of inventory, temporary investments, or other current assets, under which losses inherent in declines of the market prices of items held below their costs are recognized in the period in which such declines become apparent.

Management Discussion and Analysis (MD&A)
A section of a company's annual report in which management reviews the results for the year and explains what happened in some detail. The MD&A is used by many analysts to supplement ratios and other forms of analysis.

Marginal Analysis
Focusing on revenues or expenses that change between two alternatives, rather than including all revenues and expenses, so as to highlight effects.

Marginal (or Incremental) Cost
A calculation showing the change in total cost as a result of a change in volume. For example: if one more item of output increases the total cost by $25, the marginal cost is $25.

Marginal Tax Rate
The ratio of the increase in tax to the increase in the tax base (i.e., the tax rate on each additional dollar of income). For example, in the case of an individual with a marginal income tax rate of 33 percent, each additional dollar of income above a threshold would be subject to an income tax of 33 cents.

Marketable Securities
Investments having a ready market for resale and held as a way of earning a return from temporarily unneeded cash.

Market Capitalization
The total dollar value of all outstanding shares. It is calculated by multiplying the number of shares times the current market price. The term is commonly referred to as "market cap."

Market to Market
Daily settlement of obligations on futures positions.

Markup
The difference between the enterprise's selling prices for its products and the unit costs it incurs for those products.

Matching Concept
The accounting principle that requires the recognition of all costs that are directly associated with the realization of the revenue reported within the income statement.

Material, Materiality
In accounting, material means that the magnitude of an omission or misstatement of accounting information makes it probable that, in the light of surrounding circumstances, the judgment of a reasonable person relying on the information would have been changed or influenced by the omission or misstatement.

Mean
The measure of central tendency; also called the "average." It is calculated by the sum of the data points divided by the number of data points.

Median
The value of the midpoint variable when the data are arranged in ascending or descending order.

Memorandum of Association
The charter of a company which indicates nationality, the nature of its business, and the share capital it is authorized to issue. It is a statutory document that effectively governs the company's relations with the outside world.

Merger
The joining together of two corporations such that the owners of both become the owners of the combined corporation.

Minority Interest
The interest or percentage ownership of a group of stockholders who, in total, own less than 50 percent of the shares in the corporation.

Miscellaneous Income
That income realized that is not directly related to the sale of standard products and services.

Monetary
Anything pertaining to or having to do with money, money creation, money supply, and the government management of money.

Money Market Instruments
Short-term debt securities maturing in one year or less. Examples: treasury bills, bankers' acceptances, commercial paper, discount notes, and guaranteed investment certificates.

Mortgage
A form of security on a loan in which the lender has a direct claim on title to property specified in the mortgage.

Mortgage-Backed Security (MBS)
A debt security that gives a share in a pool of mortgages. An MBS pays monthly income, which is a combination of interest and a portion of the principal of the underlying mortgages.

Multiple
Same as Price/Earnings Ratio.

Negative Goodwill
Arises where the net assets at the date of acquisition, fairly valued, exceed the cost of acquisition. It is reflected on the balance sheet net of other intangible assets.

Net
In general, the figure remaining after all relevant deductions have been made from the starting, or gross, amount. Examples: net book value, net income, net-of-tax analysis, and net realizable value.

Net Asset Value (NAV)
The market value or price of one fund share in securities, except in money market funds, which always have a NAV of $1.00. The total value of the fund's portfolio less liabilities divided by the number of shares.

Net Book Value
The cost of an asset minus any accumulated depreciation, amortization, allowance for doubtful accounts.

Net Income
The difference between a business's total revenue and its total expenses, usually found at the bottom of a company's Profit and Loss statement. Also called net profit.

Net Leases
Typically, there are three net leases: net lease, double-net lease, and triple-net lease. A net lease is a base rent plus an additional charge for taxes. A double-net lease is a base rent plus an additional charge for taxes and insurance. A triple-net lease is base rent plus an additional charge for taxes, insurance, and common area expenses.

Net Loss
Negative net income.

Net-of-Tax Analysis
A method of determining the impact of management decisions or accounting changes in which the effects of income tax are included to produce the net after-tax effect of the decision or change.

Net Operating Income (NOI)
Income after deducting for operating expenses but before deducting for income taxes and interest.

Net Operating Loss (NOL)
Experienced by a business when business deductions exceed business income for the fiscal year.

Net Present Value (NPV)
The difference between the discounted value of an investment's market value and its cost. Used in evaluating investments, whereby the net present value of all cash outflows (such as the cost of the investment) and cash inflows (returns) is calculated using a given discount rate.

Net Present Value Profile
A graphical representation of the relationship between an investment's NPVs and various discount rates.

Net Profit
See Net Income.

Net Profit Margin (NPM after Tax)
Measures profitability as a percentage of revenues after consideration of all revenue and expense, including interest expenses, non-operating items, and income taxes.

Net Purchases
Those items purchased less returns, discounts, and allowances on those purchases.

Net Realizable Value
The fair market value that an asset will bring if it is sold through the usual product market minus any completion or disposal costs.

Net Receivables
A company's accounts receivable (money owed to the company) minus any provisions for bad debts.

Net Revenue
Gross Revenue minus discounts, allowances, sales returns, freight out, etc.

Net Sales
Gross sales less discounts, allowances, sales returns, freight out, etc.

Net 10, 30, etc.
Refers to payment terms on an invoice. For example: 'Net 10 2 percent, 30,' means that if purchaser pays the invoice within 10 days they receive a 2 percent reduction in invoice. Otherwise, full invoice amount is due within 30 days.

Net Worth
The difference between total liabilities and total assets.

New Issue
A company coming to the market for the first time or issuing additional shares.

New Shares
Shares newly issued by a company.

Nominal Rate of Interest
The stated rate of interest applied to an investment.

Non-Cash Items
Expenses charged against revenues that do not directly affect cash flow, such as depreciation.

Non-Current Assets
Assets expected to bring benefit for more than one fiscal year such as property, plant, and equipment, as opposed to current assets, which include cash,

cash equivalents (e.g., securities, short-term notes, etc.), inventory, and accounts receivable.

Non-Current Liabilities
Liabilities expected to be repaid or otherwise removed more than one year in the future.

Non-Operating Cash Flows
Cash inflows and outflows related to non-current investments, financing, and dividends.

No-Par (shares)
Shares having no legal minimum issue price (par value). Proceeds are added to share capital at whatever price the company obtains for each issue.

Normal Distribution
Asymmetric, bell-shaped frequency distribution that can be defined by its mean and standard deviation.

Notes Payable
Accounts payable that are supported by signed contracts or other agreements and usually carry interest.

Notes Payable — Short Term
All short-term note obligations, including bank and commercial paper. Does not include trade notes payable.

Notes Receivable
Accounts receivable supported by signed contracts or other agreements specifying repayment terms, interest rate, and other conditions.

Notes to the Financial Statements
A detailed set of Notes immediately following the financial statements contained in the annual report that expands upon and/or explains in some depth the information contained in the financial statements.

Not-for-Profit Accounting
Procedures used to account for non-business, non-government entities. These procedures increasingly follow GAAP.

NPV
An acronym for Net Present Value.

Objectivity
The notion that the information in financial statements must be as free from bias as possible, in order that all user groups can have confidence in it.

Off-Balance Sheet Financing
Methods of obtaining financing that avoid having to record the sources as liabilities or equity.

Operating Cash Flow
Cash generated from a firm's normal business activities.

Operating Cycle
The time period between the acquisition of inventory and when cash is collected from receivables.

Operating Expenditures
The amount used during a particular period directly in support of day-to-day operations such as wages, maintenance, office supplies, etc.

Operating Expenses
All selling and general and administrative expenses, including depreciation, but not interest expense.

Operating Income
Revenue minus cost of goods sold and related operating expenses that are applied to the day-to-day operating activities of the company. Excludes financial related items (i.e., interest income, dividend income, and interest expense), extraordinary items, and taxes.

Operating Lease
Usually a shorter-term lease where the lessor is responsible for insurance, taxes, and upkeep. Often cancellable on short notice.

Operating Loan
Loan negotiated with banks, usually by small business, for day-to-day operations.

Operating Profit
Gross Profit minus Operating Expenses.

Operating Return
The return earned by an enterprise before considering the cost of financing and nonrecurring items.

Option
A contract that gives its owner the right (but not the obligation) to buy (call option) or sell (put option) some asset at a fixed price on or before a given date. For that right, the option holder (or buyer) pays the option writer (or seller) a premium.

Order of Liquidity
When items on a balance sheet are listed in order of liquidity. After cash, the other current assets are listed in order of liquidity or nearness to cash (i.e., accounts receivable first, then inventory . . .).

Order of Permanence
Where fixed assets are entered in the balance sheet in descending order of permanence (i.e., land first, then buildings, then equipment . . .).

Ordinary Shares
The most common form of share. Holders receive dividends, which vary in amount in accordance with the profitability of the company and recommendations of the directors. The holders of the ordinary shares are the owners of the company.

Organization Cost
Amounts spent to begin a business entity, e.g., business filing fees, franchise acquisition, and legal fees.

Original Issue Discount
When a long-term debt instrument is issued at a price that is lower than its stated redemption value; the difference is called Original Issue Discount (OID).

Other Assets
A catch-all category used for non-current (and occasionally current) assets that do not fit into other categories, that are not material individually but aggregate to a material total.

Outstanding Shares
The number of shares that are currently owned by all investors. It also includes restricted shares (shares owned by officers and insiders of the company) as well as shares held by the public. Shares that the company has repurchased or retired are not considered outstanding stock.

Overhead Costs
The costs associated with providing and maintaining a manufacturing or working environment. Examples: renting the building, heating and lighting the work area, supervision costs, and maintenance of the facilities. Includes indirect labour and indirect material.

Overleveraged
A balance sheet condition where the entity is incapable of servicing its debt load (interest payments) with available capital sources.

Owner's Capital
The owner's equity of the proprietor of an unincorporated business.

Own Work Capitalized
Represents the value of work performed for own purposes and capitalized as part of fixed assets.

Pacioli Luca
Pacioli's *Suma* is the first known book describing double-entry bookkeeping. Published in 1494, it was influential in the development of accounting and business in Europe.

Parent Corporation
The dominant corporation in a corporate group linked by ownership, the name of which is usually used in the consolidated financial statements.

Partners' Capital
The owners' equity section of a partnership's balance sheet.

Partnership
An unincorporated business formed by two or more co-owners in a relationship with a view to profit.

Par Value
A value set as the legal minimum amount for which a corporation's shares may be issued. Canadian companies typically have no-par shares, but par value is still used in many other jurisdictions, including some in the United States.

Patent
A legal form of protection that provides a person or legal entity with exclusive rights to exclude others from making, using, or selling a concept or invention for the duration of the patent. There are three types of patents available: design, plant, and utility.

Payback Period
In capital budgeting, is the length of time needed to recoup the cost of Capital Investment. The payback period is the ratio of the initial investment (cash outlay, regardless of the source of the cash) to the annual cash inflows for the recovery period.

Payout Ratio
Dividends paid divided by company earnings over some period of time, expressed as a percentage.

P/E Ratio
See Price-Earnings Ratio.

Percentage Lease
A type of lease where the landlord charges a base rent plus an additional percentage of any profits realized by the business tenant.

Period Expenses
Expenses that are related to the passage of time rather than to the level of sales volume or other activities. Examples: interest, salaries.

Periodic Inventory Control Method
A method of calculating inventory that uses data on beginning inventory, additions to inventory, and an end-of-period count to deduce the cost of goods sold.

Periodic Reporting
A basic convention of financial accounting that holds that accounting information must be assembled and presented to users at regular intervals (at least yearly and often quarterly or monthly).

Perpetual Inventory Control Method
A method of controlling inventory that maintains continuous records on the flow of units of inventory. Thus, there are figures on record for beginning inventory, each unit added to inventory, and each unit removed from inventory for sale.

Perpetuity
An annuity in which the cash flows continue forever.

Personal Tax
Tax on personal income in Canada, including both personal income taxes and the employee portion of social security contributions, such as unemployment insurance premiums and Canada/Quebec Pension Plan contributions.

Petty Cash
A small fund of cash kept on hand by an employee for paying small expenses such as postage, minor supplies, and courier charges.

PITI
An acronym for Principal, Interest, Taxes, and Insurance when dealing with property mortgages.

Plug
The double-entry system requires that debits equal credits. If adding up all the debits and the credits does not produce two equal figures, the statements must be adjusted so that a balance occurs. The amount of adjustment needed is often called a "plug."

Portfolio
A collection of securities held by an investor.

Portfolio Investments
Debt or equity investments in a corporation that do not provide the investor with substantial ownership or influence in the management of the corporation. Typically, equity ownership of less than 10 percent of a corporation is considered to be a portfolio investment.

Preference Share Capital
Capital raised by an entity through the sale of preferred shares.

Preferred Shares
Usually, non-voting shares that pay dividends at a specified rate and have preference over common shares (but not over debentures and loans) in the payment of dividends and the liquidation of assets.

Premium
(1) If the market price of a new security is higher than the issue price, the difference is the premium. If it is lower, the difference is called the discount; (2) The cost of purchasing a traded option.

Premium on Bonds
Arises when bonds are issued at a price above their legal face value, such as a $100 bond being issued for $105 cash, indicating a $5 premium.

Prepaid Expenses
Amounts that are paid in advance to a vender or creditor for goods and services. Example: insurance premiums paid in advance of the coverage contained in the policy.

Present Value
The current value of one or more future cash payments, discounted at some appropriate interest rate.

Present Value Analysis
Analysis of future cash flows done by removing the presumed interest components of those flows.

Price-Earnings Ratio (P/E ratio)
The current share price divided by the last published earnings per share, where earnings per share is net profit divided by the number of ordinary shares.

Price to Book
A financial ratio derived by dividing a stock's capitalization by its book value. Also called Market-to-Book.

Price to Revenue
A financial ratio derived by dividing current stock price by revenue per share (adjusted for stock splits).

Principal
In interest calculations, the principal is the amount of money initially borrowed, lent, or invested and on which interest is calculated.

Private Company
A company that does not have a listing on the Exchange and is barred from offering its shares to the general public.

Professional Ethics
Codes of conduct to guide professionals in applying their professional judgment and that are conducive to their professional activities.

Professionalism
Acting according to the levels of competence, ethics, independence, etc., expected of professionals.

Professional Judgment
The judgment of professionals about problems in their domain, for example, that of accountants or auditors about financial accounting matters.

Profit
See Net Income.

Profitability
A company's ability to generate revenues in excess of the costs incurred in producing those revenues.

Profitability Ratios
Measures of performance showing how much the firm is earning compared to its sales, assets or equity.

Profit after Tax (PAT)
The net profit earned by the company after deducting all expenses like interest, depreciation, and tax.

Profit and Loss Statement (P&L)
Shows business revenue and expenses for a specific period of time. The difference between the total revenue and the total expense is net income.

Profit before Taxes
Operating profit minus all other expenses (net).

Profit Centre
A section of an organization that is responsible for producing profit, e.g., a division of a corporation that is not a stand-alone entity but is required to produce profits within the corporation.

Profit Margin on Sales
A profitability ratio calculated by dividing net income by average total assets.

Pro Forma
To provide in advance to a prescribed form or to describe items, e.g., *pro forma* financial statement or *pro forma* invoice.

***Pro Forma* Financial Statements**
Financial statements projecting future years' operations.

***Pro Forma* Invoice**
A price quote written as an invoice that says, in effect: "This is the purchase price and terms we are offering."

Promissory Note
Usually just called a "note," is a negotiable instrument wherein the maker agrees to pay a specific sum at a definite time.

Proprietary Asset
Usually, any asset that is considered in the realm of intellectual property that should not be disclosed. Examples: information having to do with clients/customers, trade secrets, and undisclosed inventions.

Proprietor's Draw
When a business proprietor draws money for personal needs, but is taxed on business results (at marginal rate for individuals) regardless of drawings.

Proprietorship
A firm that is neither a corporation nor a partnership but is under the sole control of one individual. Such a firm is not legally separate from that individual.

Protective Covenant
Part of the indenture limiting certain transactions that can be taken during the term of the loan, usually to protect the lender's interest.

Provision
Another phrase for a usually non-current accrual such as for future pension costs or warranties.

Prudence Concept
Otherwise known as conservatism. Whenever there are alternative procedures or values, choose the one that results in a lower profit, a lower asset value, and a higher liability value.

Public Accounting, Public Accounting Firms
Offering auditing, accounting, tax, consulting, and related services to the public on a professional basis.

Public Company
A corporation whose shares and related securities are sold widely, to members of the public and other investors, and whose securities are traded on stock exchanges and other capital markets. See also Listed Company.

Put Option
The right to sell stock at an agreed price at or within a stated future time. The opposite of a Call Option. See, generally, Option.

Put Warrant
A security that, in contrast to a conventional warrant, gives the holder the right to sell the underlying or to receive a cash payment that increases as the value of the underlying declines. Put warrants, like their call warrant counterparts, generally have an initial term of more than one year.

Qualified Opinion
The auditor's opinion accompanying a financial statement that calls attention to limitations in the audit or exceptions the auditor has taken with the audit of the statements.

Quick Ratio (or Acid Test Ratio)
A more rigorous test than the Current Ratio of short-run solvency, the current ability of a firm to pay its current debts as they come due. This ratio is calculated by dividing total liquid assets, such as cash, marketable securities (cash equivalents), and accounts receivable by current liabilities.

R&D
Research and development activities.

Rate of Return
The gain or loss for a security in a particular period, consisting of income plus capital gains relative to investment, usually quoted as a percentage.

Ratios, Ratio Analysis
Numbers produced by dividing one financial statement figure by another figure, such as the working capital ratio, which is the total current assets figure divided by the total current liabilities figure.

Real Interest Rate
The nominal interest rate minus the rate of inflation.

Realization Principle
That revenue should be recognized at the time goods are sold and services are rendered.

Realized Capital Gains
The increase in value of an investment converted to cash upon sale.

Realized Income
The return or profit that is actually earned or collected over a given time period.

Recaptured Depreciation
The taxable difference between adjusted proceeds of disposal and UCC when UCC is greater.

Receivable
Funds expected to be collected by the enterprise.

Receiver
A court-appointed person who takes possession of, but not title to, the assets and affairs of a business or estate that is in a form of bankruptcy called Receivership.

Receiver General for Canada
The chief financial officer of the federal government, who receives all revenues from the government and deposits them in the consolidated revenue fund.

Receivership
An equitable remedy whereby a court orders property placed under the control of a receiver so that it may be preserved for the benefit of affected parties.

Recourse
In finance, the right to demand payment from the maker or endorser of a negotiable instrument (as a check).

Redeemable
A feature of an investment security (e.g., shares or bonds) that gives the issuer (company) the right to buy the investment back from the holder at a specified price during a specified period prior to maturity.

Redemption Date
The date on which a security (usually fixed interest stock) is due to be repaid by the issuer at its full face value. The year is included in the title of the

security, the actual redemption date being that on which the last interest is due to be paid.

Refundable Tax Credit
Where a tax credit is refundable, a portion of the credit that is not needed to reduce a taxpayer's tax liability (because it is already zero) may be paid to the taxpayer.

Regular Cash Dividend
Cash payment made by a firm to its owners in the normal course of business, usually made four times a year.

Reorganization
Financial restructuring of a firm to attempt to continue operations as a going concern or in a new structure.

Replacement Cost (of an asset)
The price that will have to be paid in order to replace an existing asset with a similar asset.

Reporting Entity
The legal entity for which financial reports are prepared and made available.

Reserve Accounts
Generally, those accounts where retained earnings are set aside to satisfy dividends, improvements, contingencies, retirement of preferred stock, etc.

Residual Claim
A claim to a share of earnings after debt obligations have been satisfied.

Residual Value
(1) Realizable value of a fixed asset after deducting costs associated with its sale; (2) Scrap value or the value to a junk dealer; (3) The amount remaining after all depreciation has been deducted from the original cost of a depreciable asset.

Resources
In financial accounting, the recognized assets of the enterprise as shown on the balance sheet.

Restricted Assets
Assets/resources which are restricted by legal or contractual requirements for use under specific circumstances or purposes.

Retained Earnings
Earnings not yet distributed to owners; the sum of net incomes earned over the life of a company, minus distributions (dividends declared) to owners.

Retention Ratio
Retained earnings divided by net income. Also called the plowback ratio.

Retractable
A feature of an investment security (e.g., shares or bonds) which gives the holder the right to sell (put) the investment back to the issuer at a specified price during a specified period prior to maturity.

Return
Some amount of gain (income or performance) usually measured in relation to the amount invested to get the return.

Return on Assets (ROA or ROA(ATI))
Net income, before considering interest expense or the tax saving provided by interest expense, divided by total assets. This measures the operating return before the cost of financing.

Return on Assets (ROA)
Shows the after tax earnings of assets.

Return on Capital
The distribution of cash from depreciation tax savings, the sale of a capital asset or securities, or any other transaction not related to retained earnings.

Return on Equity (ROE)
Net income after interest and taxes divided by average common shareholders' equity.

Revenue
The amount of benefit received or promised from the sale of goods or services, before any deductions for the cost of providing the goods or services.

Revenue Recognition
The entering into the accounts of the amount of revenue determined, according to the firm's accounting policies, to be attributable to the current period.

Revenue Reserve
A fund that is not a capital reserve, i.e., the funds are distributable.

Reverse Split
Procedure where a firm's number of shares outstanding is reduced. The opposite of a Stock Split.

Review
A report prepared on an enterprise's financial statements by a public accounting firm that is less than an audit but more than a compilation. The accounting firm studies the statements' contents and compliance with GAAP

to determine if there are any apparent problems but does not verify individual accounts or the underlying records.

Revolving Collateral
Accounts receivable or inventory which change from day to day.

Revolving Financing
Financing secured by collateral.

Revolving Line of Credit
In commercial banking, a contractual agreement between a bank and, usually, a company where the bank agrees to provide loans up to a specified maximum over a specified period, usually a year or more. In consumer banking, it is a loan account requiring monthly payments less than the full amount of the loan, and the balance is carried forward with a finance charge on that balance.

Right
A temporary privilege allowing investors who already own common shares to purchase additional shares directly from the company at a specified price.

Rights Issue
An invitation to existing shareholders to acquire additional shares in the company in proportion to the number of shares they already own — usually at a preferential price.

Royalty(ies)
The term "royalties" generally refers to amounts paid for the use of personal property (usually, but not always, intangible property), such as industrial, commercial, scientific, or artistic property.

Sale and Leaseback
A financial lease in which the lessee sells an asset to the lessor and then leases it back.

Sales Invoice
A document containing the details of a sale of goods or services from a *vendor* to a *customer*.

Sales Order
Also known as sales contract, a contract by which buyer and seller agree to the terms and conditions of a sale.

Sales Return
The ratio of net income to revenue.

Salvage Value
(1) Realizable value of a fixed asset after deducting costs associated with its sale; (2) Scrap value or the value to a junk dealer; (3) The amount remaining after all depreciation has been deducted from the original cost of a depreciable asset.

SCFP (Statement of Changes in Financial Position)
See Cash Flow Statement.

Secured Liability
A liability that has a degree of protection towards satisfaction if unpaid because the debtor has pledged personal/company assets towards satisfaction of that liability.

Securities
Shares, bonds, and other financial instruments issued by corporations and governments and usually traded on capital markets.

Securities and Exchange Commission (SEC)
An agency of the US government that supervises the registration of security issues, prosecutes fraudulent stock manipulations, and regulates securities transactions in the United States.

Senior Debt/Note
Loans or debt securities that have a claim prior to junior obligations and equity on a corporation's assets in the event of a liquidation.

Sensitivity Analysis
Investigation of what happens to NPV when only one variable is changed.

Setoff
The discharge of a debt by setting against it a distinct claim in favour of the debtor.

Settlement
The process of exchanging money, or some other value, for shares.

SG&A
Refers to the indirect overhead costs contained within the sales, general, and administrative expense/cost categories.

Share Capital
The portion of a corporation's equity obtained by issuing shares in return for cash or other consideration.

Shareholder(s)
The holders of a corporation's share capital, and so the owners of the corporation.

Shareholder Rights Plan
Provisions allowing existing shareholders to purchase stock at some fixed price should an outside takeover bid take place, discouraging hostile takeover attempts.

Shareholder's Equity
The sums of shareholders' direct investment (share capital) and indirect investment (retained earnings). Calculated as total assets minus total liabilities. It is the same as equity, net worth, and stockholder's equity.

Shares (stock)
Units of share capital, evidenced by certificates and, for public companies, traded on capital markets with other securities.

Short Term Asset
An asset expected to be converted into cash within the normal operating cycle (usually one year), e.g., accounts receivable and inventory.

Short Term Liability
A liability that will come due within one year or less.

Signature Loan
A loan secured by the borrower with nothing more than the signature of that borrower.

Simple Interest
Interest earned only on the original principal amount invested. Does not include interest on the interest. Compare to Compound Interest.

Sinking Fund
A sum set apart periodically from the income of a government or a business and allowed to accumulate in order ultimately to pay off a debt. A preferred investment for a sinking fund is the purchase of the government's or firm's bonds that are to be paid off.

Soft Costs
Those extraneous costs that are not readily foreseen or budgeted for, e.g., legal fees, loan fees and interest, etc.

Sole Proprietor
An individual that owns a business as opposed to stock in a corporation.

Sole Proprietorship
A form of business organization. The distinguishing characteristics of a sole proprietorship include: only one owner for the business (hence, "sole") and the business is unincorporated.

Solvency
The condition of being able to meet all debts and obligations.

Sources
The right-hand side of the balance sheet (liabilities and equity) are the sources of the enterprise's assets.

Sources of Cash
A firm's activities that generate cash.

Specific Identification
Accounting for inventories according to the specific cost of the items, which therefore requires some sort of identification of the items, such as by serial number.

Spread
(1) The gap between the interest rate a bank pays on deposits and the rate it charges on loans; (2) Compensation to the underwriter, determined by the difference between the underwriter's buying price and offering price.

Stag
One who applied for a new issue in the hope of being able to sell the shares allotted to them at a profit as soon as dealing starts.

Stakeholder
Anyone who potentially has a claim on a firm.

Standby Fee
Amount paid to underwriter participating in standby underwriting agreement.

Standby Underwriting
Agreement where the underwriter agrees to purchase the unsubscribed portion of the issue.

Stated Capital
The declared total amount of money or other resources owned or used to acquire future income or benefits.

Stated or Quoted Interest Rate
The interest rate expressed in terms of the interest payment made each period.

Stated Value
A value provided to shares that is similar to par value but less legally binding.

Statement of Cash Flows
See Cash Flow Statement.

Statement of Changes in Financial Position (SCFP)
See Cash Flow Statement.

Statement of Financial Position
A synonym for Balance Sheet.

Statement of Retained Earnings
A financial statement that summarizes the changes in retained earnings for the year. Change in retained earnings equals net income minus dividends plus or minus any retained earnings adjustments.

Statement of Source and Application of Cash
See Cash Flow Statement.

Step Lease
A type of lease that outlines or stipulates the expected annual increases in the tenant's base rent based on an approximation of what the landlord believes the landlord's expenses may be.

Stock Dividend
A dividend paid by issuing more shares to existing shareholders rather than paying them cash.

Stock Exchange
A place where shares and other securities are traded.

Stock Exchange Bid
Corporate takeover bid communicated to the stockholders through a stock exchange.

Stockholder
An alternative term for shareholder, particularly used in the United States.

Stock Market
A capital market in which equity shares are traded. Often used as a generic term for stock exchanges and capital markets.

Stock Option(s)
Promises, usually made to senior managers, to issue shares to them at specified prices.

Stocks
Usually used to mean shares, but also used to mean inventories, as in "stock-taking" for counting inventories.

Stock Split
An increase in a firm's shares outstanding without any change in owner's equity. This involves reissuing shares in which the number of new shares is some multiple of the previous number.

Stocktaking
The process of counting and evaluating stock-in-trade, usually at an organization's year end, in order to value the total stock for preparation of the accounts.

Straight Bond Value
The value of a convertible bond if it could not be converted into common stock.

Straight-Line Amortization (Depreciation)
A method of computing amortization (depreciation) simply by dividing the difference between the asset's cost and its expected salvage value by the number of years the asset is expected to be used.

Strike Price
The fixed price in the option contract at which the holder can buy or sell the underlying asset. Also the exercise price or striking price.

Stripped Bond
A bond that has been separated into its component parts (namely the principal and the coupons) and each part sold separately at a large discount.

Stripped Common Shares
Common stock on which dividends and capital gains are repackaged and sold separately.

Subordinated Debt
Where there is a pecking order determining the sequence in which a company will pay off its debt instruments, subordinate (or junior) issues will not be repaid until unsubordinated (or senior) debt has been repaid in full.

Subsidiary
A company a majority of whose voting shares are owned by another company (the parent).

Sunk Cost
A cost that has already been incurred and cannot be removed and therefore should not be considered in an investment decision.

Surplus
Generally means any excess amount, but in finance it is the remainder of a fund appropriated for a particular purpose. In a corporation, surplus means

that assets left after liabilities and debt, including capital stock, have been subtracted.

Sweeteners or Equity Kickers
A feature included in the terms of a new issue of debt or preferred shares to make the issue more attractive to initial investors.

Tangible
Normally refers to assets that can be held or seen and that are capable of being appraised at an actual or approximate value (e.g., inventory, land and buildings, etc.).

Tax Deferral
A deferral of income taxes from the current year to a later taxation year through the use of provisions, such as deductions for RRSP contributions.

Tax Equivalent Yield
The yield that must be offered before factoring in taxes so that an investment pays off a certain after-tax yield.

Tax Shelter
Any investment sold on the basis that the investor can receive accelerated deductions and/or credits.

Temporary Investments
Investments made for a short term, often used as a place to put temporarily excess cash to work.

Term Deposit
Debt security issued by a bank with terms ranging from several weeks to several years.

Term Loans
Direct business loans of, typically, one to five years.

Term Preferred Shares
Preferred Shares issued with a fixed term and dividend rate, and therefore having some of the characteristics of debt.

Times Interest Earned (TIE)
Measures the extent to which operating income can decline before the firm is unable to meet its annual interest costs.

Time Value of Money
Money can earn interest, so money received in the future is worth less in "present value" terms because the lower amount can be invested to grow to the future amount. Money has a time value because interest accrues over time.

Total Asset Turnover
Measures management's efficiency in managing all of a firm's assets—specifically the generation of revenues from the firm's total investments in assets.

Total Current Assets
Total of cash and equivalents, trade receivables, inventory, and all other current assets.

Total Current Liabilities
The total of short-term notes payable, current maturities LTD, trade payables, income taxes payable, and all other current liabilities.

Total Liabilities & Net Worth
The sum of all liability items and net worth.

Trade Discount
A producer discount given to retail trade members to assist them in increasing sales of the producer's product.

Traded Options
Transferable options with the right to buy and sell a standardized amount of a security at a fixed price within a specified period.

Trade Name
A distinctive name used to identify a product or company and build recognition. Examples: Apple, Coca Cola, Ford, IBM, etc.

Trade Payable
An amount owed to a creditor for goods and services received; also known as an account payable.

Trade Receivables
These are Accounts Receivable arising in the normal course of business with customers.

Trade Receivables (Net)
All accounts from trade, net of allowance for doubtful accounts.

Trading Concern
An entity that derives its products for sale, and thereby its revenue, through purchasing products for sale from other producers/manufacturers for resale to their customer base.

Trading Profit
Profit earned from the short-term trading of securities that were held for less than one year.

Trading Range

Price range between highest and lowest prices at which a stock is traded.

Transfer Form

The form signed by the seller of a security authorizing the company to remove their name from the register and substitute that of the buyer.

Transfer Price

The price charged by an individual entity in a multi-entity corporation on transactions among the entities involved.

Transfer Pricing

Transfer pricing seeks to adjust taxable profits between related entities in different countries to reflect arm's length pricing policies and thereby yield a fair return to each taxing authority.

Treasury Bill (T-Bill)

Short-term debt security issued by federal or provincial governments. T-bills are sold at less than face value (at a discount) and mature at their face value. The difference is the investor's profit.

Treasury Shares (Stock)

Share capital issued and then reacquired by the firm that issued the shares. The result is a reduction of shareholders' equity because resources have been used to reduce the actual amount of outstanding equity.

Turnover

The number of times an asset is replaced during a financial period; often used in terms of inventory turnover or accounts receivable turnover.

Unallocated Costs

Represents corporate costs not associated either directly or indirectly in providing a product or service for sale. Unallocated costs are not included in the calculation of cost of goods sold.

Unearned Revenue/Income

Represents money received in advance of providing the goods or services to customers.

Units-of-Production Amortization

An amortization (depreciation) method in which the annual amortization expense varies directly with the year's production volume.

Unrealized Income ("paper profit")

Profit that has been made but not yet realized or collected through a transaction, such as a stock that has risen in value but is still being held.

Unrealized Loss
A term that commonly refers to the write-down of an investment portfolio resulting from applying the lower of cost or market value on an aggregate basis.

Unrestricted Assets
Assets/resources that are not restricted for use by legal or contractual requirements and may be used for any purpose.

Unusual Items
Unusual revenues or expenses that are large enough to be worth identifying separately in the income statement.

Users
People who use financial statements to assist them in deciding whether to invest in the enterprise, lend it money, or take other action involving financial information.

Uses of Cash
A firm's activities in which cash is spent; also called applications of cash.

Valuation
Determining the amounts at which assets, liabilities, and equity should be shown in the balance sheet.

Valuation Date
The date when the value of a fund is calculated for a purchase exchange or redemption.

Value
A term that defines the worth of a thing. The term is usually preceded by the word, or words such as "Fair" or "Fair Market."

Variable Costs
Costs that change when the quantity of output changes.

Variable Expenses
Those business expenses that usually fluctuate dependent upon production or sales volume. Contrast with Fixed Expenses.

Venture Capital
Capital committed to an unproven venture. The initial start-up money is referred to as "seed money" and entails the greatest risk.

Verifiability
Ability to trace an accounting entry or figure back to the underlying evidence of its occurrence and validity.

Vertical Financial Analysis
Allows comparison of the financial ratios of a company in time — past, present, and future.

Warrant
In securities, it is a security entitling the holder to buy a proportionate amount of stock at some specified future date at a specified price, usually one higher than current market.

Weighted Average
One in which different data in the data set are given different "weights."

Weighted Average Cost of Capital (WACC)
The weighted average of the costs of debt and equity.

Weighted Cost of Capital
The expected return on a portfolio of all a firm's securities. Used as a hurdle rate for capital investment.

Wholly Owned Subsidiary
An entity whose parent owns virtually 100 percent of its common stock.

Window Dressing
The act or an instance of making something appear deceptively attractive or favourable.

WIP
An acronym for Work in Process/Progress. Usually refers to inventory that has value added from labour or additional processing.

Working Capital (WC)
The difference between current assets and current liabilities that measures the margin of protection for current creditors.

Working Capital Management
Planning and managing the firm's current assets and liabilities.

Working Capital Ratio
See Current Ratio.

Write-Off
To decrease the value of an item. For example: a tax write-off decreases tax liability.

Yield
The annual income from an investment expressed as a percentage of the investment's current value.

Zero Based Budget

Where the expenses or costs of the prior year are not taken into consideration when establishing expense or budgetary levels looking forward. Each expense category starts from zero.

Zero Coupon Bonds

Bonds priced at a large discount from face value. The bonds mature at full face value so the difference between the original issue price and the face value represents interest income. Sometimes called Stripped Bonds.

Zero Coupon Convertible Debenture/Security

A Zero Coupon Bond that is convertible into the common stock of the issuing company after the common stock reaches a certain price.

Index

T after a page number indicates a table

About the Author

Vern Krishna, CM, QC, FRSC, FCPA, has earned a B Comm (Manchester), MBA, LLB (Alberta), DCL (Cambridge), and LLM (Harvard). He is now a Professor of Law at the University of Ottawa. He is also Of Counsel, Tax Chambers LLP (Toronto). Professor Krishna is Queen's Counsel, a member of the Order of Canada, a recipient of the Queen's Diamond Jubilee Medal, the Governor General's 125th Anniversary Medal, and a Fellow of the Royal Society (Canada). He has been a Bencher of the Law Society of Upper Canada since 1991 and served as its Treasurer from 2001–03.

Professor Krishna is the author of seventeen texts in law, including, most recently, Volumes 1 (Personal) and 2 (Corporate) of *The Fundamentals of Canadian Income Tax*, *Income Tax Law* (2012), three volumes on general taxation, corporate taxation, and international taxation in *Halsbury's Laws of Canada*, and the Editor of *Canada's Tax Treaties*. He is listed in *Who's Who*, and *Lexpert* has recognized him in Best Lawyers in Canada in Tax Law, Estates and Trusts, and Appellate Advocacy.

FSC
www.fsc.org
MIX
Papier | Fördert
gute Waldnutzung
FSC® C083411

Kolibri 360 GmbH
Ferdinand-Jühlke-Straße 7
99095 Erfurt, Deutschland
produktsicherheit@kolibri360.de